Those Who Can, Teach

Eighth Edition

Kevin Ryan
Boston University

James M. Cooper
University of Virginia

Instructor's Resource Manual with Test Items

Leslie A. Swetnam
Metropolitan State College of Denver

HOUGHTON MIFFLIN COMPANY BOSTON NEW YORK

Senior Sponsoring Editor: Loretta Wolozin
Associate Editor: Lisa Mafrici
Editorial Assistant: Jean Zielinski DeMayo
Project Editor: Julie Lane
Senior Manufacturing Coordinator: Marie Barnes
Marketing Manager: Pamela Laskey

Printed in the U.S.A.

ISBN: 0-395-858755

123456789-VG-01 00 99 98 97

Contents

Preface

The first section of this Instructor's Resource Manual provides instructors with model syllabi for the introduction to education course for both a 10- and 16-week semester schedule.

The section on instructional resources includes, for each chapter of the text, learning objectives, a chapter overview, a chapter outline, supplementary lecture and discussion topics, additional resources for instructors, media resources, student activities, and ready-to-use assignments, including:

- Observe/interview a teacher
- Reflections on current events
- A presentation or paper on a controversial issue in education
- Write your own philosophy of education

The learning objectives and chapter overview orient the instructor to the purposes of the chapter and its contribution to students' professional development. The supplementary lecture and discussion topics offer a sampling of suggestions for elaborating on the chapter's contents. The annotated references—both print and media—show where additional information or insights can be found. The student activities are designed to engage students in reflective thinking and role-plays that simulate aspects of a teacher's work.

The student resources section is new and was designed to provide study aids that can be copied and distributed to students. It includes the same statement of learning objectives found in the instructor's resources, study guide questions that focus on the recognition and comprehension of major points in the chapter, and a practice quiz with answer key on page 261. There are no answer keys included for the study guide since the answers are clearly indicated in the chapter and the intent of this section is to provide a study aid for students, not an assignment for the instructor to grade.

The evaluation section for each chapter contains 30 to 40 multiple-choice items. The distractors for each item have been formed with the intention of stimulating careful thought; to reject a distractor is to have reviewed its meaning and recognized its inappropriateness. Items have been developed according to accepted principles of test construction and are designed to elicit student thinking at various levels. The evaluation section also contains two or three short-answer and essay questions per chapter, along with guided responses, and alternative assessment tools such as papers, readings, and journal prompts.

To supplement the cases presented in the text and the short cases in some of the activities in the Instructor's Resource Manual, the Appendix contains four longer case studies that present interesting dilemmas or issues that prospective teachers may encounter in their professional career.

It is included at the end of the manual. Discussion questions help to guide the analysis of the cases and to bring the prospective teachers to some resolution of the issue at hand.

The test items contained in the Instructor's Resource Manual are also available in a Computerized *Test Bank* for use with IBM or Macintosh microcomputers.

Our goal in providing these materials is to help students learn about themselves and the teaching profession. We strongly believe that the student activities should include follow-up. In addition, tests should be reviewed in class, with correct answers made available and alternative responses discussed. Such follow-up and discussion allow for clarification and consolidation of new information.

Although many individuals helped develop this manual, we express special gratitude to Leslie Swetnam, who revised and prepared this edition of the *Instructor's Resource Manual with Test Items;* and to Lee McCanne, who reviewed the materials for Chapter 7. We also thank Cathleen Kinsella Stutz, Susan Tauer, Mary S. Leighton, Gloria Thompson, Kathryn Rabinow, and Debra Hallock Phillips, whose work on earlier editions was most valuable. To those readers who took the trouble to comment on previous editions, we also offer thanks. The changes made for this edition are based on their helpful advice.

Information regarding your own experience with this manual will be used in preparing future editions. Comments may be recorded on the instructor evaluation sheet at the end of the manual. If you develop or discover activities that you would like to recommend to us, we would be delighted to hear of them.

Good luck in your teaching!

A Guide to Your Examination of *Those Who Can, Teach,* Eighth Edition

Purpose

Those Who Can, Teach is a book of questions. In fact, it was written in the first place to answer the question "What are the things people beginning their formal study of education should know?" We have organized the chapters of our book around a series of questions that are likely to be of special concern to prospective teachers, and which we believe are keys to the central issues and concerns of teaching and learning. We hope that these questions provide direction and focus to readers' study well beyond the time they spend with this book. In addition, for those who are considering careers in teaching, we believe that the search for answers to these questions will help them clarify their career goals.

Audience

This is the eighth edition of *Those Who Can, Teach.* It is intended as a basic text for courses variously titled "Introduction to Education" or "Foundations of Education." We originally wrote this book because we couldn't find the kind of textbook our students and the students of many of our colleagues needed and wanted—a book that involves prospective teachers in the real issues of schooling and education and gives them a clear view of the skills and knowledge they will need to be successful professionals.

Content of the Eighth Edition

Those Who Can, Teach, Eighth Edition, presents a frank and up-to-date examination of the field and foundations of education, and especially of the teaching profession. Although the text is firmly based in educational research and scholarship, it seeks to convey the important knowledge and issues in the field of education in a way that effectively bridges educational research and classroom practice. For this purpose, we rely heavily throughout the book on a narrative style, attempting to place the book's content in very human terms.

We have organized the book around five themes, each theme representing one of the five parts. The five parts are as follows:

Part One, "Schools," opens with an examination of the various motivations for teaching, and then looks at the dynamics of school life from many different angles to give the prospective teacher a multilayered view of schools. *Part Two,* "Students," attempts to provide the reader with a vivid grasp of the diverse and changing nature of today's students and examines the critical social issues that affect American students and schools today. *Part Three,* "Teachers," begins with the knowledge base about effective teaching and looks at what is taught. Part Three also includes our brand new chapter on the teacher and technology, since technology has become so central to both the content and process of teaching. *Part Four,* "Foundations," contains chapters on topics that are "foundational" to the practice of teaching: the economic and political issues underlying the control and governance of schools, the philosophy of education, the history of American education, and the ethical and legal issues facing teachers. It is in this mix of our educational past and current issues that we have also placed an important chapter on educational reform. In *Part Five,* "Careers," we provide timely information on salaries and employment opportunities, try to give the reader a behind-the-scenes look at what we know about the experiences of beginning teachers, and examine teaching as a profession.

Features of the Revision

Teaching and learning and the condition of our schools have been in the headlines almost continually in the three years since our last edition. Education is big news from Main Street to Pennsylvania Avenue. As the link between education and the well-being of both the individual and the nation becomes more obvious, both real change and proposals for change become apparent. This edition, therefore, tries to sort out the most significant developments without losing sight of the enduring issues facing students and teachers. Among the most significant changes in this edition are the following:

***New* educational technology chapter.** An entirely new chapter has been written about the exciting field of technology and teaching: Chapter 7 entitled "What Should Teachers Know About Technology and its Impact on Schools?" For decades schools have lagged behind much of the rest of society in the use of technologies. Business, industry, and even the home have outstripped the schoolhouse. While the rest of the country has been easing onto the information highway, most teachers are still in their driveways. Some are still in their garages. The most obvious example of this is the teacher with a new computer either letting it gather dust or having to rely on students to run it. This new chapter will take someone who is computer-illiterate or just uncertain and give him or her a clear, basic understanding of the technological possibilities in the classroom. In addition, individuals who are computer-comfortable will find many educational resources and important sites on the World Wide Web in this chapter. As more and more instructional materials are becoming available on videotapes, CD-ROMs, and software programs, and as computer skills become more central both to learning and the world of work, teachers must have mastery of these new developments. We believe you will find the chapter to be comprehensive, detailed, and "user friendly."

***New* School Observations.** Bridging the gap between education theory and school practice has been an aim of our text from the first edition. However, since more and more introductory courses have some sort of field component or built-in school observation activity, we have developed a new feature to help students better see the relationships between what is studied in the college classroom and what happens in schools. In this eighth edition, we have incorporated a school observation activity for each of the chapters—an activity that is related to the chapter topic and that will help the student make connections between the chapter content and what is going on in the field.

***New* Voices from the Classroom: "The Stories of Five New Teachers" insert.** Again, to give the reader the richest and fullest sense of what it is like to become a teacher, we have added another feature to this edition. Five new teachers (all former student-users of this book) give their candid views on their experiences as beginning teachers. The topics range from handling classroom management to finding support from colleagues and administrators. The stories include their personal struggles with dealing with stress and learning about time management. We believe you will find their frank view of teaching a valuable source for your own reflection.

Websites. Congruent with the new focus on technology and the teacher, websites have been added to all chapters (except for Chapter 10 on the philosophy of education, where we were unable find a suitable site). Relevant website addresses have been added to the "For Further Information" sections at the end of the chapters. We have made every effort to include stable sites, and we have screened sites to judge their quality. Given the rapidity of change in this rapidly evolving, emergent technology, we cannot guarantee the constancy of sites included in this book.

Chapter organization. Based on our own experiences teaching this text, we have decided to reorder the chapters. Our basic reasoning was to conform the chapter sequence more to the new "field experience" emphasis in so many courses today. We wanted students to get some fresh perspectives early in the course on topics like schools and students, since most go into the field shortly after a term begins. Therefore, we put some of the more abstract or theoretical chapters later in the book. We believe this will be a benefit to both instructors and teacher education students.

Full-color design. This edition has an entirely new, visually dynamic, four-color design. The most noticeable result is the approximately seventy color photos of teachers, students, and life in classrooms. These fine photos were specifically shot or selected to coordinate with the book's major themes. We hope the reader looks upon these pictures as a source of information and insight into the work of the teacher. These elements of the text's new design—individually and all taken together—significantly facilitate students' learning.

More concise chapters. Over the course of the first seven editions, our chapters became longer and longer. For this edition, we used scalpels, carving knives, and, in some chapters, chain saws to shorten and tighten the book. F. Scott Fitzgerald once remarked that cutting one's prose was like murdering your children. Although the process of paring down was painful, we believe we have a better, more readable book. We hope you agree. At the same time, every chapter has been changed and updated, some quite substantially.

World View deleted. This was part of the effort to trim the chapters.

Specific changes in the chapters of the eighth edition include the following:

Part One: Schools

Chapter 1: "Why Teach?"

The chapter was updated to maintain currency and was streamlined by dropping two of the four case studies in the previous edition.

Chapter 2: "What Is a School?"

The baby-sitter model was dropped and the factory model was renamed "trainer of workers."

Chapter 3: "What Is Life in Schools Like?"

Additions include a summary of the Carnegie/NASSP Report *Breaking Ranks: Changing an American Institution,* which makes suggestions for improving the quality of American high schools, and Lawrence Steinberg's study *Beyond the Classroom: Why School Reform Has Failed and What Parents Need to Do.* The gender difference information was moved to Chapter 5.

Part Two: Students

Chapter 4: "Who Are Today's Students?"

More information on the controversial aspects of both multiculturalism and full inclusion was added. The section "New American Family Patterns" was moved to Chapter 5, and the section on Maslow's hierarchy of needs has been deleted.

Chapter 5: "What Social Problems and Tension Points Affect Today's Students?"

"New American Family Patterns" and gender issues were moved to this chapter from Chapters 4 and 3, respectively. This chapter also contains new information regarding gangs and the recent Supreme Court rulings dismantling school desegregation plans.

Part Three: Teachers

Chapter 6: "What Makes a Teacher Effective?"

The coverage of reflective teaching has been increased, and a section on wait time has been added. References to interactive, prescriptive, proactive, and retroactive decisions have been deleted.

Chapter 7: "What Should Teachers Know About Technology and Its Impact on Schools?"

This is a brand new chapter that responds to the rapidly increasing use of technology in the schools. The chapter provides a broad-based introduction to how computers can be used by teachers and students and how they affect the curriculum.

Chapter 8: "What Is Taught?"

The chapter includes increased coverage of student academic performance as measured by the NAEP tests. It also provides greater coverage of international comparisons of student achievement, including the most recent TIMSS (Third International Mathematics and Science Study). Block scheduling has been added to the influences on curriculum, and a new section on current curriculum controversies has been included. Mastery learning as an influence on curriculum has been deleted.

Part Four: Foundations

Chapter 9: "How Are Schools Governed, Influenced, and Financed?"

A section on private schools and public funding has been added. The emphasis has been changed from "controlled" to "influenced."

Chapter 10: "What Are the Philosophical Foundations of American Education?"

The basic structure and content of this chapter have remained the same. A special section on constructivism and behaviorism has been included.

Chapter 11: "What Is the History of American Education?"

No major significant changes were made to this chapter.

Chapter 12: "What Are the Ethical and Legal Issues Facing Teachers?"

Information in this chapter reflects the changes and additions to the legal issues surrounding students, teachers, and schools. New information on software and Internet-related law as well as laws regarding religious activity in and around schools has been added.

Chapter 13: "How Should Education Be Reformed?"

This chapter was reorganized to better communicate the relationship between what ought to drive the reform and what is being reformed. There is a new emphasis on constructivism. Goals 2000 is given a much lower profile, and there is more emphasis on national standards.

Part Five: Careers

Chapter 14: "What Are Your Job Options in Education?"

Statistics have been updated and reorganized.

Chapter 15: "What Can the New Teacher Expect?"

This chapter is essentially the same.

Chapter 16: "What Does It Mean to Be a Professional?"

The emphasis has been changed from whether or not teaching is a profession to how a professional behaves. Information from and about the professional teacher associations has been updated. The letter from Al Shanker (AFT) was one of the last formal statements he made before his death.

Learning Aids and Special Qualities

Although much is new in the eighth edition, many other features have been retained. Chief among them is the book's *informal writing style.* We have tried to communicate the seriousness surrounding professional topics and at the same time weave in humor and create a sense of conversing directly with the reader. Besides the new "Voices from the Classroom: Stories of Five New Teachers" insert, the text describes extensively the experiences of classroom teachers, often in their own words. Frequently these experiences happened directly to the authors when we were teaching in public schools. We believe (and hope) that this writing style and heavy use of narrative gives the text a greater sense of reality.

Many pedagogical features have been included to enhance the student's learning and the text's usefulness. *Dialogues* between the two authors appear periodically both to highlight controversial points and to make clear to the reader that education is not a field where all the issues are settled with cut-and-dried answers. *Special inserts* are included in each chapter to focus in depth on topics or research findings of particular interest to prospective teachers. As mentioned, *School Observation* activities have been added to help bridge the gap between theory and practice. *Biographies* of distinguished educators and teachers, such as Socrates, John Dewey, Anne Sullivan, and Jaime Escalante, have been placed throughout the text. Further, the book is extensively illustrated with *cartoons, color photographs, graphs, charts, and thought-provoking quotations.* In addition, *marginal notes* highlight the important points of every page, and each chapter begins with a capsule *overview* and a *list of key points.* Each chapter concludes with a *list of key terms* (new to this edition), a series of *discussions questions,* and an annotated *list of suggested readings and web resources.* The book concludes with a *glossary of terms* and a very detailed text *index.*

Accompanying Teaching and Learning Resources

The eighth edition of *Those Who Can, Teach* is accompanied by an extensive package of instructor and student resources. *Kaleidoscope: Readings in Education,* Eighth Edition, is a companion book of readings that can be used either in conjunction with the text or as a separate volume. This collection of more than seventy selections contains works by some of the most distinguished scholars in education, along with the writings of practicing teachers. A mixture of topical and classical studies, the readings include diary entries, letters, teacher accounts, journal articles, and reports. Many of the authors and reports of research cited in *Those Who Can, Teach* are included in this book of readings. Also, an easy-to-use chart cross-references topics discussed in *Those Who Can, Teach* with the readings in *Kaleidoscope.* Finally, there is a teaching video: *In Classrooms:* A Houghton Mifflin Teacher Education Video (6 segments: Orientation, 6 min., *Diversity,* 12 min., *Teacher Decision Making,* 12 min., *Cooperative Learning,* 7 min., *Communication and Relationship,* 8 min., *Learning Environment,* 10 min.). This video was developed to accompany Houghton Mifflin Company education texts.

Accompanying the text is an *Instructor's Resource Manual with Test Items.* The IRM contains a transition guide from the seventh edition to the eighth; model syllabi, instructor support resources, including chapter outlines; student study guide materials, including study guide questions and sample chapter quizzes; and assessment materials, including multiple-choice, short answer, essay, and alternative assessment ideas. The test items contained in the *Instructor's*

Resource Manual are also available in new computerized form in a computerized test bank for use with IBM and Macintosh. On-line testing and ESAGRADE are now available with this package. Finally, a set of seventy-five overhead color transparencies is free to instructors upon adoption of the text. The transparencies include figures from the text as well as new material generated specifically for this set.

Student Resources

An entirely new section to provide study guides and practice quizzes has been created and included for each chapter.

Part I Model Syllabi

Note to Instructors: We have provided you with model syllabi for an introduction to education course, one for a 16-week semester and another for a 10-week semester. It is our hope that these syllabi will give instructors some idea on how *Those Who Can, Teach* can be used in an introductory course. Readings from the companion book *Kaleidoscope* are also included in the syllabi.

INTRODUCTION TO EDUCATION
16-Week Syllabus

Instructor:
Office:
Telephone:
Office hours:

Objectives

Students will:

- deepen their understanding of education by focusing on four interrelated topics: themselves as teachers and learners, teachers and teaching, students and schools, and schools and society.
- improve their academic analytical writing skills through writing assignments and field journals.
- refine their problem-solving skills in preparation for educational leadership roles.
- gain knowledge of current educational issues related to the philosophy, history, and politics of education, particularly in the United States.
- demonstrate professional behavior in their roles as observers and assistants in field placements.
- examine their commitment to the teaching profession through reflection on their classroom and field experiences.

Course Structure

Section: Students meet for small group discussions of the readings and of field experiences. Students are expected to have completed the assigned readings and to be ready to discuss ideas and topics found in the readings. Their weekly journal entries based on the readings will be used as discussion starters.

Class: Students meet with the professor—after the section sessions for lectures and other learning experiences. ***Regular and punctual attendance is required for section and lecture.***

Field: Each student is assigned to an elementary or middle school classroom to serve as the apprentice to a cooperating teacher. Students are expected to dress, behave, and speak in a professional manner. They must attend all field visits and should be punctual. Students will keep a field journal in which they will write a weekly entry related to their experiences in the classroom.

Texts (available at the bookstore)

Required:

Ryan, K., and J. M. Cooper (1998). *Those Who Can, Teach* (8th ed.). Boston: Houghton Mifflin.

Ryan, K., and J. M. Cooper (Eds.). (1998). *Kaleidoscope: Readings in Education* (8th ed.). Boston: Houghton Mifflin.

In addition:

One book to be read for a book critique. Students will be provided with more information about this assignment and should wait before purchasing any of these books.

Recommended:

Hairston and Ruszkiewicz (1991). *The Scott, Foresman Handbook for Writers* (2nd ed.). New York: HarperCollins.

or any reliable college-level grammar and writing handbook.

Grading and Assignments

Semester grades will be based on your knowledge of educational concepts and theories and your ability to express yourself orally and in writing. Knowledge of educational concepts and theories will be evaluated through periodic quizzes and two exams: a midterm and a final. Both exams will consist of multiple-choice, short-answer, and essay questions. The midterm will deal with material covered in the textbooks, discussions, and lectures during the first half of the semester, and the final exam will be cumulative, covering material from both halves of the course.

Because it is so important these days for teachers to communicate their ideas to colleagues, parents, and administrators effectively, writing clear and error-free English is a priority at the School of Education. Therefore, your ability to express your knowledge of educational concepts and theories within the conventions of academic discourse will be assessed through oral presentations and written assignments. Criteria for evaluation will be based on content and mechanics. Integration of information from lectures, readings, discussions, and field experiences will also be taken into consideration. A guide to academic writing as well as specific instructions for each assignment will be distributed.

Assignment	***Due Date***	***Value***
An influential teacher		10%
Educational issue investigation		20%
Introductory paper		
Literature review		
Position paper		
Book critique		10%
Journal and journal summary		10%
Midterm examination		15%
Final examination		20%
Participation		15%
Quizzes		
Article critique		
Professional interview		
Total		**100%**

Course Schedule

Date	*Topic*	*Those Who Can*	*Kaleidoscope*
Part I: Schools			
Week 1	Introduction Why Teach?	Ch. 1	Metzger Csikszentmihalyi & McCormack
Week 2	What Is a School?	Ch. 2	Wynne
	Life in Schools	Ch. 3	Powell Raywid
Part II: Students			
Week 3	Today's Students	Ch. 4	Minicucci Shanker
Week 4	Social Problems and Tension Points	Ch. 5	Cates Edelman
Part III: Teachers			
Week 5	Effective Teachers	Ch. 6	Brophy Rogers
Week 6	Technology in Education	Ch. 7	Mehlinger Postman
Week 7	Curriculum	Ch. 8	Hirsch Dewey
Week 8	**Midterm Exam**		
Part IV: Foundations			
Week 9	Governance and Finance	Ch. 9	LoVette Comer
Week 10	Philosophy	Ch. 10	Hutchins
Week 11	History	Ch. 11	Ravitch
Week 12	Ethical and Legal Issues	Ch. 12	Strike McDaniel
Week 13	School Reform	Ch. 13	Hill David

Part V: Careers

Date	*Topic*	*Those Who Can*	*Kaleidoscope*
Week 14	Job Options	Ch. 14	Haberman Darling-Hammond
	New Teachers	Ch. 15	Finders & Lewis Shively
Week 15	Professionalism	Ch. 16	Darling-Hammond Wise
Week 16	**Final Exam**		

Note to Instructors: Although it is probably most effective to keep the chapters of each part together, Parts I through V can be interchanged to meet your needs.

INTRODUCTION TO EDUCATION
10-Week Syllabus

Instructor:
Office:
Telephone:
Office hours:

Objectives

Students will:

- deepen their understanding of education by focusing on four interrelated topics: themselves as teachers and learners, teachers and teaching, students and schools, and schools and society.
- improve their academic analytical writing skills through writing assignments and field journals.
- refine their problem-solving skills in preparation for educational leadership roles.
- gain knowledge of current educational issues related to the philosophy, history, and politics of education, particularly in the United States.
- demonstrate professional behavior in their roles as observers and assistants in field placements.
- examine their commitment to the teaching profession through reflection on their classroom and field experiences.

Course Structure

Section: Students meet for small group discussions of the readings and of field experiences. Students are expected to have completed the assigned readings and to be ready to discuss ideas and topics found in the readings. Their weekly journal entries based on the readings will be used as discussion starters.

Class: Students meet with the professor—after the section sessions for lectures and other learning experiences. ***Regular and punctual attendance is required for section and lecture.***

Field: Each student is assigned to an elementary or middle school classroom to serve as the apprentice to a cooperating teacher. Students are expected to dress, behave, and speak in a professional manner. They must attend all field visits and should be punctual. Students will keep a field journal in which they will write a weekly entry related to their experiences in the classroom.

Texts (available at the bookstore)

Required:

Ryan, K., and J. M. Cooper (1998). *Those Who Can, Teach* (8th ed.). Boston: Houghton Mifflin.

Ryan, K., and J. M. Cooper (Eds.). (1998). *Kaleidoscope: Readings in Education* (8th ed.). Boston: Houghton Mifflin.

Recommended:

Hairston and Ruszkiewicz (1991). *The Scott, Foresman Handbook for Writers* (2nd ed.). New York: HarperCollins.

or any reliable college-level grammar and writing handbook.

Grading and Assignments

Semester grades will be based on your knowledge of educational concepts and theories and your ability to express yourself orally and in writing. Knowledge of educational concepts and theories will be evaluated through periodic quizzes and two exams: a midterm and a final. Both exams will consist of multiple-choice, short-answer, and essay questions. The midterm will deal with material covered in the textbooks, discussions, and lectures during the first half of the semester, and the final exam will be cumulative, covering material from both halves of the course.

Because it is so important these days for teachers to communicate their ideas to colleagues, parents, and administrators effectively, writing clear and error-free English is a priority at the School of Education. Therefore, your ability to express your knowledge of educational concepts and theories within the conventions of academic discourse will be assessed through oral presentations and written assignments. Criteria for evaluation will be based on content and mechanics. Integration of information from lectures, readings, discussions, and field experiences will also be taken into consideration. A guide to academic writing as well as specific instructions for each assignment will be distributed.

Assignment	***Due Date***	***Value***
An influential teacher		10%
Educational issue investigation		20%
Literature review		
Position paper		
Book critique		10%
Journal and journal summary		10%
Midterm examination		15%
Final examination		20%
Participation		15%
Quizzes		
Total		
		100%

Course Schedule

Date	*Topic*	*Those Who Can*	*Kaleidoscope*
Part I: Schools			
Week 1	Course Introduction Why Teach?	Ch. 1	Metzger Csikszentmihalyi & McCormack
Week 2	What Is a School?	Ch. 2	Wynne
	Life in Schools	Ch. 3	Powell Raywid
Part II: Students			
Week 3	Today's Students	Ch. 4	Minicucci Shanker
	Social Problems and Tension Points	Ch. 5	Cates Edelman
Part III: Teachers			
Week 4	Effective Teachers	Ch. 6	Brophy Rogers
	Technology in Education	Ch. 7	Mehlinger Postman
Week 5	Curriculum	Ch. 8	Hirsch Dewey
	Midterm Exam		
Part IV: Foundations			
Week 6	Governance and Finance	Ch. 9	LoVette Comer
	Philosophy	Ch. 10	Hutchins
Week 7	History	Ch. 11	Ravitch
	Ethical and Legal Issues	Ch. 12	Strike McDaniel
Week 8	School Reform	Ch. 13	Hill David

Date	*Topic*	*Those Who Can*	*Kaleidoscope*
Part V: Careers			
Week 9	Job Options	Ch. 14	Haberman Darling-Hammond
	New Teachers	Ch. 15	Finders & Lewis Shively
	Professionalism	Ch. 16	Darling-Hammond Wise
Week 10	**Final Exam**		

Note to Instructors: Although it is probably most effective to keep the chapters of each part together, Parts I through V can be interchanged to meet your needs.

CORRELATIONS FOR *KALEIDOSCOPE*

I. TEACHERS

			TWCT Chapters
1.	Mihaly Csikszentmihalyi & Jane McCormack	*The Influence of Teachers*	6, 13
2.	Margaret Metzger	*Calling in the Cosmos*	1, 6
3.	Martin Haberman	*Selecting "Star" Teachers for Children and Youth in Urban Poverty*	6, 13, 14
4.	Mary Catherine Buday & James Kelly	*National Board Certification and the Teaching Profession's Commitment to Quality Assurance*	16
5.	Judith Shively	*Why I Entered Teaching, Why I Stay*	15, 16
6.	John C. Crowley	*Letter from a Teacher*	15, 16
7.	Edward R. Ducharme	*The Great Teacher Question: Beyond Competencies*	6, 13, 14
8.	Kenneth Wolf	*Developing an Effective Teaching Portfolio*	14
9.	Arthur E. Wise	*Six Steps to Teacher Professionalism*	9, 14, 16
10.	Robert Fried	*The Heart of the Matter*	1, 6

II. STUDENTS

11.	Robert D. Barr	*Who Is This Child?*	4, 5
12.	Marian Wright Edelman	*Defending America's Children*	4, 5
13.	Robert J. Sternberg	*Investing in Creativity: Many Happy Returns*	8, 13
14.	Richard Strong, Harvey F. Silver, & Amy Robinson	*What Do Students Want (and What Really Motivates Them)?*	6, 13
15.	D. Stanley Eitzen	*Problem Students: The Sociocultural Roots*	4, 5
16.	M. Mark Wasicsko & Steven M. Ross	*How to Create Discipline Problems*	2, 6, 15
17.	Dennis L. Cates, Marc A. Markell, & Sherrie Bettenhausen	*At Risk for Abuse: A Teacher's Guide for Recognizing and Reporting Child Neglect and Abuse*	5, 12

			TWCT Chapters

III. SCHOOLS

18.	David C. Berliner	*Mythology and the American System of Education*	4, 13
19.	Edward A. Wynne	*Looking at Good Schools*	2, 3, 13
20.	Deborah W. Meier	*The Big Benefits of Smallness*	13
21.	Jean Johnson & John Immerwahr	*First Things First: What Americans Expect from the Public Schools*	2, 5
22.	Arthur G. Powell	*Being Unspecial in the Shopping Mall High School*	2, 3
23.	Joe Nathan	*Early Lessons of the Charter School Movement*	13
24.	Alex Molnar	*Charter Schools: The Smiling Face of Disinvestment*	13
25.	David A. Squires & Robert D. Kranyik	*The Comer Program: Changing School Culture*	2, 3, 4, 13

IV. CURRICULUM

26.	J. Abner Peddiwell	*The Saber-Tooth Curriculum*	8
27.	William Glasser	*The Quality School Curriculum*	8
28.	Arthur W. Combs	*Affective Education or None at All*	3, 6, 8
29.	Mortimer J. Adler	*The Paideia Proposal: Rediscovering the Essence of Education*	8, 10
30.	Albert Shanker	*Developing a Common Curriculum*	3, 8
31.	E. D. Hirsch, Jr.	*The Core Knowledge Curriculum—What's Behind Its Success?*	8
32.	Nel Noddings	*Teaching Themes of Care*	8, 13
33.	James A. Beane	*Curriculum Integration and the Disciplines of Knowledge*	8
34.	Kevin Ryan	*Mining the Values in the Curriculum*	8, 13
35.	Elliot W. Eisner	*Standards for American Schools: Help or Hindrance?*	13

V. INSTRUCTION

36.	Margaret M. Clifford	*Students Need Challenge, Not Easy Success*	6, 13
37.	Jere Brophy	*Probing the Subtleties of Subject-Matter Teaching*	6, 8, 13

			TWCT Chapters
38.	Geaea Leinhardt	*What Research on Learning Tells Us About Teaching*	6, 13
39.	Robert E. Slavin	*Cooperative Learning and the Cooperative School*	8
40.	Frank Betts	*What's All the Noise About? Constructivism in the Classroom*	6, 10, 13
41.	Anne Wescott Dodd	*Engaging Students: What I Learned Along the Way*	6, 13
42.	Nancy Sato & Milbrey W. McLaughlin	*Context Matters: Teaching in Japan and in the United States*	16
43.	Thomas R. Guskey	*Making the Grade: What Benefits Students?*	8, 13
44.	Richard S. Marsh & Mary Anne Raywid	*How to Make Detracking Work*	3

VI. FOUNDATIONS

45.	John Dewey	*My Pedagogic Creed*	2, 8, 10
46.	Ernest L. Boyer	*The Educated Person*	8, 10
47.	Robert Maynard Hutchins	*The Basis of Education*	8, 10
48.	B. F. Skinner	*The Free and Happy Student*	10
49.	Carl Rogers	*Personal Thoughts on Teaching and Learning*	6, 10
50.	Kenneth A. Strike	*The Ethics of Teaching*	12
51.	Thomas R. McDaniel	*The Teacher's Ten Commandments: School Law in the Classroom*	12
52.	Otis K. LoVette	*You Ask, "Why Have School Costs Increased So Greatly During the Last 20 Years?"*	9
53.	Thomas Lickona	*The Return of Character Education*	13
54.	Theodore R. Sizer	*New Hope for High Schools: Lessons from Reform-Minded Educators*	13
55.	Linda Darling-Hammond	*What Matters Most: A Competent Teacher for Every Child*	6, 13, 14, 16
56.	Jane L. David	*The Who, What, and Why of Site-Based Management*	9, 13
57.	Lauren Resnick & Kate Nolan	*Where in the World Are World-Class Standards?*	8, 13
58.	Robert Lynn Canady & Michael D. Rettig	*The Power of Innovative Scheduling*	3, 8
59.	Paul T. Hill	*The Educational Consequences of Choice*	13

			TWCT Chapters
60.	Kevin B. Smith & Kenneth J. Meier	*School Choice: Panacea or Pandora's Box?*	13
61.	Daniel L. Burke	*Multi-Year Teacher/Student Relationships Are a Long-Overdue Arrangement*	3, 13

VII. EDUCATIONAL TECHNOLOGY

62.	Howard D. Mehlinger	*School Reform in the Information Age*	7, 13
63.	Vicki Hancock & Frank Betts	*From the Lagging to the Leading Edge*	7
64.	James A. Levin & Cathy Thurston	*Research Summary: Educational Electronic Networks*	7
65.	Mary Anne Mather	*Exploring the Internet Safely—What Schools Can Do*	7, 12
66.	Michael N. Milone, Jr. & Judy Salpeter	*Technology and Equity Issues*	5, 7
67.	Neil Postman	*Making a Living, Making a Life: Technology Reconsidered*	7, 10

VIII. SOCIAL CURRENTS

68.	James P. Comer	*Parent Participation: Fad or Function?*	4, 9, 15
69.	Diane Ravitch	*Multiculturalism: E Pluribus Plures*	4, 11
70.	Albert Shanker	*Where We Stand on the Rush to Inclusion*	4
71.	Michael F. Giangreco	*What Do I Do Now? A Teacher's Guide to Including Students with Disabilities*	4
72.	Susan McGee Bailey	*Shortchanging Girls and Boys*	5
73.	Catherine Minnicucci, et al.	*School Reform and Student Diversity*	4
74.	Margaret Finders & Cynthia Lewis	*Why Some Parents Don't Come to School*	4, 9, 15
75.	Patricia M. Lines	*Home Schooling Comes of Age*	12, 13

Part II Instructional Resources

FOR EACH CHAPTER

Learning Objectives
Chapter Overview
Chapter Outline
Supplementary Lecture and Discussion Topics
Additional Resources for Instructors
Media Resources
Student Activities

Chapter 1 Why Teach?

Quickly rate week (1)
1 - terrible
2 - okay
3 - wonderful
and explain why as briefly as possible (2)
Now, I have another question for you - ARE YOU SURE YOU WANT TO DO THIS ... TEACH??
WHY ... Let's create PRO/CON List

Share in groups of (3)
- 10 minutes
Overall Sharing
(2) Continue ... point out Intrinsic and Extrinsic distinction made in text
(3) So, based on this list what do YOU think? Is teaching your place? so far?? I'll leave you w/ this question -

...be able to

...s for want...

...ations for

...eachers g...

...nd intrins...

- list and explain sources of useful experience regarding teaching.
- explain a potential difficulty faced by teachers whose primary motivation is to teach a particular content or subject matter.
- explain the potential difficulty of using teaching as a means to work out one's own problems.
- explain how teachers can aid in the renewal of society through their teaching.
- apply the concepts introduced to their own perspective on teaching.
- think, speak, and write with greater clarity and insight about why they are considering (or not considering) a career in teaching.

Chapter Overview

Everyone has gone to school, so everyone knows what it must be like to be a teacher. Right? Wrong. Although recalling one's own experiences in school may be helpful, prospective teachers need to base their career choice on more than just memories. Prospective teachers need to explore their desire to teach in more depth, and Chapter 1 encourages them to do just that. Teaching is a very satisfying career for thousands of people, yet to be satisfied in the career, prospective teachers must think about why they are becoming a teacher and whether their career aspirations can be fulfilled in teaching.

Chapter 1 presents factual data as well as case studies for prospective teachers to mull over as they begin their teacher education program. Too often, students are willing to rely on outside information without testing it against their own knowledge or frame of reference. The textbook's intent is to engage the students so that reading it becomes a more reflective experience than just reading and memorizing.

Basic facets of the teaching profession are highlighted in the chapter. One part discusses the rewards of teaching. We point out that teaching yields both extrinsic and intrinsic rewards, yet the extrinsic rewards are often downplayed. Intrinsic rewards, because of their highly individualistic nature, vary in degree from teacher to teacher. Considering both the extrinsic and intrinsic rewards of teaching, the authors suggest, is a realistic way of assessing if a person would be content as a teacher.

Four categories of experience, as well as case studies depicting common motivations for people to teach, are included for students to consider as they begin their teacher education.

Chapter Outline

Chapter 1 *Why Teach?*

I. Examining Your Motives for Teaching

  A. Knowing Your Motives
  B. Engaging the Questions
  C. Motives for Becoming a Teacher
  D. Motives for Not Becoming a Teacher
  E. Discuss the consequences of sliding into teaching without making a considered choice.

II. The Rewards of Teaching

  A. Extrinsic Rewards
  B. Intrinsic Rewards

C. Rewards in Perspective

III. Sources of Useful Experience

A. Real Encounters

B. Vicarious Experiences (brainstorm, fictional teachers your students are familiar with)

C. Guidance

E. Reflection

Supplementary Lecture and Discussion Topics

1. **Mixed motives for teaching** In Chapter 1 we examine a few motives for teaching and list others. Students may get the wrong impression that most teachers have a single and clear reason for doing certain things. Point out that people engage in most activities for a mixture of motives and that having mixed motives is not a moral failing. Also, forewarn them that motives for teaching tend to change over time. The article by Fuller and Bown listed in the "Additional Resources for Instructors" for this chapter may help here.

2. **Pitfalls in choosing teaching** We are convinced that many people simply "slide" into teacher education programs. Teaching represents a nonchoice. People "know" schools, they can meet the standards, and teaching doesn't look overly taxing and has plentiful vacations distributed throughout the year. So why not give it a try? The personal cost of a casual approach to such an important decision should be spelled out.

Additional Resources for Instructors

Bogue, Ernest Grady. *A Journey of the Heart: The Call to Teaching.* Bloomington, Ind.: Phi Delta Kappa Education Foundation, 1991. This short volume explores the reasons and the motives attracting people to teaching.

Fuller, Frances F., and Oliver Bown. "Becoming a Teacher." In *Teacher Education: The Seventy-fourth Yearbook for the Study of Education*, ed. Kevin Ryan. Chicago: University of Chicago Press, 1975. Fuller and Bown discuss research on the personal context of becoming a teacher, including their own theory of the stages of teaching.

Jersild, Arthur T. *In Search of Self.* New York: Teachers College Press, 1955. This classic in the field provides much insight into why people become teachers.

Johnson, Susan Moore. *Teachers at Work: Achieving Success in Our Schools.* New York: Basic Books, 1990. Johnson provides an analysis, based on interviews with teachers, of why the best teachers are leaving the classroom.

Joseph, Pamela Bolotin, and Gail E. Burnaford (Eds.). *Images of School Teachers in Twentieth-Century America: Paragons, Polarities, Complexities*. New York: St. Martin's Press, 1994. This book makes explicit those things that most often are implicit in the common cultural experiences of teachers and students.

Perrone, Vito. *A Letter to Teachers: Reflections on Schooling and the Art of Teaching.* San Francisco: Jossey-Bass, 1991. This respected scholar on teaching articulates his understanding of schooling and the importance of teaching.

Schubert, William, and William Ayers (Eds.). *Teacher Lore: Learning from Our Own Experiences.* White Plains, N.Y.: Longman, 1992. This edited volume contains essays by various teachers discussing what they have learned from their teaching experiences and the myths and lore surrounding teaching.

Swetnam, Leslie A. "Media Distortion of the Teacher Image." *The Clearing House* (September/October 1992): 30–32. This article describes some of the most common representations of the "stereotypical" images of teachers.

Weber, Sandra, and Claudia Mitchell. *That's Funny, You Don't Look Like a Teacher: Integrating Images and Identity in Popular Culture.* Washington, D.C.: Falmore Press, 1995. This is a book about the images of teachers and teaching that infiltrate our lives, shaping in important but unrecognized ways our notions of who teachers are and what they do.

True Accounts of Teaching

Ashton-Warner, Sylvia. *Teacher*. New York: Simon and Schuster, 1963.

Collins, Marva, and Civia Tamarkin. *Marva Collins' Way*. Los Angeles: Tarcher, 1982. This book takes the reader inside the world of one of America's most inspiring and controversial teachers. Marva Collins describes her method of educating the children others forgot.

Finnegan, William. *Crossing the Line*. New York: Harper and Row, 1986.

Freedman, Samuel G. *Small Victories*. New York: Harper and Row, 1990. This book chronicles life in a New York City high school and its staff in the late 1980s. The highs and lows of teaching in urban schools are pictured, and the major problems affecting life in these schools are vividly presented.

Greenstein, Jack. *What the Children Taught Me: The Experience of an Educator in the Public Schools*. Chicago: University of Chicago Press, 1983.

Herndon, James. *Notes from a Schoolteacher*. New York: Simon and Schuster, 1985.

Hohler, Robert. *I Touch the Future. . . The Story of Christa McAuliffe*. New York: Random House, 1989. The story of the "first teacher in space."

Kammeraad-Campbell, Susan. *Teacher: Dennis Littky's Fight for a Better School.* New York: Plume, 1991. The book chronicles the work of Dennis Littky in a rural New Hampshire high school and the changes that his innovative methods as an administrator brought to a poor, rural, troubled school.

Kane, P. R. (Ed.). *My First Year As a Teacher.* New York: Penguin Books, 1991. This book is a collection of accounts by twenty-five teachers of their first year in teaching, describing their struggles and triumphs as they grappled with their new profession.

Keizer, Garret. *No Place But Here: A Teacher's Vocation in a Rural Community.* New York: Penguin, 1988. Keizer writes evocatively of his experience teaching in a rural high school in northern Vermont. His faith in the students and the people of that rural Vermont town is countered by his skepticism toward the values and driving force of U.S. society at large.

Kidder, Tracy. *Among Schoolchildren.* Boston: Houghton Mifflin, 1989. Kidder spent the entire school year in Chris Zajac's classroom, observing her teach every day. His account shows the demands, rewards, and realities of teaching elementary children in an urban, distressed environment by one teacher, and her impact on the children.

Lathrop-Hawkins, Frances P. *Journey with Children: The Autobiography of a Teacher.* Boulder, Colo.: University Press of Colorado, 1996. This autobiography integrates personal experiences in the classroom with educational teaching practice and theory.

Marquis, David Marshall (Ed.). *I Am a Teacher: A Tribute to America's Teachers.* New York: Simon and Schuster, 1990. The book presents in photographs and interviews why people became teachers and why they stayed in the profession. A moving tribute to real teachers across the United States.

Mathews, Jay. *Escalante, Best Teacher in America.* New York: Holt, 1990. This is the biography of Jamie Escalante, an inspiring math teacher who is the subject of the film *Stand and Deliver.* Escalante wins his students, largely urban Hispanics, with a combination of challenges to pride, demands of dedicated hard work, and demonstrated love.

Millstone, David H. *An Elementary Odyssey.* Portsmouth, N.H.: Heinemann, 1995. Millstone outlines his successful thematic integrated teaching of social studies and his interdisciplinary weaving of the arts, writing, and storytelling.

Natkins, Lucille. *Our Last Term: A Teacher's Diary.* Landem, Md.: University Press of America, 1986.

Paley, Vivian Gussin. *White Teacher.* Cambridge, Mass.: Harvard University Press, 1989. Paley describes her progress in learning to deal more openly with her own perceptions of race.

Palonsky, Stuart. *900 Shows a Year.* New York: Random House, 1986.

Parkay, Forest. *White Teacher, Black School: The Professional Growth of a Ghetto Teacher*. New York: Praeger, 1983.

Rofes, Eric. *Socrates, Plato, and Guys Like Me: Confessions of a Gay Schoolteacher*. Boston: Alyson, 1985.

Ryan, Kevin (Ed.). *The Roller Coaster Year: Stories of First Year Teachers*. New York: HarperCollins, 1991. This book presents the stories of twelve first-year teachers and their struggles and triumphs as they discovered who they were as teachers and why they taught.

Twiss, Ruth. *Morning, Noon, and Night*. Smithtown, N.Y.: Exposition Press, 1982.

Welsh, Patrick. *Tales Out of School*. New York: Viking, 1986.

Wigginton, Eliot. *Sometimes a Shining Moment: The Foxfire Experience*. Garden City, N.Y.: Anchor Press/Doubleday, 1985.

Media Resources

Career Close-Ups: School Teacher (Insight Media, 27 min., 1994). As classrooms become more dangerous and crowded, teachers are challenged to find creative ways to motivate their students. This video, hosted by Whoopi Goldberg, profiles extraordinary teachers who entertain as they educate, tailoring their lessons to fit their students' interests.

Career Encounters: Teaching (Insight Media, 28 min., 1992). This documentary-style program looks at the career of teaching and includes practical information about educational and certification requirements. Teachers explain what they do, how they became involved in education, and what they find most rewarding about their careers.

The Dead Poets' Society (Touchstone, 1989). Robin Williams stars in this highly acclaimed film about a dynamic, iconoclastic English teacher in a prestigious preparatory boys school in New Hampshire during the late 1950s. Not unlike other famous teachers of the past, the English teacher pays a bitter price for encouraging his students to think about, question, and revel in life.

Educating Educators (Insight Media, 20 min., 1989). What are the challenges facing teachers today? What challenges will teachers face in the future? Prominent educators join host Dr. John Goodlad to explore ideas that will help to set the agenda for reform in teacher education.

Making a Difference: Great Teachers (Films for the Humanities and Sciences, 28 min., 1994). This documentary focuses on three teachers who have made a positive impact—academically or personally—on their students' lives. Selected as a result of an essay contest that asked students to write about the teacher who had most challenged and inspired them, the teachers are shown at work in the classroom.

Making a Difference: Great Teachers, II (Films for the Humanities and Sciences, 28 min., 1996). This video follows three teachers and shows how they motivate students and affect their self-esteem.

Mr. Holland's Opus (Buena Vista, 1996). Richard Dreyfuss stars in this highly acclaimed film about a high school music teacher's career over three decades. Changes in students, society, and the curriculum are portrayed as well as the evolution of one teacher's career.

Stand and Deliver (Warner Brothers, 1988). This film depicts the story of real-life math teacher Jaime Escalante, who teaches in a tough, urban area of California. He takes a class of potential dropouts and transforms them so that by the end of the year all his students not only think differently about school but all pass a college-level calculus exam. A moving story.

Teachers (CBS/Fox, 1984). This is a movie that is harshly comic yet poignant. It depicts the dedicated as well as the burned-out teachers in a tough, urban neighborhood. This movie, with its biting observation of teachers and the current educational system, usually provokes strong responses.

Wanted: A Million Teachers (PBS video, 60 min., 1989). This program looks at some of the crises in teaching today, including "burnout," poor pay, low morale, and an overload of administrative duties. These elements in the school work environment may contribute to the sharp decline in the number of teachers entering the profession at a time when attracting talented individuals to the field may be more important than ever.

Student Activities

1. The Fictional Teacher and the Fictional School

As the authors mention, countless depictions of the fictional teacher exist. Although these may be food for one's imagination, real teaching is usually different. Show one of the films listed in Media Resources and analyze the accuracy of the portrayal. Fictionalized teachers can appear to be anything from saviors to burned-out robots to comical pals. A supplementary lecture could focus on a character analysis of teachers illustrated in books, films, and television. Information on the way teachers are presented in the media would be enriching material to present to students. (See "Additional Resources for Instructors.")

2. Real Teachers and Real Schools

An additional topic that may be presented is the real experiences of actual teachers. The accounts of real teachers in such books as *Small Victories, Among Schoolchildren*, *Marva Collins' Way*, and *No Place But Here* present four vivid accounts of teaching. The lecture could also touch on local news about teachers. As an additional presentation for class, the lecturer can invite several local teachers to discuss with students their motivations for teaching and their experiences as teachers. (See references under *True Accounts of Teaching* in "Additional Resources for Instructors.")

3. A Few Thoughts on Teaching and Education

The objectives of this exercise are for students to consider various statements regarding teaching and education, to compare those perceptions with their own, and to share their reflections on the quotations with those of their classmates.

Instructions

a. Give the students a sheet with the quotations about teaching listed below.
b. Ask the students to read the sheet carefully and to consider the implications of each quotation. If the quotation were followed, or could be taken to be true, what are the implications for teaching? Also ask the students to choose which of the following statements, if any, *most* reflects their thoughts about education and teaching. Ask them which of the statements *least* reflects their notions of teaching and education. Tell them to be prepared to share their observations with a partner.
c. When all the students have had enough time to consider the statements, ask them to write one sentence that they think best represents their thoughts about teaching.
d. Ask the students to form groups of about four to discuss their responses and to share their sentences about teaching. Allow about fifteen minutes.
e. Debrief with the whole class.

List of Quotations

- "You cannot teach a man anything; you can only help him find it within himself." (Galileo)
- "One good schoolmaster is worth a thousand priests." (Robert Green Ingersoll)
- "A child . . . must feel the flush of victory and the heart-sinking of disappointment before he takes with a will to the tasks distasteful to him and resolves to dance his way through a dull routine of textbooks." (Helen Keller)
- "That type of scholarship which is bent on remembering things in order to answer people's questions does not qualify one to be a teacher." (Confucius)
- "The teacher is one who makes two ideas grow where only one grew before." (Elbert Hubbard)
- "Her job [the teacher's] is limited to offering the materials and suffices if she demonstrates their use; after that, she leaves the child with his work. Our goal is not so much the imparting of knowledge as the unveiling and developing of spiritual energy." (Maria Montessori)
- "The man who can make hard things easy is the educator." (Ralph Waldo Emerson)
- *More:* Why not be a teacher? You'd be a fine teacher. Perhaps—a great one.
  Rich: And if I were, who would know it?

More: You, your pupils, your friends, God—not a bad public, that. (Robert Bolt, *A Man for All Seasons*)

- "I see the mind of the 5-year old as a volcano with two vents: destructiveness and creativeness." (Sylvia Ashton-Warner, *Teacher*)
- "A poor surgeon hurts 1 person at a time. A poor teacher hurts 130." (Ernest Boyer, president, Carnegie Foundation for Advancement of Teaching)
- "We have inadvertently designed a system in which being good at what you do as a teacher is not formally rewarded, while being poor at what you do is seldom corrected nor penalized." (Elliot Eisner, professor, Stanford School of Education)
- "I have one rule—attention. They give me theirs and I give them mine." (Sister Evangelist, RSM, teacher in Montana)
- "The most important function of education at any level is to develop the personality of the individual and the significance of his life to himself and to others. This is the basic architecture of a life; the rest is ornamentation and decoration of the structure." (Grayson Kirk, president, Columbia University)
- "What a teacher doesn't say . . . is a telling part of what a student hears." (Maurice Natanson, professor of philosophy, Yale University)
- "I cannot join the space program and restart my life as an astronaut, but this opportunity to connect my abilities as an educator with my interests in history and space is a unique opportunity to fulfill my early fantasies." (Christa McAuliffe, teacher, Concord, N.H.; from her winning essay in NASA's nationwide search for the first teacher to travel in space)
- "I had learned to respect the intelligence, integrity, creativity, and capacity for deep thought and hard work latent somewhere in every child; they had learned that I differed from them only in years and experience, and that as I, an ordinary human being, loved and respected them, I expected payment in kind." (Sybil Marshall, on eighteen years as a teacher in a one-room schoolhouse in rural England)
- "A teacher must believe in the value and interest of his subject as a doctor believes in health." (Gilbert Highet, *The Art of Teaching*)
- "Teaching is an instinctual art, mindful of potential, craving of realization, a pausing, seamless process." (A. Bartlett Giamatti, president, Yale University)
- "Much that passes for education . . . is not education at all but ritual. The fact is that we are being educated when we know it least." (David P. Gardner, president, University of Utah)

- "A primary reason for my success in the classroom was that I couldn't forget that schooling was changing me and separating me from the life I enjoyed before becoming a student." (Richard Rodriguez, writer, scholar, in his autobiography, *Hunger of Memory*)

- "I didn't know anything about educational theory, and I have often thought that worked in my favor. Without preconceived ideas and not bound by rules, I was forced to deal with my students as individuals, to talk to them, to listen to them, to find out their needs. I wasn't trying to see how they fit into any learning patterns or educational models. I followed my own instincts and taught according to what felt right." (Marva Collins)

4. The Professional Interview (group work)

Using the professional interview activity outlined in point 6 below, debrief that activity with your whole class. Ask students either individually or in groups to present the ideas they found from doing their interviews. Were there any recurring themes in the teachers' responses? A helpful technique may be to have groups of students write important themes on transparencies or on poster paper to display to the class as a whole. Discuss with the students what insights they gleaned from considering this body of interviews.

5. An Analysis of Teacher Portrayals (for individual or group work)

Ask your students to watch several hours of television portraying teachers, to view a movie with a teacher as a central character, or to listen to songs with references to teaching or teachers in them. Have the students write up what they find. Discuss the portrayals, stereotypes, and depictions of teachers presented through popular culture and ask the students to reflect, either in writing or in small-group discussion, how the image that popular culture presents of teaching matches that of what they see in their field-site schools. (Use the sources regarding media portrayals in the "Additional Resources for Instructors" listing as well as the videos in "Media Resources" as a starting point.)

6. Shifting from Student to Teacher: The Professional Interview

See ready-to-copy assignment sheet.

Often a good teacher is easy to observe, but the data on what makes the teaching effective are difficult to collect. The good teacher's "machine" runs so smoothly that the individual parts are indistinguishable to the novice observer. This activity helps the student obtain critical data about someone's teaching. The activity helps students begin to structure their professional thinking while sharpening their observation skills.

It is difficult to conduct a focused interview that yields complete information. For this reason, we encourage you to model the interview process first in class. The students should interview a teacher of their choice. Perhaps the best selection criterion is to choose a significant teaching influence from their past. Usually students welcome the opportunity to chat "professionally" with one of their former teachers. In doing so, they begin the transition from student to teacher, a role in which they must soon feel comfortable.

TEACHER INTERVIEW / OBSERVATION REFLECTION ASSIGNMENT

Purpose:

The student will investigate the career of teaching by observing and interviewing a teacher and reporting his or her reaction to the interview.

Requirements:

- Interview and observe a current teacher.
- Describe the contexts in which this teacher teaches.
- Include the following:
  - Teacher's motivation for deciding to enter the profession
  - Advantages and disadvantages of the profession as portrayed by this teacher
  - Teacher's style, philosophy, and values
  - Teacher's specific environment
  - Teacher's experience
  - Teacher's expectations for the future
  - Teacher's philosophy regarding making educational decisions (how?)
  - Teacher's greatest challenges
  - Teacher's best advice for a new teacher
  - Teacher's greatest rewards
- Observe, describe, and interview the teacher about at least three decisions you observed the teacher make during your time in the classroom.
- Conclude with a description of what you've learned about teaching, decision making, and diverse educational contexts that you didn't know before.
- Describe your reaction—questions, concerns, feelings, and so on.

Evaluation:

- Depth of detail (probably around 5 pages, typed)
- Clear and error-free communication
- Demonstration of reflection

Due date: ______________________

Chapter 2 *What Is a School?*

Learning Objectives

After studying the chapter, students will be able to

- distinguish between education and schooling.
- describe the purposes of schooling.
- apply and analyze a school's formal statement of purpose.
- explain, apply, and analyze the school models described in the text: worker trainer, college prep, social panacea, social escalator, shopping mall, family, human potential developer, acculturator.
- describe how schools function as representatives and transmitters of culture.
- identify, explain, and discuss some elements of American dominant culture evidenced in schools.
- describe how schools could operate as vehicles for social reconstruction.
- describe some of the similarities and differences among schools.
- list and explain some of the features of schools that are effective with respect to academic outcomes and those that are considered effective on the basis of more holistic outcomes.

Chapter Overview

This chapter highlights some of the more common conceptions of schools. Each model is briefly described, but we also acknowledge that each model is useful only in its ability to explain or describe what exists. No one model, then, can completely explain a school; however, as long as we recognize the limitations of models, we can draw on what the models can offer to form a fuller understanding of schools.

Our intent in this chapter is to demonstrate that schools are human inventions, created and sustained to enable children to learn what they need to function effectively. Schools were created so that students can master key skills. We change and modify schools constantly because—like all other human inventions—schools are imperfect. As times change and as we change our minds about what schools should be accomplishing, we change school goals and curriculum.

Schools also reflect and transmit a culture. This aspect of schooling is one that has come under increased scrutiny in the recent past. Should schools tacitly or overtly support the dominant culture of the society? Should schools be structured so that they are encouraging students to fit into the social structure as it exists, or should schools demonstrate to students how they can be agents of change? As public schools exist now, they pass on a community's values, which are imparted through the work of teachers, who are cultural transmitters. The ways schools are organized, the content of the curriculum, the methods of instruction—all reflect current national norms. It must be noted, though, that teachers may also be participants in the debate regarding the interpretation and redefinition of norms.

Student readers should recognize the range and diversity of schools. For that reason, we encourage them to compare their own experiences of schooling with the models shown in the chapter. We expect that class discussion will highlight differences and similarities in their schooling. Understanding the differing, and at times competing, conceptions of schools is vital for a prospective teacher.

Chapter Outline

Chapter 2 *What Is a School?*

I. Education and Schooling

  A. Education

  B. Schooling

  C. The Role of the School

II. Discovering the Purposes of School

  A. Formal Statements

  B. Personal Experiences

III. Models of Schools

  A. Trainer of Good Worker

B. Preparer for College
C. Shopping Mall
D. Social Escalator
E. Social Panacea
F. Developer of Human Potential
G. Acculturator
H. Family

IV. Schools As Transmitters or Re-creators of Culture

A. Transmitting Culture
B. Reconstructing Society
1. Social
2. Democratic
3. Economic

V. What Are Schools Like Today?

A. Similarities
B. Differences

VI. What Is a Good School?

A. Characteristics of an Effective School
1. Teacher Expectations
2. Communication
3. Task Orientation
4. Time on Task
5. Behavior Management
6. Instructional Leader Principal
7. Parents
8. School Environment

B. Characteristics of an Effective School: Another View
1. Coherence
2. Good Communication
3. Teacher Subgroups
4. Student Incentives
5. Student Discipline

6. Extracurricular Activities

VII. The Unfinished Work of the Schools

Supplementary Lecture and Discussion Topics

1. **Teacher: the creator or transmitter of culture?** In more detail, present to your class how the teacher can be either the creator or transmitter of culture. Explain how a teacher can also embody some of the models of schools described in the chapter. Explore in greater detail the realities of a teacher being either a transmitter or a creator of culture. What obstacles does one face as a teacher fully committed to the cause of reconstruction? To what extent can a teacher be a convincing transmitter of the culture? You can refer to any of the research recently done on teachers and their perceptions of their workplace. (Susan Moore Johnson's book is listed in the reference section.) Are the elements of a teaching job and the requirements for social reconstructions too disparate to expect teachers, in general, to work actively to change society? Is there a basic mismatch between (a) anyone who would stay with teaching because of the stability of the profession, (b) tenure, and (c) the active participation and risk taking required of those committed to social reconstruction? You can also provide examples of well-known teachers and analyze what seems to be their conception of being a teacher.

2. **An international perspective on schools** Describe the typical school in several other countries. (If you have international students, this is an excellent time for them to make a presentation about the schools in their own countries.) Describe the physical layout of the schools, the roles of teachers and students, the length of the school day and school year, the content of the curriculum, and the goals of education. Show how differences in schooling practices reflect differences in national culture or ideology.

3. **The meaning of school: different people** Use excerpts from ethnographies and biographies to highlight the differences in the ways people from different subcultures in the United States experience schooling. Explain the relationship between home culture and school culture.

4. **The school as a workplace** Describe the organizational structure of elementary, middle, and high schools. Review the kinds of jobs that people hold in each. Invite discussion about the contribution of each kind of worker to the school's mission.

5. **Privatization** Discuss how privatization groups like the Edison Project affect the model and decision-making process in the schools they take over.

Additional Resources for Instructors

Freedman, Samuel G. *Small Victories: The Real World of a Teacher, Her Students, and Their High School.* New York: Harper and Row, 1990. The author spent a year with a teacher and her class in a school in the Lower East Side of New York. The book presents a grim portrayal of life in poor, urban schools.

Good, Thomas, and Jere Brophy. *Looking in Classrooms.* 6th ed. New York: HarperCollins, 1994. This text offers a popular, class-tested examination of strategies for observing and describing classroom teaching. This edition features a concise and authoritative review of classroom research combined with specific teaching recommendations.

Goodlad, John I. *A Place Called School.* New York: McGraw-Hill, 1984. Goodlad and his team of researchers spent several thousand hours collecting data on what schools are actually like. The book is a detailed, scholarly look at the events, forces, and philosophies that shape U.S. schools.

Goodlad, John I., and Pamela Keating (Eds.). *Access to Knowledge: An Agenda for Our Nation's Schools.* New York: College Entrance Examination Board, 1990. This book contains articles by scholars and educational researchers prescribing directions for U.S. public education for the future.

Hampel, Robert. *The Last Little Citadel.* Boston: Houghton Mifflin, 1986. This modern history has much to say about the nature of high school and, indirectly, the elementary school. What emerges is a laissez-faire world of schools where it is difficult to determine who is in charge.

Johnson, Susan Moore. *Teachers at Work: Achieving Success in Our Schools.* New York: Basic Books, 1990. Johnson provides an analysis, based on interviews with teachers, of why the best teachers are leaving the classroom.

Lawson, Robert, Val D. Rust, and Susanne Shafer (Eds.). *Education and Social Concern: An Approach to Social Foundations.* Ann Arbor: Praeger, 1987. The text explores the social dimensions of schooling, developing in more detail the varying models of schools and their social functions.

Lightfoot, Sara Lawrence. *The Good High School: Portraits of Character and Culture.* New York: Basic Books, 1983. Sara Lawrence Lightfoot creates a highly readable account of life in several exemplary high schools.

Peterson, Ralph. *Life in a Crowded Place: Making a Learning Community.* Portsmouth, N.H.: Heinemann, 1992. This text discusses how schools struggle with the factors that work against education and how schools can build their own communities.

Media Resources

All-American High (Direct Cinema, 58 min., 1985). This video is a documentary about Finnish foreign exchange student Rikki Rauhala, who spent her senior year in high school in Torrance, California. It shows her various classes, the pep rallies, and the prom. The video counterpoints the frantic pace of U.S. high schools with Rikki's sharp observations of U.S. high schools and U.S. youth.

High School Stories: One Day in America's Schools (PBS video, 60 min., 1993). Explores the impact of community and school environments on the lives of students and their ability and willingness to learn and achieve in school. In this documentary, public television stations in seven different locations across America document a day in the life of high school seniors. See how students thrive in a variety of learning situations.

Marshall High Fights Back (Prod: Drew Associates, Dist: Direct Cinema Ltd., 58 min., 1985). An inner-city high school once declared "out of control" makes a crucial turnaround in this story of how a school, a community, and its children find the power within themselves to make changes for the better under a new principal and his successor.

The Nongraded School (AIT, 30 min., 1993). Robert H. Anderson is president of a nonprofit organization for leadership development, former Dean of Education at Texas Tech University, and coauthor of *The Nongraded Elementary School.* Barbara Nelson Pavan was principal of the first nongraded team-teaching school in the United States. Currently working on a major study of continuous progress schools, Anderson and Pavan discuss how students learn more and teacher satisfaction increases when schools move to nongradedness.

The Quality School (Insight Media, 207 min., 1993). Dr. William Glasser discusses how reality therapy and control theory can be applied to schools. He provides practical suggestions for creating a quality school where administrators, teachers, counselors, parents, and students work together to provide all students with an education based upon cooperation and established standards.

Renewing a Place Called School (Insight Media, 90 min., 1989). These six fifteen-minute videos focus on methods for improving American education by renewing individual schools. Dr. John Goodlad offers practical suggestions for starting, maintaining, and evaluating site-based renewal programs.

The School As the Unit of Change (EBEC, 15 min., 1988). John Goodlad explores the importance of school environment in creating change in schools.

Schools (PBS video, 29 min., 1985). Children spend more of their waking hours in school than anywhere else, and they cope with situations and personalities in school that will have a profound effect in their later lives. Are they learning what we're teaching, or are they getting a different message?

Schools and the Freedom to Change (EBEC, 15 min., 1988). Professor John Goodlad, noted educational researcher, asks, "How much freedom do we have in our schools?" He answers by pointing to a national definition of an agenda for schools. He shows evidence that the national response falls short of expectations.

Success! The Marva Collins Approach (Films Incorporated, 29 min., 1981). Through her teaching, Marva Collins communicates a seemingly absolute faith to students that they can and will succeed in their learning tasks. The film shows how she handles discipline problems in her school, which she founded in an upstairs room in her west side Chicago home in 1975.

Why Do These Kids Love School? (Insight Media, 60 min., 1990). This documentary visits schools around the country that have introduced bold, innovative programs in which students, teachers, parents, and administrators join together to create a vibrant and supportive educational environment. The video underscores the strong student and faculty morale and the improved test scores that have resulted from these programs.

Student Activities

1. Transmitter of Culture? Social Reconstructionist?

Based on the number of students in your class, divide them into groups of four to six. Assign each side as a supporter of the "transmitter of culture" model or the "social reconstructionist" model. Allow each group adequate time to research the theory it supports. At a scheduled date, conduct a debate between the groups that support the view of schools as transmitting the culture and the groups that support the view of schools as reconstructionist. If you will have more than one debate, stagger the debate times so that no one observes the debate before his or her team debates. After students have conducted their debate, they may sit in on other teams' debates. Videotape each debate, and schedule some time outside of class so that the students can watch the debates they missed. As a class, discuss the issues debated. What are the relative merits of each of the theories? Which points made were particularly strong? Did the debates change or modify people's views on one conception of schools or another?

2. What Are Schools For?

Have students ask four or five people of different ages and situations the following questions: "What are schools supposed to do? What do you think schools actually do?" Students should write up the responses and comment on similarities, differences, and implications. If possible, ask your students to interview five teachers with the same questions. What are the results? What are the implications? What are the similarities and differences between the teachers' responses and those of the general public?

3. What Is a School? (for group work)

Videotape a fifteen- to twenty-minute segment depicting "What is a school?" You may want to have a montage, a series of people describing their thoughts, scenes of various activities occurring, or a piece that is journalistic. Present your video to the whole class. What does your video say about schooling in general?

4. Students' Perspectives on Schooling (for individual or group work)

Interview approximately a dozen students about their schooling. How do they describe their school? Learning? Education? Schooling in general? Collate your findings to write up or to present to class. What kinds of conceptions of schooling have emerged from your work?

5. Field Site School Analysis (for individual or group work)

As the text indicates, the models of schools are abstractions of daily realities of schools. Few schools, if any, are completely one model. Analyze the school in which you are doing fieldwork. Describe the elements of the school model that exist. Document through written text, photographs, audiotape, or videotape. Present to the class. How does your analysis reflect upon the mission of the school and the community in general?

6. The School As Transmitter of Culture (for individual or group work)

Culture is a powerful word with numerous connotations. In recent years, heated debates have erupted over what American culture is—if there is *an* American culture—and how culture should be presented in schools. Look at the arguments from a number of representatives who support various positions (perennialists, traditionalists, multiculturalists [who hold a number of different positions], feminists, reconceptualists, and so on). Select three strands or arguments. Research the arguments and present your findings to class.

7. Create a School (see copy-ready assignment sheet on the following page)

CREATE-A-SCHOOL ASSIGNMENT

Purpose:

To explore the relationship between philosophy, educational goals, and school models. Students will describe a school of their own creation.

Assignment:

Select a specific vocation, subject area, or educational goal and create a school to produce students who are equipped to meet the goal or to satisfy the requirements of the vocation. A well-focused goal will help simplify the complexity of the task.

Describe your school's
- goals or purpose.
- philosophy.
- most appropriate model.
- essential skills and/or content.
- necessary resources and materials.
- most effective methods.

Evaluation:

- Satisfaction of requirements
- Detail and support of ideas
- Rationale for decisions
- Ability to communicate the model orally or in writing

Note to Instructors: You may want to start this activity in small groups or individually in this chapter with a due date after the philosophy chapter has been presented.

Chapter 3 What Is Life in Schools Like?

Learning Objectives

After studying the chapter, students will be able to

- explain how the school serves a socialization function through the explicit and implicit curricula.
- explain why students in elementary classrooms learn to deny desire, delay gratification, cope with interruptions, and work through distractions.
- describe the range of educational experiences for middle-grade students, based on the grade configuration of the school, the size of the school, the administration's and teachers' orientations, the goals of the school, and the staffing patterns.
- explain how conflicting goals of the high school require numerous elective courses that often strain the resources of the institution.
- explain how the instructional practices in high schools have remained largely unchanged over the past century.
- explain how secondary students experience high school differently from each other, based on tracking, the courses in which they enroll, the feedback they receive from teachers, and the tacit agreements they make with their teachers.
- describe the nature and role of peer groups and adolescent subculture in shaping the attitudes and behaviors of secondary students.
- explain how teachers' expectations of students are formed and how they affect teachers' interactional patterns with students.

Chapter Overview

Chapter 3 focuses on many different studies that have examined life in classrooms. Much research is cited in order to present to prospective teachers an accurate portrait of what life in school is like. In this way, prospective teachers can broaden their perception of school life beyond their own experiences and can think about their role in the classroom. By understanding peer cultures and teacher-student interactional patterns, prospective teachers will be better equipped to respond to students and their needs.

The studies reported look at school life at different levels: elementary, middle, and high school. Philip Jackson's study of life in elementary classrooms explains how daily routines shape the experiences of both teachers and students. The dearth of research on middle schools leaves many questions unanswered; nevertheless, student experiences in the middle grades, between sixth and eighth grades, are strongly influenced by the configuration of grades, the size of the school, and the goals and objectives set out by the administration. Studies of high schools by Boyer and Cuban highlight the unchanging nature of these environments and offer recommendations for change. The chapter also discusses instructional aspects of schools, such as how students spend their class time, how student access to knowledge varies, and how students and teachers make tacit agreements for peaceful coexistence. We provide a sampling of major research studies that cite the practices of teachers and the practices of schools in educating students.

An integral part of any school is its social life. The chapter discusses the subcultures and social elements of schooling, particularly for adolescents. In high school, the powerful influence of the student peer group dictates "appropriate" behaviors that, in some cases, run counter to the aims of the school. We focus on Penelope Eckert's extensive study of a high school culture in which students identified with either the "jocks" or "burnouts" to highlight the impact these groups have on the experience of students in school. The adolescent need to identify with a group has a profound effect on the ways in which students perceive themselves and interact with others. We include a summary of the findings in Lawrence Steinberg's study, *Beyond the Classroom: Why School Reform Has Failed and What Parents Need to Do,* which reviews the aspects of teen culture that prevent students from doing well academically. We assert that teachers need to be cognizant of the subcultures at work within schools and need to develop ways to respond to student needs and wants.

We conclude the chapter by briefly discussing the ways in which teachers affect students' motivation. Teacher-student interactional patterns in the classroom are shown to be linked to student performance. By including information about these interactional patterns, we hope to encourage students to make their own observations of teachers' behavioral patterns in classes and compare their findings to those in the text.

Chapter Outline

Chapter 3 *What Is Life in Schools Like?*

I. The School As an Environment

II. The School As an Agent of Socialization
   A. Formal—Explicit Curriculum
   B. Informal—Implicit Curriculum

III. Studies of Life in Elementary Schools
   A. Routine
   B. Teachers' Role
      1. Gatekeeper
      2. Supply Dispenser
      3. Granter of Privileges
      4. Timekeeper
   C. Students' Experience
      1. Delay
      2. Denial of Desire
      3. Interruptions
      4. Social Distraction

IV. More About Life in Elementary Schools
   A. Ability Grouping or Tracking

V. Studies of Life in Middle and Junior High Schools

VI. Studies of Life in High Schools

VII. Some Common Characteristics

VIII. A New Call for High School Reform

IX. Peer Groups and Teen Subcultures
   A. Jocks and Burnouts
   B. Influences on Achievement

X. The Role of Teachers' Expectations

Supplementary Lecture and Discussion Topics

1. **The hidden curriculum** Much has been written about the hidden curriculum by educational researchers who think that schools, through their hidden curricula, support and maintain the status quo. Such educational writers harshly criticize public schools for the illusion they create of an institution where all are encouraged to succeed. For such researchers, the hidden curriculum negatively affects students. The hidden curriculum is also said to negatively affect female students and minorities. You may want to explore this interpretation of the hidden curriculum with your students in greater detail. Finally, discuss with them—assuming that the hidden curriculum does work in negative ways on students' self-concept—why such an agenda exists. Explore the positive effects of the hidden curriculum.

2. **Teachers' expectations** Devote some time to discussing teachers' expectations of students and what the research indicates about teachers' expectations. Some research has found that in the lower elementary grades, teachers set expectations of students and tend to have higher expectations for students who are clean, well dressed, and attractive. What are the problems with such a scenario? Many teachers also have higher expectations of children who are the same race as the teacher. Describe some of the research findings in greater detail with the students, and indicate ways to foster teacher expectations that can improve the experiences of all children.

3. **Values in the curriculum** Discuss the explicit and implicit curricula of your school. Have students list school requirements and identify the values transmitted by their inclusion. Talk about the less visible requirements, such as supporting some athletic teams, joining social groups (fraternities, sororities), or hanging out in certain places. Distinguish between the implicit curriculum that might reasonably be ascribed to school intentions and the implicit curriculum that probably originates with the students, by virtue of factors such as their economic status or hometown.

4. **Future instruction in high school** Boyer and Cuban studied high school programs and came up with very different recommendations for change. Boyer advocated revitalizing programs by sweeping changes in teaching; Cuban advocated strengthening teacher-centered instruction. Review the work of these authors, and discuss the implications for students if either approach were adopted. Review points made in Chapters 12 and 15 about different teaching strategies and their influence on learning.

5. **School climate** Describe how schools differ in climate, and review some of the features of structure and organization that affect climate.

6. **Tracking in the high school** Although much has been written criticizing the use of tracking in the high school, many, if not most, public high schools still do some tracking. Examine the arguments for and against tracking. Explore some of the common questions surrounding tracking. How does tracking affect a student's self-image? How can a teacher provide enough challenge for a bright student in a mixed-ability class so that he or she won't be held back? How can a teacher effectively teach a classroom of heterogeneous

students? What are the differences in class size in the different tracks? How do teachers view teaching "honors" or "general"-level classes? Finally, you may want to share with your students a curriculum of a high school that uses tracking. Look at the curriculum, for example, of the ninth-grade general science class and the ninth-grade college preparatory science class. What are the differences in activities? Textbooks? Skills to be covered?

Additional Resources for Instructors

Bruckerhoff, Charles. *Between Classes: Faculty Life at Truman High.* New York: Teachers College Press, 1991. An interesting look at some aspects of faculty life that rarely get observed.

Eckert, Penelope. *Jocks and Burnouts: Social Categories and Identity in the High School.* New York: Teachers College Press, 1989. Penny Eckert spent several years in a high school, and her sociological analysis of the importance of peer group subcultures makes for fascinating reading.

Marshall, Catherine (Ed.). *The New Politics of Race and Gender.* Bristol, Pa.: Falmer Press, 1993. The shifting demographics of the 1990s have brought about new thinking in the politics of race and gender in the schools. The author shows how the politics of race and gender enter proposals for school choice, leadership questions, and curriculum debates.

Rottier, Jerry, and Beverly Ogan. *Cooperative Learning in Middle-level Schools.* Washington, D.C.: National Education Association, 1992. This book provides several sample lesson plans, staff development workshop material, and project planning forms for middle school students.

Sadker, Myra, and David Sadker. "Sexism in the Classroom: Grade School to Graduate School." *Phi Delta Kappan* 67 (March 1986): 512. Based on the belief that unequal treatment yields unequal results, this article points out the inequities in interactions between teachers and their male and female students and shows how these inequities can be reduced.

Siskin, Leslie. *Realms of Knowledge: Academic Departments in Secondary Schools.* Bristol, Pa.: Falmer Press, 1994. This book explores why teachers find academic departments to be crucial to their high school setting. Departments are seen as boundaries for dividing the school, centers of social interaction, decision-making forums, and knowledge centers.

Stevenson, Chris, and Judy F. Carr. *Integrated Studies in the Middle Grades: Dancing Through the Walls.* New York: Teachers College Press, 1993. Stevenson and Carr invited middle-level teachers to design and implement innovative teaching units that would be more interesting to the students they teach. They provide the reader with dozens of detailed examples of integrated curriculum units to encourage the reader to try them out or to develop his or her own.

Wexler, Philip. *Become Somebody: Toward a Social Psychology of School.* Bristol, Pa.: Falmer Press, 1992. Wexler discusses the need to pay attention to the students as "whole people" and to be aware of their needs as members of society as well as learners.

Media Resources

The Breakfast Club (MCA, 1985). This movie centers around a Saturday morning detention that a group of students from different cliques must serve. Throughout the morning, they talk and challenge each other's perceptions of who they really are. The movie captures much of the uncertainty teenagers have about their social position, while revealing their aspirations for the future.

The End of a Morning (EDC, 16 min.). Made at Hilltop Head Start Center in Roxbury, Massachusetts, this film shows a classroom of four-year-olds completing their morning activities. A final segment catches the teachers talking to each other about how the day went.

Mondays, Marbles, and Chalk: A Video Course on Classroom Management (8-part series, BFA, video). One title in the series is *Children Are . . .* (49 min.): the child's basic human needs and how the child's behavior is affected by them are discussed. Four goals of misbehavior and how to deal with each are examined. Another title is *How to Give a Room a Class* (38 min.): the use of space, time, and the affective climate in the classroom are examined.

Schools of Thought I (The Learning Source, 30 min., 1992). A series of six videos, each lasting 30 minutes, *Schools of Thought* presents topics related to classroom and student management. These topics include tracking, the nongraded school, quality schools, restructuring schools, and classroom discipline.

Schools of Thought II (The Learning Source, 30 min., 1992). A series of six videos, each lasting 30 minutes, *Schools of Thought* discusses the latest theories and findings in education. It presents instructional innovations and gives suggestions for implementing them in the classroom. Topics include performance assessment, parental involvement, multiple intelligences, conflict resolution, reading styles and whole languages, and creating caring classrooms.

Speaking for Ourselves: The Challenge of Being Deaf (Campus, 26 min.). The film traces the daily activities and progress of a class of deaf twelve-year-olds during a typical school year. Through their temporary setbacks and later achievements, the film examines the integration of deaf children into the hearing world.

Teacher, Lester Bit Me! (EDC, 9 min., 1975). In this animated version of a preschool day, everything seems to go wrong. The teacher arrives at school anticipating a happy and productive day, but mischief and mishaps overturn all her plans. By exaggerating some of the worst fears of people who work with young children, this film provides an opportunity to discuss some common difficulties and ways they might be solved.

They Can Do It (EDC, 35 min.). Made in the Pastorius Public School in Philadelphia, this film documents the school experiences of 26 first-graders who had never been to school before. Starting with the second day of school, the film records the class on six separate occasions throughout the school year.

The Tunnel (Dist: university film libraries, 25 min., 1975). This film is based on real incidents surrounding a young man's violent encounter with a gang and the subsequent pressures surrounding his day at school. Various people play a role during his agonizing day: police, school administrators, peers, rival gang leaders, counselors, teachers, and parents.

Who Needs Boys? (ABC, 15 min., 1992). A John Stoessel report for *20/20* that demonstrates how even in young grades boys dominate classroom participation.

Student Activities

1. The Typical Day of a Teacher

Have each student get permission to spend the day with a teacher at the grade level or subject area in which the student aspires to teach. The students should keep track of how the teacher spends his or her day by noting the activity and the time spent on each activity. The results of the day's activities can be shared and discussed in class. Use the following chart as a guide for the students. *Note:* You might tell your students that some activities listed, such as "teaching—whole class" or "teaching—small group," may happen several times during the day for various lengths of time. It would be expected that they might have several entries for certain activities.

Activity	Time	Minutes Used on Task
Example: *Lunch duty*	*11:30*	*22 minutes*
1. filling out forms: attendance paperwork from main office		
2. reading/correcting student work		
3. teaching—whole class		
4. teaching—small group		
5. teaching—individual		
6. lunch		
7. faculty meetings: whole school		

Activity	Time	Minutes Used on Task
8. team planning (grade or subject)		
9. duties—hall, lavatory, lunch		
10. meeting student outside of class for discipline problem		
11. free time—coffee break, chatting with colleagues		
12. planning lessons		
13. preparing materials		
14. library research		
15. talking to other teachers or counselors about a student who is having trouble		
16. IEP meetings or child study team meetings		
17. calling/conferencing with parents		
18. supervising extracurricular activities/ coaching		
19. other		

2. Case Studies of Student Life

Have each student "shadow" an elementary or secondary school pupil for the duration of the school day. (If necessary, this might be a "day" pieced together from separate short visits.) Be sure students have the permission of the pupil and his or her teacher. Invite comments and analysis regarding the observations. Suggest using a stopwatch to document the number of minutes the student spends in academic on-task time.

3. Peer Cultures in Different Schools (group activity)

Have the students form groups according to their high school experience: prep school, private school, public school, parochial school. Each group can create a profile of the peer culture in the given setting. Ask the students to speculate on the origins of the culture as well as the effects of the culture on the future careers of the students who attend the school.

4. Tracking

Students should interview three or more elementary and/or secondary school teachers to learn their views on tracking. Does the school they teach in track students? In what subjects?

How do they (the teachers) feel about this practice? What effects do they see on their students' affective or cognitive development?

5. Teacher Experience

In groups of four or five, have the students discuss their experiences with teacher expectations when they were in elementary or secondary school. What were the teacher expectations for them? For their classmates? How did they respond to the expectations set for them?

Chapter 4   Who Are Today's Students?

Learning Objectives

After studying the chapter, students will be able to

- explain the concepts of cultural diversity and cultural pluralism, and their implications in the classroom.
- describe the demographic trends of U.S. minorities and describe how ethnic and cultural differences between public school teachers and students may foster misunderstanding.
- identify and explain William Glasser's control theory and describe how this theory can influence a teacher's behavior with students.
- explain Howard Gardner's theory of multiple intelligences and relate that theory to teaching.
- describe the concept of learning styles and their potential influence on teachers.
- discuss the opposing positions in the debate on multicultural education.
- describe the salient elements of the IDEA, including the key terms *appropriate public education* and *least-restrictive environment.*
- describe the term *gifted and talented* as applied to students, and explain how gifted and talented students are identified and educated.
- explain the impact of the *Lau* v. *Nichols* Supreme Court decision on bilingual education.
- describe the models of bilingual education.
- describe the work of Dr. James Comer in the school intervention project of New Haven, Connecticut.

Chapter Overview

This chapter focuses on the students who fill classrooms across the country and the diversity these students represent. The chapter first explores who is being educated in our schools and seeks to understand what their background is and what an optimal learning environment looks like for them. The chapter then looks to understand how these students learn and describes programs to facilitate their learning. The chapter closes with a look at who is teaching these students and whether teachers and learners can understand one another. Throughout the chapter, prospective teachers will appreciate the range of ethnic, cultural, and linguistic backgrounds found in our schools; the different degrees of parental involvement in school; and the challenging and diverse needs, abilities, and learning styles of today's school-age population.

The overwhelming majority of public school teachers remain white, middle-class women while the student population becomes more and more diverse. Prospective teachers need to be aware of the wide range of backgrounds represented in a given class. For that reason, we spend considerable time discussing the demographics of the school-age population, which is dominated by a steady growth in the minority population while the white population remains relatively stable. We link this discussion to the concept of cultural diversity and pluralism.

The theories of psychiatrist William Glasser provide rich sources for thought for prospective teachers, who can make sense of their students' behaviors once they understand their students' needs. It is our hope that teachers will use some of the findings in planning and implementing their lessons.

The chapter also presents theories on how students learn. Howard Gardner's theory of multiple intelligences is described and complemented by a discussion of individual learning styles. We strongly believe that teachers should try to incorporate an appreciation for diverse capabilities and an awareness of learning styles into their lessons so that they can facilitate the learning of all students, no matter what their strengths may be.

A portion of the chapter is devoted to discussing programs designed to enhance the learning of identified groups of students. We describe multicultural and bilingual education programs that are geared to help students from different cultural or linguistic origins. The special needs of disabled children are served through a variety of individualized programs that strive to provide "free, appropriate public education in the least restrictive environment." We also note that programs for gifted and talented students tend to be underfunded because of the elitist connotation of such programs.

By discussing the needs of each type of child, we also emphasize that a student is more than a label. It is important for teachers to look beyond the category and teach the person. The most helpful way to teach the individual is by gaining sound knowledge of the students along with strong pedagogical training.

Chapter Outline

Chapter 4 *Who Are Today's Students?*

I. Diversity in the Classroom

II. Diverse Needs

III. Diverse Abilities

- A. Multiple Intelligences
- B. Differing Learning Styles
- C. Students with Disabilities
- D. Gifted and Talented Students

IV. The School's Response to Diversity

- A. Multicultural Education
- B. Bilingual Education
    - 1. Models
        - a. Transitional
        - b. Immersion
        - c. Submersion
        - d. English As a Second Language
- C. Special Education
- D. Programs for the Gifted and Talented
- E. Nontraditional Programs
- F. Diversity: A Complex Phenomenon

V. The Teacher's Response to Diversity

- A. Teacher-Student Disparity
- B. Implications for Teachers

Supplemen…

1. **Multicu…** …ıcation
circles tc… …
concepts… …that
minimizı… …f
knowled… …r
multicul… …y learn
about im… …Those
who do… …
multicul… …tial
events, p… …
students… …ean
influence… …is. In
addition, they argue that schools cannot teach everything, so they need to select the most important issues. The debate most likely will rage on. You may want to examine the premises of each argument as well as explore the highly political nature of the debate. Include recent issues such as the California adoption of an American history book for its public schools and the process by which it was selected.

2. **The cost of educating children with special, particular needs** In an ideal world, the cost of education would not be a concern. However, particularly given the economy in the 1990s, the funding of educational programs has become a looming problem. The federal government is backing away from heavy financial commitments to fund specific programs, and taxpayers repeatedly reject the budgets of their local school districts. Because of budgetary constraints, schools are not able, and probably will not be able in the near future, to meet the needs of all students. What are the actual costs of particular programs for students? How much can a particular program per student cost? In a typical school, how much money is spent on special education programs? Bilingual or ESL programs? Gifted and talented programs? Explain how particular programs, such as special education programs, are mandated by federal legislation, yet federal funding is insufficient to cover the costs of these programs. Speculate on the resentment that these expenditures may cause among residents who see other programs that may serve a large portion of the student body being eliminated due to lack of resources. Explore the various aspects of the problem with your students. You may want to invite a local superintendent to discuss the impact of funding difficulties on his or her school district.

3. **Life before PL 94-142** Before special education programs were implemented in the United States, how were children with learning disabilities educated? Trace the history of education for disabled children, and explain the changes and benefits that special education programs have made for children with special needs.

4. **"Special" teachers** Invite several local teachers in who teach gifted and talented students and who teach special needs children. Ask them to conduct a panel discussion with your class. What education is necessary to teach gifted and talented or special needs students? What are the biggest rewards of working with such students? What are the

biggest challenges? What do they think will happen to their field in the future? What are their most pressing concerns as teachers of special needs children? Ask your class to prepare questions for the teachers.

5. **Bilingual education** Invite a colleague (or you, if you are fluent in another language) to teach part of a lesson in a language other than English—perhaps a language spoken at home by a member of the class, if possible. Have the guest speak only in the other language, responding in that language to questions or comments made in English. (This is the immersion model.) After a period of instruction, break to discuss how students feel about the experience. Ask them to project how they might feel in the submersion model, where the instructor responds only to comments made in the instructor's language. If time permits, demonstrate how other models might work. End with a general discussion of *Lau* v. *Nichols* and the implications of bilingual education.

6. **School intervention** Describe in detail James Comer's school intervention model in New Haven, Connecticut. What is his underlying philosophy regarding school intervention and reform? How did he create his design? What are the various components of the plan, and how does it all work? Describe the changes in the New Haven schools in which Comer's model has been implemented. You may also compare the Comer model of school intervention with the school intervention developed by Boston University for the schools of Chelsea, Massachusetts. How does that plan work? What is its underlying philosophy? How is it working? What are the challenges faced by any school intervention model?

7. **Psychological needs of humans** Explore Glasser's theory of human needs and people's motivation for behavior. Describe in greater detail the elements of both and compare them. If those theories were implemented in classrooms, how would that affect the teacher's perception of students' behavior? What are some competing psychological theories of human behavior, and how do they reflect on the work of Maslow and Glasser? Imagine what a classroom would look like if the teacher were a firm believer in the theory of either Maslow or Glasser.

8. **Learning styles and multiple intelligences** How could these two concepts dramatically change the nature of public school education? Explore the possibilities with your students.

Additional Resources for Instructors

Cambone, Joseph. *Teaching Troubled Children.* New York: Teachers College Press, 1994. Cambone's story of a teacher in a residential treatment center for emotionally disturbed and learning disabled boys highlights the practices of special education with troubled children. The account raises questions about current special education practices as well as regular education practices for children with diverse needs.

Comer, James. *School Power: Implications of an Intervention*. New York: Free Press, 1980. Comer explains his theory of school intervention and reform in detail.

Crawford, J. *Bilingual Education: History, Politics, Theory, and Practice*. Trenton, N.J.: Crane Publishing, 1989. A thorough, yet easy-to-read analysis of bilingual education from a historical, theoretical, and practical perspective.

Dyson, Anne Haas. *Social Worlds of Children: Learning to Write in an Urban Primary School.* New York: Teachers College Press, 1993. Dyson's research helps broaden our vision of how language experience contributes to school literacy success. She supports efforts to make literacy more accessible to all children by taking into account the children's cultural background.

Gardner, Howard. *The Unschooled Mind: How Children Think and How Schools Should Teach.* New York: Basic Books, 1983. The Harvard psychologist applies his innovative ideas on children's natural learning mechanisms to educational practice.

Glasser, William. *The Quality School: Managing Children Without Coercion.* New York: Perennial Library, 1990. Noted psychiatrist William Glasser presents his vision of how schools could be conducted. He also spends considerable time explaining his control theory and its implications for students.

Grant, Carl (Ed.). *Research and Multicultural Education.* Bristol, Pa.: Falmer Press, 1992. Grant brings together authors who consider the challenges and issues relating to multicultural research. Sixteen articles around three topics are presented: multiculturalism in education, the research process, and the social impact of multiculturalism as reflected in school practice.

Kolb, David A. *Learning Styles Inventory*. Boston: McBer, 1981. Kolb has created several exercises to allow an individual to identify his or her learning style. The packet includes the inventory as well as the interpretation for the score.

Ravitch, Diane. "Diversity and Democracy: Multicultural Education in America." *American Educator: The Professional Journal of the American Federation of Teachers* 14 (Spring 1990): 16–20, 46–48. The article discusses the controversy over multicultural education. It contrasts California's pluralistic approach with New York's particularistic approach. Ravitch argues for a multiculturalism that provides students with both an appreciation for America's racial and cultural diversity and a commitment to the common culture that unites us all.

Rossi, Robert. *Schools and Students at Risk.* New York: Teachers College Press, 1994. This book provides an examination of reform efforts aimed at students at risk for failure in our schools. The four parts of the book cover the historical perspective of the reform efforts, the context in which reform must take place, current reforms, and a new framework for change.

Media Resources

All Our Children (PBS videos, 90 min., 1990). Journalist Bill Moyers examines the efforts of several programs and schools that have developed effective innovations in curriculum and counseling to help at-risk students.

Appreciating Diversity (Insight Media, 22 min., 1992). Educators from around the world share their ideas about how they can instill in their students an awareness of and respect for cultural and ethnic diversity. The video suggests ways to incorporate this multicultural material into the curriculum.

Dealing with Diversity in the Classroom (Insight Media, 23 min., 1991). The video examines some of the requisites for effectively teaching, motivating, and evaluating culturally diverse student populations. Leading educational specialists teach how to apply instructional strategies for working with diverse groups in the classroom.

The Demographics of American Education (Insight Media, 25 min., 1991). This video examines the impact of changing demographics on the nation's schools. It presents the views of researchers and demographers, as well as teachers, students, and parents, on such issues as career opportunities and the direction of education in the coming years.

Educating Peter (Insight Media, 30 min., 1993). There are 60,000 students being mainstreamed into the public school system in the United States. This program examines how education can prepare for inclusion, showing how Peter, a child with Down's syndrome, was integrated into a "normal" third-grade class.

Focusing on Sociocultural Appropriateness (Insight Media, 60 min., 1991). This video examines how different cultures interact in today's multicultural society. It discusses how the language and the class values that often define a school's culture may conflict with the values and backgrounds of ESL students. The program alerts teachers to the needs of ESL students and helps them prepare their classrooms to meet these special needs.

Giftedness (Insight Media, 30 min., 1991). This video reviews how the concept of giftedness has changed over the last century. Robert Clasen of the University of Wisconsin at Madison explains why the term *able learners* is better than the term *gifted*. The video also differentiates among five types of able learners—intellectually gifted, academically gifted, creatively gifted, artistically gifted, and leadership gifted.

The Inclusion Dilemma (Insight Media, 22 min., 1995). Using examples from two schools, this program examines what it means to include special needs children in regular classrooms and discusses how inclusion can be beneficial for all students and teachers.

Learning Disabilities (Gannett, 29 min., 1986). This video explores the signs and symptoms of learning disabilities and what is currently known about them. It shows how learning disabilities affect the lives of millions of Americans. It also examines how learning-disabled children and parents cope with school and social problems. The video also identifies famous learning-disabled people.

Learning Styles (Philip I. Goodman, 30 min., 1980). The film shows how to develop an awareness of one's learning styles and gives specific ways to adapt to them.

Mainstreaming in Action (Insight Media, 28 min., 1980). Filmed entirely in public schools, this film takes the viewer into classes at the elementary and secondary levels to observe teachers at work with handicapped children in response to PL 94-142. At discussion time, educators review the concept of mainstreaming: what it means and how it affects them and their classroom.

Multiple Intelligences in the Classroom (Insight Media, 31 min., 1995). Profiling a program at a Massachusetts elementary school, this video introduces multiple intelligence theory and defines seven kinds of intelligence.

Reaching Potential (EBEC, 26 min., 1982). The experiences of four visually impaired students are examined, raising such concerns as the children's need for constant special care, teachers who feel poorly prepared to deal with these children, and educators and child care workers who are anxious to integrate the disabled into society.

Self-Esteem and Social Development (Insight Media, 2 volumes, 18 min. each, 1991). This two-part program explores how self-esteem develops in children. Examining why children need to develop social skills, it discusses six principles that promote self-esteem and social skills development in children.

The Talented, the Gifted, the Bright (NEA, 30 min.). Are students of unusual ability getting a fair shake? The film includes interviews with teachers, students, parents, and school administrators. Dr. Charles Bish, the director of NEA Talented Pupil Project, expresses his reaction to what is being done for gifted students.

Typewatching Tape Series (Fairfax, Va.: Otto Kroeger Associates, 1985). This set of tapes includes a tape for each personality type as defined by the Myers-Briggs personality inventory. It describes the personality type, including the ways in which the personality type best learns.

The Under-Represented Gifted (Insight Media, 30 min., 1991). Minorities are underrepresented in programs for the gifted. This video shows how a magnet elementary program has attempted to remedy the problem by offering an extended day, talent area classes, and programs for children as young as three. It examines how the STREAM program helps gifted middle school minority students by identifying them in the sixth grade and offering continuous programming and counseling. The video also profiles a magnet high school.

Understanding Our Frames of Mind: Unique Learning Styles (Insight Media, 2 volumes, 60 min., 1989). This two-part program presents an overview of modality and learning-style research. The first part examines the characteristics of visual, auditory, and kinesthetic learners and shows multimodality teaching techniques. The second part describes the right brain and the left brain and shows adaptive teaching techniques that accommodate the right-brained child. It explores the role that color plays in learning and describes the theory of multiple intelligences.

Student Activities

1. Learning Styles and Personality Inventory

Get copies of David Kolb's Learning Styles Inventory and the Myers-Briggs Personality Inventory for your class or use the Swassing/Barbe instrument provided at the end of this chapter. Ask your students to work through each inventory, identifying their own learning styles and their personality styles. Then provide time for them to read or listen to descriptions of their learning style and of their personality type.

2. Field Site Journal Entry

Ask your students to review carefully Glasser's control theory before going to their field site school; then tell them to observe the behavior of the pupils in the classroom in light of Glasser's control theory. Students can focus on the following questions for their observation: To what extent are children motivated by their need for power or self-esteem? Can you come to any conclusions about these pupils based on Glasser's theory? Have students share their observations with one another during class.

3. Embracing the Multiple Intelligences of Students

Divide your class into small groups of no more than four. Ask your students to design and create a curriculum unit drawing on the seven forms of intelligence described by Howard Gardner. The curriculum unit should be designed so that it could be taught in one or two weeks. Ask the students to select one lesson or one activity that they will teach to the class as a whole. The lesson may draw on one or several of the intelligences described by Gardner. You may ask them to present a cover sheet on their project, including the following information:

Names ____

Title of curriculum unit

Grade level

Goals of unit

Time needed to teach unit

Activities

Lesson/activity presented to class

Goal of lesson/activity

4. Bilingual Education Program

Divide students into five groups and assign each group one model of a bilingual education program that the group will research extensively, presenting its findings to the class. The groups could be asked to teach a minilesson that would reflect the philosophy of the model they are presenting.

5. Handicap Accessibility

In groups of two, students can investigate the handicap accessibility of educational institutions. Students should visit an institution and note what facilities are available and then arrange an interview with administrative personnel in charge of overseeing compliance with the ADA. In the interview, the students should find out about what facilities must be made available, how the institution complies with these guidelines, and the consequences of noncompliance. Students report their findings to the class.

6. Nontraditional Programs

The chapter talks about Dr. Comer's work in New Haven with a nontraditional model of school. Have students investigate other nontraditional models of schools. The students can describe the model and then comment on its effectiveness in achieving its stated goals for learning.

SWASSING-BARBE CHECKLIST OF OBSERVABLE MODALITY STRENGTH CHARACTERISTICS

Area Observed	Visual	Auditory	Kinesthetic
Learning Style	• Learns by seeing; watching demonstrations	• Learns through verbal instructions from others or self	• Learns by doing; direct involvement
Reading	• Likes description; sometimes stops reading to stare into space and imagine scene; intense concentration	• Enjoys dialogue, plays; avoids lengthy description, unaware of illustrations; moves lips or subvocalizes	• Prefers stories where action occurs early; fidgets when reading, handles books; not an avid reader
Spelling	• Recognizes words by sight; relies on configuration of words	• Uses a phonics approach; has auditory word attack skills	• Often a poor speller; writes words to determine if they "feel" right
Handwriting	• Tends to be good, particularly when young; spacing and size are good; appearance is important	• Has more difficulty learning in initial stages; tends to write lightly; says strokes when writing	• Good initially, deteriorates when space becomes smaller; pushes harder on writing instrument
Memory	• Remembers faces, forgets names; writes things down, takes notes	• Remembers names, forgets faces; remembers by auditory repetition	• Remembers best what was done, not what was seen or talked about
Imagery	• Vivid imagination; thinks in pictures, visualizes in detail	• Subvocalizes, thinks in sounds; details less important	• Imagery not important; images that do occur are accompanied by movement
Distractibility	• Generally unaware of sounds; distracted by visual disorder or movement	• Easily distracted by sounds	• Not attentive to visual, auditory presentation so seems distractible
Problem Solving	• Deliberate; plans in advance; organizes thoughts by writing them; lists problems	• Talks problems out, tries solutions verbally, subvocally; talks self through problem	• Attacks problems physically; impulsive; often selects solution involving greatest activity
Response to Periods of Inactivity	• Stares; doodles; finds something to watch	• Hums; talks to self or to others	• Fidgets; finds reasons to move; holds up hand
Response to New Situations	• Looks around; examines structure	• Talks about situation, pros and cons, what to do	• Tries things out; touches, feels; manipulates
Emotionality	• Somewhat repressed; stares when angry; cries easily, beams when happy; facial expression is a good index of emotion	• Shouts with joy or anger; blows up verbally but soon calms down; expresses emotion verbally and through changes in tone, volume, pitch of voice	• Jumps for joy; hugs, tugs, and pulls when happy; stamps, jumps, and pounds when angry, stomps off; general body tone is a good index of emotion
Communication	• Quiet; does not talk at length; becomes impatient when extensive listening is required; may use words clumsily; describes without embellishment; uses words such as see, look, etc.	• Enjoys listening but cannot wait to talk; descriptions are long but repetitive; likes hearing self and others talk; uses words such as listen, hear, etc.	• Gestures when speaking; does not listen well; stands close when speaking or listening; quickly loses interest in detailed verbal discourse; uses words such as get, take, etc.
General Appearance	• Neat, meticulous, likes order; may choose not to vary appearance	• Matching clothes not so important, can explain choices of clothes	• Neat but soon becomes wrinkled through activity
Response to the Arts	• Not particularly responsive to music; prefers the visual arts; tends not to voice appreciation of art of any kind, but can be deeply affected by visual displays; focuses on details and components rather than the work as a whole	• Favors music; finds less appeal in visual art, but is readily able to discuss it; misses significant detail, but appreciates the work as a whole; is able to develop verbal association for all art forms; spends more time talking about pieces than looking at them	• Responds to music by physical movement; prefers sculpture; touches statues and paintings; at exhibits stops only at those in which he or she can become physically involved; comments very little on any art form

From *Teaching Through Modality Strengths: Concepts and Practices* by Walter B. Barbe, Ph.D. and Raymond H. Swassing, Ed.D., with Michael N. Milone, Jr., Ph.D. Used with permission of Zaner-Bloser, Inc.

Chapter 5 What Social Problems and Tension Points Affect Today's Students?

Learning Objectives

After studying the chapter, students will be able to

- identify the impact of poverty, homelessness, and child abuse on children's classroom behavior and learning.
- describe the structures of U.S. families today, identifying the difficulties that single parents and working parents face in raising children.
- describe the impact that alcohol abuse, drug abuse, and suicide have had on students in recent years.
- describe the problems of school violence and vandalism, and summarize some of the aspects that contribute to student aggression.
- discuss some of the things that schools, principals, and teachers can do to reduce the incidence of school violence.
- understand the reasons for students dropping out and discuss successful preventive measures.
- explain the effect of *Brown* v. *Board of Education of Topeka* on American education.
- describe the methods used to bring about school desegregation based on race, especially busing and magnet schools, and their effectiveness in achieving integration.
- explain how gender bias leads to unequal educational opportunities for females and how federal legislation, in particular Title IX, seeks to reduce these inequalities.

Chapter Overview

Social issues and problems in the world constitute a looming element in public education. In fact, a major portion of the school's work devotes itself to responding, directly or indirectly, to students whose lives are challenged by social ills, such as poverty or violence. Such problems, including homelessness, teen parenting, substance abuse, child abuse, and youth suicide, complicate students' efforts to learn. Other social problems, such as vandalism, school violence, and the drop-out rate, are exacerbated when students feel alienated from the school structure. The chapter briefly discusses each of these topics and the ways in which public education is responding as an introduction for prospective teachers, not as a detailed analysis.

We also look at U.S. family structure, which has undergone considerable modification in recent years. The traditional family, made up of a working father, a homemaker mother, and two children in school, represents only 6 percent of the U.S. households today. Family structures today include single-parent families, blended families, older parents, and working parents. Family structure can play a significant role in a child's school experiences and can affect his or her learning.

The chapter then looks at the tension points in U.S. education, beginning with a key issue in education: equality of educational opportunities in regards to race, social class, and gender. The historical perspective on racial desegregation of schools is examined, and methods to bring about greater integration, both mandatory (busing) and voluntary (magnet schools), are presented and their effectiveness analyzed. Equal educational opportunities for disadvantaged children is the focus of Chapter I, Compensatory Education, part of the Elementary and Secondary Education Act of 1965. Chapter I provides federally funded educational support for low-income students to compensate for their educational opportunities. The worth and efficacy of these programs are debated as both sides of the issue are presented. Inequality in educational opportunities is a recently recognized problem, and Title IX was an attempt to legislate equality of opportunity based on gender. Although Title IX met with mixed results, new federal legislation is currently working its way through Congress that seeks to provide gender equity programs in all phases of society, not just in schools.

Finally, the issue of sex education in the schools is revisited in light of the growing concern over the spread of sexually transmitted diseases and the problem of teen pregnancies. The appropriateness of sex education in schools is debated, as is the approach to sex education.

Our purpose in this chapter is not to overwhelm prospective teachers with all the problems affecting schools but to sensitize them to the connections between teaching and social issues of national concern. Although teachers spend a good deal of time absorbed in meeting the challenges of their own classrooms, they must be aware of the conditions outside the classroom in order to participate fully in the advancement of the democratic process.

Chapter Outline

Chapter 5 *What Social Problems and Tension Points Affect Today's Students?*

I. Social Problems Affecting the Young

A. New American Family Patterns
B. Poverty
C. Homelessness
D. Teenage Pregnancy
E. Abused and Neglected Children
F. Alcohol and Drug Abuse
G. Adolescent Suicide
H. School Violence and Vandalism
I. School Dropouts

II. Tension Points in American Education

A. Equality of Educational Opportunity
B. Desegregation
C. Magnet School Programs
D. Compensatory Education
E. Gender Issues
F. Sex Education

Supplementary Lecture and Discussion Topics

1. **School as one social agency among many** The social problems presented in this chapter are addressed primarily by social agencies that may develop working relationships with the schools. Select a subset of problems, such as poverty-related problems or teen problems, and describe the local agencies that work on them. Explain the relationships that local teachers might have with other agencies, either directly or through school teams. Invite a local teacher who has been successful in working with the problems to come and describe his or her work.

2. **Youth problems: yesterday, today, and tomorrow** Choose three distinct historical periods—for example, colonial times, post–Civil War era, and modern times—and describe the differences that characterize a single issue. For example, what kinds of work were expected of a ten-year-old of a particular social class in each period? Did these

expectations differ in urban and rural settings? Or what kind of education (if any) might a child of the lowest social class have received in each period? Who might have paid for it? Or how were language differences accommodated in different periods?

3. **Crack, gangs, and kids who kill** Each day across the country a dozen or so teens and children are killed on the street. Some may have been involved as drug runners; others may have been walking down the street to a convenience store; still others may have been sitting on their front steps. Their deaths are particularly horrifying because in many instances the killers are themselves children. Not infrequently, the child who pulled the trigger was a member of a gang. Analyze gangs and their philosophy. How do they operate? Why is violence a given? How do drugs play a role in the lives of gang members? What can public schools do for these youth? What do experts think needs to be done to stop the killings and the madness?

4. **Gender bias in school** Choose two editions of a basal reader, a social studies text, or a math book—one edition somewhat older than the other. For each, or for a matched segment of each, tally the number and kinds of characters that are male or female. Present information to the class, and discuss how textbooks support inappropriate sex-role stereotyping. Reinforce the fact that gender bias not only leads to economic disability for women but artificially restricts options for both men and women. You may also want to explore other issues concerning sexism in schools: generic use of male pronouns and its effects on shaping the consciousness of both men and women; the representation of women in history, science, and literature; and the hierarchy in schools and its male dominance.

Additional Resources for Instructors

Crosby, Emeral. "The 'At-Risk' Decade." *Phi Delta Kappan* 75 (April 1993): 598–604. Crosby argues that little has been done in the ten years since *A Nation at Risk* to reduce the risks that face American children and threaten their learning.

Donmoyer, Robert, and Raylene Kos (Eds.). *At Risk Students: Portraits, Policies, Programs, and Practices.* New York: SUNY Press, 1992. This books explores the circumstances of at-risk students and argues that well-intentioned policymakers and educators run the risk of making matters worse rather than better for these students.

Fine, Michelle. "Of Kitsch and Caring." *School Administrator* 45 (September 1988): 16–18, 23. A look at national and particularly urban drop-out rates reveals that the disadvantages of high school dropouts, relative to their graduate peers, are confounded by race, ethnicity, social class, and gender. Their troubles in terms of employment and earnings are more devastating today than they were twenty years ago.

Havinghurst, Robert, and Daniel Levine. *Society and Education*. 8th ed. Boston: Allyn and Bacon, 1992. An examination of many of the social issues touched on in this chapter. The authors summarize recent research.

Hodgkinson, Harold L. *All One System: Demographics of Education—Kindergarten Through Graduate School*. Washington, D.C.: Institute for Educational Leadership, 1985. Based on the assumption that the educational system must be viewed as a continuum of people moving through it rather than as discrete levels in a hierarchy, this report presents the demographics to enable educators and policymakers to make predictions about, and therefore better provide for, future schools.

How Schools Shortchange Girls: The AAUW Report. Washington, D.C.: National Education Association. The findings of this report show that girls are not receiving the same quality of education as boys. This landmark report has led to policy endeavors to bring about greater equity in education.

National Board of Inquiry into Schools. *Barriers to Excellence: Our Children at Risk.* Boston: National Coalition of Advocates for Students, 1985. An investigation into topics such as racial, class, cultural, and sex discrimination. The study identifies 104 strategies to achieve fair and excellent schools.

Plunkett, Virginia R. L. "From Title I to Chapter I: The Evaluation of Compensatory Education." *Phi Delta Kappan* 66 (April 1985): 533–37. This article describes the development of federally funded compensatory education programs initiated during the 1960s and their role in the current "excellence in education" movement.

Scherer, Marge. "On Savage Inequalities: A Conversation with Jonathan Kozol." *Educational Leadership* 50 (December 1992/January 1993): 4–9. Kozol describes the conditions that face our nation's urban students and proposes ways to eradicate the inequities.

Stevens, Linda, and Marianne Price. "Meeting the Challenge of Educating Children at Risk." *Phi Delta Kappan* 74 (September 1992): 18–23. Stevens and Price suggest that strategies exist that schools can use to improve the conditions of at-risk students. They focus on the curriculum, the context, and the community to ameliorate the plight of these students.

Media Resources

Poverty and the Disadvantaged

Documentaries made for broadcasting include the following classics:

American Promise: Dreams on Hold (NBC, 20 min., 1986). This presentation examines the growing gap between rich and poor in America, and the nation's shrinking middle class. It looks at social trends and changes in the economy—the shift to a service economy, the high consumer debt, the dependence of families on two paychecks, and how the dream of upward mobility is disappearing.

America's Schools: Who Gives a Damn? Part II (PBS video, 60 min., 1991). The problems in America's public schools seem inseparable from our societal diseases—poverty, drugs, crumbling families, and racial tensions. Will a student's difficult environment sabotage his or her success in the classroom or can school save the child?

Down and Out in America (MPI Home Video, 57 min., 1985). This video focuses on farmers who cannot hold on to their land, the homeless, and the twenty million Americans who go hungry every day.

The Migrants, 1980 (Prod: NBC, Dist: Films Incorporated, 52 min., 1980). A follow-up of the NBC White Paper of 1970, the film finds very little improvement in the conditions of the migrants.

Other films on poverty include the following:

Growing Up Poor (PBS video, 58 min., 1986). Half of the children in Chester, Pennsylvania, are poor. They are plagued by poor health, malnutrition, drugs, and family problems. This *Frontline* segment follows the children through the maze of social services available to them and shows what it is like to grow up poor.

The Outskirts of Hope (New Day, 54 min., 1982). Poverty in the United States in the 1980s is studied through portraits of six people and their families in different parts of the country. The film documents the successes and failures of the "war on poverty."

Unequal Education: Failing Our Children (Insight Media, 21 min., 1992). This student-produced documentary goes into the classrooms of New York City's public schools to show the disproportionate educational opportunities that exist. Focusing on a school in a middle-class neighborhood and a school in a working-class neighborhood, it contrasts the quality of the staff and the resources available to students. Interviews with teachers, principals, and parents place this local crisis in the context of a nationwide educational crisis.

Family Issues

Family and Survival (FFHS, 52 min., 1986). The video focuses on the changing role of the American family: changes brought about by unprecedented stress and changing societal needs. Less than 5 percent of American households still fall into the "traditional" family mold. This film looks at the effects of broken homes, battered wives, and estrangement on children growing up in these environments.

Family of Strangers (Prod: LCA, Dist: university film libraries, 31 min., 1980). This sensitive drama concerns two single parents who marry. The family of strangers does not become a family of friends until each member recognizes the care and respect that building a new life together entails.

Home, Sweet Homes: Kids Talk About Joint Custody (Filmmakers Library, 20 min., 1982). Five articulate children share their thoughts and feelings about joint custody.

Jen's Place (Beacon Films, 52 min., 1982). On returning from summer camp, fourteen-year-old Jen learns that her parents have separated and have arranged for her to live with her mother during the week and with her father on the weekend. Unable to get either parent to communicate with her, she acquires the services of a child advocacy lawyer and has the case reopened.

Single Parent Families (KIRO–TV, video, 30 min., 1982). Students and parents look at divorce. Six episodes, each produced, written, and edited by a high school representative, tell a different story about the single-parent family.

Single Parenting: A New Page in America's Family (BARR, 25 min., 1986). The video surveys numerous types of single-parent arrangements: the divorced mother who often ends up in poverty, the single-parent father, women who choose to have children without marriage, and divorced parents who share joint custody.

Teenage Mothers—Beyond the Baby Shower (Planned Parenthood, 27 min., 1987). This video examines the lives of three teen-age girls—Amy, Candy, and Nicole—who became parents in their teens. It shows the realities of teens dealing with the pressures of growing up themselves and caring for a child. Although all three mothers love their children, they all admit they wished they had done things differently.

TeenDads (FFHS, 52 min., 1988). A study of a group of teenage fathers, some single and some married, and their psychological and financial responsibility for their children.

Vanishing Family: Crisis in Black America (Prod: Ruth Streeter/CBS News, Dist: Carousel and university film libraries, 64 min., video, 1986). *CBS Reports* with correspondent Bill Moyers examines the disintegration of the black family structure. Statistics—that nearly 60 percent of all black children are born out of wedlock—come to life.

Other Social Problems

AIDS—What Everyone Needs to Know (Churchill Films and university film libraries, 18 min., 1986). Made in cooperation with the UCLA AIDS Center, this film examines the threat of AIDS coolly, thoughtfully, and authoritatively.

America: Hooked on Drugs, ABC News Nightline (ABC Wide World of Learning, 24 min., 1986). ABC News covers the drug habits of the U.S. public by crossing all lines: ethnic, social, economic, and professional.

Boyz N the Hood (Columbia Pictures, 1991). This film portrays the grim, violent life in a low-income neighborhood of Los Angeles. It shows how several young men grow up, some seeking to get out, some seeking to make their own way. The film shows the brutal realities of living where gangs, drugs, and violence are an everyday part of life.

Cocaine Country (FI, 32 min., 1987). Tom Brokaw investigates crack, a powerful cocaine derivative that gets to the brain in five to ten seconds and can cause immediate addiction. Cocaine is now twice as potent as it was a decade ago. Most doctors believe cocaine is the most addictive substance known. Cocaine can be bought for the price of a movie ticket, and most kids know where they can get it.

Racism and Anti-Racism Education (Films for the Humanities and Sciences, 58 min.). This program looks at issues that have stirred the education establishment of late. The issues it covers are drawn from contemporary England but are just as applicable to the United States.

The Road to Brown (California Newsreel, 47 min., 1990). This video dramatizes the events and legal rulings that preceded the desegregation decision in *Brown* vs. *Board of Education.*

Streetwise (Prod: New World Video, Dist: university film libraries and video stores, 92 min., 1985). This film tells the true story of nine desperate, runaway teenagers. All old beyond their years (all underage survivors fighting for life and love on the streets of downtown Seattle), they are learning the hard art of street survival.

Three Schools: Drug Free (Prod: Ginny Durrin, Dist: American Council for Drug Education, 28 min., 1986). This film features the principals of three schools describing how the combination of a clear and consistently enforced policy, an age-appropriate curriculum, and involvement by the community has enabled them to reduce drug and alcohol problems significantly in their schools.

When Society's Problems Walk Through the Door (Insight Media, 30 min., 1993). Students do not leave problems such as drug abuse, homelessness, violence, or unrealistic parental expectations at the door when they enter school. In order for instruction to be effective, schools must address the problems faced by students. This video profiles three schools that have instituted programs to address the nonacademic concerns of their students.

Child Abuse and Neglect

Breaking Silence (Theresa Tollini, Dist: Film Distribution Center, 58 min., 1985). Through the juxtaposition of interviews, photographs, and children's drawings, this film reveals the dynamics of incest and child sexual abuse.

Child Sexual Abuse: What Your Child Should Know (Indiana University, 1983–84). This series of five programs provides children and adults with techniques and information to identify and avoid child abuse. In one film, *A Program for Parents* (90 minutes), a panel of experts explains sexual abuse of children: who falls victim, who are the perpetrators, and what the viewer can do to prevent it. Designed for parents, teachers, pediatricians, and school nurses. There are also programs for grades K–3, grades 4–7, grades 7–12, and senior high.

Silent Shame: The Sexual Abuse of Children (NBC News, Dist: Films Incorporated and university film libraries, 50 min., 1984). This NBC News documentary examines the nationwide spread of the sexual abuse of children and child pornography. It presents material showing that the sexual abuse of children and child pornography feed on each other; that sex with children causes them psychological, emotional, and physical damage; and that sexual abuse of children is a crime after which the victim often grows up to become a molester.

Talking Helps (ODN, 27 min., 1985). To accompany ODN's 1982 release *No More Secrets* (grades K–6), this film features a teacher using the 1982 film to teach children sexual abuse prevention skills. The film addresses parents', teachers', and counselors' concerns about teaching this sensitive topic.

Gender Bias and Stereotyping

Killing Us Softly: Advertising's Image of Women (Cambridge Documentary Films, 30 min., 1979). Based on a multimedia presentation created by Jean Kilbourne, this film is a critique of advertising as a powerful form of cultural conditioning, an industry that uses the fears and insecurities of U.S. consumers and is especially exploitative of women.

The Pinks and the Blues (Time-Life Multimedia, 57 min., 1982). Even after a decade of sex-role redefinition, boys and girls are still treated in stereotypical fashion. This film demonstrates that "from the moment parents wrap a newborn baby in either a pink or blue blanket, they start a socialization process that lasts a lifetime." So subtle is this process that parents and teachers deny it.

She's Nobody's Baby (Coronet/MTI, 55 min., 1981). Narrated by Alan Alda and Marlo Thomas, this documentary traces the evolution of U.S. women in this century. We see how the U.S. woman has been girdled and gartered, lectured to and discriminated against, romanticized and ostracized by all kinds of "authorities." But through it all, the woman of conscience and courage has fought to be heard—to shape the nation's history and define her role.

Shortchanging Girls, Shortchanging America (Insight Media, 19 min., 1992). This program interviews educators and business leaders to illuminate the effects of gender bias in schools. It investigates the loss of self-esteem in girls and shows how they are often tracked away from math and science programs.

Vandalism and Violence

Combat in the Classroom (Coronet/MTI, 27 min., 1981). This film examines current problems in today's schools, where 110,000 teachers are assaulted every year and property worth over $600 million is destroyed through vandalism. The most tragic result of classroom violence is that students can't learn and teachers can't teach. Several effective ways to respond to the violence are illustrated by showing schools where things are working and explaining why.

Declining Student Performance

American Schools: Flunking the Test (CRM/McGraw-Hill, 51 min.). Through the case study of "Peter Doe," this film dramatizes the charge that U.S. schools are failing to equip graduates with basic skills. Issues examined include the lack of uniform goals and standards, budget cutbacks, teacher militancy, and the complexities of accountability and evaluation.

Part-Time Work, Part-Time School (from the *Your Children, Our Children* series, KTCA-TV, 29 min., 1984). Today's teenagers participate in the adult world, holding jobs while going to high school. This documentary explores how these jobs prepare children for the future and asks about the tradeoffs.

Project Second Chance (PBS video, 60 min., 1986). One out of every four Americans drops out of school before receiving a diploma. This program focuses on high school dropouts who are given a second chance to take advantage of local graduate equivalency degree programs.

Student Activities

1. The "Normal" Family and Its Variations

First, have the class participate in generating the "normal" family model for itself. Ask each student to indicate on an *unsigned* paper how many parents are now at home, how many siblings there are and whether they are older or younger than the student, how many other adults are at home, and the employment status of the parents. The following form might be provided for their use (sample answers given):

a. Number of parents at home:	2
Stepparents at home?	Yes—father
b. Siblings (older? younger?)	1 older, 2 younger
c. Other adults:	1 grandmother
d. Parents' job(s):	Father and mother employed

From these responses, a class "norm" may be determined by taking the most frequently given response to each question. For example, the most common family constellation might be "mother, stepfather, one sibling (younger), both parents working." Using this model as the basis for discussion, break the class into small groups of three to five, and have each group create the set of expectations that might reasonably be held for such a family by a teacher of one of the children. When each group has generated the list of expectations, have members brainstorm ways in which other family constellations (represented by their own real families) might differ in the ability to meet those expectations. Finally, have each group write a list of warnings for a teacher. What kinds of assumptions about families should teachers be aware of making, given the diversity?

2. Role Stereotyping Simulation (Sex, Age, Ethnicity)

Divide the class into groups of from five to eight members. Be sure the groups are heterogeneous. Supply each group with the following scenario and set of résumés. Direct each group to reach consensus on the three items:

a. Select the person best qualified.
b. Select the person with the most executive potential (can be the same person as in item a).
c. Develop three questions to ask in an interview.

From each group, select an observer who is willing to forgo participation in the group discussion. Give separate instructions to observers, out of hearing of the others in the groups, to record any instances of (a) assumptions made by participants about the influence of gender on the suitability of candidates for a position, (b) comments or assumptions about race, (c) comments or assumptions about age, (d) questions or concerns about women that did not arise with respect to men. Observers are not to name group members making comments, only to record comments. At the end of a time, compare group findings and observer records.

Remind the class that it is illegal to ask certain questions in a job interview—for example, one cannot ask questions of a female that would not be asked of a male counterpart. Such questions include plans for marriage, plans for raising a family, and child care arrangements. Comments on physical attractiveness are also illegal.

BIG OIL SCENARIO

You are members of the executive personnel committee in the regional office of the Big Oil Corporation. The home office is in New Jersey, with refineries and diversified manufacturing plants throughout the world. Your regional office has an opening for a regional manager of personnel. This is a Level 10 position, the first level with company executive rank. People in Level 10 positions are the first ones to be considered to fill vacancies for such top executive positions as regional managers, vice president, and so on. The position of regional personnel manager carries the following job description:

> Manage and assume responsibility for the equitable and efficient conduct of routine personnel activities regarding initial employment, recordkeeping, evaluations for pay increases, promotions, and terminations. In addition, plan, organize, and supervise professional recruitment, orientation, and ongoing training of company employees throughout the region. Salary: $55,000 or commensurate with experience.

The regional office is located in Houston, Texas, and the region encompasses the states of Texas, New Mexico, Arizona, Oklahoma, Kansas, Arkansas, and Louisiana. Employee orientation and training sessions must be conducted periodically in all the regions' branches, and at hours that will not interfere with routine plant or office activities. Recruitment strategies involve establishing recruitment centers on university and college campuses throughout the country. Although the personnel manager is not required to actually conduct training, orientation, or recruiting sessions, it is his or her responsibility to plan and supervise such sessions and to see that they meet the needs of the growing corporation.

Corporation executives are expected to be free to relocate in any of the international branches. They are expected to be loyal to the corporation and to conduct themselves socially in a manner that will enhance the corporate image. People who fill Level 10 positions invariably are promoted to executive positions. It is important that they show dedication to the corporation.

Applicants

- John P. Morgan, B.S. in general business administration. Age 43. Married (wife: Jane A. Morgan, homemaker), four children ages 18, 16, 12, 9. NAACP Fellowship. Previous experience: twelve years with a rival company in sales department—seven years as sales agent, five years as area sales manager. Came into our corporation eight years ago in the position of area manager for region. Duties involved recruitment and training of sales agents for all regional branches. Considered stable, good with people, with executive potential.

- Mona S. Hickey, B.S. in business management science; M.S. in personnel management. Age 36. Married (husband: William S. Hickey, physicist, Ph.D., employed by NASA). Three children, ages 14, 8, 5. Previous experience: six years with Exxon USA in New Orleans. Four years as executive secretary to vice president in charge of support personnel. Has been with our corporation three years as assistant personnel manager in charge of support personnel and beginning professional trainees. Came to our office when husband was transferred to NASA. While in our employ, has been taking courses in petroleum engineering at nearby university. Extremely intelligent, very articulate, with excellent organization and management skills. Energetic, in good health, one child with chronic illness.

- Michael J. Martinez, B.S. in business management science. Age 45. Divorced, single parent, two children, Michael, age 16, and Linda, age 14. Previous experience: ten years in army recruiting and training positions and ten years personnel manager for Texas division of corrections. Efficient, organized, enthusiastic, and well liked.

- John T. Miller, B.S. in business management science. Age 26. Second marriage (wife: Sun Li, reporter for CBS local affiliate). One child, age 2. Presently working toward M.S. degree in management psychology. Now employed by family-owned department store chain, in personnel records. Has been with present company since graduation from college three years ago. Previous experience: retail sales with present company, two years while working toward degree; three summers as roughneck in oil fields. Is extremely ambitious and eager for opportunities for advancement, which he feels are limited with present employers. Is mobile, can relocate. Bright, energetic, honor graduate with membership in several professional and civic organizations.

- James R. Stadtmueller, B.S. in business administration. Age 58. Widowed, two children—both married. Previous experience: personnel director of small Southwest-area oil company, fifteen years. Responsibilities included planning and conducting executive training programs for company. General office manager of accounting department (same company) nine years. Twelve years experience in billing and accounting departments, with three promotions during period. References from previous employer are excellent.

- Jaclyn S. Young, B.A. in psychology. M.B.A. Age 27. Single. Ford Foundation Fellowship. Mary Lyon Scholar. Previous experience: faculty member of Mount Holyoke College Department of Social Science. Youngest appointment; chair of the Presidential Commission on Women and Minorities in Business. Bright, articulate. References are glowing, especially those from the National Feminist Caucus and NOW. Considered a "high flyer."

3. The Media and Social Issues

This activity could take on two different strands.

a. *"Killing Us Softly . . ."* Show the film of that name to your class (listed in reference section). After viewing the film, spend some time discussing it. What are Jean Kilbourne's prominent themes? What does she want us to see? How does she accomplish her ends? Is her message compelling? The movie was made in 1979, and some of her themes may be familiar to students now; other implications may not be as familiar. Have we heard or accepted her message?

For the next part of the activity, ask students to collect magazines targeted for teen-age girls. Allow students to work in pairs or groups of three to analyze the advertisements in one magazine. To what degree do these ads mirror what Kilbourne points out? What messages do these ads suggest to young girls? What is their role in society? What is the conception of the "good life"? Ask them to categorize the most prominent themes and collect the ads that promote such themes. When your class is done, have each group share its conclusions.

b. "The Good Life." A long-held view of education is that it would propel one to seek the good. Schools, however, are in heated competition with other elements of society in informing students what the good is. Have your students do an analysis with both commercials and magazines. With the magazines, pick ones that are targeted to particular populations: news magazines, finance magazines, family magazines, sports magazines. What lifestyles are the commercials selling? How do advertisements market alcohol? Particular companies have been sharply criticized for their beer advertisements directed at young people. What songs are used to promote the "good life"? Compare the vision of the good life with the traditional purposes of education. Have your students share their conclusions.

4. "Real-Life" Simulation

Have your students assume the perspective of either Darice, a seventeen-year-old single mother of a five-month-old infant, or Benjy, a sixteen-year-old male. Both of them are dropouts. If these two teenagers wanted to survive in the world, how would they do it? Assume that they cannot live with their families; they are on their own. Students should answer the following questions.

- Employment
  a. Find the local classified section of the paper. Identify the number of jobs that an unskilled worker could fill. What kinds of jobs are they? Is the pay listed?
  b. Follow up on several of them with a phone call for information. What are the requirements of the job? What are the hours? What benefits, if any, are included with the job?
  c. Check with a local employment office. What possibilities exist for Darice or Benjy?
  d. Calculate the annual salary Darice or Benjy would make if hired for a particular job.
- Housing

a. Where are apartments located in the area? What is the span in the rents? What is the appearance of the least expensive apartments? What is the surrounding neighborhood like? How much money would Darice or Benjy need immediately; for example, how many months' security deposit does the landlord want?
b. To what extent are low-income apartments available? What is the process for obtaining one? Where are they located? What do they look like?

- Food
  a. What is the average cost of feeding an adult or an adult and a child in the area?
  b. What kinds of support services are in the area? Food banks, food cooperatives?
  c. What is the procedure for getting food stamps? What will they buy?
- Medical Facilities
  How would Darice provide health care for her infant? What facilities are available? What is the process for enrolling in Medicaid? What are its requirements? Would Darice meet those?

5. Social Programs in the Curriculum

As mentioned in the text, schools must face the complexity of educating students challenged by numerous social problems. In groups of four, choose one of the following programs and investigate that program at a given school. Find out what the curriculum of the program is, which students are taught the curriculum, why it is taught in that school, and whether the program is perceived as being successful by students, faculty, and the community. If no such program exists, try to find out why.

a. Substance abuse prevention program (They can concentrate on a specific substance, such as cocaine or alcohol.)
b. Suicide prevention program
c. Teen pregnancy prevention program
d. AIDS education program
e. Programs for at-risk students or drop-out prevention

6. You may want to use the more detailed case study "Leigh Scott" on pp. 471–473 in Appendix I.

7. Educational Current Event Assignment

<u>Purpose</u>: To be able to discuss current controversial issues in education intelligently, the student needs to be able to locate professional resources that shed light on issues reported in the popular as well as professional press. The student will develop the ability to consult research and professional literature, using it to analyze the contexts that influence these issues, and to express these ideas orally and in writing.

<u>Requirements</u>: The student will locate _____ current events concerning education in newspapers or popular periodicals within the semester. For each current event the student will do the following:

- Submit a copy of the current event article or a summary of the broadcast report (with a complete bibliographical reference)
- Attach at least one professional source that sheds light on the issues (include complete annotated bibliographical reference and ERIC designation)
- Present an analysis of the issue including the relevant contexts (historical, economical, philosophical, legal, sociological, governance, etc.) and express his or her own informed opinion in no more than one and a half pages typed

Evaluation:

- Satisfaction of all requirements
- Demonstration of use of professional sources
- Depth of analysis
- Completeness of references
- Mechanics of communication
- (Oral presentation)
- Due date ______________________

8. Group Controversial-Issue-in-Education Assignment

Purpose: To discuss current controversial issues in education intelligently, the student needs to be able to locate resources to obtain information on all sides of the issue, to recognize the diverse contexts that influence these issues, and then, considering personal values and experiences, to make an informed decision—and if necessary to persuade others.

Requirements: Each group of five students will do the following:

- Select an issue and receive instructor approval of the topic
- Using ERIC, research the issue in not less than six sources
- Present the issue in a 20-minute class presentation
  Include the following sections:
  - Introduction and description of the issue
  - Discussion of the appropriate historical, social, economical, political, financial, governance, etc., contexts of the issue
  - Pro's and con's of the issue
  - Various proposed solutions
  - Current trends
  - Recognized authorities in the field
  - Your own opinions and recommendations
  - Standard bibliography citations, annotated
  - One- to two-page summary of the issue, class handout sheets

Sample issues:

- Unequal funding
- Bilingual education
- Teacher strikes
- Year-round schools

- Inclusion
- Character education
- Home schooling
- Charter schools
- Sex education
- Censorship
- Uniforms
- and many others

<u>Evaluation</u>:

- Organization
- Participation
- Satisfaction of all requirements
- Insight into the contexts influencing the issue
- Coherence and detailed support
- Class presentation
- Two-page handout
- Creativity in written and oral presentation

Chapter 6 What Makes a Teacher Effective?

Learning Objectives

After studying the chapter, students will be able to

- describe the teacher's role as a decision maker.
- explain how teachers' attitudes toward themselves, their students, their colleagues and other adults, and their subject matter affect teaching.
- identify and explain attitudes that can foster effective teaching and those that can hinder it.
- describe how knowledge of a discipline, the disciplinary knowledge covered in the curriculum, and pedagogical content knowledge contribute to effective teaching.
- identify and explain the characteristics of effective teachers.
- describe what reflective teaching is.
- describe what a constructivist view of learning is.
- identify and explain the implications of recent cognitive research on teaching and learning.
- explain the relationship between academically engaged time and learning.
- define Jacob Kounin's terms (*with-it-ness, smoothness,* and *momentum*) in terms of their meaning in classroom management.
- summarize guidelines for effective classroom management.
- explain how questioning, wait-time, and planning contribute to teaching effectiveness.

Chapter Overview

The purpose of Chapter 6 is to introduce the prospective teacher to some current research on teacher effectiveness. The chapter, by its nature, is more theoretical than many other chapters of the textbook, and for this reason it may be more difficult for some students. However, we think that prospective teachers should recognize the importance of theory for education for every teacher. We agree with John Dewey: "Nothing is so practical as a good theory." Novice teachers, though, often fault their preparation for being too theoretical—a complaint their more experienced colleagues sometimes echo. In our view, the problem is not an oversupply of theory; it lies with an undersupply of how to use theory in the classroom. Reflective teaching involves the use of theory to determine the effectiveness of instruction as well as to find ways to improve it. Teacher education programs need to provide opportunities for beginning teachers to view classroom events and to interpret them by using relevant theories.

We review the findings of research and explore the implications of theory in several areas: teachers' attitudes, subject-matter knowledge, learning and human behavior, instructional strategies, and classroom management. The opening story about Carol Landis provides a reference point for showing how theory may be applied. This chapter covers a lot of ground; if time permits, you might wish to spend extra time elaborating many of the topics we simply introduce.

Chapter Outline

Chapter 6 *What Makes A Teacher Effective?*

I. The Teacher As Decision Maker

  A. Aspects of Effective Decision Making

II. What Attitudes Does the Effective Teacher Possess?

  A. The Teacher's Attitude Toward Self: Self-Understanding
  B. The Teacher's Attitude Toward Children
  C. The Teacher's Attitude Toward Peers and Parents
  D. The Teacher's Attitude Toward the Subject Matter

III. What Subject-Matter Knowledge Does the Effective Teacher Need?

IV. What Theoretical Knowledge Does the Effective Teacher Need?

  A. Theories-in-Use
  B. Why Study Educational Theory?
  C. How Can Theoretical Knowledge Be Used?

V. What Teaching Skills Are Required of an Effective Teacher?

A. Knowing Versus Doing
B. Classroom Management Skills
C. Questioning Skills
D. Planning Skills

Supplementary Lecture and Discussion Topics

1. **Decision making** Using one of your own recent classes as an example, discuss the planning, implementing, and evaluation decisions you made. List the elements that affected your choices: coverage, prior lessons, knowledge of other experiences of the students, and so on. Then describe the interactive decisions you made while teaching—when to pause in a lecture, when to ask for questions, whom to call on, when to stop a small-group activity. After you list the decisions, invite the class to help you generate examples relevant to the grade levels they plan to teach.

2. **Self-fulfilling prophecy** Elaborate on the research on self-fulfilling prophecies. Describe the early experiments and the later work that established the behavioral connections between expectations and learning.

3. **The importance of enthusiasm** Most students find the studies of enthusiasm intriguing. Summarize the origins of the research, and describe the organization of the projects designed to measure the effects of enthusiasm. Discuss the need to balance teachers' interests against curricular necessities.

4. **How a historian becomes a history teacher** Choose one of the case studies published by the Stanford University group (headed by Lee Shulman) that describes the changes experienced by people whose undergraduate studies were in a given discipline when they began work as secondary teachers. Several of the cases involve teachers who were expert in social science content areas yet discovered that they needed to learn a new perspective on their discipline in order to be effective teachers.

5. **Theories-in-use** Elaborate on the idea of theories-in-use as it is defined and described by Argyris and Schon in *Theory in Practice* (1974). You may also extend your discussion of Schon's later work by including *The Reflective Turn* (1991).

6. **Classroom management or discipline** One area that beginning teachers (and many others) typically find difficult is classroom management or discipline. Present some of the current theories regarding management or discipline and discuss them in more detail. What are the implicit values behind each management style? You may want to ask your students to recall the management style of their teachers. Which teachers were effective? Which weren't? What do they think they will find difficult in managing a classroom?

7. **Theory in practice** Choose a set of recommendations about teaching—such as Kunin's on classroom management, Rowe's on wait-time, Wilen's and Clegg's research on effective questioning—and then review how they work in the classroom. Show a videotape

of a teaching episode that illustrates use or nonuse of the recommendations. At the beginning of the tape, stop the tape whenever evidence appears and show students how to spot instances where the theory might have been practiced. As the tape continues, invite students to tell you when to pause so they can practice identifying when theories apply.

8. **The beginning teacher evaluation study** This study has provided the basis for much ongoing research about instructional methods and engaged time. Describe the details of the study, its relevance to beginning teachers, and some of the work on engaged time that has followed.

9. **Wait-time** Explain in greater detail the work of Mary Budd Rowe on wait-time and its implications for teaching.

10. **Creating an environment for effectiveness** The effective teacher needs support. Many attributes of effectiveness and the skills of behavior management mentioned in this chapter depend on supports in the school or class environment. Discuss the ways a teacher can influence his or her school and peers to be supportive—for example, by finding a colleague to provide coaching in some skills. Describe the way effective management strategies depend on external supports. The program of rewards might work best with a student who is also moved to a less distracting place, for instance.

11. **Constructivist approaches to learning** The impact of constructivism in educational circles is significant. Elaborate upon the philosophy underlying constructivism—its essential positions on meaning and acquiring knowledge. Explain in greater detail how something like think-aloud protocols support constructivism. Contrast the theories and practices of contructivism and other approaches to teaching and learning.

12. **Reflective teachers** Elaborate on the importance that reflection has in teaching. Discuss the work of Donald Schon and its subsequent impact on education. Also identify how the emphasis on reflective teachers parallels the work of teachers collaborating with university professors in research on teaching.

Additional Resources for Instructors

Anderson, Lorin W. *Increasing Teacher Effectiveness*. Paris: UNESCO International Institute for Educational Planning. A fairly concise presentation of the latest research findings on teacher effectiveness and classroom implications.

Bedwell, Lance E. *Effective Teaching: Preparation and Implementation*. Springfield, Ill.: C.C. Thomas, 1991. Bedwell presents a helpful guide for those practitioners who want to incorporate the principles of effective teaching into practice.

Brubaker, Dale L., and Laurence H. Simon. *Teacher As Decision Maker*. Newbury Park, Calif.: Corwin Press, 1993. A book of real life that examines several different models and approaches to classroom management.

Cruickshank, Donald R. "Profile of an Effective Teacher." *Educational Horizons* 63 (Winter 1985): 90–92. Culminating in a description of an effective teacher, this article provides an overview of research on teaching effectiveness before 1960 that focuses on personal characteristics, and of research done since, which includes presage, context, process, and product variables.

Doyle, Walter. "Classroom Organization and Management." In *Handbook of Research on Teaching*. 3d ed. Ed. Merlin C. Wittrock. New York: Macmillan, 1986. Doyle presents important themes in the research on the nature and functions of classroom management and organization.

Gail, Meredith. "Synthesis of Research on Teachers' Questioning." *Educational Leadership* 42 (November 1984): 40–47. This article highlights research on the effects of both factual and higher-level questions; it also suggests reasons for the effectiveness of recitation.

Highet, Gilbert. *The Art of Teaching*. New York: Vintage, 1977 (originally published 1950). Highet writes a little gem of a book on the art of teaching. He describes the teacher, the methods, great teachers and their pupils, and teaching in everyday life.

Jackson, Philip W. *The Practice of Teaching*. New York: Teachers College Press, 1986. In this collection of six essays, Jackson deals with some of the complex issues surrounding the teaching profession, such as why many people view teaching as a simple task, whether teaching can be defined systematically, and what progress the profession has made in improving the quality of its practice.

Newman, Judith (Ed.). *Finding Our Own Way: Teachers Explore Their Assumptions*. Portsmouth, N.H.: Heinemann, 1990. In this collection of essays, teachers describe the assumptions they had about teaching, students, and themselves and how these affected their lives as teachers.

Oser, Fritz K., Andreas Dick, and Jean Luc Patry. *Effective and Responsible Teaching: The New Synthesis*. San Francisco: Jossey-Bass, 1992. A scholarly volume detailing recent findings of research on effective teaching.

Perrone, Vito. *A Letter to Teachers*. San Francisco: Jossey-Bass, 1991. Drawing on his conversations with teachers across the country and his own experience working in public schools, Perrone offers insights and practical advice designed to help teachers renew their commitment to their profession and to inspire a love of learning in their students. He shows teachers how to restore the intellectual challenge to their work and to avoid slipping into routine.

Ross, Wayne C., Jeffrey Cornett, and Gail McCutcheon (Eds.). *Teacher Personal Theorizing: Connecting Curricular Practice, Theory, and Research*. Albany: SUNY Press, 1992. An edited volume of essays illustrating how teachers' own theories are buttressed or contradicted by current theory and research.

Seymour, Daniel, Terry Seymour, and 30 Teachers of the Year. *America's Best Classrooms: How Award Winning Teachers Are Shaping Our Children's Future*. Princeton, N.J.: Petersen's Guides, 1992. A highly readable collection describing how award-winning teachers work with students. The volume includes numerous bibliographical references.

Shulman, Lee S. *Research in Teaching and Learning: A Project of AERA*. New York: Macmillan, 1990. One of the nation's foremost researchers on teaching presents the findings of an AERA research project. A scholarly, dense volume for those interested in the current research theory and findings.

Van Manen, Max. *The Tact of Teaching: The Meaning of Pedagogical Thoughtfulness*. Albany: SUNY Press, 1991. Drawing from the traditions of qualitative research, this volume explores the implications and ramifications of *pedagogical thoughtfulness,* a term grouped with *teacher reflection*.

Media Resources

Cognitive Coaching: A Process for Teaching and Learning (Films for the Humanities and Sciences, 39 min., 1994). This video describes and demonstrates specific examples of instructional conversation and other types of cognitive coaching; identifies instructional arrangements that are used to promote active learning by students; models questioning techniques and student interactions, including the ways in which cognitive coaches keep student discussion focused and productive; and considers the role that authentic and ongoing assessment plays in cognitive coaching.

Connecting with Kids (Films for the Humanities and Sciences, 26 min., 1994). Teachers talk about how they communicate effectively with students by showing they care and taking an active interest in their students' lives. In the classroom, teachers demonstrate ways of building a team feeling and making students feel successful without compromising standards.

Convergent Thinking (AIT, 30 min., 1986). This video demonstrates classroom techniques for helping students reach higher levels of abstract thinking.

Divergent Thinking (AIT, 30 min., 1986). Divergent questions usually have no correct answers. They require creative responses. This video shows the kinds of questions and activities the teacher can use to propel students to think divergently.

Getting Ready (Films for the Humanities and Sciences, 26 min., 1994). This video shows how teachers plan to create a classroom that is conducive to student learning. Through interviews and classroom demonstration, teachers present how they organize the classroom, introduce themselves to students, define and meet objectives, and address student needs.

Making a Difference: Great Teachers (Films for the Humanities and Sciences, 28 min., 1994). This documentary focuses on three teachers who have made a positive impact—academically or personally—on their students' lives. Selected as a result of an essay contest that asked students to write about the teacher who had most challenged and inspired them, the teachers are shown at work in the classroom.

Planning for Prevention (Films for the Humanities and Sciences, 26 min., 1994). To stop problems before they start, teachers must clearly define what is expected of students from the outset and establish routines that make the best use of classroom time. Teachers explain and demonstrate unique, effective styles of communicating expectations and initiating class procedures.

Responding to Misbehavior (Films for the Humanities and Sciences, 26 min., 1994). This program examines various classroom disruptions and analyzes some techniques that enable the teacher to deal with misbehaving students without interrupting the class.

Take an Idea and Go Creative: The IMPACT II Series (Prod: IMPACT II, 5 programs, 15 min. each, 1986). This series takes the viewer into the workplaces of five teachers who have created award-winning ideas for better teaching and shows the teachers putting the ideas into action.

Teaching: A Problem Solving Venture (Hubbard, 30 min., 1985). This film illustrates how teachers can assess and remedy children's academic and behavior problems in a classroom setting by using the problem-solving process.

Student Activities

1. A Gauge of Your Attitudes Toward Teaching

Part of the chapter deals with the significance of a teacher's attitudes toward himself or herself, other teachers, students, and others in the school. To be an effective teacher, she or he needs to know what attitudes she or he has concerning those areas. Ask your students to complete the following gauge of their attitudes about a range of issues. When the students have completed their own, put them in small groups to debrief.

Self-Gauge of Your Attitudes Toward Teaching and Related Areas

---

Respond to each question as honestly and as thoroughly as you can. This exercise is designed for you to think about your attitudes, especially if they are unexamined ones.

1. Your ideal class would look like...
2. Your ideal lesson would be...
3. Are you a competitive person? Why? Why not? Are there particular circumstances in which you are more competitive than others?

4. How easily do you collaborate with your supervisor? How do you respond to someone directing or guiding your actions?

5. Do you get easily annoyed with or are you judgmental of people? What is your biggest pet peeve about people?

6. What would make you lose your temper in a classroom?

7. Are you especially drawn to particular "types" of children? The "underdog"? The class comedian? The earnest, bright student?

8. What is your attitude toward grading and evaluating student work?

9. What is your biggest worry about teaching?

10. How long in your life do you plan to be a teacher? Do you have other possible career goals?

11. What is your attitude toward classroom management or discipline? What are your underlying thoughts regarding discipline?

2. The Qualities of an Effective Teacher

Considering what you have learned abut the characteristics of an effective teacher, this activity is designed to help you observe these qualities in a real setting. For this activity, you need to observe a teacher in action. You must tell the teacher what this assignment is and ask for permission. When you explain the project, make sure you emphasize that this observation is not to critique his or her teaching style, but to see particular skills in action.

As you observe the teacher over the course of the day, check off the number of times he or she behaves in a certain way. You probably will not be able to use some of the listed abilities. In that case, write "N.A." for "not applicable." Note to yourself what was happening as you made your tally mark. At the end of the day, review your list. You may, if appropriate, want to share your list with the teacher for further discussion.

Qualities of an Effective Teacher

a. The ability to ask different kinds of questions, each of which requires different types of thought processes from the student
b. The ability to reinforce certain kinds of behaviors
c. The ability to diagnose student needs and learning difficulties
d. The ability to vary the learning situation continually to keep the student involved
e. The ability to recognize when students are paying attention and to use this information to vary behavior and possibly the direction of the lesson
f. The ability to use technological equipment, such as microcomputers
g. The ability to judge the appropriateness of instructional materials

h. The ability to define the objectives of particular lessons in terms of student behaviors
i. The ability to relate learning to each student's experience

3. The Roots of Professional Training

Have the students read the following two accounts of effective teaching. Have them compare each to the advice given in the chapter. Ask them to list similarities and differences and to comment on what things remained the same while others changed. Ask them to write a similar list of do's and don't's for the year 2000.

How to Keep the Class "On Task"—Advice to Teachers (1867)[1]

1. The teacher must be well acquainted with the work to be done; must know well how to do it; must be well acquainted with the wants of the class or school and of its individual members; and must be inspired with a love for teaching and filled with the enthusiasm which such love generates.

2. The capacity of the class or the individual should be so clearly understood and carefully considered that the lesson given may be fully mastered within the limits of proper, healthful exercises. For pupils six to eight years of age, I think the limit may be put at 5 to 10 minutes; from eight to ten, 15 minutes, with 3 to 5 minutes for review at the end of a half hour; from ten to twelve, 20 minutes with a like review; for older pupils, the time of study may be increased until one hour shall not be too long.

3. THE RECITATION SHOULD NOT BE PROLONGED BEYOND THE PROPER LIMIT OF HEALTHFUL EXERTION. While studying the pupils should give the whole force of their mental powers to the acquisition of the lesson, so while reciting, they should be thoroughly busy—should perform every mental operation required of anyone. Whatever plan of conducting the recitations is found the best adapted to fix attention should be followed, and any plan that does not secure the undivided attention of every pupil should be discarded or modified at once. The teacher's own attention should be directed to observing whether the pupils are thoroughly interested and absorbed in the work to be done, and the moment the interest abates the recitation should be closed. Better no recitation at all than one continued while the pupils are thinking of something else or nothing at all—dreaming, as so many do. Many complain of want of time to conduct the recitation. The trouble is not want of time, but want of proper employment of time. More time is wasted than used, if my observations may form a proper basis of judgement.

4. THE TEACHER SHOULD NEVER ALLOW ANY PORTION OF A RECITATION TO PASS WITHOUT GIVING IT TO HIS OWN PERSONAL AND UNDIVIDED ATTENTION. The habit of assisting individual pupils to do "sums" is hard to find. The habit of assisting individual pupils to do "sums" or to find localities on a map while others

---

[1]Thanks is given to the Education Museum of the Department of History in Education Foundations and Research at The Ohio State University, Columbus, Ohio, for the use of its primary source collection of education materials.

are reciting cannot be too pointedly condemned. If the recitation is not worthy of the teacher's attention, how can he expect to command the attention of the pupils?

5. WHILE THE RECITATION IS IN PROGRESS, THE TEACHER MAY ASK FREQUENT QUESTIONS FOR THE CLASS TO ANSWER IN CONCERT. Let the questions be such as all can answer, and let the teacher see that all do answer.

6. Many more like suggestions might be added, but I forbear. Enough has already been said to set the LIVE TEACHER to thinking; and more might only serve to harden the plodder to his dullness.

The Art of Questioning—Teacher Training Course, Summer 1918[2]

Mrs. Boober

Good questioning is considered one of the greatest achievements of the successful teacher, since this is the only method by which she can get at the best possible results of her work.

In questioning a class, the teacher should first take into consideration the age and intellectual powers of the pupils. Then she should endeavor to adapt her language to their age and understanding. Questions asked in words so difficult as to impede comprehension on the part of the pupils are, of course, useless in stimulating thought. In the lower grades the teacher's language must be very simple, indeed, while in the upper grades the pupils have a larger vocabulary and the teacher may feel that she may use more difficult words. Having this in mind, she should then ask her questions in an encouraging, animated manner. She has, of course, prepared her lesson beforehand, so that her eyes are free from the text, which is used only as a reference book.

Questions should be definite and free from ambiguity. They should be clear, concise, and direct to the point. Indefinite questions lead to indefinite answers; or, if the answer is correct, it is invariably a reproduction of the text, which, in reality, is developing the verbal memory, rather than encouraging the pupil to use his judgement.

One of the teacher's greatest desires should be to stimulate thot [sic]. Text questions lack interest. If the words of the teacher are well chosen they will create pictures in the mind of her pupils, which leads us to inquiry on their part. Thus they result in their understanding the subject. Of course, there are exceptions, but as a rule the teacher should avoid questions that may be answered by a "yes," or "no" as they lead to guessing on the part of the pupil. Of course, if she is developing a lesson, "yes" and

[2]Thanks is given to the Education Museum of the Department of History in Education Foundations and Research at The Ohio State University, Columbus, Ohio, for the use of its primary source collection of education materials.

"no" questions are permissible, but invariably the pupils will answer offhand without much meditation; thus the teacher is obliged to "pump" her lessons from her class.

Unity and continuity are two important factors in good instruction. The teacher should seek to have one lesson, a continuation of the previous day's, and one question to have some bearing on the one before it. This results in assimilation of the lesson on the part of the pupil.

4. Advising Carol Landis

Divide the class into small groups to discuss the case of Carol Landis in the text. Ask each group to identify the decision points used by Carol to plan and react. Have groups either affirm Carol's decision at each point or propose some advice on how she should do things differently or what she should do on the following day. Each affirmation or bit of advice should be supported by the appropriate text citation on sensible practice.

5. Developing Questioning Skills

Much emphasis has been placed on the need for teachers to vary the kinds of questions they ask students. This activity is designed to help prospective teachers develop their questoning skills.

In a small group, select a topic or skill to teach (e.g., a particular folktale, hibernation, adding three-column numbers, etc.) for a particular age of students. Draft a set of questions that you think would help those students understand the new concept through varying levels of difficulty. Review and revise your set of questions with your group members.

After the questions are completed, debrief with the whole class. Each group should present their set of questions to the class. Have each group explain their choices, and have the class as a whole analyze the questions, making suggestions for changes or revisions.

6. Minilesson

Design a minilesson on a topic of your choice that operates from a constructivist point of view about learning. Your may choose either to write up the minilesson, describing the lesson and explaining how it exemplifies constructivism, or to conduct the minilesson and videotape it. (This activity could easily be used in cooperative learning groups.) Present this lesson to the whole class and debrief.

7. Class Observation and Analysis

Record a set of questions that a teacher asks while teaching a particular skill or concept. After reviewing them, analyze them and write up your findings. How would you categorize them? Which type of question elicited the largest number of student responses? Which kind received the most correct answers? Which kind seemed to get the longest student responses? Which kind received the greatest variety of responses? Based upon your analysis of the data, can you make generalizations?

8. Improvisation (for several students)

Improvise a scene either on videotape or live in front of your education class portraying a teacher's response to a classroom disturbance. Present and debrief with your class. Here are the characters needed, but others may be added:

Jo(e) Marley, a teacher who usually demonstrates effective teaching
Sandy, a student who is easily distracted
Shawn, a student who resists authority and who often acts out
Several other students

Chapter 7 What Should Teachers Know About Technology and Its Impact on Schools?

Learning Objectives

After studying the chapter, students will be able to

- describe some of the events in the historical evolution of the audiovisual and computer technologies used in the classroom.
- identify the sources of pressure on schools to use more technology.
- discuss a variety of ways that technology can be used to assist student learning.
- summarize how technology changes the teacher's role in instruction and contributes to the teacher's productivity.
- explain several ways computers may be "deployed" for use within a school.
- debate the issues surrounding the use of computers in education.
- analyze the equity issues regarding equal access to technology for disadvantaged students and girls.
- use computer terminology with greater understanding.

Chapter Overview

We believe that educational technology is having an increasingly significant impact on instructional delivery and effectiveness. Because of the fast pace of adoption of technological methods and resources in our schools, it is important to introduce prospective teachers to this information early in their teacher preparation. To this end we created an entirely new chapter for this edition to provide a broad-based introduction to how telecommunication technology and computers can assist the work of the teacher and student learning.

In this chapter we briefly review the historical development of the use of educational technology. Varied applications of computers are introduced. The changes that educational technology makes in instructional methods and the applications that contribute to teacher productivity are described.

Technology affects student learning in four ways: as cognitive tools, tools for facilitating instruction, communication tools, and assistive technology for students with special needs.

The teacher's role is changed by new methods of instruction, the availability of additional resources, and new ways of communicating and managing productivity.

Students are introduced to the key issues in educational technology: the infrastructure and budgeting issues, the challenges of integrating technology into the curriculum, the necessity of preservice as well as in-service teacher education, and issues of equity involving students of all genders, races, and socioeconomic classes.

Chapter Outline

Chapter 7 *What Should Teachers Know About Technology and Its Impact on Schools?*

I. A Brief Look at Education's Technological Past

II. How Are Schools Being Pressured to Change?

III. How Are Technologies Affecting Student Learning?

- A. Cognitive Tools
- B. Tools for Facilitating Instruction
- C. Communication Tools
- D. Technology for Students with Special Needs

IV. How Are Technologies Affecting Teaching?

- A. A Different Role for the Teacher
- B. Professional Resources and Communication
- C. Management: Teacher Productivity Tools

V. How Are Computer Technologies Organized for Student Use?

A. Computer Labs

B. Single-Computer Classrooms

C. Classroom Clusters

VI. What Are the Key Issues in Educational Technology?

A. Infrastructure and Budgeting

B. Integration into Curriculum

C. Education of Teachers

D. Equity

Supplementary Lecture and Discussion Topics

1. **The Internet** The Internet has vast implications for data access and communication. What possible instructional applications does this type of technology immediately bring to mind for your own teaching? What other possibilities can you envision in other fields of education?

2. **Extending learning beyond school walls** Connecting schools and classrooms to the Internet will in effect extend learning beyond the confines of the school walls. How might this in fact be true or not true? Under what conditions do you think this vision will be realized?

3. **The influences of networking** Telecommunication offers educators a new tool, a new technology for advancing learning in exciting ways. The dynamic is that the process of learning will not just be enhanced as a consequence of having this new technology but will evolve into an activity that is more meaningfully enriched. How do you see networking among schools, other institutions, agencies, and corporations influencing the way learning takes place?

4. **Software and Internet copyright issues** The use of the Internet in education brings to mind additional areas that teachers need to be cognizant of regarding fair use and copyright law. Discuss with students in more detail the stipulations regarding how and under what conditions teachers can use information gained from the various computer on-line services available.

Additional Resources for Instructors

Betts, F. "On the Birth of the Communication Age: A Conversation with David Thornburg." *Educational Leadership,* 51(7) (1994): 20–23. David Thornburg provides insight into trends in educational technology and how it may shape classroom instruction.

Carey, D. M. "Teacher Roles and Technology Integration: Moving from Teacher As Director to Teacher As Facilator." *Computer in the Schools,* 9(2/3) (1993): 105–117. Carey outlines the assumptions that need to be rethought with regard to the teacher's role and technology integration.

Devallar, R., and F. Christian. *Computers and Cultural Diversity: Restructuring for School Success*. New York: SUNY Press, 1993. This book examines the topic of computer-aided instruction and the increasingly important role of technology in the instructional process.

Means, B., and K. Olson. "The Link Between Technology and Authentic Learning." *Educational Leadership* 51(7) (1994): 15–18. In this article the researchers discuss their observations about effective use of technology in the classroom, and the need for technology to be applied to authentic, meaningful tasks.

Miller, L., and J. Olson. "How Computers Live in Schools." *Educational Leadership* 53(2) (1995): 74–77. This article explores issues relating to how computers are used in schools and how technology can yield unexpected results.

O'Neil, J. "Teachers and Technology: Potential and Pitfalls." *Educational Leadership* 53(2) (1995): 10–11. This short article alludes to the gap between the potential of technology in education and current practice.

Rockman, S. "In School or Out: Technology, Equity, and the Future of Our Kids." *Communication of the ACM* 38, no. 6 (June 1995): 25–29. This article bring up important issues regarding equity of technology resources and use.

Selby, L., and K. Ryba. "Creating Gender Equitable Computer Learning Environments." *Journal of Computing in Teacher Education* 10(2) (1994): 7–10. This article discusses learning approaches for gender-equitable learning with technology.

Swan, K., and M. Mitrani. "The Changing Nature of Teaching and Learning in Computer-Based Classrooms." *Journal of Research on Computing in Education* 26(1) (1993): 41–53. Reports the findings of a study on teaching and learning behaviors when using an integrated learning system.

VanDusen, L.M., and B. R. Worthen. "Can Integrated Instructional Technology Transform the Classroom?" *Educational Leadership* 53(2) (1995): 28–33. Reports the findings of a two-year study of integrated learning systems and discusses key points.

Watson, J. G. "Educational Technology: A Necessity for the 21st Century—Why the Delay?" *Network News & Views* (August 1996), 84–91. An excellent article outlining the justification for using technology in instruction.

Media Resources

Cyber Classroom—Now and in the Future - Number 6 of the *Imagine II* series (Apple Computer, 30 min., 1996). Combines snapshots of today's technologies with glimpses of what's in store for the future.

Enhancing Curriculum with Technology; Number 4 of the *Imagine II* series (Apple Computer, 30 min., 1996). This video demonstrates that technology works best when it supports what teachers are already doing. This episode chronicles the work of educators integrating technology into their curriculum.

How Important Is Technology for the Classroom Teacher? (Insight Media, 60 min., 1992). Leading educators debate the use of technology in the classroom. They consider how different forms of technology are best applied, as well as the misuse of technology.

Integrating Technology: More Than an Electronic Blackboard? (Insight Media, 60 min., 1992). This program visits an elementary school that integrates technology into the schoolwide curriculum and a Native American reservation school where technology enhances cross-cultural communication.

Multimedia in Education (Insight Media, 20 min., 1993). This program shows how educators are using multimedia technology to explore new ways of teaching and learning. It discusses the use of videotapes, laser disks, information networks, virtual reality systems, and computer modeling in education.

The New ABC's: Classrooms of Tomorrow (Films for the Humanities and Sciences, 58 min., 1992). This program visits several "classrooms of tomorrow" to examine how technologies stimulate smart students, involve young children, reduce truancy, aid special education students, and simulate real-world job tasks.

Power Teaching: How to Develop Creative Teaching Techniques Using CD-ROM Technology (Insight Media, 25 min., 1995). Profiling an overview of CD-ROM technology, this video explains how to integrate CD-ROMs into the curriculum. It emphasizes that CD-ROMs not only allow students access to extensive information, but also enable them to adapt the interactive program to their needs and ability levels. The video features samples of CD-ROM programs and demonstrates the use of CD-ROMs by students practicing basic skills.

Technology and the Role of the Teacher: How to Integrate Technology into the Classroom (Insight Media, 20 min., 1996). This fast-paced video addresses technology not as a cure for problems in the classroom but rather as a tool for effective instruction. It shows how to restructure the classroom to incorporate technology and discusses both the pedagogical and emotional issues raised by its growing use in schools.

Technology Education: The New Basic (Insight Media, 10 min., 1990). Visiting many of North America's leading technology education classrooms, this video teaches new ideas for integrating technology into the curriculum.

Technology in the Classroom (Insight Media, 60 min., 1993). This video shows how technology can be used to motivate students and considers how it can make schools and teachers more efficient and effective.

Your School and the Internet (Films for the Humanities and Sciences, 45 min., 1996). An overview of the effective use of the Internet in the classroom.

Student Activities

1. Inventory of Technology Skills

Before you start this chapter, use the technology inventory (included here) to assess your students' level of technology background and to raise their awareness of their own skills and needs in this area.

2. Safe and Effective Use Guidelines

The Internet is a mixed bag for students. It opens up some wonderful resources, but it also exposes students to unverified information and in some cases inappropriate or dangerous materials and opportunities. In small groups have your students develop guidelines for the safe and effective use of the Internet. Each group should also develop at least one teaching activity that could be used with students to teach them these safe and effective skills. Have the small groups share their ideas with the rest of the class.

3. Integrating Technology

Find a professional in your field who is integrating technologies into his or her teaching—this is not always an easy task. This may be the cooperating teacher (if he or she is integrating technology) or any K–12 educator. Talk with the teacher about his or her media tools of choice. Inquire how the teacher was trained to use the tools and how they were acquired for the classroom. Ask if the teacher has plans to integrate different or additional media in his or her teaching. What does the teacher feel the future holds for media tools in the classroom? And lastly, how is technology affecting classroom instruction; if it is not, should it, and why?

4. Software Review

Use a Liquid Crystal Display (LCD) or other computer projection system and select several pieces of educational software to review with your students. Ask them to evaluate the software's:

Usability

Is it easy to use for both student and teacher? What level of teacher involvement is necessary? Can it be used for students at more than one achievement level? Is it "adjustable"?

Instructional Design

What audience is it appropriate for? What are the instructional objectives it is designed to achieve? At what level of Bloom's taxonomy does it require the student to operate? How much learner control is there? Is it interesting and motivating for the learner? How much learner interaction does it require? Can work be saved and/or recorded?

Evaluation

Does it accomplish what it claims to? Is it worth the time and expense for what it accomplishes?

You may want to select contrasting software: one "good" and one "bad" example, or one elementary and one secondary in the same subject area, or one at a low level of Bloom's taxonomy and one at a higher level.

5. Telecommunications

Have students use telecommunications technology to research and seek resources for an issue in teacher education or their subject field. This could be done individually but would be of more value if done in small groups. Groups of individuals should produce a two-page outline with an introductory paragraph that describes the issue or subject field and a brief close-up description of the telecommunications resources located.

Some of the possible avenues for completing this activity include the use of the following:

Newsgroups:	Post an inquiry to an appropriate newsgroup about the issue or subject field.
Telnet:	Use an on-line library catalog resource to research your issue or subject field.
File Transfer Protocol (FTP):	Download and incorporate an existing file into a multimedia report or presentation.
Gopher:	Search for information using a gopher site.
Browser:	Use Netscape, the Internet Explorer, or another browser to find two or three appropriate sources of information.

At this point it is important to develop the idea that technology should support the learning process and should not be the focal point around which the lesson is developed. That is not to say, however, that use of technology shouldn't change some things about how learning takes place. Telecommunications technology places a rich variety of resources in the hands of teachers. This activity demonstrates a type of learning in which students are responsible for conducting their own investigations and constructing their own knowledge.

INVENTORY OF PERSONAL TECHNOLOGY SKILLS

Please complete the following inventory of your previous knowledge and experience using technology. If you are not familiar with the terminology in one of the questions, answer in the "never" column.

I own a home computer.	Yes	No	Type ______________
I frequently use a computer at work or school.	Yes	No	Type ______________
I am connected to the Internet at home.	Yes	No	

	Frequently	Occasionally	Never
Communication Tools			
I use e-mail.	_____	_____	_____
I use the Internet to find information.	_____	_____	_____
I know how to use hypertext to get more information when I need it.	_____	_____	_____
I have used Power Point, Persuasion, or another presentation tool.	_____	_____	_____
I use search engine(s).	_____	_____	_____
I have participated in distance education.	_____	_____	_____
I have produced my own computer graphics.	_____	_____	_____
Cognitive Tools			
I use word processing.	_____	_____	_____
I use databases.	_____	_____	_____
I use spreadsheets.	_____	_____	_____
Instructional Tools			
I have reviewed software for use.	_____	_____	_____
I have used tutorial software (as a student).	_____	_____	_____
I have used a computer simulation.	_____	_____	_____
I have used interactive multimedia (ex: a multimedia encyclopedia).	_____	_____	_____
I have generated a test or worksheet using software designed for that purpose.	_____	_____	_____
I have created multimedia presentations.	_____	_____	_____

I am familiar with the following types of assistive technologies for students with special needs.

____

____

____

Chapter 8 What Is Taught?

Learning Objectives

After studying this chapter, students will be able to

- define the formal and informal curriculum and differentiate between the two, giving specific examples.
- explain how shifting purposes have affected school curriculum throughout American history.
- describe recent trends in curriculum reform.
- discuss international comparisons of achievement.
- summarize debates about curricular changes in language arts, science, math, social studies, foreign languages, art, physical education, and vocational studies.
- explain the relationship between textbook adoption practices, textbook content, and a national curriculum.
- describe several instructional approaches—interdisciplinary teaching, cooperative learning, critical thinking, writing across the curriculum, and block scheduling.

Chapter Overview

This chapter provides an overview of the major curricular emphases in American education, tracing the development from the colonial period to the 1990s. It highlights the shifting purposes that have led schools to change their curriculum to respond to the changing needs of American society and examines the effects of these shifts. Students will understand that until the nineteenth century, schools adhered to a perennial philosophy, but in the late 1800s and early 1900s, many schools adopted a progressivist approach that favored the student-centered or society-centered curriculum. By the 1950s, the curriculum in schools had become very broad and diverse in response to competing priorities: vocational training, societal reform, and personal development. After the launching of the Soviet satellite *Sputnik* in 1957, the curriculum shifted quickly to a more discipline-based focus. Math and science instruction received heightened scrutiny and funding as Americans searched for the most efficient way to teach those disciplines. The prosperity of the late 1950s and 1960s brought about significant innovation in the curriculum, particularly in light of the postwar knowledge explosion and the growing middle class. The flexibility of the curriculum in the 1970s gave way to a back-to-basics movement in the 1980s as report after report called for curricular reform.

This chapter reviews the curricular changes and reforms that occurred after *Sputnik* and presents key figures such as Jerome Bruner (discovery method, spiral curriculum). The methods, results, and implications of international achievement comparisons are presented and analyzed. The chapter explores the hot topics on curricular reform, including block scheduling, cultural literacy, multiculturalism, core curriculum, centralizing versus decentralizing the curriculum, and outcomes-based education.

The chapter discusses current curricular trends in different subject areas and describes other influences on the curriculum, in particular the role of textbooks in curriculum development. The chapter concludes by presenting some of the innovative instructional techniques now being used in schools.

Chapter Outline

Chapter 8 *What Is Taught?*

I. Where Does the Existing Curriculum Come From?

- A. Shifting Purposes: From Colonial Times Through the 1970s
- B. Curriculum Reform in the 1980s and 1990s

II. What Is the Present Curriculum?

- A. Language Arts and English
- B. Mathematics
- C. Science
- D. Social Studies
- E. Foreign Languages
- F. The Arts
- G. Physical Education, Health, and Recreation

H. Elective Courses
I. Vocational Courses

III. Student Academic Performance

A. International Comparison

IV. Additional Influences on Curriculum

A. Textbooks
B. Innovative Instructional Approaches
1. Interdisciplinary Curriculum
2. Cooperative Learning
3. Critical Thinking and Problem Solving
4. Writing Across the Curriculum
5. Block Scheduling
C. Current Curriculum Controversies
1. Multicultural Curriculum versus Core Curriculum
2. Cultural Literacy
3. Outcomes-Based Education

V. Is the Existing Curriculum Relevant to Today's Society?

VI. The Curriculum in a Changing World

Supplementary Lecture and Discussion Topics

1. **Curriculum and values** Analyze a given curriculum and show how it supports particular values. Categorize the course credit requirements for earning a degree in teacher education, and identify the value system implicit in that distribution of effort. Categorize the activities of a child's school day and identify the social directive implied by those activities.

2. **Multiculturalism and the curriculum** Discuss the impact multiculturalism has had on various curricula at either the elementary or secondary level. Present the arguments of the proponents of multicultural curriculum and those of the opposing view. Then have the students suggest compromise approaches.

3. **Significance of *Sputnik*** Discuss in greater depth the U.S. reaction to *Sputnik*. Bring in clippings or pictures of headlines and copies of newspaper stories. Present how the U.S. Congress and the president reacted to *Sputnik*. Show the educational projects, movements, and trends that resulted from *Sputnik*.

4. **"Camelot," "the Great Society," and the end of the dream** Discuss in greater depth the idealism, the hope, and the efforts the nation put into education in the 1960s. Describe the types of educational research conducted, the new approaches developed and implemented in the classroom, and the rationale for them. Compare the spirit of the time in the 1960s with that of the 1980s, particularly in light of the outcry in the early 1980s over the ineffectiveness of American education.

5. **Textbooks, publishing, and textbook adoption** Discuss in greater detail the factors that contribute to the writing of a textbook and the factors that publishing companies must consider when developing a textbook. In addition, discuss in more detail the vocal groups, such as those in Texas, that wield power over the contents of textbooks. Provide a background sketch of those involved in these vocal special-interest groups.

6. **Instructional approaches** Demonstrate the differences between a discovery lesson and a lecture-and-discussion lesson on a given topic in science.

7. **International comparisons** Explain the value and cultural differences among modern countries and their conceptions of the curriculum. Present information on a country (Korea, France, and so on) that follows a national curriculum, and discuss that country's goals for the education of its students. Discuss the vocational education and apprenticeship programs other modern countries have for students who want to learn a trade. What are some other countries' ways of preparing all students to become productive citizens?

8. **Scheduling** Discuss traditional 50-minute period scheduling and compare it to several of the block scheduling structures. Illustrate the relationship to educational goals and methods.

Additional References for Instructors

Adler, Mortimer. *The Paideia Proposal: An Educational Manifesto.* New York: Macmillan, 1982. This book provides a basis for strengthening the academic curriculum in public schools.

Boyer, Ernest L. *High School: A Report on Secondary Education in America.* New York: Harper and Row, 1983. This report presents recommendations for improving U.S. secondary schools, based on a study of fifteen public high schools in the United States.

Castenell, Louis A., Jr., and William Pinar. *Understanding Curriculum As Racial Text: Representations of Identity and Difference in Education.* New York: SUNY Press, 1993. This book examines the issues of identity and difference, both theoretically and as represented in curriculum materials. The debates over curriculum are characterized as debates over the American national identity.

Clemson, Rochelle, and Jay McTighe. "Teaching Teachers to Make Connections: The Challenge of Teacher Educators." *Action-in-Teacher-Education* 12 (Spring 1990): 55–60. The article outlines basic concepts of three prominent instructional approaches: cooperative learning, direct instruction, and learning styles. The relationship between each model and developing student thinking skills is explored.

Connelly, F. Michael, and D. Jean Clandinin. *Teachers As Curriculum Planners.* New York: Teachers College Press, 1988. Connelly and Clandinin place curriculum planning and development at the center of teacher activity and responsibility. The book presents a number of case studies to illustrate the teacher-centered approach to the curriculum.

Hawthorne, Rebecca K. *Curriculum in the Making: Teacher Choice in the Classroom Experience.* New York: Teachers College Press, 1992. The book presents case studies of four English teachers who base their curriculum on the "role of teacher values, beliefs, experience, and expertise." The author discusses the struggle between personal and professional autonomy and obligations to mandated curricula.

Howard, V. A. *Learning by All Means: Lessons from the Arts.* New York: Peter Lang Publishing, 1994. This book presents a modern philosophy of arts education that stresses the personal struggle for competency and creativity.

Kleibard, Herbert M. "Three Currents of American Curriculum Thought." *Current Thought on Curriculum: 1985 ASCD Yearbook,* pp. 31–44. Kleibard sees the development of contemporary curriculum not as a bipolar grapple between traditionalists and progressives but as a culminating mixture of "three currents of curriculum reform"—social efficiency, human development, and social meliorism—tempered by the traditional humanist curriculum.

Klein, M. Frances (Ed.). *The Politics of Curriculum Decision-Making.* Albany, N.Y.: SUNY Press, 1991. An edited volume that explores the political processes and issues in centralizing the public school curriculum.

McNeil, John D. *Curriculum: A Comprehensive Introduction.* 4th ed. Glenview, Ill.: Scott, Foresman/Little, Brown Higher Education, 1990. A comprehensive overview of major curriculum issues, including brief descriptions of new directions in the various subject fields.

Schifter, Deborah, and Catherine T. Fosnot. *Reconstructing Mathematics Education.* New York: Teachers College Press, 1993. The book recounts the difficulties of teachers who have been guided by a constructivist understanding of mathematics learning and who work to bring that vision to life in their classrooms.

Slavin, Robert. *Cooperative Grouping for Interactive Learning: Students, Teachers, and Administrators.* Washington, D.C.: National Education Association, 1990. This book takes cooperative learning beyond the classroom and provides ways to build productive grouping among students.

Walker, Decker F. "Curriculum and Technology." *Current Thought on Curriculum: 1985 ASCD Yearbook,* pp. 91–102. This chapter explores the implications of advancing technology for curriculum theorists in helping schools develop curricula to meet the needs of contemporary society.

Media Resources

Censorship or Selection: Choosing Books for Public Schools (PBS video, 60 min., 1982). Who determines what belongs in textbooks, the teacher or the parents? This video includes the creationism versus evolution controversy.

The Changing Role of Testing and Evaluation (Phi Delta Kappan, 35 min., 1985). Ralph Tyler, one of the foremost experts and scholars of curriculum theory, expresses his views on the subject.

Cross-Subject Teaching (Insight Media, 60 min., 1992). This video considers ways that a teacher, a school, or a community can adopt a general theme for study. It shows how pursuing a theme that includes many subject areas can increase students' appreciation for the scope of learning.

Cultural Literacy and Interactive Language Instruction (Insight Media, 60 min., 1989). This video focuses on strategies to integrate language and literature into all levels of foreign language learning. Instructors demonstrate effective and ineffective techniques for teaching literature in a foreign language classroom.

Curriculum Innovations (Insight Media, 60 min., 1993). This program explores innovative ideas about how to reach students and how to make the classroom an exciting place.

Developing Student Understanding: The New Direction in Curriculum (ASCD, 40 to 60 min., 1993). This three-cassette series focuses on what schools should be teaching in order to help people be successful in the twenty-first century.

Enhancing Student Thinking in the Classroom (ASCD, 40 to 60 min., 1993). This three-cassette series presents instructional and assessment strategies that can help students become problem solvers and lifelong learners.

The Great Horseshoe Crab Field Trip (Togg Films, 28 min., 1982). This film reveals ways of both learning and teaching as students in a seventh-grade science class from Harlem take a field trip to the seashore.

Making Whole Language Happen (Insight Media, 22 min., 1991). The video teaches how to incorporate developmental learning, oral language, reading, writing, and evaluation into practical methods that can be used in an elementary school classroom. It explains how to incorporate aspects of a whole language approach.

New Venues for Learning: Authentic Materials (Insight Media, 22 min., 1993). This video examines school programs that draw on materials from everyday life and surroundings. It visits a Minnesota high school that uses a local river as a source of interdisciplinary learning and a New Mexico middle school where students run businesses and the government in their own simulated city.

Problem Solving Strategies: The Synectics Approach (Prod: CRM, Dist: university film libraries, 27 min., 1980). Synectics Incorporated is a consulting firm that specializes in teaching the process of creative problem solving. This film documents the process.

What Should We Do in School Today? (Insight Media, 22 min., 1992). This video explores some of the most pressing issues facing educators today. It examines problems with curriculum, discipline, teacher evaluation, and children at risk, and visits innovative programs around the country that aim to improve the quality of education.

Student Activities

1. The Saber-Tooth Curriculum

Have students list five social changes they anticipate will occur in the next decade. Next to each prediction, have them write a short explanation of how schools might (or should) respond to these changes. If time permits, have students pair and discuss lists. Using chart paper, make a master list of all the anticipated changes.

2. The Knowledge Most Worth Having

Have each student select a grade level and write two paragraphs identifying what he or she thinks is the most important knowledge for a student of that age to learn in school and why.

3. The Little Red Schoolhouse

Copy pages from a *McGuffey Reader* and pages from a current basal reader and have the students compare the content of the two readers. Have them discuss the values and philosophy implicit in each reader.

4. Innovative Instructional Approaches

Divide the students into groups and assign one of the following instructional approaches to each group: interdisciplinary teaching, critical learning, writing across the curriculum, and multiage grouping in elementary school. Have each group prepare a short (10-minute) minilesson in a subject area using the approach.

5. The Ideal Curriculum

Based on a particular philosophy (your choice), design an ideal curriculum that embodies the beliefs of that philosophy, not just about subject matter, but also the role of the teacher, the student, the school, and even society in the educational process. (This activity could be done as a group activity.)

6. Curriculum Analysis

Collect several examples of curricula. Divide the class into groups of three or four and provide each group with a distinct curriculum. Ask the students to analyze the curriculum by looking at the goals and the objectives of the curriculum and answering questions such as: What appears to be the underlying educational philosophy governing this curriculum? Are the goals realizable and age-appropriate? To what extent are the goals affective or cognitive? Are learning activities specified? Is there any evidence of innovative instructional methods? Then have each group present its findings to the entire class.

7. Role Play

Divide the class into groups of seven. Assign one person in each group one of the roles listed below. Have the groups hold simulated meetings for 15 minutes, during which they discuss the "textbook controversy."

At the end of the time period, discuss the following questions:

a. What pressures were exerted on the superintendent?
b. Was the group able to reach a consensus?
c. Is consensus practical or possible in this situation?
d. What alternatives did the group develop?
e. Who should have the greatest influence on what a student learns?
f. How can different values and beliefs coexist in a school setting?

The Textbook Controversy

Scenario: The superintendent of schools has worked in a crisis situation for the past year. The books that were to bring innovation to the school system have resulted in violence and turmoil. Parents are deeply divided over the types of books their children should be using in the class. Many teachers are also divided over the textbook controversy. The superintendent is told by the "fundamentalist" parents that they intend to take their children out of the schools unless objectionable textbooks are removed from the classrooms. The "liberal" parents are pressing the superintendent and the school board to keep the books. A meeting has been called, attended by representatives of each of the following groups:

Task: The group is expected to resolve the conflict and develop some alternative plans for the remaining three months of school and for the next year. Roles are presented for either sex.

Roles:

a. Oliver/Olivia Tavares, **superintendent** of schools (chairperson). You have been the head of the school district of fifty thousand students for the past year. You have tried to bring some innovations into the system through very realistic and innovative paperback and hardback texts. You want the books to remain in the classroom, but you realize the need to compromise. You are the chairperson for the meeting.

b. Lynn Kaiser Conrad, **principal** (secondary or elementary school). There has been a great deal of disruption in your school. You have received several belligerent calls from unidentified parents. Absenteeism is about 30 percent higher than normal. The strain is beginning to affect the teachers and the students. Your main concern is to bring the school back to normal.

c. John/Bonnie Morgan, **teacher**. Most of the turmoil created by the use of the textbooks in the classroom has had little effect on your own teaching. Most parents of students in your classroom favor the new approach to teaching and the use of the controversial books. You feel other materials could be used to avoid the conflict now occurring.

d. Ray/Rana Bonanno. The **union representative**, who is a teacher in the system, feels the textbook issue has the potential for creating havoc in the classroom. If parents can dictate which texts to use, then they could also dictate what to teach and how it should be taught. You feel the teachers, who have been trained as professionals, should decide educational matters, not the "fundamentalist" or "liberal" parents.

e. Charles/Charlotte Kravulski, **fundamentalist parent**. You feel that your basic values are being betrayed by "those liberals who dare to bring filth and anti-Americanism" into the classroom. If the books remain in the schools, you will remove your three children and send them to a private school.

f. Frank/Frannie Scheuer, **liberal parent**. You feel the new books reflect the reality of life in our society. It is better for the students to learn about this life in the classroom than in the streets. You see the textbooks as preparation for the future, while the "fundamentalists" seem to want reality to go away.

g. Kevin/Lynne McCreanor, **school board member**. You feel the community is being unnecessarily divided by the conflict, and your main aim is to soothe both sides until time passes and heals the rift.

Chapter 9 How Are Schools Governed, Influenced, and Financed?

Learning Objectives

After studying the chapter, students will be able to

- describe and identify the contributions to public education from the state and local districts.
- identify and explain the influence that the state legislature and governor's office have upon educational policy.
- define the source of authority and particular responsibilities of the state board of education, the chief state school officer, the state department of education, the local school board and superintendent, and the school principal.
- describe the demographic data relating to school superintendents, principals, and school board members and explain the significance of those data.
- describe some ways school officials exercise informal influence in education.
- identify and explain the historical influence business has had upon public education.
- describe the current business interest in public schooling and analyze its effects.
- explain the strengths and shortcomings of standardized tests as measures of school effectiveness.
- explain the implications of several court cases regarding state and local funding of education, including the *Serrano* case and cases in Kentucky, Texas, and New Jersey, and the alternative plan to finance public education in Michigan.

- describe the typical pattern of school funding by local, state, and federal agencies, and explain the relationships among the local economy, tax structure, and the quality of education.
- describe the trends in federal support of education from the 1960s through the 1990s.

Chapter Overview

Few prospective teachers probably think at length about the governance, forces of influence, or finance of public schools. To someone enthusiastically learning how to become a teacher, such issues may seem far removed from life in classrooms. Yet issues involving the governance, influence, or finance of schools directly and indirectly affect a teacher's job because they define the parameters of public education and the roles of those involved in public education. For that reason, we describe some of the features of formal school governance that are common to all the states, as well as some aspects that may differ. We think prospective teachers should know how the organizational structure of a school works and how they, as teachers, will fit into that structure. Their effectiveness as teachers can be enhanced by the knowledge of the forces that shape other formal roles.

In addition, we want student readers to be cognizant of the ways informal influences affect school operation. As teachers, they will assume informal authority daily through the decisions they make about their classes. Department chairs, supervisors, and other teacher-administrators will exercise informal authority, often out of necessity. What beginning teachers may be less aware of is the informal influence that parents, business groups, and political organizations will try to exert in running the schools. New teachers ought to know what to expect and what limitations are set by law and custom.

We also discuss in the chapter the sources of funding for education. We describe the local, state, and federal contributions to education, also pointing out the historical changes in the federal funding of education. It is important to explain where money for school budgets comes from and what services each funding source has agreed to finance. Because of recent court cases finding that funding schemes in some states were unconstitutional, public funding and educational equity will be linked tightly in the near future. Such court cases and their implications could have a powerful influence on public education in the near future.

Chapter Outline

Chapter 9 *How Are Schools Governed, Influenced, and Financed?*

I. Who Legally Governs Public Education?

   A. State Offices and Administrators

   B. The Local School District

II. Who Influences American Public Education?

A. Professional Education Organizations

B. Parents

C. Business

D. Standardized Testing

E. The Federal Government

III. How Are Schools Financed?

A. State and Local Funding

B. School Finance Reform and the Courts

C. Federal Funding

Supplementary Lecture and Discussion Topics

1. **Changes in financing schools** Discuss in more detail the recent court cases determining that the existing system of school financing is unconstitutional. For example, what impact will the Texas court decision have nationally? Describe the differences among school support structures in two states—one state with an equation that equalizes resources among districts, another state with an equation that allows significant per-pupil variations in expenditures. Explain something about the cost-of-living differences that may account for some of the variations in expenditure among states and the differences in the quality of education. Explain in more detail what "redistribution" of funds would mean. What are the advantages? Any disadvantages? How would you explain the inequity in school funding to a low-income parent who hopes that his or her child will have an opportunity to succeed? How would you explain the court decisions to middle- or upper-income parents whose decision to move to a particular town was based on the reputation of its school system?

2. **An international comparison** Compare the federal government's role in U.S. education to the government's role in education in several other industrialized countries. Compare the similarities and differences in financing and in governing the public schools.

3. **Superintendent/principal/school board member** Invite a local superintendent, principal, and school board member to your class to discuss their roles and their perspectives on being a superintendent, principal, or school board member. If possible, have each person come from a different school district so that each can talk about his or her position and answer students' questions without any awkwardness. What are some of the speakers' greatest satisfactions in their role? What are some of their greatest frustrations? What do they spend most of their time doing on the job? Ask your students to prepare some questions beforehand for each speaker.

4. **Role of the state education agency** Describe the role of the state education agency in your state. Name the chief school officer and tell something about the people and programs that are particularly relevant to the students—for example, the teacher certification or licensure office or the staff development office. Many states are currently offering beginning teacher induction programs. If yours is, perhaps a person from that program could be invited to discuss it.

5. **Site-based management of schools** In the recent past, educational journals and research have discussed the benefits of site-based management of schools. Describe this concept in more detail to your students, outlining the changes in school hierarchy and the changes in roles and functions.

6. **Role of the PTO** Invite the president of a local parent-teacher organization to describe the responsibilities and activities of the group.

7. **U.S. Department of Education** Describe the budget of the department—the size of the budget in relation to the budgets of other cabinet-level departments and the programs it funds. Identify any programs that affect your college or community. Explain some of the arguments made for and against the continued existence of the department.

8. **Property tax** If you live in a community that funds schools through property taxes, use the following Property Tax Chart and Formula to walk your students through the calculations that determine mill levy and property tax amount.

JEFFERSON COUNTY COLORADO

Property Tax Statement

Tax Dist. 7015 Schedule No. 408809 1996 TAXES PAYABLE 1997

DOING BUSINESS AS: **BLDG 4 UNIT 102**	PROPERTY LOCATION		FIN. INST. **RD**
SEC.TWN.RNG.QTT SQ,FT. LAND BLK LOT KEY BOOK PAGE	TAX AUTHORITY	TAX LEVY*	TAX AMOUNT
JEWELL LAKE CONDOS 4TH SUPP	SCHOOL	39.6610	344.65
28 04 69 NE 004 0102 91093779	SCHOOL GEN	10.3000	89.51
	SCHOOL BND		
	COUNTY	14.2220	123.57
	CNTY GEN'L	.5000	4.35
	DEV DISABL	3.4130	29.66
	R&B SRVCS	2.1160	18.39
	SOC SERVCS	2.2040	19.15
	CAP'TL EXP	3.5000	30.42
	LIBRARY	.0230	.20
	CNTY OTHER	4.7110	40.94
RESIDENTIAL	LKWD	1.7460	15.17
	B-CLW&SD	4.0680	35.35
	FR&PD	.7800	6.78
	UDFCD	11.4130	99.18
	WMFPD		
PROPERTY VALUATION	DUE FIRST HALF	**TAX LEVY***	FULL AMOUNT DUE APRIL 30
ACTUAL LAND AND BUILDING.... 83,900			
ASSESSED LAND AND BUILDING.. 8,690	FEB 28 428.66		
	-------------------	98.6570	
	DUE SECOND HALF		857.32
ASSESSMENT PERCENTAGE RESIDENTIAL PROPERTY 10.36% ALL OTHER PROPERTY 29.00%	JUNE 428.66		

Example:

$$\$83{,}900 \times 10.36\% \times \frac{98.657}{1{,}000} =$$

Assessed Value of a House	Legislatively set/assessment percentage	Mill Levy Formula: 1 mill - 1/1000 of a dollar or 1/10 of a cent

$$83{,}900 \times .1036 \times .098657 = 857 = \text{Tax}$$

Additional Resources for Instructors

Burke, Fred G. *Public Education: Who's in Charge?* New York: Praeger, 1990. An account of the different forces that control public education. A readable book that details the issues of control and governance in public schools.

Callahan, Raymond. *Education and the Cult of Efficiency: A Study of the Social Forces That Have Shaped the Administration of Public Schools.* Chicago: University of Chicago Press, 1962. Although it was published three decades ago, Callahan's book provides important insights into how the administration of public schools during the early twentieth century progressed as it did. It examines how various forces, including the scientific management theory designed to increase production, influenced the management and direction of schools. The book provides powerful ideas for anyone interested in administration or reform of schools.

Campbell, Roald, et al. *The Organization and Control of American Schools.* 6th ed. Columbus, Ohio: Macmillan, 1990. A good overview of the American educational system, including both governance and control issues.

Chubb, John E., and Terry Moe. *Politics, Markets and America's Schools.* Washington, D.C.: Brookings Institute, 1990. A critical analysis of the ways in which politics, the market, and choice affect the public schools. This book captured immediate attention from the education community when it was published.

Eaton, William Edward. *Shaping the Superintendency: A Reexamination of Callahan and the Cult of Efficiency.* New York: Teachers College Press, 1990. Eaton returns to the work of Raymond Callahan and discusses Callahan's analysis and its applicability in the 1990s.

Fuller, Bruce, and Richard Rubinson (Eds.). *The Political Construction of Education: The State, School Expansion and Economic Change.* New York: Praeger, 1992. A detailed account of the intricacies and political complexities of funding schools.

Gainey, Donald B. *Education for the New Century: Views from the Principal's Office.* Reston, Va.: National Association of Secondary School Principals, 1993. A highly readable narrative describing the life of a principal.

Kozol, Jonathan. *Savage Inequalities: Children in America's Schools.* New York: Harper Perennial, 1992. A portrait of the schooling provided for children in some of America's most financially depressed cities. A disturbing account and highly recommended reading.

LoVette, Otis K. "You Ask, 'Why Have School Costs Increased So Greatly During the Last 20 Years?'" *Phi Delta Kappan* (October 1995): 169–172. LoVette lists the reasons under the general headings of court decisions, federal legislation and regulations, state legislation and regulations, and social expectations and demands.

McGonagill, Grady. "Board/Staff Partnership: The Key to the Effectiveness of State and Local Boards." *Phi Delta Kappan* 69 (September 1987): 65–68. McGonagill offers a four-step solution to the problem of developing a more viable partnership between boards of education and staff members.

Robinson, Glen E., and Nancy Protheroe. *Cost of Education: An Investment in America's Future.* Arlington, Va.: Educational Research Services, 1987. A scholarly appraisal of education and its economic costs.

Sergiovanni, Thomas J., et al. *Educational Governance and Administration.* Needham, Mass.: Allyn and Bacon, 1992. This text provides a balanced overview of the development of thought in educational administration. It emphasizes both school governance and administration.

Toch, Thomas. *In the Name of Excellence: The Struggle to Reform the Nation's Schools, Why It's Failing and What Ought to Be Done.* New York: Oxford University Press, 1991. Toch presents a critical analysis of the quest to make the nation's schools "excellent" by analyzing some flaws within the existing reform movement. He also proposes some alternative approaches that would improve the nation's schools.

Media Resources

Are We Shortchanging Our Schools? (PBS video, 60 min., 1992). Is increased federal spending necessary, or can reforms be accomplished by requiring schools to cut administrative costs?

Changing Schools Through Shared Decision Making (ASCD video, 30 min., 1994). This video shows the benefits of a shared approach to decision making on curriculum, instruction, and management policies. It shows how schools and districts successfully seek input from teachers, school support staff, parents, and students.

Children in America's Schools, with Bill Moyers (ETV Marketing, 2 hrs., first 60 min. most informative, 1996). Using Jonathan Kozol's book, *Savage Inequalities: Children in America's Schools,* as a starting point, this video depicts the undeniable inequities in American schools today.

Inner City vs. Suburban Schools (Films for the Humanities and Sciences, 28 min., 1993). This specially adapted Phil Donahue program provides a platform for parents as well as for Jonathan Kozol. Both the parents and Kozol claim that America's educational system is savagely unequal and discriminatory.

A Matter of Trust (IDEA, 32 min.). This film shows the difficulties that typically prevent decisions from being made by the appropriate school personnel. Examples include communities that did not trust school staffs to make educational decisions, reluctance of principals to trust teachers to make instructional decisions, and reluctance of teachers to trust children to make decisions.

Unequal Education (PBS video, 60 min., 1992). This video examines the political rhetoric versus the reality of American schooling. A video profile of students at two different public schools in the Bronx points out the inequities of our current system and how the discrepancies affect the quality of education. Includes comments from John Chubb and Jonathan Kozol.

Student Activities

1. Budget Role Play

The purpose of this exercise is to simulate the problems that school boards and educators deal with annually to balance the budget. Divide students into groups of two or three.

A student or group of students will be given an assignment that requires a presentation to the school board in order to retain or improve the current level of services for various program areas. Ask the students to assume the role of one of the influence groups (students, parents, taxpayers, professional education organizations, etc.) for their rationale and presentation.

BOARD OF EDUCATION (one group of three)

1. Elect a chair for the board.
2. Evaluate the various presentations to the board.
3. Recess, discuss, and vote on the proposals.
4. Final decisions must allow only a $6 million increase in the budget.
   Note to Instructors: Adjust the budget amount if you don't use all the requests.

PRESENTATIONS TO THE BOARD

1. Plan a 2-minute presentation that gives the best rationale for keeping a program or increasing the services of that program.
2. Present alternatives that indicate that you are trying to save the board money or are willing to compromise.

COMPUTER LABS

Need $0.7 million to keep programs at current levels, or the district will have to halt plans for putting a computer lab in each elementary school and for adding IBM computers at each high school to go with the current Macintosh computers.

INSTRUMENTAL MUSIC

Need $0.5 million to maintain elementary music teachers, or the district will have to

1. Eliminate one-half of the current music teachers at the elementary school level.
2. Eliminate elementary band and orchestra for this year.

DROPOUT PROGRAMS

Need $0.75 million to retain this program at the current level, or the district will have to

1. Cut the dropout prevention staff by 50 percent.
2. Eliminate this year's purchase of additional materials for the high school retention programs.
3. Cut the elementary bilingual staff by 25 percent.
4. Eliminate the community liaison position.

TEACHER SALARY INCREASES

Need $2 million to grant the increase, or the district will have to cut the 3.5 percent salary raise that was approved at the last board meeting provided that funds were available at this last round of cuts. If there is no salary raise, this will be the second year in a row.

SPORTS

Need $0.75 million to maintain remaining services, or the district will have to

1. Eliminate all varsity sports. Community would assume financial support of all continuing sports programs.
2. Cut back 15 percent in high school P.E. teachers.
3. Cut back 25 percent in elementary P.E. teachers.
4. Operate intramurals on a volunteer basis.

ARTS

Need $0.5 million to keep remaining programs, or the district will have to

1. Eliminate all elementary art teachers.
2. Cut back 35 percent in secondary art teachers (7–12).

FOREIGN LANGUAGE PROGRAMS

Need $0.75 million to continue this program, or the district will have to

1. Cut junior high teachers by 25 percent.
2. Not replace any senior high teachers who leave their positions.

GIFTED AND TALENTED

Need $0.75 million to

1. Establish a part-time pullout program in each elementary school.
2. Hire traveling gifted and talented specialists to operate the pullout programs.

ELEMENTARY TEACHER AIDES

Need $1 million to retain the current ratio of 2 hours a day per teacher, including paperwork, student assistance, and lunch and recess supervision.

ELEMENTARY CLASS SIZE REDUCTION

Need $1 million to reduce the primary ratio of 1:25 to 1:22, and the intermediate ratio of 1:30 to 1:26.

INCLUSION/MAINSTREAMING SUPPORT

Need $1.5 million to provide support for the classroom teacher.

1. Add teacher aides to assist inclusion of pupils in their regular classrooms.
2. Institute a weighing system to reduce pupil-teacher ratios in relation to the additional time and attention required by the number of mainstreamed students in each classroom.

Allow students to prepare for a few minutes in class or to research their issue from one class period to the next. Allow the board members to study the issues ahead of time and develop a plan or philosophy for decision making. After the presentations, while the board is deliberating, discuss the rationales and tactics used by the various groups. Point out current points of view and issues that students may have omitted. Have the school board members present their decisions, their rationale, and the decision-making process they developed and chose to use.

2. Mini Debates

Five statements that can be debated are listed below. Assign one group of from four to six students to act as supporters and one group to be the opposition for each statement. Videotape the debates so that students involved in their own assignments can watch their peers debate other issues. (Alternatively, invite community leaders or members of the local school board to debate some of the issues informally.)

The following features of public schools make them particularly vulnerable to local community concerns and pressures:

a. Schools are, in effect, monopolies that serve consumers who usually have little or no choice about attendance and who are individually powerless to bring about change.
b. Schools affect many people in the community in very personal and powerful ways.
c. Schools are seen as important institutions for imparting the selected traditions and values of the community.
d. Schools are often tied to local politics, since school board members and superintendents, whether appointed or elected, represent powerful elements in the community.
e. Schools provide an important avenue to success for some students and act as repressive, alienating, and failure-orienting institutions for others.

3. Stress and Control

Many recent studies have shown that a major cause of distress (stress) is the lack of control an individual has over work events. Both teachers and administrators rank low locus of control as a major work stressor. One recent study of public school administrators revealed that the "top five stressors" involved the issues of governance and control and resultant feelings of frustration and lack of accomplishment. Those stressors included, in order of distress, complying with rules, attending meetings, completing paperwork, gaining public approval, and resolving parental conflicts.

A teacher's life in school includes an immense amount of required managerial paper shuffling. Confronting this problem through the mailbox activity helps students develop an insight into the nonteaching part of the profession. After they complete the chart, a class discussion of answers and rationales should ensue.

Instructions: This morning when you arrived in school, you visited your mailbox and found the following items. In the space to the right of each item in Table 9.1 indicate whether you consider it a matter of governance and influence or of teaching. Also indicate how much stress you think that item would generate.

Table 9.1 A Teacher's Mailbox

Item	Governance and/or Influence	Teaching	Stress Low/Med./High
A bill that needs your signature for classroom materials purchased for you	______	______	______
Two new educational journals	______	______	______
A note from the principal asking you to attend a meeting of the PTA executive committee next Thursday in his office during lunch	______	______	______
A questionnaire from a nearby teachers' college asking you about your view on mainstreaming	______	______	______
A unit plan from a fellow teacher on a topic you were planning to teach next month	______	______	______
A letter from your supervisor asking for the names of potential community volunteers who might be interested in donating some time to the school	______	______	______
A memo from the social committee asking you if you will be attending the faculty picnic Sunday and what you will be bringing	______	______	______
A thank-you note from parents for the extra help you have given their child, who was having trouble in your class	______	______	______
A note to call Mr. and Mrs. Wong about Lin's failing grade in your class	______	______	______
A note from your principal asking you to fill out a preliminary form for annual observation/evaluation—you will probably be observed sometime Friday afternoon	______	______	______
A form from the book room indicating how many supplemental texts are missing from your room	______	______	______
A form from your department chair asking you to list supplies needed next year	______	______	______

4. Channel One Analysis

Obtain permission for your students to watch several segments of Channel One. As they watch, ask them to note what strikes them. You may want to direct your students to the following issues. How many and what kind of commercials are included? How frequently are these commercials shown? What are the underlying messages promoted by the commercials? What kinds of informational programming does Channel One provide? How is it edited and presented for the viewers? After you finish watching, discuss with the students their insights and analysis.

5. Analysis of School Funding and Per-Pupil Spending (for individual or group work)

This project is ideally suited to those students in field-site schools. Collect economic and budgetary data from your field-site school and several school districts nearby. Try to collect the following information: per-pupil expenditure, teachers' salary scale, cost of instructional materials and equipment, and cost of building and grounds maintenance and improvement. See if you can collect data on how much each grade level or academic discipline receives. Can you also collect findings on student academic achievement (standardized test scores, percentage who graduate, percentage who attend and who complete postsecondary education, drop-out rate, absenteeism rate)? Also collect information on the residential and commercial tax rate. Roughly speaking, can you estimate how much money each household contributes to public schooling in this district? Also see the percentage of the school district budget that is supplied through other sources: corporate taxes, state and federal funding, and so on. What kinds of findings do you have? How does your field-site school compare to neighboring districts? Present your findings to the class in a chart or table form.

6. Alternative Funding Schemes for Schools (for individual or group work)

Research in greater detail the court cases concerning school funding in New Jersey, Kentucky, Texas, or, most recently, New Hampshire. What is the background of the state's school funding? What were the results? Based upon the court ruling, what are the alternative funding schemes being proposed or implemented? Or look at the public school funding in Michigan more closely, examining the background of this issue and how Michigan has chosen to fund its public schools.

7. Report on School Board Meeting (for individual or group work)

The school board plays an important role in local government. Each school district has different priorities, and they often reflect the interests of the school board members. Meetings are open to the public and are usually held monthly. Find out when the local school board meets and attend one meeting. If a printed agenda is provided, ask students to add to it their own notes on any hidden agenda items. After the meeting, analyze the various concerns raised, the issues presented, and the factions (if applicable). Also try to assess the relationship between the school board and the superintendent. Present your analysis to the whole class.

Chapter 10 What Are the Philosophical Foundations of American Education?

Learning Objectives

After studying this chapter, students will be able to

- describe the role of philosophical knowledge in clarifying questions of educational decision making in policy and practice.
- explain how four branches of philosophy—metaphysics, epistemology, logic, and axiology—relate to the work of the teacher.
- describe and distinguish among four philosophies of education—perennialism, progressivism, essentialism, and existentialism—and explain the implications of each for schooling.
- identify the key contributions of John Dewey to U.S. education.
- apply the information they have learned about educational philosophy to analyze existing school curricula.
- begin to formulate and articulate their personal philosophy.

Chapter Overview

Chapter 10 introduces prospective teachers to the four major branches of philosophy—metaphysics, epistemology, logic, and axiology—and demonstrates how those branches apply to education. It also provides examples of how each branch of philosophy affects decisions about education. When a faculty decides, for example, what constitutes knowledge, their goals in educating students, the content of their curriculum, or the methods their teachers will use, they are making educational decisions rooted in philosophy. The chapter presents the various implications philosophy has for education and invites readers to apply this information to their own lives as prospective teachers.

The chapter also traces the development of four major philosophies of education: perennialism, progressivism, essentialism, and existentialism. The chapter highlights the similarities and differences in each of these schools of philosophy and demonstrates how each philosophy would be manifested in schools. The chapter also includes an overview of the work and philosophy of John Dewey as it relates to U.S. education.

Perennialism. Perennialism views human nature as constant over time, asserting that people's rationality sets them apart from animals. Applied to education, perennialism asserts that the development of the intellect is the sole purpose of schooling. Perennialists believe that the best way to develop one's intellect is through rigorously studying the enduring truths of humankind contained in the classics of Western culture.

Progressivism. Progressivism views nature as being ever-changing, so knowledge must be continually redefined and rediscovered. Progressive education views learners as problem solvers who naturally develop by exploring questions of interest to them. Progressives contend that no knowledge is privileged over another and that the knowledge of the most value is the knowledge that the learner wants to know.

Essentialism. Essentialism views the mind as the central element of reality and holds that knowing requires the ability to observe and measure the physical world accurately. Essentialists claim that there is a core body of knowledge, including both classical and contemporary disciplines, that all people need to have in order to function productively in society, and that the overwhelming majority of students can learn this core. In essentialism, the worth of any knowledge is measured by how much an individual needs that knowledge to become a productive member of society.

Existentialism. Existentialism views existence as meaningless; therefore, it is up to the individual to determine the meaning he or she finds within life. In existentialism, people are free. That is, because of people's inherent freedom, they define themselves and their personal relationships with the world by their freely made choices in their quest for personal meaning. Existentialist education emphasizes the student's quest for personal meaning. Existentialist elements that appear in modern schools are values clarification exercises, individualized instruction, and other programs that emphasize personal choice as an element of development.

Chapter Outline

Chapter 10 *What Are the Philosophical Foundations of American Education?*

Our philosophy of education (values and goals) influences the decisions we make regarding education whether we are teachers, parents, students, or legislators.

I. What Is Philosophy?

II. The Terrain (Branches) of Philosophy

   A. Metaphysics
   B. Epistemology
   C. Axiology
      1. Ethics
      2. Aesthetics
   D. Logic
      1. Deductive
      2. Inductive

[Use educational philosophy test (see p. 126) here or prior to starting the lecture as preparation so that students can explore their own unrecognized but existing philosophical values before further information is presented.]

III. Schools of Education Philosophy

   A. Perennialism
   B. Progressivism
   C. Essentialism
   D. Existentialism

IV. Your Philosophy of Education

V. Eclecticism: Not an Excuse for Sloppy Thinking

VI. Philosophy and Liberal Education

Supplementary Lecture and Discussion Topics

1. **Philosophy of education in other countries** The text mentions that essentialism and progressivism are two educational philosophies that are distinctly American. They also have had considerable influence on the U.S. educational system. How do those philosophies compare with other countries' philosophies of education around the world? Describe and explain the educational philosophies of countries such as France, Korea, Kenya, or Brazil. What are they? What are the philosophical assumptions about the role of the teacher? The learner? The curriculum? If you have students in your class from other countries, you can invite them to participate in the lecture.

2. **Current issues in education and their philosophical roots** Often even the best-informed students fail to look behind educational controversies or ideas to see their philosophical origins or bases. Particular terms used in education—such as *diversity, equity, PC (politically correct), core curriculum, excellence, back-to-basics, outcomes-based education, authentic assessment, inclusion,* and *effective schools*—have philosophical as well as political roots. Choose a few of the current educational terms and analyze them in terms of the implicit educational philosophy they reflect.

3. **Schools choose eclecticism** The text mentions that many teachers are eclectic in their philosophy of education. Many schools are, too, for a variety of reasons. Some consciously choose elements of different philosophies; others demonstrate various philosophies in their educational practice because they have never clearly identified their own philosophy of education. Still others are eclectic because it is far too difficult to adhere completely to one philosophy. For example, most schools would find it quite difficult to implement a wholly existentialist philosophy of education. Explain and describe the forces that may result in an eclectic philosophy of education for a school, and explain its ramifications.

4. **Multiculturalism and educational philosophy** Examine the philosophical underpinnings of the various manifestations of multicultural education. Present the various associated educational schools of thought, such as global education, Afrocentrism, and ethnic studies, and describe the distinctions among them. In multicultural education, what are the core issues? What is the core concept of knowledge, and how it is learned by various people? What significance do the terms *knowledge* and *curriculum* have for those engaged in multicultural education? To what degree is multicultural education complementary to the educational philosophies discussed in this chapter?

Additional Resources for Instructors

Adler, Mortimer. "The Paideia Proposal: Rediscovering the Essence of Education." *The American School Board Journal* 169 (July 1982): 17–20. This article summarizes Adler's *The Paideia Proposal, An Educational Manifesto* (New York: Macmillan, 1982), which is a reformulation of perennialism.

Ayers, William. "Rethinking the Profession of Teaching: A Progressive Option." *Action in Teacher Education* 12 (Spring 1990): 1–5. This article discusses Dewey's concept of progressive education and states the experientialist assumptions that characterize progressive education as a guide in the movement toward teacher professionalism.

Barzun, Jacques. *Begin Here: The Forgotten Conditions of Teaching and Learning.* Chicago: University of Chicago Press, 1991. A selection of various essays from a well-respected scholar in education.

Bloom, Allan. *The Closing of the American Mind: How Higher Education Has Failed Democracy and Impoverished the Souls of Today's Students.* New York: Simon and Schuster,

1987. A trenchant intellectual attack on what the author sees as the collapse of the liberal arts tradition in U.S. higher education.

Broudy, Harry S. *The Uses of Schooling*. New York: Routledge, 1988. Well-known educational philosopher Harry S. Broudy argues that schools should provide only a general, or liberal arts, education. He defines the types of knowledge that he thinks constitute a general education.

Dewey, John. *Democracy and Education.* New York: Free Press, 1916. Progressive education was a ground-breaking educational theory that perhaps has had the strongest impact of any theory on U.S. education. It led to the widely adopted progressive education movement from the 1920s to the 1940s. Dewey's ideas gained ardent supporters, but the ideas were misconstrued and misapplied in public schools. Dewey's theories, though, have widely influenced scholars since that time.

Giroux, Henry (Ed.). *Postmodernism, Feminism, and Culture Boundaries: Redrawing Educational Boundaries.* Albany: SUNY Press, 1991. A collection of essays arguing for greater inclusion and diversity in the traditional spectrum of education.

Gray, J. Glenn. *Rethinking American Education: A Philosophy of Teaching and Learning.* Middletown, Conn.: Wesleyan University Press, 1984. In this reissue of a book published sixteen years earlier, *The Promise of Wisdom,* Gray sets forth the elements of educational theory, including essays on the definition and purpose of education, the curriculum, and the philosophical problems in practice. A clearly written book for anyone interested in a broad picture of U.S. educational philosophy.

Holtz, Harvey (Ed.). *Education and the American Dream: Conservatives, Liberals, and Radicals Debate the Future of Education.* Granby, Mass.: Bergin and Garvey, 1989. This volume contains essays written from differing perspectives regarding the goals and future of education.

Knock, Gary H. "Our Philosophical Heritage: Significant Influences on Professional Practice and Preparation." *NASPA Journal* 27 (Winter 1989): 116–22. The article examines the influence on student affairs of four philosophical perspectives: rationalism, neohumanism, pragmatism, and existentialism.

Noddings, Nel. *Philosophy of Education.* New York: HarperCollins, 1995. This book is a brief, clear review of the basics in educational philosophy. It would be especially helpful for instructors who don't have a strong background in this topic.

Oakeshott, Michael J. *The Voice of Liberal Learning: Michael Oakeshott on Education.* New Haven: Yale University Press, 1989. Oakeshott, a prominent educational philosopher, explores his conception of a liberal education.

Passmore, John A. *The Philosophy of Teaching.* Cambridge, Mass.: Harvard University Press, 1980. Passmore presents a highly readable philosophy of teaching that includes a discussion on the role of the teacher, as well as topics such as "wonder" in learning.

Peddiwell, J. Abner. *The Sabertooth Curriculum.* New York: McGraw-Hill, 1939. Peddiwell was the pseudonym of Harold Benjamin, who wrote this caveman parody of philosophical influence in education.

Postman, Neil. *The End of Education*. New York: Alfred Knopf, 1995. Postman describes the influential narratives in education—past, present (misguided), and proposed narratives—as guidelines for the future.

Semel, Susan F. *The Dalton School: The Transformation of a Progressive School.* New York: Peter Lang Publishing, 1992. This book tells the story of the Dalton School from its earliest beginnings through the present day. Ultimately, Semel uses the original Dalton Plan as a yardstick by which to measure what has happened to progressive education in the larger world.

Media Resources

The Americans (Insight Media, 21 min., 1988). This video discusses Noah Webster's work to improve American education, foster patriotism, and promote American literature and uniformity of speech. It explores the influence of Horace Mann's belief that a just society must educate all of its citizens, covers the contributions of Henry Barnard's *American Journal of Education,* and examines Robert Owen's emphasis on character formation and early childhood education.

The Critics (Insight Media, 25 min., 1988). Maria Montessori, John B. Watson, Margaret Naumburg, and W. E. B. Du Bois are the subjects of this video, which discusses critiques of educational orthodoxy.

Cultural Illiteracy (Films for the Humanities and Sciences, 28 min., 1987). Cultural illiteracy among today's teenagers threatens the very fabric of society, according to Professor E. D. Hirsch, Jr., author of *Cultural Literacy*. Hirsch and moderator Robert MacNeil are joined by poet Maya Angelou; Patrick Welsh, a teacher; and Dr. Robert Coles.

The End of Education (Into the Classroom video, 50 min., 1996). A presentation of Neil Postman's analysis of the narratives that have guided educational philosophy in the United States. It covers the past, the present, and proposals for the future. An ideal demonstration of philosophical thought in education.

Out of the Wilderness (Films for the Humanities and Sciences, 30 min., 1993). "Difficult" and "backward" children receive devoted attention at educator Reuven Feuerstein's Hadassah Institute in Jerusalem. Feuerstein's teaching system, "Institutional Enrichment," is being introduced into classrooms all over the world.

Perennial Philosophy: The Themes That Bind Us Together (Hartley Film Foundation, 30 min., 1985). The film maintains that the world's great spiritual traditions are strikingly similar. It uses dance, music, and poetry to illustrate the common core of perennial philosophy.

The Progressives (Insight Media, 24 min., 1988). This program explores the lives and views of four key figures in progressive educational theory: G. Stanley Hall, Francis W. Parker, John Dewey, and Ella Flagg Young.

Summerhill at 70 (Films for the Humanities and Sciences, 52 min., 1994). Summerhill, the first and last bastion of totally permissive, anti-authoritarian education, has been going strong for over seven decades. This video shows how Summerhill children, left entirely to their own devices, behave. A fascinatingly close look at an educational community that appears constantly on the edge of anarchy and at the method underlying the apparent chaos.

Too Good to Be True (CBS Television, 20 min., 1995). A *60 Minutes* segment that revisits Chicago educator Marva Collins and her students. Excellent example of a perennialist philosophy at the elementary level.

Transformation (Insight Media, 25 min., 1995). Designed to help teachers develop a personal philosophy of education, this program provides an overview of the history of educational philosophy, presenting observations from Darwin, Skinner, Piaget, Parker, Dewey, and Chomsky.

Student Activities

1. Educational Philosophy Survey

Before the students read the chapter, have them complete the short E.P.—educational philosophy test (at the end of this section)—to discover if they have already acquired a strong affinity for one philosophy or another. Emphasize that all of the answers are "right" for one of the philosophies. Reassure students whose answers are evenly spread across philosophies that with more experience their own philosophy will develop and emerge.

2. School Analysis

A number of individual schools have become well known for their educational philosophy. More generally, numerous schools adopt a particular philosophy and operate on the basis of its principles. Through text or video, provide opportunities for your students to see these various types of schools. As they find out more about particular schools, as a class, analyze each school's educational philosophy and discuss the implications of this type of schooling for students. Some suggestions include Summerhill; the Boston Latin school; various Quaker schools; the Waldorf schools; Montessori schools, the Bronx High School of Math and Science; and Stuyvesant High. More general suggestions include: single-sex schools, magnet schools, schools adopting the Paideia approach, and so on.

3. Teacher Interview

Have students interview a teacher to discover his or her philosophy of education. Suggest probes they may want to use to follow up this general question: "What is your philosophy of education?"

- "What are your learning goals?"
- "What do you believe are the most effective methods for teaching?"
- "What values do you try to foster in your teaching?"
- "How do you try to foster them?"
- "What do you think is the role of the teacher?"
- "What is the role of the student?"
- "What factors may sometimes keep you from acting in strict accord with your beliefs?"
- "What about your philosophy would you like to pass on to a new teacher?"
- "As you've gained experience, has your philosophy of education changed?"

4. Minilessons

Design a minilesson exemplifying one of the educational philosophies presented in this chapter (perennialism, progressivism, essentialism, existentialism). You may select a topic of your choice. After you present this minilesson to your class, analyze it. What were the elements within it that exemplified that particular philosophy? (This activity could easily be used in cooperative learning groups.)

5. Create a Charter School (group activity)

You and your colleagues have just been granted a charter to create your own school. Your school will operate under one of the four philosophies presented in the chapter. Given those conditions, you and your colleagues will prepare some important documents for your school. (1) Write your school's mission statement. What will your mission be, and how will your educational philosophy be reflected in your mission? (2) Construct general curricular goals/competencies—or select a particular grade and academic subject and create a more specific curriculum. (3) Provide a brief description of the topics covered (in elementary grades) or the course offerings provided for middle or high school. Present and discuss your documents with the whole class.

6. Curriculum Analysis (group or individual work)

Examine an actual school's curriculum guide, including, if they have one, a mission statement. Analyze the curriculum for the philosophical underpinnings. What are the key words and phrases that alert you to the school's philosophy? To what degree is the curriculum consistent with one educational philosophy? If it reflects eclecticism, what strands demonstrate various philosophies? What are the key activities, materials, or textbooks that indicate the school's philosophy?

7. Write Your Own Philosophy of Education

See copy-ready assignment sheet on the following page.

HOW TO WRITE YOUR PHILOSOPHY OF EDUCATION

Assignment:

Your own philosophy of education is very important because it provides focus and emphasis for your teaching. Working to communicate your philosophy helps you to become aware of your own goals and values, which prepares you to integrate them with the goals and values espoused by your district and your community.

Your statement of philosophy is a description of your own goals and beliefs as a teacher. There is no "right" philosophy. Some fit into certain settings better then others. You will refine, augment, and develop your philosophy for the rest of your career. Usually it is not successful to "change" your whole philosophy to meet the expectations of someone else.

Below are some guidelines to keep in mind to produce a well-written, focused, and articulate statement of your philosophy.

- Your philosophy should be no longer than two pages, typed and double spaced.

- Somewhere in your statement of philosophy answer the following questions:
  - What is the purpose of education? (What goals do you want your students to achieve?)
  - What is the student's role? (What are students' responsibilities?)
  - What is the teacher's role?
  - What is the teacher's role as a bridge to the community? (optional)
  - What is the teacher's role in educational renewal and reform? (optional)

- This statement of philosophy should rely on your personal beliefs and experiences. Your philosophy will be influenced by the knowledge and experience you acquire as you proceed through your licensure/certification program.

- You may want to "try on" a metaphor to more clearly and vividly describe your philosophy. Growing plants, filling a pitcher, and molding clay are some common (but stereotypical) metaphorical vehicles. You may want to create a new one to avoid previous connections associated with these three. Successful use of a metaphor may depend on using a skill, hobby, or activity you have experience with and also on knowing when to step outside the metaphor and show a contrast (e.g., unlike a bicycle, education has more than two wheels)

Due date: ____________________

The Educational Philosophy Test (E.P.)
By Patricia D. Jersin

INSTRUCTIONS

Please check the answer under each item that best reflects your thinking.

1. What is the essence of education?
   A. The essence of education is reason and intuition.
   B. The essence of education is growth.
   C. The essence of education is knowledge and skills.
   D. The essence of education is choice.
2. What is the nature of the learner?
   A. The learner is an experienced organism.
   B. The learner is a unique, free, choosing and responsible creature and is made up of intellect and emotion.
   C. The learner is a rational and intuitive being.
   D. The learner is a storehouse for knowledge and skills, which once acquired, can later be applied and used.
3. How should education provide for the needs of man?
   A. The students need a passionate encounter with the perennial problems of life: the agony and joy of love, the reality of choice, the anguish of freedom, the consequences of actions, and the inevitability of death.
   B. Education allows for the needs of man when it inculcates the child with certain essential skills and knowledge which all men should possess.
   C. The one distinguishing characteristic of man is intelligence. Education should concentrate on developing the intellectual needs of students.
   D. Since the needs of man are variable, education should concentrate on developing the individual differences in students.
4. What should be the environment of education?
   A. Education should possess an environment in which the student adjusts to the material and social world as it really exists.
   B. The environment of education should be life itself, where students can experience "living" . . . not prepare for it.
   C. The environment of education should be one that encourages the growth of free, creative individuality, not adjustment to group thinking or the public norms.
   D. Education is not a true replica of life; rather, it is an artificial environment where the child should be developing his or her intellectual potentialities and preparing for the future.
5. What should be the goal of education?
   A. Growth, through the reconstruction of experience, is the nature and should be the open-ended goal of education.
   B. The only type of goal to which education should lead is the goal of truth, which is absolute, universal, and unchanging.
   C. The primary concern of education should be with developing the uniqueness of individual students.
   D. The goal of education should be to provide a framework of knowledge for the student against which new truths can be gathered and assimilated.

6. What should be the concern of the school?
   A. The school should concern itself with man's distinguishing characteristic, the mind, and concentrate on developing rationality.
   B. The school should provide an education for the "whole child," centering its attention on all the needs and interests of the child.
   C. The school should educate the child to attain the basic knowledge necessary to understand the real world outside.
   D. The school should provide each student with assistance in his or her journey toward self-realization.

7. What should be the atmosphere of the school?
   A. The school should provide for group thinking in a democratic atmosphere that fosters cooperation rather than competition.
   B. The atmosphere of the school should be one of authentic freedom where a student is allowed to find his or her own truth and ultimate fulfillment through nonconforming choice making.
   C. The school should surround its students with "Great Books" and foster individuality in an atmosphere of intellectualism and creative thinking.
   D. The school should retain an atmosphere of mental discipline, yet incorporate innovative techniques that would introduce the student to a perceptual examination of the realities about him or her.

8. How should appropriate learning occur?
   A. Appropriate learning occurs as the student freely engages in choosing among alternatives while weighing personal responsibilities and the possible consequences of his or her actions.
   B. Appropriate learning takes place through the experience of problem-solving projects by which the child is led from practical issues to theoretical principles (concrete to abstract).
   C. Appropriate learning takes place as certain basic readings acquaint students with the world's permanencies, inculcating them in theoretical principles that they will later apply in life (abstract to concrete).
   D. Appropriate learning occurs when hard effort has been extended to absorb and master the prescribed subject matter.

9. What should be the role of the teacher?
   A. The teacher should discipline his or her pupils intellectually through a study of the great works in literature in which the universal concerns of man have best been expressed.
   B. The teacher should present principles and values and the reasons for them, encouraging students to examine them in order to choose for themselves whether or not to accept them.
   C. The teacher should guide and advise his or her students, since the children's own interests should determine what they learn.
   D. The teacher, the responsible authority, should mediate between the adult world and the world of the child, since immature students cannot comprehend the nature and demands of adulthood by themselves.

10. What should the curriculum include?
   A. The curriculum should include only that which has survived the test of time and which combines the symbols and ideas of literature, history, and mathematics with the sciences of the physical world.
   B. The curriculum should concentrate on teaching students how to manage change through problem-solving activities in the social studies, empirical sciences, and vocational technology.
   C. The curriculum should concentrate on intellectual subject matter and include English, languages, history, mathematics, natural sciences, the fine arts, and also philosophy.
   D. The curriculum should concentrate on the humanities—history, literature, philosophy, and art—where greater depth into the nature of man and his conflict with the world is revealed.

11. What should be the preferred teaching method?
   A. *Projects* should be the preferred method whereby the students can be guided through problem-solving experiences.
   B. *Lectures, readings,* and *discussions* should be the preferred methods for training the intellect.
   C. *Demonstrations* should be the preferred method for teaching knowledge and skills.
   D. *Socratic dialogue* (drawing responses from a questioning conversation) should be the preferred method for finding the self.

Scoring the Test:

This test is self-scoring. Circle the answer you selected for each of the questions checked on the test. Total the number of circles below each column. The more answers in one column, the stronger your inclination toward that philosophy.

Test #	Progressivism	Perennialism	Essentialism	Existentialism
1	B	A	C	D
2	A	C	D	B
3	D	C	B	A
4	B	D	A	C
5	A	B	D	C
6	B	A	C	D
7	A	C	D	B
8	B	C	D	A
9	C	A	D	B
10	B	C	A	D
11	A	B	C	D
Total				

If your answers are more evenly distributed, your philosophy has not yet fully evolved through your education and experience. As you continue your program, your experiences will influence the development of your philosophy.

Excerpted from "What Is Your E.P.?" by Patricia D. Jersin, *Clearinghouse* 46, January 1972, pp. 274–278.

Chapter 11 What Is the History of American Education?

Learning Objectives

After studying the chapter, students will be able to

- identify, explain, and analyze the six key forces that have shaped the history of American education: local control of schools, universal education, public education, comprehensive education, secular education, and the changing ideas of the basics.
- identify and describe the purposes of the various types of elementary schooling available during the colonial period and be able to associate particular types of schooling with the geographical region in which it was most common.
- identify and describe the purposes of various types of secondary schooling available, from the colonial period through the present.
- locate on a time continuum the introduction of the following major developments in U.S. education: grammar schools, public (common) schools, academies, kindergarten, and secondary schools.
- identify, explain, and apply the educational ideas and methods of several key European educators.
- identify, explain, and apply the educational ideas and methods of several key American educators.
- articulate the major arguments supporting and opposing the establishment of common schools in the United States.
- define and explain the impact that several key rulings or laws have had upon expanding education: the Old Deluder Satan Act, the Northwest Land Ordinances, the *Kalamazoo* case, the Morrill Acts, *Plessy* v. *Ferguson*, and *Brown* v. *Board of Education.*

- explain and apply the general principles of the Progressive Education Association.
- describe the evolution of education for women, for African Americans, for Hispanic Americans, for Asian Americans, and for Native Americans.

Chapter Overview

The history of American education spans more than 250 years. In this chapter on the history of American education, we paint in broad brush strokes to provide prospective teachers with the general landscape of educational history. In this way, we hope that future teachers will become familiar with significant ideas, events, and people that have shaped American education. Moreover, we also hope that prospective teachers can gain perspective on contemporary educational practices and their relationship to earlier practices. Tracing the growth of public education from the dame schools of colonial New England to the advent of middle schools in the mid-twentieth century, this chapter highlights how access to educational opportunities has gradually widened over the course of U.S. history. In that vein, we identify and discuss significant events that have helped educational institutions include a greater number and variety of people.

We identify six forces that have had an impact on shaping education in this country: local control of schools, universal education, public education, comprehensive education, secular education, and the changing ideas of the basics. Each of the subtopics we present can be related to those broad forces.

Chapter Outline

Chapter 11 *What Is the History of American Education?*

I. Themes in American Education
   - A. Local Control
   - B. Universal Education
   - C. Public Education
   - D. Comprehensive Education
   - E. Secular Education
   - F. Changing Ideas of the Basics

II. Elementary Education
   - A. Colonial Origins
     1. Home Schools

2. Town Schools
3. District Schools

B. The Common School

C. Other Developments in Elementary Education

1. European Influences
   a. Kindergarten
2. Curriculum Changes
3. Consolidation
4. Progressive Education Association
5. Post–World War II
   a. Special Education
   b. New Curriculum
   c. Back to Basics

III. Secondary Education

A. Early Forms
1. Latin Grammar
2. English Grammar

B. The Academy
1. Female Academies

C. The Public High School

D. Growth of Junior High and Middle School

IV. Private Education

V. Education of Minorities

A. Education of African Americans

B. Education of Native Americans

C. Education of Hispanic Americans

D. Education of Asian Americans

Supplementary Lecture and Discussion Topics

1. **Historical textbooks** Assemble from a local library collection a sample of textbooks used in various periods of our nation's history. The *New England Primer* and McGuffey readers are widely available. Compare the features of these books to the features of modern textbooks. Or assemble comparable samples of old and modern teacher education texts.

What do the old teacher education texts emphasize? What qualities did they say a teacher should have? What are the differences between training then and now?

2. **Historical overview of the education of various ethnic/racial groups** Trace the development of education for one or several groups in our country—for example, African Americans, Native Americans, or a newly arrived immigrant group. How did this group first obtain formal education in America? What were the underlying purposes of formal education for this group? To what degree did its members have autonomy in their choice of education? What were some key events in their achievement of formal education? What is this group's access and achievement today in regard to formal education?

3. **Private and parochial education** Trace the development of private or religious schools in the United States, paying particular attention to the nineteenth and twentieth centuries. Include discussions of contemporary religious fundamentalist schools.

4. **Educational personalities** Discuss significant but perhaps not-too-well-known historical figures who made important contributions to education in your local area. Regional historical societies are likely to have information about the people who started the first school, those who extended services to the underserved, or teachers whose influence was felt strongly for a long time.

5. **Higher education** Trace the development of American higher education from colonial days to the present. Include changes in the student body, relevant legislation, curriculum, and accessibility. Explain how your own institution was affected by these factors.

6. **Education and wartime** In 1917, numerous public school districts dropped German from their curriculum and emphasized patriotic American literature. Shortly after World War II, the G.I. bill was passed, allowing veterans to continue their schooling with the help of the federal government. At the height of the Cold War, math and science programs in high schools were expanded and bolstered. Wartime tensions usually have a direct impact on public education. Describe the influences various wars (or the threat of war) have had upon American education in the twentieth century.

Additional Resources for Instructors

Butts, R. Freeman, and Lawrence Cremin. *A History of Education in American Culture.* New York: Holt, Rinehart and Winston, 1953. This book gives a view of American education within the surrounding society and culture spanning the years 1607 to 1950.

Cremin, Lawrence. *The American Common School.* New York: Teachers College, Columbia University, 1951. Cremin's book traces the development of the common school movement.

Cuban, Larry. *How Teachers Taught: Constancy and Change in American Classrooms: 1890–1990.* New York: Teachers College Press, 1993. A respected educational historian, Cuban presents a scholarly account of the teaching methods of the last one hundred years. His findings are striking.

Curti, Merle. *The Social Ideas of American Educators.* New York: Littlefield, Adams, 1959. Curti examines the ideas of educational thinkers such as Thomas Jefferson, Benjamin Franklin, and Horace Mann.

Power, Edward J. *A Legacy of Learning: A History of Western Education.* Albany: SUNY Press, 1991. This comprehensive volume provides important events and their analyses for anyone interested in understanding the major themes and goals of Western education.

Pulliam, John P. *History of Education in America.* 5th ed. Columbus, Ohio: Merrill, 1991. A clearly written history of the major events in American education.

Ravitch, Diane. *The Troubled Crusade: American Education 1945–1980.* New York: Basic Books, 1983. Ravitch traces the history of U.S. education from directly after World War II to the beginning of the 1980s. She analyzes the fall of progressive education, the *Brown* v. *Board of Education* decision, the controversies surrounding public education during the 1960s, and the politicization of education during the second half of the twentieth century.

Rippa, S. Alexander. *Education in a Free Society: An American History.* New York: Longman, 1992. This book presents educational history through a political framework, interpreting key events in educational history.

Spring, Joel. *The American School: 1642–1990.* New York: Longman, 1990. Spring writes a history of the social, political, and ideological forces that have shaped American education from the 1600s to the present.

Tyack, David, and Elisabeth Hansot. *Learning Together: A History of Coeducation in American Schools.* New Haven: Yale University Press, 1990. Tyack and Hansot trace the development of coeducation in American education, analyzing the factors that have contributed to coeducation.

Warren, Donald R. (Ed.). *America's Teachers: Histories of a Profession at Work.* New York: Macmillan, 1989. This volume presents absorbing accounts of the varieties of ways in which teachers have conducted their work.

Media Resources

Common Threads (Insight Media, 20 min., 1995). This video chronicles the history of education in the United States from the colonial period to the present. It examines how curricula have evolved, how the purposes of education have changed over time, and how technology affects modern education.

Contributions of School in Developing a Literate Citizenship (Phi Delta Kappan, 35 min., 1985). Ralph Tyler discusses his views with Bob Cole. Tyler's insights on education from his perspective of more than fifty years make this tape an ideal resource for educational history students.

Eyes on the Prize (Prod: CCBlackside Inc., Dist: PBS and Boston University, 6-part series, 60 min. each, 1986). The civil rights struggle between 1954 and 1965 is covered by this documentary series. Included in the series: *Fighting Back* (1957–1962). The law has been used both to promote change and to resist change, particularly educational change. This episode explores the lawsuits brought by parents on behalf of their children, with special emphasis on the crucial 1954 Supreme Court *Brown* v. *Board of Education* decision.

The Fateful Decade: From Little Rock to the Civil Rights Bill (Films for the Humanities and Sciences, 27 min., 1994). This program begins at Little Rock's Central High School, when soldiers had to provide safety for black children exercising their legal right to go to school. Martin Luther King, Jr., appears in 1958 at a meeting of black leaders with President Eisenhower. The civil rights movement accelerated: marches, clashes with the police and the jailing of demonstrators, the murder of Medgar Evers, the bombing of the Baptist church in Birmingham, sit-ins and protests, the Montgomery march, the Mississippi Freedom march, King's famous "I Have a Dream" and "I Have Been to the Mountaintop" speeches, his funeral, and President Johnson's signing of the Civil Rights Bill of 1968.

Learning in America: Education on Trial (PBS video, 3-part series, 1992). This series explores the critical issues facing American education. Using the intense and dramatic setting of a courtroom, the series features Judge Connie L. Peterson of the District Court, Second Judicial District, Denver, Colorado, overseeing the trial. Host Richard Dysart defines the issues at stake in each trial.

Saviors (Films for the Humanities and Sciences, 47 min., 1994). This program provides insight into the role of the federal government in legislating and enforcing rights for African Americans. It tells the story of the Supreme Court's decision in *Brown* v. *Board of Education of Topeka*, a landmark in the battle to end segregation in the public schools.

Teaching Indians to Be White (Films for the Humanities and Sciences, 28 min., 1994). Schools are where children are taught to integrate into society, and schools represent a major problem for native children—whether they are religious schools with native teachers; residential schools that tear children away from their families and traditional values; or public day schools, where native children find it nearly impossible to balance the white view they are taught in school with the language and values they learn at home. The results are that the Seminole of Florida resist being integrated, the Miccosukee decided not to fight but to join, and the Cree took back their own schools.

Upstairs/Downstairs (PBS video, 60 min., 1989). Has the United States created a two-tiered educational system consisting of well-funded public and private schools on the one hand and urban and rural schools lacking the resources necessary to provide an equal standard of education on the other? *Upstairs/Downstairs* examines this and other questions and explores strategies that are effective in dealing with the problems of poverty, parental illiteracy, a lack of nutrition in the home, and language barriers.

Student Activities

1. Analysis of Key Issues in Education

Ask students to collect news articles on local schools. These should be articles about educational issues (the introduction of a new curriculum, the school budget, a push for school vouchers, etc.) rather than articles about educational personnel. After the students have collected and read these articles, ask them (either individually or in small groups) to analyze the stories in terms of the historical forces discussed in Chapter 11. To what degree are these news articles implicitly or explicitly linked to some of the key educational issues throughout American educational history? What conclusions can the students make?

2. Cultural Perceptions of Education/Schooling

Ask your students to research how a particular ethnic or racial group perceives schooling. A group's overall success in traditional forms of American schooling has much to do with how closely traditional American schooling mirrors that group's own cultural mores. For instance, in some cultures, children are not expected to compete with each other; in others, children are expected to remain quiet much of the time. Children from those cultures might have difficulty performing in a school where they were expected to compete against other children on tests, or "participate" by speaking frequently in front of the class. Ask your students to research a particular culture's conceptions about schooling and present their findings to the class.

3. Historical Research

Teams of three or four students can choose or be assigned different historical periods on which to do research on schooling. Each group makes a class presentation in which the members describe some important features of the larger society that affected schools. For example, presentations could answer questions such as: Who was in the student body (immigrant waves might affect this)? What developments of science and technology were influencing school life? What great artists were affecting the cultural climate? How was the shape of the country changing, and how, therefore, were geography lessons changing? What heroes or heroines of the time were functioning as role models for students?

4. Historical Research of a School or School District

Have students, either individually or in small groups, research the history of a particular school or a particular school district. Have students visit local libraries to discover when formal schooling first took place in the community and what type of schooling it was. How did formal education change over the years in the district? What were some of the major events in the district? If they are researching a school, find out when it was built and what purpose(s) it has served over the years. What were the plans when the school was built? Were there particular reasons why it was designed as it was? What does the structure of the school building reveal about the community's philosophy of education? Is the building named after someone? Who is the person, and what is his or her significance?

The students can either write a paper chronicling the history of a school district or school building or make a group presentation. A multimedia presentation including slides and taped interviews can be particularly effective.

5. History in Community Names

Assemble a list of the names of local public schools. Assign pairs of students to find out about the person for whom a particular school was named and about the date and circumstances under which the school was built. For example, why is there a grammar school in Boston named after Robert Gould Shaw? Have students present their findings to the class, in the order when the schools were established, from first built to last built.

6. "Pestalozzi taught here" (individual or group work)

Research one or two of the prominent educators presented in the chapter to understand more fully their educational philosophy and their teaching methods. Then demonstrate through simulations, oral presentation, your own video, or your active direction of the class how a class would look if taught by Pestalozzi, Herbart, Montessori, etc. After the presentation, debrief with the class. What elements of that person's educational methodology are still present today?

7. Oral History (individual or group work)

Ask each student to interview the oldest person he or she knows or can contact. (It would be best if all the interviewees were older than sixty.) Ask that person his or her memories of school. Sample questions might include the following: What did the school look like? What was the inside like? What subjects did you study? What was a typical day like? What do you remember about your teachers? What were some of the school's rules? Present to the class and discuss. An interesting whole-group project might be to construct a chart of commonalities found among the people interviewed or to look at the different experiences women had from men, various ethnic groups had from each other, or the college-bound student had from the commercial or vocational student.

Chapter 12 What Are Ethical and Legal Issues Facing Teachers?

Learning Objectives

After studying the chapter, students will be able to

- distinguish between ethics and the law and explain the proper province of each.
- list, explain, and apply the six dimensions of ethical teaching, as defined by Kenneth Howe.
- give examples of some ethical problems that teachers commonly face and explain how to think about resolving them.
- define due process, liability, assault, and battery as they relate to teaching.
- explain in general terms the laws relating to copyright, self-defense, religion in the classroom, lifestyle choices, and academic freedom.
- describe the rights of students regarding privacy, corporal punishment, access to public education, and access to their own school records.

Chapter Overview

Teaching is full of ethical and legal issues, and all teachers need to know how both ethics and the law play an integral part in their work. This chapter explains the difference between ethics and law, and it begins to explore the particular ethical and legal questions teachers must answer. It presents to prospective teachers ethical guidelines as they begin their career and also highlights particular laws that are germane to the classroom teacher. The purpose of this chapter, then, is to examine both the ethical and the legal aspects of teaching.

We begin with a discussion of ethics: the system of morality that people adopt to help them develop productive relationships with others in their communities. Because teachers can powerfully influence their students, trainees ought to be aware of the formal statements of ethics developed by the profession. We also recount several stories, right out of the experiences of practicing teachers, that illustrate the variety and intensity of ethical dilemmas.

Next in the chapter is a discussion of legal issues that teachers need to know for their own protection and for the protection of their students. Without attempting to cover all aspects of the law and teaching, we introduce some of the most common problems and sketch the implications of recent court decisions.

Our aim in this chapter is to stimulate students to think about how their own moral imperatives will mesh with the code of the profession. We want them to know something about the ways in which the law protects and restricts them. And we want them to think about the ways in which ethics and law contribute to community life.

Chapter Outline

Chapter 12 *What Are Ethical and Legal Issues Facing Teachers?*

I. The Ethics of Teaching

- A. The Characteristics of Ethical Teaching
- B. Ethical Dilemmas in Teaching
- C. The Everyday Ethics of Teaching
- D. Codes of Professional Ethics

II. The Teacher and the Law

- A. The Teacher and Due Process
- B. Contracts, Tenure, and Dismissal
- C. The Teacher and Liability
- D. Self-Defense
- E. Freedom of Expression
- F. Lifestyle and the Teacher
- G. Copyright Laws
- H. Reporting Child Abuse
- I. Law, Religion, and the School

III. Students and the Law
   A. *In Loco Parentis:* Due Process and the Student
   B. Suspension and Expulsion
   C. Corporal Punishment
   D. Search and Seizure
   E. Freedom of Speech
   F. Students with AIDS
   G. Records and the Student's Right to Privacy

Supplementary Lecture and Discussion Topics

1. **Formal ethical codes** Discuss the terms of the NEA's Code of Ethics, the AFT Bill of Rights, and the Boston University Educator's Affirmation. Compare and contrast their contents. Describe how each came to be written.

2. **The "everyday ethics of teaching" and the everyday ethical conflicts in teaching** Discuss with students in greater detail how ethics permeates the life of the teacher. Discuss in detail some of the everyday ethics of teaching, such as taking a "mental health day" to spend a day in solitude out-of-doors. For example, is there a difference between taking a "mental health day" because a teacher needs some time to rest and "regroup" and taking a "mental health day" because it is the first day of deer-hunting season? Are ethical differences involved when teachers comment hastily on papers because they want to give immediate feedback to students and when they do so because they just want to finish grading? Teachers are human, too, so how should teachers respond if they realize that they truly delight in a particular student? How can teachers make sure they aren't "playing favorites"? What should teachers do if they just cannot get along with another teacher on their team? How can they hide the friction they feel toward certain colleagues from the students that they share? There are numerous everyday, but important, ethical aspects of a teacher's job that you may want to discuss in more detail with students.

3. **Teachers and the law** Explain the way the courts have defined teachers' rights in recent decisions. Show how certain broadly defined rights—for example, due process—come to have specific meaning in professional situations. Also discuss how particular legal issues, such as reporting suspected child abuse, have influenced the job of teaching. In addition, you can discuss the impact the Buckley Amendment has had on the role of teachers. To what extent has the Buckley Amendment created positive change? To what extent has it inhibited teachers and their autonomy?

4. **Students and the law** Explore the reasons for a change from an *in loco parentis* position to a due process orientation regarding student rights. Review court decisions that protect the rights of students.

5. **Religion, secular humanism, education, and the law** Although public schools are not allowed to establish any religion, some influential groups decry the secular humanist bias they see in textbooks, teaching materials, and classroom procedures. Explain to students what secular humanism is and show some instances of texts in which a secular humanist bias is said to be found. Is secular humanism a religion? Is there an antireligion bias in public schools? Have public schools reacted too strongly against any hint of religion in their environment? Explore and consider these questions with your students.

6. **Technology and copyright laws** The advent of the information superhighway raises additional areas that teachers need to be cognizant of regarding fair use and copyright law. Discuss with students in more detail the stipulations regarding how and under what conditions teachers can use information gained from the various computer on-line services available.

Additional Resources for Instructors

DelFattore, Joan. *What Johnny Shouldn't Read: Textbook Censorship in America.* New Haven: Yale University Press, 1992. DelFattore focuses on recent federal lawsuits involving attempts to censor or ban biology, geology, history, home economics, literature, psychology, reading, and social studies textbooks. She recreates the story behind each lawsuit, describing how politically sophisticated national organizations turn local controversies into nationally publicized court cases.

Deskbook Encyclopedia of American School Law. Rosemount, Minn.: Data Research, 1996. This excellent annual reference book is an easily accessible source on the current law and the legal issues surrounding all phases of public and private education.

Goodlad, John I., Roger Soder, and Kenneth A. Sirotnik (Eds.). *The Moral Dimensions of Teaching.* San Francisco: Jossey-Bass, 1990. The book is a collection of essays from educational writers. The premise of the book is that all questions concerning public education are moral ones and that teaching is a moral craft. Through the various articles, the book considers the moral role of educators in a democratic society.

McCarthy, Martha M., and Nelda Cambron McCabe. *Public School Law: Teachers' and Students' Rights.* Boston: Allyn and Bacon, 1992. This volume clearly sets forth how teachers' and students' rights are currently seen and ruled upon by the courts.

Mills, Cheryl D. "Important Education-Related U.S. Supreme Court Decisions." In *Challenges and Achievements of American Education.* Ed. Gordon Cawalti. Association for Supervision and Curriculum Development, Alexandria, Va., 1993, pp. 187–191. This brief article summarizes the recent changes in school law.

Ryan, Kevin. "Teacher Education and Moral Education." *Journal of Teacher Education* 39 (September/October 1988): 18–23. This article states that teachers play a crucial role in communicating the values of the community and society to students. Therefore, teacher education programs have a responsibility to equip student teachers with an awareness of their role as moral educators and with the skills to implement a moral curriculum.

Sockett, Hugh. *The Moral Base for Teacher Professionalism.* New York: Teachers College Press, 1993. Sockett connects how teacher professionalism is linked to a teacher's understanding and practice of the moral elements within teaching itself. A helpful exploration of the subject.

Strike, Kenneth. "Teaching Ethics to Teachers: What the Curriculum Should Be About." *Teaching and Teacher Education* 6 (1990): 47–53. Strike describes what a teacher education curriculum in professional ethics might be like. He argues that a curriculum for educators needs to emphasize specific moral concepts that are central to what educators do.

Strike, Kenneth, and Jonas Soltis. *The Ethics of Teaching.* New York: Teachers College Press, 1985. This short book gives an illuminating discussion of practical ethics and is filled with illustrations of the types of moral problems classroom teachers regularly encounter.

Strike, Kenneth, and P. Lance Ternasky (Eds.). *Ethics for Professionals in Education: Perspectives for Preparation and Practice.* New York: Teachers College Press, 1993. This volume is particularly practical for use with prospective teachers.

Tom, A. R. *Teaching As a Moral Craft.* New York: Longman, 1984. A highly influential book in which Tom describes his theory of teaching and how it intrinsically contains a moral element.

Valente, William (Ed.). *Law in the Schools.* New York: Macmillan, 1994. This third edition sets forth important legal issues and precedents concerning education and the law. It has been updated and expanded to include recent legal issues within education.

Zirkel, Perry Alan, and Sharon Nalbone Richardson. *A Digest of Supreme Court Decisions Affecting Education.* Bloomington, Ind.: Phi Delta Kappa Press, 1993. Zirkel, who has an educational law column in the educational journal *PDK*, and Richardson present a concise, highly readable digest of the court cases that have affected education. A useful reference for teachers.

Media Resources

Battle over the Blackboard (WNET/Thirteen, 28 min., 1985). This program focuses on the controversy among parents and educators over whether the school's role is to teach students how to think or what to think. It explores the campaign by conservative Christians to eliminate "secular humanism" from the school curriculum. The film features parents, church leaders, teachers, and students.

Books Our Children Read (Prod: Michelle Marder Kamhi, Dist: Films Incorporated, 30 min., 1984). An impartial but probing treatment of the complexities surrounding book censorship is presented in this film, which focuses on the Fort Frye local school district in southeastern Ohio.

While exploring the logic and beliefs of the parents who want certain books banned, the film also covers the parents who disapprove of the censorship, the teachers' views, and finally the feelings of students most affected by the decisions.

Censorship or Selection: Choosing Books for Public Schools (PBS video, 60 min., 1982). This video still has currency. It describes the censorship controversies that have erupted in America's public schools. Who should determine what goes on the shelves of libraries and in the textbooks of public schools? Learn the complex issues with this recorded-live debate among authors, librarians, educators, and legal experts. Panelists include Kurt Vonnegut, Judy Blume, Judith Krug from the American Library Association, and the Moral Majority vice president, Ronald Godwin.

Child Abuse: It Shouldn't Hurt to Be a Kid (Insight Media, 27 min., 1985). Educators, school personnel, and day care providers are required by law to report suspected child abuse. This video advises these mandated reporters of these legal responsibilities. It defines child abuse, teaches how to recognize it, and explains where to report suspected abuse.

Child Molestation: Breaking the Silence (Prod: Disney, Dist: university film libraries, 20 min., 1985). Designed for anyone who spends time with or supervises children, this film offers guidelines on how to identify symptoms in a child who has been sexually abused and on how to respond, stressing the importance of the situation.

Classrooms, Courtrooms, and Common Sense (Insight Media, 3 parts, 30 min. each, 1991). This series on administrative liability helps teachers understand the legal implications of their actions. An attorney who has defended educators explains school law using on-site simulations.

Copyright: What Every School, College, and Public Library Should Know (Prod: A.I.M.E., Dist: Boston University, 21 min., video, 1987).

Learning in America: Education on Trial (PBS video, 3-part series, 1992). This series explores the critical issues facing American education. Using the intense and dramatic setting of a courtroom, the series features Judge Connie L. Peterson of the District Court, Second Judicial District, Denver, Colorado, overseeing the trial. Host Richard Dysart defines the issues at stake in each trial.

The Management of School Disruption and Violence (Prod: BFA in cooperation with the U.S. Department of Justice, video, four parts, 1984). The *Constitutional Issues and Liability* (18 min.) segment details the constitutional rights of students, teachers, and administrators, as determined by the U.S. Supreme Court. Issues include search and seizure, due process, censorship, and corporal punishment. The *Police/School Relations* segment (28 min.) examines a "memo of agreement" between a local school district (the Southeast Delco District outside Philadelphia) and the surrounding law enforcement agencies, presenting a series of scenarios. Police and educators are asked whether each incident is a situation for police involvement. The other titles in the series are *Management System for School Disruption and Violence* (26 min.) and *Conflict Management: Youth* (12 min.).

Professional Ethics: A Guide for Educators (Insight Media, 22 min., 1990). Explains that legal behavior is not necessarily ethical behavior. Describes sensitive situations and how to make ethical choices.

Safe Speech, Free Speech and the University (PBS video, 60 min., 1991). Does the First Amendment provide the right to shout slurs in a college dorm or to make racist, sexist, and discriminatory remarks? This program explores the issues of "fighting words" on college campuses and the attempt to legislate "politically correct" speech through an enforced code.

Toward an Ethical Learning Community (Insight Media, 35 min., 1994). This video considers the importance of regarding relationships with students as essential elements in the creation of an effective learning environment. Faculty and students discuss ethical teaching.

Student Activities

1. Legal Issues and Teaching

Select one strand of legal decisions, such as free speech, or one particular legal ruling and research it in more depth. What were the underlying conditions that gave rise to this particular legal issue? If you are researching a topic such as free speech, explore how the courts' decisions have developed over time. What has the impact of these legal rulings been upon education? What are the ramifications for future educational practice regarding some of the more recent court cases? Students may present their work either as a paper or as a presentation to the entire class.

2. Tenure

Review the provisions for tenure in local districts. Then assign students to a "pro" team and a "con" team to argue the merits of having tenure. (You may ask students' preferences, if opinions seem to be evenly divided.) Give each team time to pull together arguments for its position. Either invite a colleague in to judge or assemble a panel of judges, using some students from each side. Have each team make an opening statement and then debate the issue. Announce a winner on the basis of logical argument.

3. Student Teacher Code of Ethics

Preservice teacher trainees have a more limited range of classroom responsibilities than real teachers, but they also have responsibilities as students. To be an ethical student teacher is arguably different from being only a student or only a teacher. Have students write a "code of ethics" that represents their individual perspectives on the rights, responsibilities, and priorities of student teachers. Have them form partnerships or small groups and draft a single document from their individual documents. Copy the group-written documents for the whole class, and discuss similarities and differences.

4. Ethical Deliberation

Kenneth Howe discusses how teachers must have the capacity for moral deliberation. Have your students consider the following scenarios to help them enhance their ability for ethical deliberation. Divide the students into small groups of no more than five. Have each group do the following:

- Define the problem
- List the relevant moral or legal imperatives
- Brainstorm a few solutions
- Determine the pros and cons of each proposed solution.

Have the groups try to reach a consensus on one solution. Ask each group to present its findings to the class. Compare strategies used by each group.

Case 1
To Strike or Not to Strike

You are a tenured, first-grade teacher who has been teaching in an urban area for five years. You, like many of the other teachers, are frustrated and angry at the city's and the school board's treatment of teachers. You have seen oceans of the taxpayers' money going toward civic projects (a domed athletic stadium, a newly renovated city hall and downtown area), while teachers' salaries and the conditions in the schools have deteriorated. Like your colleagues, you are desperate to get the attention of the citizens, so you support your professional association's decision to strike.

The teachers walked out three days ago, and gradually you are realizing that the real losers in this strike are your twenty-eight first-graders, most of whom come from disorganized, poverty-ridden homes. Whereas many children in other parts of the city, and especially older children, can probably afford to lose the time in school, you believe yours cannot. They are at a critical point in their basic skills development. Also, they have just learned to settle down and really become engaged in their work. You are sure that prolonging the strike will mean disaster for the students. Then, on the strike's fourth day, several of your students' parents approach you, saying that they have secured a church basement and, if you will only come and teach, classes can go on there. However, such action might undermine the strike and would appear to be a betrayal of your coworkers. What do you do?

Case 2
Pressure to Perform

You are a fourth-grade teacher in a suburban elementary school, which caters to the children of a largely professional population. Most parents are quite interested in the school's keeping to high academic standards and expect good performance from their children. It is late in the school year, and you have been approached by the parents of a third-grade boy named Derek. They would like you to tutor their son for the rest of the spring and possibly during the summer. You tell the parents that you would like to think it over for a week. Since Derek's current third-grade teacher is a close friend, you speak to her.

She seems to know Derek well, and a picture emerges of a pleasant, cooperative, and hard-working boy who is performing right up to his capacities. He is a slow reader, has trouble with abstractions, and experiences difficulty with instructions when they become at all complex. His second-grade teacher says basically the same things. The school psychologist tells you that Derek's performance and these difficulties are confirmed in his test data. Everyone who knows Derek says that if there is a problem, it is the unrealistic expectations of his rather intense parents. One is a lawyer and the other is an accountant. They are convinced that Derek is performing at "C level," as they call it, simply because he is being lazy and not applying himself. They dismiss the psychologist's views as "just so much silly psychobabble" and claim that Derek simply needs to be given more work to do and to be held to higher standards. Further, they feel that if Derek doesn't "catch fire" soon, he will get accustomed to mediocrity and will lose all chance of attending a good college. They have not asked you for your opinion, but you support the professionals: Derek is working well up to his capacities.

Derek's parents want you to tutor him after school two days a week and for five hours on Saturday. They have offered you $250 a week to do so. You have the time, and the money would mean that you could buy a dependable car to replace the clunker you currently drive. You also are aware that if you do not accept the assignment, there are several other teachers who will, teachers who are not as skilled and conscientious as you are. What is the right thing to do?

Case 3
The Games Children Play

Four months ago you began your first year of teaching in a fairly rural part of the state. The community is spread out, but the people are closely knit, which you soon discover has pluses and minuses. Newcomers like you are noticed by all and welcomed by most. As the new fifth-grade teacher in a strange community, you were naturally sympathetic to Denise, a shy young girl who transferred in from out of state a few weeks after the school year started. After the students' initial curiosity wore off, they left Denise to herself. At lunch and on the playground, she was always alone, and, from her appearance, she was not happy about it. You made efforts to weave her into different cliques of girls, but nothing seemed "to take." Twice you tried to speak to her about it privately, but the first time she clammed right up, and the second time she cried and fled the room. Not sure what to do, you had this problem on the back burner and were watching it when things began to boil.

First, Denise started missing a good deal of school, and she apparently was not sick. Then, for no visible reason, she would sometimes burst into tears or turn and yell at her classmates, "Leave me alone!" Some students seemed surprised; others laughed at her.

Yesterday as school was letting out, Denise came up to you with a reproachful look on her face and said, "I found my gloves," and showed you what seemed to be new gloves with the fingers cut off. You called her mother last night, and she said that Denise is convinced all the kids hate her and are trying to punish her for something.

You think the apparent hazing is the work of a very popular, strong-minded girl with whom you have had your own struggles of will this year. The girl is a natural leader, as is her mother, the president of the Parent-Teachers Association. The mother has let you know in half a dozen ways that she is not thrilled with her child having "an inexperienced teacher."

Now, you have finally decided that you are going to send Denise to the library and talk to the entire class about whatever is going on. However, when the children come back from lunch and begin to take out their books, you first hear Denise gasp and then see her staring wide-eyed into her desk. After a moment, she lets out a terrifying scream. You rush over and discover the cause. In her desk is a large paper bag inside of which is a dead rat caught in a trap. There is also a note saying "You're next!!!" You recognize the handwriting as belonging to your chief suspect who, when you glance her way, is looking very pleased with herself. What should you do?

Case 4
A Tale of Two Students

You enjoy teaching, but not testing. You are proctoring the final exam for your freshman algebra class. It is hard to watch students you like and know have worked hard struggling with and being stumped by your test questions, which you were sure were going to seem easy. It is a little hard, too, to see the students who have coasted all year gliding right through your exam as if it were so much whipped cream. In the midst of your musing, you glance across the room and see Floyd stuffing what looks like a crib sheet up his sleeve. He has been trouble all year. You are certain he copied 90 percent of his homework assignments on the bus; he was mouthy and disruptive in class, and you are fairly sure he cheated on two of the other major tests. Now, finally, you've got the drop on him.

As you move quickly across the room toward Floyd, you see that Judith is copying formulas from a ribbonlike spool of paper. You cannot believe it! Judith is your favorite student, and she recently was elected secretary of next year's sophomore class. She is a very conscientious, diligent girl who gets good grades, but not out of natural brilliance. She gets them the old-fashioned way—through hard work. She has very high standards and puts a good deal of pressure on herself. Although you cannot imagine what has led her to cheat, you suspect that the pressure for good grades she puts on herself is the root cause. You are standing in the middle of the room, trying to decide what to do.

Case 5
Academic Moonlighting

You are just beginning your third year of teaching in a school district you like a great deal. Your first two years of teaching were hectic but by and large successful. Your principal has recently asked you to move from the fifth grade, where you were comfortable, to the third grade, where you are not. However, he has confidence in you, and you are coming up for tenure at the end of this year. You are also working toward a master's degree in education at the state university, and you need to take a course this semester. If you get three more graduate credits during this fall semester and three next semester, you will not only be closer to the degree but will also have a total of fifteen credits, automatically moving you up $900 on the district's salary scale.

The only graduate course open to you this semester is a very demanding and time-consuming educational statistics course, about which you have heard nothing but bad news. You have to take the course sometime, but this semester could not be worse. You know very little about the third-grade curriculum or, for that matter, about third-graders. You think that even without the course, you will be scrambling to prepare and stay a jump ahead of the children. You are sure you can bluff your way through, but you are worried about shortchanging the students. Still, the course is part of your graduate requirements. What do you do?

Case 6
For the Good of the Team

You teach in a city in which many of the students drop out of school, and the only type of job they are qualified for is unskilled work. The city also struggles to keep its youth off the streets and out of criminal activity. You are a history teacher in senior high, and most of your students are seniors. One student you particularly admire is Bruce. One of four children, he was raised by his mother. His father left when he was eight, and Bruce has been treated like the "man of the family" ever since. You think he has borne his responsibility admirably. He is a kind and mature young man.

Bruce is also a star athlete. In fact, as captain of the football team and as quarterback, he led his team to the state championship, the most positive news for the high school in twenty years. Bruce's coach has told you that college scouts are quite interested in Bruce, and that all he needs to do is graduate from high school with a C average and he will be admitted to any one of the major universities that have nationally ranked athletic programs. Bruce could be heading for a professional football career.

As much as you admire Bruce, he never has been a strong student. He is courteous in class, participates in discussions frequently, but his writing and test-taking ability are weak. He has not been identified as having any learning disabilities. You have worked with him individually after class several times, and his improvement has been slight. In your class, he has been running a C-minus average, and U.S. history is a requirement for graduation. You have figured that he needs a least a C-plus to earn a C for the year.

When you correct Bruce's exam, you see he earned a 68, which is a D. Both the coach and Bruce have said they will stop by later in the day to find out his grade. You check over his exam twice to see if you made any mistakes in correcting. You didn't. Then you consider curving the exam, even though the grades seem to be evenly distributed. When Bruce and the coach arrive, what will you do?

Case 7
Social Promotion

You are a first-year teacher in a poor, urban public middle school. Some of your students, despite all your hard work, have remained beyond your reach. Consequently, a number of your eighth-graders still cannot read near grade level and have mastered only the most elementary computing skills. You and several other eighth-grade teachers are reviewing the students' files to see who will be promoted to ninth grade. During the middle of the meeting, the principal enters. His agenda, you learned quite early, is far different from yours. Central office judges his performance not on the students' real academic achievement but on the percentage of students promoted and on the number of student suspensions and expulsions. His goal is to keep students quiet and out of trouble. He listens to the teachers' recommendations for a moment without comment and then interrupts.

"Look," he says bluntly. "I would strongly encourage you to promote your students if they have met state attendance requirements." He continues on for several minutes, talking about how important it is for the eighth-graders to feel successful and to go to the high school.

You look at him dumbfounded. Essentially, he's telling you to pass all of your students, whether they are literate or not. What will you do?

Case 8
Sex Education

You have taught for several years in Greenpond, a small rural town, and have developed a good rapport with most of your students, especially those students who seem to need to a caring adult in their lives. One such student is Jessye. At thirteen, she is already sexually mature and looks to be nineteen to twenty, rather than just beginning her teen years.

Several months into the school year, Jessye lingers in your room after school. Without speaking, she starts to help you straighten the room, and after you finish, you sit down to share some cookies for a snack. You let Jessye speak. It's just small talk at first; then she tells you details about her family life. Then she says she wants to know what form of contraception you use.

You look at her and say nothing for a moment. Jessye continues unself-consciously: "I figured you're about my mom's age, and you don't have any kids. So either there's something wrong with you or you do something so you don't have kids."

You ask Jessye why she is so curious, and she tells you that she has slept with "four or five guys," and she has just started going out with Pete, an eighteen-year-old who graduated last year. She hasn't "gotten caught" so far, but she's "not dumb." "I figure sooner or later, I'll get pregnant, but I'd rather it come later," she tells you with a chuckle.

You mention to Jessye that she should talk to her mom about her questions, but Jessye looks at you and snorts, "Are you kidding? She's never around, and she said she'd kick me out if she found out I was doing anything." What should you do?

Note to Instructors: Two additional cases are included in Chapter 12 of the text.

The following more detailed, extensively developed case studies in Appendix I are appropriate for use with this chapter.

Leigh Scott, pp. 471–473
Erica Kaiser, pp. 479–482
Karen Washington, pp. 483–485

Chapter 13 How Should Education Be Reformed?

Learning Objectives

After studying the chapter, students will be able to

- recognize the complexity of educational reform in the United States.
- identify and describe seven elements that are essential to true and lasting school reform.
- explain national efforts to bring about educational reform.
- describe state reform efforts, identifying common elements found in these efforts.
- identify successful state efforts to bring about educational reform.
- explain the constraining factors that restrict local reform efforts.

Chapter Overview

Chapter 13 looks at the school reform movement, discussing both what it should be and what it has been. We preface our discussion on the reform of education by reminding prospective teachers of the complexity of trying to reform public education in America, especially in light of the range of views about what constitutes a "good" education.

We introduce the reform movement by reminding prospective teachers of the three aims of education: to develop the democratic citizen, the good worker, and the private person. With these three aims as an ideal, we propose seven components that we feel are essential to true and lasting school reform. These components, present to varying degrees in successful reform projects, include a call to excellence, active learning, authentic assessment, community, choice, learning to learn, and character education. Each of these elements is described to provide prospective teachers with an understanding of what each element incorporates and how we feel it can improve the quality of education in our schools.

The second part of the chapter discusses the actual reform initiatives that are being carried out. We present reform efforts from the national, state, and local level. At the national level, proposals are being formulated by the federal government, such as the Goals 2000: Educate America Act, a reformulation of America 2000. National groups of scholars in different disciplines and fields are developing curriculum frameworks, standards, or in some cases entire curriculum plans that attempt to identify essential skills and knowledge that students should possess in these disciplines. State reform efforts have emphasized structural change, promoting more time in schools, stricter graduation requirements, better accountability of student learning, and more qualified teachers. We also note that state reform efforts tend to involve top-down reform with changes that may be more cosmetic than effective and that have led primarily to a loss of local autonomy and authority. Local efforts have been limited primarily because of lack of funding, not lack of interest.

We close the chapter with a reminder that educational change is a slow, demanding process, but one that cannot be successful without the involvement of teachers, who are at the very heart of the educational process.

Chapter Outline

Chapter 13 *How Should Education Be Reformed?*

I. What Ought to Be the Elements of Educational Reform?

- A. Excellence
- B. Active Learning: The Constructivist's Approach
- C. Authentic Assessment
- D. Community
- E. School Choice
- F. Learning to Learn
- G. Reclaiming Character Education

II. Current Reform Initiatives

- A. National-Level Reform Efforts
- B. State Educational Reform
- C. Local-Level School Reform

III. School Reform and the Teacher

Supplementary Lecture and Discussion Topics

1. **State educational reform** What has been done in your state in the way of educational reform? Present the reform efforts that are being discussed or have been implemented in your state. What is the focus of these reform efforts? Ask the students to identify which of the nine essential principles are evidenced in the state reform proposal.

2. **Goals 2000: Educate America Act** Explain in greater depth the history of this act. Discuss the Education Summit of 1989, explaining why it was held, who attended, and what the outcome of the summit was. Relating back to Chapter 9, you may want to evoke the idea that the federal government has no authority over education in the United States. How then, can the Goals 2000 act be constitutional? Have the students identify the overriding goals of the act and ask them to speculate on whether these goals will be achieved.

3. **Values in schools** Explain in greater depth the debate around character education. Present the historical perspective of character education, highlighting the 1960s and 1970s, when values clarification became the most widely practiced approach to teaching values in school. Compare that period to the renewed interest in character education. Ask students to identify factors that affect the teaching of values in schools.

4. **Local reform efforts** Try to locate a school or school district in your area that has successfully implemented reform efforts. Ask a well-informed participant, a teacher, principal, or superintendent, to come to class and talk about the reform proposal. Your guest could talk about the content of the reform proposal and the process for implementing the proposed changes.

5. **Community building** If there is a middle or high school in your area that has instituted houses, ask someone who is familiar with the structure to come and talk to the students. The guest speaker should focus on the rationale behind creating houses and what the effect of these houses has been on the school environment. Has he or she seen any improvement in the academic performance of the students? How has the social and emotional climate of the school been affected?

6. **Site-based management and total quality management (TQM)** Introduce your students to the concepts of site-based management and TQM. Explain that these ideas originally came from business and are being tried out in the school setting. Discuss the principles behind them and how they are to affect school effectiveness, at least from a theoretical standpoint. As more research is carried out on the effectiveness of these approaches, a more solid position can be formulated.

Additional Resources for Instructors

Clark, David, and Terry Astuto. "Redirecting Reform. Challenges to Popular Assumptions About Teachers and Students." *Phi Delta Kappan* 75 (March 1994): 512–20. Clark and Astuto maintain that responsibility for reforming schools must be a grassroots effort. They examine the assumptions underlying reform efforts and show why these efforts have been unsuccessful to date.

Darling-Hammond, Linda. *Professional Development Schools.* New York: Teachers College Press, 1994. One of the trends in the school restructuring and reform movement is the professional development school. This book explains the function, structure, and philosophy of the professional development school. A number of case studies are included that have been written by participants in school reform projects.

Fine, Michelle. *Chartering Urban School Reform.* New York: Teachers College Press, 1994. This book is designed to provoke a radical rethinking of educational practice and research for school-based change in urban America. A series of essays written by school reformers, it presents the development of a reform movement in an urban district.

Fullan, Michael. *Changing Forces: Probing the Depths of Educational Reform.* Bristol, Pa.: Falmer Press, 1993. Drawing on research from successful organizations in business and education, Fullan identifies eight basic lessons about why change is seemingly chaotic and what to do about it.

Fullan, Michael. *The New Meaning of Educational Change.* New York: Teachers College Press, 1991. Fullan describes educational change and how it can be achieved and then presents successful programs designed to bring about change in schools.

Likona, Thomas. "The Return of Character Education." *Educational Leadership* 51 (November 1993): 6–12. Likona presents a historical overview of character education in the United States and explains why character education has received a groundswell of support in the last ten years.

Madsen, Jean, and Lewis Smith. *Educational Reform at the State Level.* Bristol, Pa.: Falmer Press, 1994. This book is an account of how a state's educational agency had difficulties in implementing new legislation because of limited resources, lack of consensus on program goals, and bureaucratic lethargy.

Moffett, James. "On to the Past: Wrong-headed School Reform." *Phi Delta Kappan* 75 (April 1994): 584–90. Moffett questions the assumptions of the business world that educational reform based on free-market competition can bring about effective change in American schools. He argues that educators need to look at what works best in education, not in business or bureaucracy, to reform schools.

Newmann, Fred, and Gary Wehlage. "Five Standards of Authentic Instruction." *Educational Leadership* 50 (April 1993): 8–12. Newmann and Wehlage present a framework based on five standards for assessing student learning more authentically.

O'Neil, John. "Aiming for New Outcomes: The Promise and the Reality." *Educational Leadership* 51 (March 1994): 6–12. O'Neil reviews the progress made to date on outcomes-based education and discusses the major challenges that outcomes-based education faces.

"Realizing the Promise of Technology." *Educational Leadership* 51 (April 1994). This edition of *Educational Leadership* is devoted to technology in the school, examining the purpose of technology use and proposals for integrating computers in the curriculum.

Starratt, Robert. *Building an Ethical School: A Practical Response to the Moral Crisis in Schools.* Bristol, Pa.: Falmer Press, 1994. Starratt argues for greater attention to ethical education. He provides a conceptual foundation for ethical education that is broad enough for building consensus among teachers and parents, yet focused enough to provide guidance for specific learning activities.

Tanner, Daniel. "A Nation 'Truly' at Risk." *Phi Delta Kappan* 75 (December 1993): 288–97. Tanner responds to the proposals in America 2000 and reproduced in Goals 2000, contending that some of them need to be challenged in light of the other reports of studies carried out by different groups, in particular the Sandia Report. Tanner compares the findings and recommendations of the two reports and concludes that the priorities of educational reform must be clearly focused on improving the educational quality of our schools, not meeting the political goals of diverse groups.

Wiggins, Grant. "Assessment: Authentic, Context, and Validity." *Phi Delta Kappan* 75 (November 1993): 200–14. Wiggins suggests that test makers recognize their obligation to link their tests to the tasks, contexts, and "feel" of real-world challenges.

Media Resources

American Heroes: The Future Belongs to the Educated (PBS video, 60 min., 1993). A collection of gifted educators who make a positive difference in their students' lives despite the obstacles of poverty, crime, and apathy. A common theme emerges: caring and respect for the dignity of students.

America's Education Revolution: A Report from the Front (PBS video, 60 min., 1993). This program takes a first-time look at education reform efforts in the country's public schools and the impact the political system can have on educational change. The documentary examines reform efforts in New York City; Rochester, New York; Gainesville, Florida; and Kentucky.

America's Schools: Who Gives a Damn? Part I (PBS video, 60 min., 1991). The role of the teacher is examined as one factor in the continuing dilemma of a failing public school system. The "bureaucracy" and the "system" are also suspected culprits.

Common Miracles: The New American Revolution in Learning (MPI home video, 60 min., 1993). This video tells stories of local innovation and accomplishment that offer a vital new perspective on educational reform.

Learning in America: Education on Trial (PBS videos, 3-part series, 60 min. each, 1992). This three-part series explores the critical issues facing American education. Individual titles include

Do We Need a National Report Card?, *Are Our Public Schools Beyond Repair?*, and *Are We Short-Changing Our Schools?*

Liberating America's Schools (PBS video, 60 min., 1993). This documentary shows the school choice movement through the eyes of parents, students, teachers, administrators, and community activists who have tried choice as a means to achieving better schools.

Teaching Values in Schools (Insight Media, 60 min., 1992). This video features a debate by educators, business people, and government officials on whether or not values should be explicitly taught in school and, if so, how they should be presented.

Towards a Community of Learners: Strategies for Cultivating a Climate for Reform (ASCD, 40 to 60 min., 1993). This four-cassette series discusses how educators can build community-wide support for school reform efforts. It offers perspectives from educators involved in reform efforts.

Unequal Education (PBS video, 60 min., 1992). This program examines the realities of American schooling. It profiles students at two different public schools in the Bronx and points out the inequities of our current system and how discrepancies affect the quality of education. Advocates for educational reform discuss possible solutions.

Upstairs, Downstairs (PBS video, 60 min., 1989). This video examines the questions of equality of educational opportunities and explores programs that are effective in dealing with problems such as poverty and parental illiteracy.

Why Is Change So Hard? (Insight Media, 22 min., 1995). Systematic school change is a difficult process, even when staff members are committed to it. Designed to help school administrators facilitate change, this video shows the change process as a "work in progress."

Student Activities

1. National Curriculum Reform

Have the students form groups according to their subject area of interest to investigate what has been done in that subject area or discipline to standardize and harmonize the learning of essential skills and knowledge. In some areas like science, there is more than one group developing curriculum guides or frameworks. (Elementary education majors should focus on the elementary goals in the subject area of their choice.)

The students can also look at the feasibility of the standards that have been set. Based on their experience and on the textbooks available or other instructional materials, do the students believe that the proposals developed or the standards set can be realized?

Each group will present its findings to the class.

2. Keys to Educational Reform

Students are divided into seven groups, with each group assigned one of the key elements of true educational reform. The students can think about the specific desired effects that these elements are to bring about. For example, how will authentic assessment or active learning help improve the quality of education? Students may find a flow chart a helpful way of organizing their thinking.

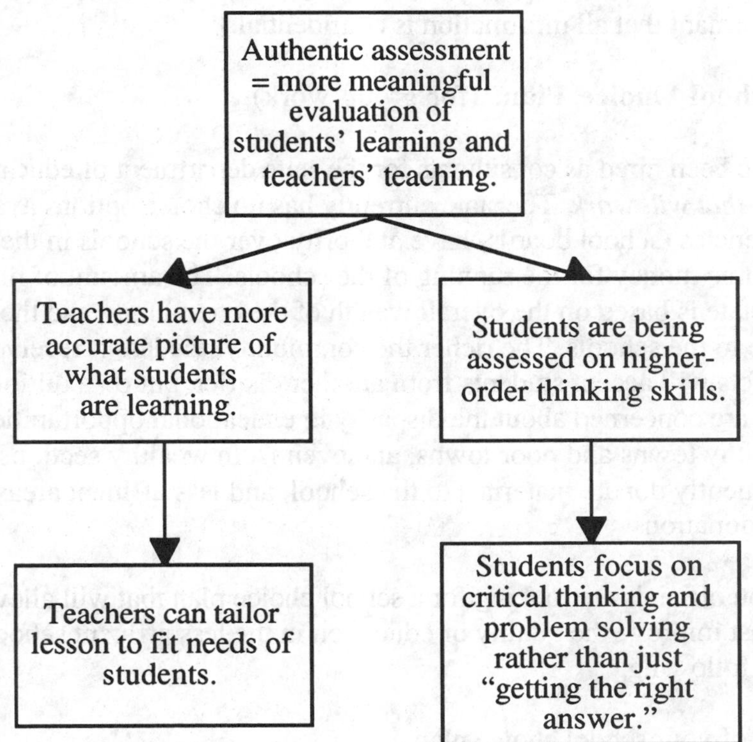

3. Model Reform Projects

Although national or state reforms have brought about limited improvement in public education, there are a number of success stories in individual schools or districts. The Comer School and Sizer's Essential Schools are examples of successful reform projects. Have the students research a successful reform project carried out at either the school or the district level. In their research, they would want to consider the following questions:

- Who initiated the project?
- What kind of support was there for the project—from the faculty, administration, central office administration?
- Who participated in the development and implementation of the project?
- Where did the funding for the project come from?
- What did the project focus on? What were its goals? Why was there a need for this reform project?
- What have been the effects of the project on student learning and school climate?

- Have any attempts been made to replicate the project in another school or district? With what results?

4. Local Reform Efforts

What reform projects, if any, do the students see happening in their field site? The students can interview a knowledgeable person at their field site to learn about reform at the local level. What is the school doing? Who is initiating it? How do the teachers feel about it? (Students may want to remind their informant that all information is confidential.)

5. Design a School Choice Plan (for group work)

Scenario: You have been hired as consultants for the state department of education to draft a school choice plan *that will work.* The state currently has no choice options available at all—local education agencies (school boards) have authority over the schools in their district. The state contributes some money for the running of the schools. The amount of money a district receives from the state is based on the overall wealth of the community and the financial resources available to the schools. The richer the community, the less it receives from the state. Some school districts will accept students from another district, but on a tuition basis only. State education officials are concerned about the disparity in educational opportunities afforded students from wealthy towns and poor towns, and even from wealthy sections of urban areas, where parents frequently donate materials to the school, and less affluent areas, which do not benefit from such donations.

State education officials are looking for a school choice plan that will alleviate the disparities or at least improve the quality of education in the less affluent schools. Your proposal should include the following:

- A description of your school choice plan
- The underlying philosophy of the plan and its stated goals
- The rationale for the plan (What will it accomplish? How?)
- Necessary resources—financial, material, and human—to implement the plan
- Implementation strategies, including:
  - A timeline for the plan
  - Changes to be made in existing structure
  - Key people responsible for tasks
  - Public relations activities
  - Key events or activities
- Anticipated outcomes of the plan
- Evaluation plan to assess progress toward articulated goals

Students present their plans to the class, which can debate the viability and feasibility of each plan.

Chapter 14 What Are Your Job Options in Education?

Learning Objectives

After studying the chapter, students will be able to

- describe the current and projected job market in education.
- explain factors that affect the supply and demand of teaching positions.
- identify and explain effective job search strategies.
- describe the purpose of both traditional-route and alternative-route licensure.
- identify competencies and areas of specialized knowledge that may enhance their employment opportunities.
- identify other occupations for which they may be qualified on completion of a teacher education program.

Chapter Overview

As prospective teachers begin to contemplate a career in teaching, they are plagued by many questions. Two of the more crucial ones are "Where will I find a job?" and "How will I find a job?" This chapter attempts to answer these questions by presenting a portrait of the current job market in education, discussing the factors that influence that job market, and then providing prospective teachers with some advice about job hunting.

The chapter first describes the current job market in education, which we see as rather promising. Although the anticipated teacher shortage of the 1990s has yet to materialize, there are openings in most districts as more and more teachers retire and the student population grows. We warn prospective teachers of the mediocre economic climate of the early 1990s that has led to tight fiscal budgets and fewer teachers leaving teaching to venture into other fields. Still, we expect to see the number of teachers increase by 13 percent to keep up with similar projected increases in student enrollment. The greatest need for teachers continues to be minority teachers, who represent only 13 percent of the teaching population, even though the minority student population will be 38 percent early in the twenty-first century.

The second part of the chapter discusses the various factors that influence the supply and demand of teachers in the job market. While the unpredictability of the job market is highlighted, we explain factors that impact on the availability of teaching positions, such as subject area, geographic location, community demographics, and type of school (public or private). Next we look at trends in teachers' salaries and benefits as well as salary schedules to help prospective teachers understand the financial complexities of teaching.

We give prospective teachers some helpful job search strategies, recommending that they develop a plan for their search and that they campaign actively for teaching positions. Necessary materials that job applicants need to prepare include a résumé, cover letter, credentials, and interview skills. We also suggest that prospective teachers construct a teaching portfolio to be presented to possible employers.

The chapter also presents important information on licensure, both in traditional and alternative routes. We make note of the wide range of requirements for either route of licensure, depending on the state. We also acquaint prospective teachers with the Teach for America program as one alternative program. We remind prospective teachers of the reciprocity agreements for licensure that exist between many states, but also encourage them to pursue more than one licensure area in order to make themselves more attractive candidates.

Finally, we explore options for those teacher candidates who are unsuccessful in finding a teaching position or decide that teaching is not for them. We identify some of the teaching skills that are transferable to other jobs, making teachers attractive candidates for those jobs as well.

Chapter Outline

Chapter 14 *What Are Your Job Options in Education?*

I. Will There Be Job Openings in Education?

   A. Factors Influencing Teacher Supply and Demand
   B. The Severe Shortage of Minority Teachers
   C. Employers Besides the Public Schools

II. What Are Teachers Paid?

III. How Do You Obtain a Teaching Position?

IV. How Do You Become Licensed?

A. Traditional Licensure Programs

B. Alternative Licensure

V. If You Don't Teach, What Then?

Supplementary Lecture and Discussion Topics

1. **Merit pay for teachers** This concept, promoted as a way to retain and reward expert teachers, is by no means universally hailed. The National Education Association was and is opposed to the concept because of the difficulty of implementing it fairly. Because of its potential to change fundamental aspects of the teaching profession and because it provokes such heated debate, this is a topic well worth exploring with your class.

2. **Public school versus private school teaching** The advantages and disadvantages of teaching in private schools, as opposed to public schools, can be examined. Discussion can include salaries, job availability, licensure, personal rewards, discipline, student motivation, and parental support.

3. **Job interviews** Invite one or more personnel officers from local school districts to visit your classes to describe what they look for when hiring new teachers. They can also discuss the kinds of teaching positions that are most in demand.

4. **Educational jobs besides teaching** Other college staff or school personnel can be invited to describe various educational jobs besides teaching that are available in local school districts. Qualifications for these positions can also be described. Examples might include counselors, principals, supervisors, curriculum coordinators, or special education consultants.

5. **Information on your state's requirements** You may want to detail for students the licensure/certification procedures and requirements in your state.

6. **Alternative and traditional teaching certification** Since the mid-1980s, alternative routes to teaching licensure have been gaining strength. A class lecture devoted to further explanation of this change in teaching licensure is helpful. The text mentions that these licensure programs vary widely. It is a useful exercise to examine several states' alternative teaching licensure programs to discern their underlying notions of what constitutes adequate preparation to teach. You can also devote some time to the traditional licensure requirements and explain the recent changes in many states' licensure procedures.

Additional Resources for Instructors

Albrecht, Kay. "Helping Teachers Grow: Separating Competency from Compensation." *Child Care Information Exchange* 70 (December 1989): 37–38. Albrecht presents a design for how teachers could be compensated, discussing why competency and compensation need to be distinctly assessed.

Alexander, Lamar. "Time for Results." *Phi Delta Kappan* 68 (November 1986): 202–204. Alexander summarizes the work of seven National Governors' Association task forces on education, including the state's role of public and teacher education, and the "action agenda" proposed.

ASCUS Annual: A Job Search Handbook for Educators. Evanston, Ill.: Association for School, College and University Staffing. An annual publication designed to assist both new and experienced educators in their job searches, and the single most important reference in this topic. The *Annual* is usually distributed through career planning and placement offices in colleges and universities, but it may also be obtained from the ASCUS Office, 1600 Dodge Ave., S-330, Evanston, Ill., 60201-3451, (847) 864-1999.

Braun, Joseph A., Jr., Arnie Williams, Max Brown, and Kathy Green. "A Survey of Hiring Practices in Selected School Districts." *Journal of Teacher Education* 38 (March/April 1987): 45–49. This article looks at variables considered by school administrators in reviewing applicants' credential files, qualities they note in interviewing applicants, and how administrators structure interviews.

Ciscell, Robert E. "The Salary Expectations of Elementary Education Majors." *Illinois Schools Journal* 68 (1989): 3–10. Ciscell presents the findings of a survey conducted on elementary education majors and their perspectives on how school reform would relate to financial issues. The survey presents the data on their perspectives on salary issues, and the article discusses their dissatisfaction.

Hawley, Willis D. "Toward a Comprehensive Strategy for Addressing the Teacher Shortage." *Phi Delta Kappan* 67 (June 1986): 712–18. Hawley presents a pattern of teacher preparation, certification, and improvement in working conditions that he feels would enhance teaching as a profession and thereby alleviate teacher shortages.

Mangan, Katherine S. "Growing Number of Teachers Beginning Their Careers Without the Traditional Education School Training." *Chronicle of Higher Education* 9 (May 1990): A13, 19. This article describes the alternative-route certification plans offered by thirty states and their purpose in diversifying and expanding the pool of teachers.

Rickman, Bill D., and Carl D. Parker. "Alternative Wages and Teacher Mobility: A Human Capital Approach." *Economics of Education Review* 9 (1990): 73–81. The authors posit that teachers' current wages and the wages of alternative occupations influence teachers' decisions to leave the field. The authors argue for a merit-based, market-sensitive teacher salary schedule.

Root, Paul, and Rob Kennedy. "Black Teacher Recruitment." Paper presented at the Joint Annual Meeting of the Arkansas Association of Colleges for Teacher Education and the Arkansas Association of Teacher Educators, April 6, 1990. Root and Kennedy explain the reasons for the low percentage of black teachers and suggest ways of recruiting blacks into teaching. Projecting that blacks may constitute only 5 percent of the teaching force by 2000, the authors discuss the role that black teachers can fill by serving as role models, teaching cultural diversity, and supplementing the general teacher shortage. The paper is available from EDRS.

Salaries Paid Professional Personnel in Public Schools, 1996–1997. Arlington, Va.: Educational Research Services, 1997. This document presents the results of a survey of the annual salaries of people in professional and support positions in over a thousand school districts. The data are reported separately for large, medium, small, and very small school districts, and for eight different geographical regions.

Media Resources

To Be a Teacher (Prod: Tom Spain/NBC News, video, 1987). This NBC News documentary covers the present teaching situation in the United States, following four student teachers from Georgian Court College in New Jersey through their teaching assignments. The program focuses on the motivation, problems, and future not only of these student teachers, but also of their supervising teachers and the profession as a whole.

Where Have All the Teachers Gone? (Prod: Cornell University, video, 29 min., 1987). Originally aired on public broadcasting stations, this program focuses on the problems of the United States's elementary and secondary schools, where 1.3 million new teachers were expected to be needed by 1990.

Who Will Teach for America? (PBS video, 60 min., 1993). This documentary is about Teach for America, an organization that is modeled to bring 500 college graduates who deferred their careers to teach for two years in urban schools.

Student Activities

1. Writing Your Résumé (out-of-class activity)

Have students write their own résumé out of class and then bring it in for review and discussion with classmates. They may refer to the résumé in the text and the one included here as models.

2. The Teaching Application: A Professional Step

The teaching application is a vital communication instrument between the teaching candidate and the prospective school system. A sample teaching application (from Worthington City Schools, Worthington, Ohio, and developed by Dr. Arnold E. Skidmore, Assistant Superintendent for

Personnel and Evaluation) is included to spark class discussion and individual reflection on the process of applying for a job.

3. The Professional Me

Before students can feel confident in interviews, they need to reflect on their own expectations and assumptions. After students have completed each of the fifteen items for the teaching application provided, focus class discussion on the impact their answers might have on an interviewer. Allow 30 to 45 minutes for this activity.

4. The Job Interview

This activity allows students to experience a simulated job interview. Allow 25 minutes for it. Have one person role-play the personnel director and the other the prospective teacher. Identify the grade level or content area for the job opening. *After 10 minutes, reverse the roles.*

Instructions: You are the personnel director of a medium-size school district. A few job openings are available because teachers have retired and left the school system. Here are your main criteria for hiring new teachers:

a. The prospective teacher must have only a bachelor's degree and little or no teaching experience (because you can hire almost two new inexperienced teachers for the price of each veteran teacher retiring from the system).
b. The prospective teacher must be able to handle classroom discipline.
c. The prospective teacher should be able to discuss many of the recent innovations in education.
d. The prospective teacher should be a model for the students.

Here are some questions you may ask the prospective teacher:

a. Why did you choose this school district over others?
b. What would you do on the first day in class?
c. What are some advantages and disadvantages of ability grouping or tracking?
d. What do you think is the mission of the public schools? What abilities and competencies should they emphasize?
e. What should be the role of the teacher in establishing moral standards?
f. What is your philosophy of education?
g. How do you visualize your classroom? What will you and the students be doing on a typical day or during a typical period?
h. What are your views on discipline?
i. We start our teachers at $25,000 and prohibit them from taking other jobs. How will this affect your decision on taking a position in our district?
j. Where do you see yourself in five years? Ten years? What are your career goals?
k. Why should we hire you?

5. Salary Schedules

Given the nature of school financing, teachers' salaries will vary. Have students determine the beginning salary for a B.A. or B.S. teacher in the school district in which they (a) reside, (b) intend to teach, or (c) graduated. Discuss differences in salary and fringe benefits.

6. Local School District Data

Much of the chapter has been devoted to discussing the statistical data concerning teaching. Have students collect data from different school districts in your area or from their home district so that they can compare statistical information from region to region.

Objectives

On completing the exercise, participants will be able to

a. discover firsthand how national or regional educational statistical reports differ or support local trends.
b. discover firsthand how specific factors impinge on the hiring of teachers.
c. gain practical experience in conducting an information interview and in visiting schools.

Instructions for Students

Make an appointment with a local school personnel office and ask them to supply you with statistical information regarding the teaching demand or surplus they have experienced. Here are some suggested questions:

a. What is the median age of teachers employed in this district?
b. What is your pupil-teacher ratio? Do you expect it to change?
c. How many students are in your district? Has this number been increasing or decreasing?
d. If you will be hiring, are there any types of teachers for which you anticipate a particular demand? (examples: ESL, elementary, or physics teachers)
e. If you do not expect to be hiring in the next few years, what are the reasons? Shrinking school enrollment? Stable supply of teachers? Economic constraints?
f. What percentage of teachers will be eligible for retirement in the next five years?
g. (If speaking to a personnel officer) Which factors make a teaching candidate appealing to this school district? (examples: years of teaching experience, dual certification, coaching or advising ability) What factors do you actively seek in a candidate, if any?
h. Have any recent federal or state regulations affected the number of teachers hired?

7. Teacher Demographics

Ryan and Cooper speak of an aging teaching force, but is that the case in your community? Have the students form groups, and assign each group a school district to investigate. Each group will describe the teaching population of that district. What is the average age of the teachers in that district? Average number of years of teaching experience? How many teachers have been in the district fewer than five years? More than twenty years? How many male teachers are there? In the elementary school? In the high school?

Students may also want to investigate the administrative personnel. How many principals and assistant principals are there in the system? How many are men, and how many are women? Were they all teachers before? What subject(s) or level did they teach? How long did they teach before they moved into administration?

Students are encouraged to chart their information, and then each group can present its findings.

8. Teaching Contracts

Most school districts have a limited, provisional contract for the first three years of a teacher's career. After that time the contract becomes a continuing (tenured) one. Sample contracts are included for discussion and comparison with local districts.

SAMPLE RÉSUMÉ

Glen P. Stewart

School Address:
3413 Chestnut Street
Philadelphia, PA 19104
(215) 555-1234

Home Address:
15 Sea Mist Boulevard
Stone Harbor, NJ
(609) 555-9876

PROFESSIONAL OBJECTIVE

To obtain an English or language arts teaching position in middle or high school

EDUCATION

TEMPLE UNIVERSITY, Philadelphia, PA
Bachelor of Arts. Majors: Theater Arts and English; minor: Education
Cum laude. May 1992

OCEAN HIGH SCHOOL, Stone Harbor, NJ
June 1988

EXPERIENCE

STUDENT TEACHER — Springfield High School, Springfield, PA

Taught ninth- and eleventh-grade English classes. Designed a thematic unit on "Heroes in Literature" and taught it to ninth grade. Taught *Macbeth* and SAT–vocabulary building skills to eleventh-graders. Conducted writing conferences for all students. Volunteered as assistant director for student production of *The Glass Menagerie.*

February–April, 1992

LITERACY TUTOR — West Philadelphia High School

Volunteered to help high school students and adults learn to read. Also assisted others in strengthening their reading abilities.

September 1989–April 1992

LIFEGUARD — Stone Harbor, NJ

Employed as lifeguard at town beach. Assisted in several rescues.

Summers 1989–1991

SWIMMING INSTRUCTOR — Stone Harbor Y.M.C.A., Stone Harbor, NJ

Instructed several levels of swimmers, from beginner to advanced. Also instructed an advanced lifesaving course.

Summers, 1988-1991

ACTIVITIES

The Temple Players
Member of Temple University's acting troupe that performed on campus and at other locations throughout the city. Acted in *Long Day's Journey into Night, One Flew over the Cuckoo's Nest,* and *Waiting for Godot.*

September 1989–May 1992

References available on request

WORTHINGTON CITY SCHOOLS
An Equal Opportunity Employer

Personnel Office
579 High Street
Worthington, Ohio 43085
Phone: 614-846-9383

TEACHING APPLICATION
for 19____ to 19____

NAME____ DATE__________
Last First M. I. or Maiden Name

PRESENT ADDRESS______________________________ PHONE__________

______________________________ BUSINESS PHONE__________
Town State Zip Code

(To assist us in maintaining contact with you during the period of application, please complete the following. This information is optional.)

Name of Spouse______________________________ Phone__________

Name of Parent______________________________ Phone__________

Parental Address____

I am applying for the position of____
Teaching Field of Area of Certification

My grade level or subject preferences are:

ELEMENTARY (Grade) MIDDLE SCHOOL (Grade) HIGH SCHOOL (Subject)

First Choice__________ First Choice__________ First Choice__________

Second Choice__________ Second Choice__________ Second Choice__________

My assignment preference is Regular____ Substitute____ Tutor____

I would be willing to direct or assist with the following extracurricular or coaching areas:

____

____

My Ohio Certificate Number is ______________________________ Date Issued__________

The subjects listed for my certificate are ____

My training is as follows:

University and Location	Degree	Year	Major/Minor	Semester Hours Beyond Graduation Completed/In Process

I completed my student teaching experience at:

School City Grade/Subject Dates

____

____

Some highlights of my student teaching experience that I want to share:

____

____

____

My teaching experience consists of:

No. of Years	Dates From To	Assignment	Principal—Name of School—Address
1._____	________	____________	____________________
2._____	________	____________	____________________
3._____	________	____________	____________________
4._____	________	____________	____________________

Some highlights of my teaching career that I would like you to know:

____

____

____

I *have/have not* been employed under a continuing contract in Ohio. (Circle one.)

My continuing contract was granted by ________________________ on ____________

School System Date

Other work experiences that I believe have been valuable to my career are:

____

____

____

The information above is true and accurate to the best of my knowledge. (I understand that withholding or falsifying information on this form is grounds for dismissal.)

______________________________ ______________

Applicant's Signature Date

It is the policy of the Worthington Board of Education that the best qualified applicant shall be selected for each position without regard to race, color, religion, national origin, age, sex, or marital status.

WHAT I WANT YOU TO KNOW ABOUT ME AS A TEACHER

This section is designed to provide you with an opportunity to share some of your experiences and thoughts about teaching. Please respond to each item in the space provided. Since fifteen items (opportunities) have been provided to you, brief candid responses are encouraged.

1. What I want most to accomplish as a teacher

2. The way I find out about how students feel about my class

3. The kind of relationship I want with my students

4. The way I go about building the relationship just described

5. The way I go about deciding what should be taught in my class

6. What I would do if a parent came to me and complained that what I am teaching his or her child is irrelevant to the child's needs

7. My greatest pleasure in teaching

8. What I do to improve my teaching

9. How I go about finding what students are good at

10. What I consider to be my most effective teaching approaches and techniques

11. The way I go about organizing my work

12. What I would do about a student performing poorly in my class who responds to my expression of concern by saying that he or she considers me to be one of the poorest teachers he or she has ever had

13. What I would most want to do in life if there were no restrictions placed on me

14. The most important things I do to maintain discipline in my classroom

15. Some of the most effective teaching behaviors of those educators who I know really care about their students

WORTHINGTON BOARD OF EDUCATION

Worthington, Ohio

TEACHER'S LIMITED CONTRACT

This Agreement is entered into this____________ day of _____________, 19 ____, by and between the Board of Education of the Worthington City School District, Franklin County, Ohio (hereinafter the "Board") and ____ (hereinafter the "Teacher") beginning ____________________, 19______, and concluding _________________, 19__________.

The Teacher agrees to teach and to perform all duties regularly and customarily associated therewith in the Worthington City School District subject to assignment by the Superintendent of Schools. The Teacher further agrees to abide by and to maintain the rules and regulations now in effect that have been prescribed by resolution of the Board for the government of the schools and such rules and regulations as may from time to time hereafter be adopted by said Board. The provisions of this contract shall be subject to such rules and regulations.

In full consideration of the performance of said duties the Board agrees to pay the Teacher a salary in the sum of ______________________________ for the above-stated period of time, payable in equal semimonthly installments.

The execution of this contract by the Teacher constitutes acceptance of membership in the Ohio State Teachers' Retirement System.

Classification:
Years' Experience:
Basic Salary:

____
Teacher

BOARD OF EDUCATION

by ____
President

by ____
Treasurer

Return white and yellow copies to Board Office.

WORTHINGTON BOARD OF EDUCATION

Worthington, Ohio

TEACHER'S CONTINUING CONTRACT

This continuing contract is entered into this __________ day of ________________, 19____, by and between the Board of Education of the Worthington City School District (hereinafter the "Board") and ____ (hereinafter the "Teacher") beginning _____________________, 19 ________, and continuing in full force and effect until the said Teacher resigns, elects to retire, or is retired pursuant to Section 3307.37 of the Revised Code or until this contract is terminated or suspended as provided by law. Said Teacher agrees to teach in the district subject to the assignment of the Superintendent of Schools and further agrees to abide by and maintain the rules and regulations prescribed by resolution of the Board of Education for the government of the schools now in effect and such rules and regulations as may from time to time hereafter be adopted by said Board and that this contract at all times shall be subject to such rules and regulations.

In full consideration for such services, the Worthington Board of Education agrees to pay said Teacher the sum of ____ ($______________) for the school year_______________, and such sum for each subsequent year as may be established by said Board in accordance with Section 3319.12 Revised Code.

Classification:
Years' Experience:
Basic Salary:

____
Teacher

WORTHINGTON BOARD OF EDUCATION
by ______________________________________
President

by ______________________________________
Treasurer

Return white and yellow copies to Board Office.

Chapter 15 What Can the New Teacher Expect?

Learning Objectives

After studying the chapter, students will be able to

- define and discuss the culture shock experienced by first-year teachers.
- identify and explain the role of the principal and the principal's relationship to the teacher.
- identify and explain supervisors' roles in the school.
- summarize the authors' recommendations for the first day of teaching.
- identify the most reliable indicator of a teacher's success with students.
- describe the impact that other teachers can have on the first-year teacher's experience.
- describe and analyze the potential difficulties inherent in parent-teacher communication.
- identify and analyze the change that many first-year teachers undergo in their attitude toward children.
- explain and analyze the concept of "social distance" between teacher and student.
- identify and apply the practical teaching tips the authors supply for surviving the first year of teaching.

Chapter Overview

Because everyone has spent considerable time in schools, one might think that a prospective teacher's introduction to school life would be smoother than, say, that of a young trainee learning the culture of a large corporation. That sounds reasonable, but it is wrong. Our own experiences as teachers and educators of teachers have convinced us that most new teachers are surprised by the experience of becoming a teacher. The life of a teacher, they immediately discover, is worlds apart from the life of a student. Unexpected pleasures as well as unexpected problems confront every teacher during the first year of teaching.

The first year of teaching, many claim, is the most stressful of the teacher's career. *Everything*—from the school building to the teachers to the students to the job of teaching—is new. The new teacher can't refer to previous experience, so every lesson, every morning is uncharted territory. The first year is an awkward time of figuring out how to put theory into practice, how to put into effect all those good ideas collected during teacher education, and how to turn educational dreams into classroom realities.

Our purpose in this chapter is to have future teachers "walk in the shoes" of some teachers who have gone before them. There are two main reasons for taking this approach. First, if they do have a difficult time as beginning teachers, we want them to realize that "I am not alone. Others have had this problem." One of the worst adjustment difficulties many beginners face is their sense that no one else is having problems. Second, we believe that having them confront common problems at this stage in their preparation helps develop the breadth of awareness that may keep them from being undone by the nature and extent of the challenges they face. Our expectation is that such preparation will enhance their experience as new teachers.

Chapter Outline

Chapter 15 *What Can the New Teacher Expect?*

I. The School Milieu: The Shock of the Familiar

II. Administrators: Mixed Bag and Many Hats

III. Peers: A Mixed Blessing

IV. Instruction: So Much to Learn

V. Students: Friends or Fiends?

VI. Discipline

VII. Social Distance

VIII. Sex

IX. Parents: Natural Allies with Different Agendas

X. Surviving the First Year of Teaching

A. Begin Now

B. Keeping a Teaching Journal

C. The Proper Frame of Mind

D. Find a Mentor

E. Make Your Students' Parents Your Allies

F. Take Evaluation Seriously

G. Take Care of Yourself

Supplementary Lecture and Discussion Topics

1. **The world of the beginning teacher** Invite a few people from a variety of roles to describe the experience of a beginning teacher. Participants might include a second-year teacher, a principal, a personnel director, a member of the state department of education whose work involves beginning teachers, a representative from a professional association, a school secretary or custodian, and a middle school or high school student (or parent of one) who has had a recent experience with a new teacher.

2. **School structure and new teachers** Many schools have either brief orientation programs or induction programs designed for new teachers. Some systems have a mentor system where an experienced teacher is paired with a new teacher to provide support. The new teacher can talk to the mentor for special advice, feedback, and instructional ideas. Discuss some of the practices available to help new teachers in schools in your area.

3. **Assuming the role of the teacher** For many new teachers, the difficult part of becoming a teacher is learning how to assume the role of a teacher. This is not to say that teachers should not be themselves or should be artificial. However, teachers do not act the same way with their students as they do with friends and families. As easy as that separation sounds, it is not always as easy to execute. The fact that some new teachers may be only four or five years older than their students makes the transition for some teachers even more difficult. Discuss in detail the inherent authority of the "teacher" position and the expectations that students, faculty, administrators, and parents have that the teacher will assume that authority.

4. **Stress and the new teacher** The first year of teaching is exhausting for most. Briefly describe the typical demands on the time of a teacher. Explain how stress can easily cause the new teacher to feel overwhelmed and exhausted. Provide some suggestions for how to deal with the stress of being a teacher.

5. **The role of the principal** Describe the roles and functions of a principal. Show how the principal's roles and functions that relate to the beginning teacher fit into the total picture.

6. **Sociology and school relations** Explain the way sociological variables affect relationships between teachers and their colleagues or their students' parents. For example, the location of a classroom in the building to some extent predicts its place in teachers' "traffic patterns" and perhaps creates greater or lesser likelihood that teachers will pass the classroom often and thus have frequent opportunities to extend friendship. Colleagues or parents who speak with the same accent as the teacher or come from the same part of the city or attended the same church or school may be given the warmest welcome in return for friendly comments. The teacher in the next room may become a mentor just because of proximity.

7. **Research on beginning teachers** Review some of the recent research on the problems and pleasures of the first year. Discuss threats to enthusiasm and to a positive attitude about students. Describe some exemplary mentor programs.

Additional Resources for Instructors

Clandinin, D. Jean, Annie Davies, Pat Hogan, and Barbara Kennard (Eds.). *Learning to Teach, Teaching to Learn: Stories of Collaboration in Teacher Education.* This book centers on participants in a year-long alternative education program. The student teachers, cooperating teachers, and education professors collaborated to live out a new story of teacher education. Their narratives fall into five thematic areas.

Grossman, Pamela. *The Making of a Teacher: Teacher Knowledge and Teacher Education.* New York: Teachers College Press, 1990. Grossman analyzes the skills and knowledge of the beginning teacher and offers recommendations for future teachers.

Holden, Peter E. *Classroom Tactics for Teachers of Young Teens: Quelling Fear of the Classroom.* Springfield, Ill.: CC Thomas, 1989. This short, practical guide offers helpful tips, particularly for new teachers, on how to deal with students in the throes of puberty.

Kronowitz, Ellen. *Beyond Student Teaching*. New York: Longman, 1992. This volume explores the stages and transitions that new teachers go through to move beyond their conceptions as a student teacher and into the role of a teacher.

La Boskey, Vicki Kubler. *Development of Reflective Practice: A Study of Preservice Teachers.* New York: Teachers College Press, 1994. This book provides a clear conceptual framework for thinking about reflective teaching and practice. The study examines the cases of twelve preservice teachers and offers suggestions for how teacher educators might better include and accomplish reflective goals in teacher education.

Moran, Carol. *Keys to the Classroom: A Teacher's Guide to the First Month of School.* Newbury Park, Calif.: Corwin Press, 1992. This is a helpful, practical guide for establishing a successful year through the patterns and activities established during the first month.

Palonsky, Stuart. *900 Shows a Year: A Look at Teaching from a Teacher's Side of the Desk.* New York: Random House, 1986. The author recounts his experiences as a high school teacher in a small, suburban community outside New York City. The descriptions of his encounters with students, fellow teachers, and administrators are fresh and vivid.

Ryan, Kevin (Ed.). *The Roller Coaster Year: The Stories of First-Year Teachers*. New York: HarperCollins, 1991. This book contains the accounts of twelve first-year teachers as they give an honest account of the events and feelings that fill their lives as they begin their teaching careers.

Ryan, Kevin, and others. *Biting the Apple*. New York: Longman, 1980. This book is a collection of stories of first-year elementary and secondary school teachers. The stories are told by the researchers with the collaboration of the new teachers. The accounts are candid pictures of the problems and joys of beginning a career in teaching.

Schubert, William H., and William C. Ayers (Eds.) *Teacher Lore: Learning from Our Own Experience*. New York: Longman, 1992. This book emphasizes reflective teaching and the use of personal accounts as the best source for understanding.

Media Resources

Harry Wong: Inducting New Teachers into the Profession (AIT, 30 min., 1992). Harry Wong is a self-described "plain old classroom teacher" who has taught and served as director, advisor, or consultant to many professional science education agencies. Wong argues that what happens within the first several days of class each fall is critical to the success of the school year for both teachers and students. He recommends conducting induction programs for new teachers to introduce them to the school's culture and to establish classroom discipline, procedures, and routines from the first day.

Managing and Organizing the Elementary Classroom (Insight Media, 26 min., 1991). Providing practical insights into methods for managing and organizing an elementary classroom, this video teaches how to build student responsibility by setting goals, establishing individual and group behavioral norms, and creating learning partnerships. It also considers ways to monitor and assess student progress.

Managing Students Without Coercion (Insight Media, 74 min., 1993). Presenting a variety of methods designed to improve classroom management, this video explains why authoritarianism and coercive approaches are not effective. It discusses why a collaborative approach teaches students to accept responsibility both for their actions and for their learning.

Partnerships with Parents (Insight Media, 28 min., 1989). Young children benefit most from programs in which teachers and parents work together as partners. This program dramatizes the importance of the parent/teacher relationship for children and demonstrates how to establish and maintain positive communication. It also shows how to handle common problems teachers face when working with parents.

Room 109: Elementary Education (Insight Media, 15 min., 1987). Illustrating some of the unique management situations facing an elementary classroom teacher, this program provides an opportunity for teachers in training to practice making decisions about disruptive situations they are likely to face.

Room 309: Secondary Education (Insight Media, 14 min., 1987). This two-volume set depicts vignettes of scenes from a teacher's day to stimulate discussion of how to manage problematic situations. Volume 1 features situations typical of a junior high or middle school classroom, and Volume 2 focuses on senior high students.

Who Will Teach for America? (PBS video, 60 min., 1991). This documentary about 500 college graduates who deferred their careers to become teachers offers a stirring portrait of young people who are making a difference. Their organization, Teach for America, the brainchild of Wendy Kopp, who has formed a domestic teacher corps modeled on the Peace Corps, is designed to bring the best young minds to teaching.

Student Activities

1. Planning for Culture Shock

One way to decrease culture shock is to learn as much as possible about a situation from a safe distance. Some of the surprising bits of information that flood in during the first few weeks of teaching can be discovered by asking the right questions before school even begins. Here is a list of questions about some mundane and some substantial aspects of daily school life. Have the students individually or in pairs visit a teacher or a school and get answers to as many of them as possible. (Warn them that some of the questions are delicate and may not be answered. A way to avoid problems might be to have students give their teacher-interviewee a copy of the questions before the scheduled interview.) When students have completed the assignment, have them meet in groups of five or six and compare answers. Or have students who interviewed teachers in the same school compare and discuss answers.

The Nitty Gritty School Fact Sheet

a. What do you call the principal?

b. What is the proper title of the people who do custodial work on the premises?

c. Where is the copy machine? Whom should you ask to teach you how to use it?

d. How do you buy milk, soda, or coffee? Where can you drink it?

e. What are the particular tasks of the secretary? The clerk? The regular volunteers?

f. How is attendance taken?

g. Who doles out supplies? What are the policies about amounts?

h. What do you do if a student faints in class?

i. Are there any differences between the official rules for teachers and the real expectations?

j. What kinds of things do the custodians do, and what should you take care of yourself?

k. Who goes to the faculty lounge?

l. Is there an active professional organization? Should you join?

m. Is there a pencil sharpener in your room?

n. On what kinds of issues will the principal back you up? Which ones do you have to undertake on your own?

o. How do you arrange time to talk with the principal? The counselor? The supervisor?

p. Are there hall passes or student rules that you should know about on the first day?

q. Who has the keys to unlock the things that are locked?

r. Where can you find students' records?

s. What are the faculty "cliques" and on what kinds of factors are they based? For instance, are they based on age (older, younger), on grade taught, on interests?

2. Teachers' Memories

Have your students survey or interview experienced teachers, working or retired, about their memories of their first year of teaching. Many students will benefit from hearing how veteran teachers "toughed it out" the first year. You may even compile a list of questions for the whole class to use or a short form such as the following:

I now teach ______________________ *(grade/subject/courses)*

As a first-year teacher, I taught ______________________

I started my teaching career in the 1920s, 1930s, 1940s, 1950s, 1960s, 1970s, 1980s. (Circle one.)

(If applicable) My greatest anxiety about becoming a teacher was ______________________

My worst teaching moment was ______________________

My best teaching moment was ______________________

Before I started teaching, I wished I had learned ______________________

My biggest challenge as a first-year teacher was ______________________

If I had one piece of advice for any entering teacher, it would be ______________________

____

If I had to do it all over again, I ______________________

After students talk to other teachers, discuss their findings in class. Were there any themes that emerged? How did the advice correlate with the information presented in the text?

3. Faculty Orientation/Faculty Handbook

Collect some faculty handbooks from schools. Pass the handbooks out to students, asking them to read one of the handbooks. Compare the handbooks to one another. Have your students focus on the following questions:

a. What kind of information makes up most of the handbook? Is there any particular emphasis, such as classroom management or bureaucratic procedures?

b. To what degree are the handbooks similar to one another?

c. To what degree does the handbook answer the kinds of questions raised on the "Nitty Gritty School Fact Sheet"?

d. Based on the handbook, what theories can you derive about the atmosphere of the school and the teacher's position in the organization?

4. Teacher Socialization (individual or group work)

As you observe in your field-site schools, see if you can identify and categorize the kinds of social activities teachers engage in with each other. Consider all conversation or activities, even if at first they seem only related to teaching. Visit the teachers' room, the work room, the teachers' cafeteria, or any other place in the school where teachers congregate. What do teachers talk about? Are there specific activities established? (For example, a monthly breakfast, a certain time teachers meet for coffee, birthday celebrations?) What purpose does the talk serve? Is it purely personal and social? Is the talk purely job related? Do they share information about particular students or teaching activities? Do they express their feelings regarding certain school policies or curriculum work? Do they "vent" when they've had a frustrating day? How close do the teachers seem to be? Write up your findings and present them to class.

5. Teaching Tips Card File (individual or group work)

This activity could be done in conjunction with the teacher interview project. Talk to at least ten teachers. Ask them the following question: "Can you describe one or two of the most helpful teaching tips you would share with beginning teachers?" Collect their responses and create a card file presenting their "tips." The card file could take on a wide variety of styles and forms, including photographs and sayings about teaching. Divide the tips into sections for particular areas, such as grading, starting a new unit, classroom management, and the like. Also, include card file tips that you read in teaching journals or books. Present several of your favorite card file ideas or particular subject areas or topics to the class. An additional very helpful idea is to compile all "tips," print them up, and distribute them for students' future reference. Add to your card file throughout your program.

6. First Day of School

Divide the students into groups formed on the basis of their teaching goals—for example, the grade levels or subject areas to which they aspire. Have each individual group member spend some time sketching out first-day plans (built along the Jim-and-Kevin model). When each has defined some preliminary ideas for each category, have the groups collectively develop a full-scale plan that represents their best shared ideas. Have each group describe its plan to the rest of the class.

7. Teacher's Evaluations

Imagine the shock of a first-year teacher thinking he or she is doing a "good job," only to see on the written evaluation from the principal that several areas "need improvement." Collect sample evaluation forms from schools. You may also want to include your college's evaluation for student teachers. Duplicate them so each student in class has several to analyze. Allow the students to work individually analyzing them, and then place students in discussion groups.

Ask them to look for the following: What is the relative weight given to different aspects of teaching? (How many questions deal with classroom management? How many with the instructional technique?) What are some of the most surprising elements that are included on the teaching evaluation form for students? (How many forms include questions on the appearance of the room—noting, for instance, if shades were drawn evenly, or if papers were organized neatly?) What appears to be rewarded? What is censured? After the discussion groups have identified and analyzed some trends, debrief with the whole class.

You may also want to ask several evaluators—principals, curriculum coordinators, department chairs, and others responsible for evaluating teacher performance—to visit your class. What do they look for in their evaluations? What are the "red flags" for them? What do they see as the indicators of a successful teacher?

Chapter 16 What Does It Mean to Be a Professional?

Learning Objectives

After studying the chapter, students will be able to

- trace the major developments in the history of teaching and teacher education from the colonial period to the present.
- identify the defining characteristics of a profession.
- identify and describe arguments that support the position that teaching is a profession and those that support the contention that it is not.
- discuss the role of the two major professional organizations in education, the National Education Association and the American Federation of Teachers.
- explain continuous learning opportunities available to teachers.

Chapter Overview

This chapter focuses on the status of teachers in American society in order to clarify the debate over teaching as a profession. It begins with a brief overview of the history of teaching and teacher education, and then looks to identify the defining characteristics of a profession. This discussion serves as a basis for an examination of the current status of teaching. Other factors that affect the status of teaching, such as professional associations, are also discussed.

We begin the chapter with some anecdotes in order to point out the vulnerability of teachers, since most prospective teachers are so preoccupied with the act of teaching that they may not be aware of the many issues surrounding their actual work. We then trace the history of teaching and teacher education in the United States, highlighting the periods of substantial change in teaching and the events that helped to bring about these changes. The second half of this century marks a significant shift in teacher preparation: from teacher *training* to teacher *education*.

Next, we present Myron Lieberman's classic definition of a profession and make use of these eight criteria to present the debate over whether teaching is a profession. We discuss the arguments supporting the contention that teaching is a profession and those that maintain that it is not. We also propose a third option—that teaching is a semiprofession or is *becoming* a profession. We strongly encourage prospective teachers to take part in this debate, which could affect their career choice.

We help preservice teachers consider the importance of continuing education for teacher professionalism. As the social landscape becomes more complex and new knowledge and skills more abundant, teachers need to keep abreast of these changes to maintain their effectiveness and "professional" status. We describe five types of continuous learning opportunities for teachers.

We close the chapter with a look at the role of professional organizations—one of the criteria of a profession—in the teaching-as-a-profession debate. We introduce the two main teachers' organizations: the National Education Association (NEA) and the American Federation of Teachers (AFT), presenting the history of each association and the kinds of issues they choose to support or defend. Traditionally, the NEA has been more conservative than the AFT; however, changes are occurring in both organizations that make clear delineation between the two more difficult to maintain. We also present the position of those educators who are opposed to these associations, who see them as unions that are only protecting the interests of their members rather than promoting professional growth. This image of teachers, they feel, diminishes their status and professionalism. We end the debate by eliciting the potential benefits and abuses of teacher professionalism and suggest that the new teacher empowerment movement may play a key role in the professionalism debate.

The overriding purpose of this chapter is to help prospective teachers feel that they are joining an adult group with a history—one that is embedded in a particular social context. We hope that prospective teachers recognize their responsibility to the profession.

Chapter Outline

Chapter 16 *What Does It Mean to Be a Professional?*

I. The Emergence of the Modern Teacher

  A. The Colonial Period

  B. The Nineteenth Century

  C. The Twentieth Century

II. The Status of Teaching: A Profession or Not?

   A. The Case FOR Teaching As a Profession
   B. The Case AGAINST Teaching As a Profession
   C. A Third Possibility: An Evolving Profession
   D. The National Board for Professional Teaching Standards

III. Professional Development

   A. Types of Continuous Learning Opportunities

IV. Professional Associations

   A. The National Education Association
   B. The American Federation of Teachers
   C. Other Professional Associations

V. Professionalism at the Crossroads

Supplementary Lecture and Discussion Topics

1. **The history of teacher education** Trace the history of teacher education with your class. Focus on the minimal education teachers received in the colonial period, and discuss how the normal schools prepared teachers. Discuss how teacher training changed its direction in the twentieth century to teacher education. Has the shift made a difference in the professionalism of teachers? You may want to discuss this issue with your students.

2. **Is teaching a profession? A fourth alternative** You may wish to provide your own view of the teaching profession, one that may differ from the views presented in the text.

3. **What would teaching be like today without its professional organizations?** You may wish to do your own hypothesizing here, or you may find it illuminating to invite a superintendent who is unsympathetic to teachers' associations, a teachers' association representative, and teachers with strong views on the subject to speak in your class.

4. **The continuing growth of teachers** One part of the chapter deals with the ways in which a teacher can develop professionally. You may want to elaborate on how teachers can continue to develop professionally. It is particularly effective to invite veteran teachers who have maintained their love of teaching to talk to the class. How did they continue their professional development throughout the years? What advice would they give to prospective teachers?

Additional Resources for Instructors

Ayers, William. *To Teach: The Journey of a Teacher.* New York: Teachers College Press, 1993. Ayers tells the story of a teacher through the eyes of the teacher, a parent, and a student.

Berube, Maurice. *Teacher Politics: The Influence of Unions.* New York: Greenwood Press, 1988. Looking at unions from a critical perspective, Berube analyzes the effect that unionization has had on teaching as a whole.

Brandt, Ron. "On Restructuring Roles and Relationships: A Conversation with Phil Schlecty." *Educational Leadership* 51 (October 1993): 8–11. Schlecty discusses how teachers, principals, superintendents, and school board members need to become more focused on developing the capacity of students.

Firestone, William. "Why 'Professionalizing' Teaching Is Not Enough." *Educational Leadership* 50.6 (March 1993): 6–11. Firestone argues that teachers will not benefit from a more professional reputation until they have a better grounding in pedagogical content knowledge.

Fullan, Michael. "Why Teachers Must Become Change Agents." *Educational Leadership* 50.6 (March 1993): 12–17. Fullan believes that teacher education programs need to instill in prospective teachers a greater sense of moral purpose in teaching.

Huberman, Michael. *The Lives of Teachers.* New York: Teachers College Press, 1994. Huberman uses a "life cycle" framework to look at the teaching profession and answer questions about sources of career satisfaction and commitment to teaching and teacher regeneration.

Johnson, Susan Moore. *Teachers at Work: Achieving Success in Our Schools.* New York: Basic Books, 1990. Johnson takes an updated look at teachers' workplaces and describes the different factors that affect the school environment.

Lieberman, Ann, and Lynne Miller. *Teachers—Their World and Their Work.* New York: Teachers College Press, 1992. This book explores the affective world of teachers. The authors tie the social realities of school life to the process of instructional improvement.

Lortie, Dan. *School Teacher: A Sociological Study.* Chicago: University of Chicago Press, 1975. This book and an earlier book by Willard Waller, *The Sociology of Teaching*, treat many of the factors implicit in school teaching that work against teaching becoming a profession.

McDonald, Joseph. *Teaching: Making Sense of an Uncertain Craft.* New York: Teachers College Press, 1992. The book deals with the uncertainties inherent in teaching. It discusses how teachers deal with the ambiguity and complexity of teaching.

Murphy, Marjorie. *Blackboard Unions: The AFT and NEA, 1900–1980.* Ithaca: Cornell University Press, 1990. Murphy examines the history of the two major teachers' associations, describing their origins, their philosophies, and their impact on teachers.

Shanker, Albert. "The Making of a Profession." *American Educator* 9 (Fall 1985): 10–17, 46, 48. Proclaiming the second revolution in U.S. public education, the president of the American Federation of Teachers outlines a bold new plan for our children and their teachers. Furthermore, Shanker offers four recommendations for improving professional standards.

Media Resources

Try It Sometime (IDEA, 47 min.). This film shows how, when teachers begin to visit other classrooms in the school, teaching changes from a lonely profession to one in which teachers frequently discuss with one another their failures, successes, fears, and hopes. It also indicates how this mutual professional support can help improve instruction in schools.

Wanted: A Million Teachers (PBS video, 60 min., 1989). The program looks at some of the crises in teaching today, including "burnout," poor pay, low morale, and administrative duties. The program shows how these elements may contribute to the sharp decline in the number of teachers entering the profession.

Student Activities

1. Debates

Present two debate topics: "Are teachers' associations necessary?" and "Is teaching a profession?" Ask your students to select a position, either pro or con, for each debate topic. If the numbers are unbalanced, assign students to one side to provide for each position approximately the same number of people. Allow students adequate time to prepare for the debate, and tell them they will have 45 minutes to debate the issue. On the designated day, invite guests—perhaps other education students and professors—to observe and judge their arguments.

2. Who Has the Power? A Simulation[1]

Divide the class into groups of nine students. Reproduce enough of the following role descriptions so that each group has a complete set of nine different roles. The groups should spend 20 to 30 minutes in a role-played discussion to determine the answers to the following questions:

- Who will evaluate teacher classroom competency?
- How will the evaluation be done?

At the end of the small-group discussions, the class as a whole should discuss the frustrations and successes felt in their own groups, the answers they reached, and the problems inherent in being the spokesperson for a "position."

---

[1]Adapted from a paper presented at the American Association for Supervision by Emily Feistritzer, H. Jerome Freiber, and Frank Kunstel, March 14, 1976. Used by permission.

The Setting

Metro City schools serve a large urban area with a decreasing school population. In fact, enrollment is expected to decline 5 percent over the next two years, which will probably lead to a reduction of the teaching personnel. At the beginning of the current school year, a dynamic new superintendent was brought in to get the system moving again after several years of stagnation. It is now March, and the superintendent is trying to improve the quality of instruction in the schools. As part of this process, a committee has been assigned the task of revamping the teacher evaluation process for tenured and nontenured teaching staff. Most of the teachers in the Metro City district are not tenured.

In an attempt to ensure a fair evaluation process and to incorporate as many ideas as possible, the superintendent has appointed the following people to serve on the committee:

- The assistant superintendent for instruction
- The coordinator of staff development
- One representative from the state department of education
- Two professors from the city's university
- Two principals
- Two representatives from the local teachers' union

The committee is currently deliberating about the component of the evaluation process that focuses on teacher classroom competency. Two questions are of primary concern at this stage:

- Who will evaluate teacher classroom competency?
- How will the evaluation be done?

The purpose of the current meeting of the committee is to outline answers to these two basic questions so that subcommittees can proceed to work on the details.

Roles

a. *Teachers' union representatives: Nick DeLiberato and Jean Kruger.* You each have your own view about the proper procedures for teacher evaluation, but your union has taken a look at what has happened in other states and the executive board has given you two mandates:

   1. Don't allow student achievement scores to play any part in the criteria for evaluation. This would be a gross misinterpretation of the whole concept of accountability, because teachers do not control all the factors that influence student achievement.
   2. Push for a procedure that includes evaluation by several people, including union reps, rather than allowing just principals to do the evaluation.

b. *Principal A. Lee Diamond.* You have talked many hours with your associates in the principals' association and have reached the consensus that this is a chance to strengthen the quality of teaching in the Metro schools. The principals want a procedure that will finally allow them to weed out the incompetent teachers, who in some buildings represent a substantial portion of the staff. The procedure should be fair but should not require an inordinate amount of time, because most principals are already overworked. The principal must be the one to do the evaluating, because he or she knows the teachers best.

c. *Principal B. Dale Callaghan.* You are afraid that this whole task could strain teacher-administrator relations, which are already poor. You don't want the principals to get stuck with the dirty work of evaluating the teachers. It would take too much time from an already busy schedule, and it would make the principals the "bad guys." You do want to see the quality of teaching in the district upgraded, however.

d. *Community representative: B. J. Rosario.* You have for some time been actively concerned with the quality of the schools and have supported the tax levies in an attempt to improve the schools. Nevertheless, you are continually hearing about bad teachers in the system. Although these are a minority, they do a lot of damage to young boys and girls every year. When the new superintendent was hired, he pledged to improve school-community relations but neglected to appoint any community representatives to the evaluation committee. This has upset you, because you have been so active in supporting the schools. Also, you feel that community people must have some input into the teacher evaluation process, because your taxes pay their salaries.

e. *Assistant superintendent for instruction: Pat Kavanaugh.* You are trying to maintain harmonious relations on the committee, because you are the highest-ranking school official on the committee and have an overall view of the system. You sincerely want to help the committee reach a consensus so that every group feels ownership of the final product.

f. *Coordinator of staff development: Lou Gonzalez.* You have a small, overworked staff of your own with which to plan, organize, and help conduct the district's in-service program. The final evaluation procedure will have an important impact on how your department functions in the next few years, because you will have to help teachers develop competence in those areas deemed important enough to include in the evaluation process. You need to maintain good relations with all the parties because you work so closely with all the people in the system. In particular, it is important that the teachers not feel defensive about the evaluation process.

g. *State department of education representative: Sandy Lee.* This is an opportunity for you to make some real contributions to education in the state. Metro is the largest and most influential school district in the state; if you can come up with an evaluation procedure that works here, other districts will be likely to adopt similar procedures. The superintendent of instruction for the state has clearly pushed for competency-based teacher education and evaluation, and she is especially strong on behavioral objectives as the way to improve education. Discrete, observable skills, coupled with an emphasis on actual student achievement, are the key to teacher evaluation.

h. *Professor Denny Kravulski.* You believe that the current emphasis on systems approaches and behavioral objectives is pushing education into the industrial model more than ever before, and you strongly object to it. You believe that teachers, as well as students, need to be treated as human beings first.

i. *Professor Leslie Lane.* You believe that education would improve greatly if only educators would start thinking about being more efficient. You support a well-planned evaluation procedure that focuses on specific teacher competencies. Because the principal is the instructional leader in his or her building, the principal must be the one to do the evaluating. This is also an opportunity for the university to have more influence and input into the public schools, a role the dean has been pushing.

3. Playing by the Rules

This can be either a whole-class or small-group discussion. It is designed to develop the concept of teacher power while offering an opportunity to expand the issue. The power of teachers is realized in their rule-making capabilities. Often this power is limited to the managerial functions within their classrooms.

Which of the following rules have been established for the entire district? Which ones are school rules? Which are classroom rules determined by the teacher?

a. No papers or notebooks will be accepted late.
b. All papers must be dated and show the section number.
c. All written work must be in ink.
d. Pencils may not be sharpened after the bell rings.
e. Students who arrive after the bell starts to ring must report to the principal's office for a pass.
f. Student must get permission to open-enroll at a school outside their attendance district.
g. Parents must sign a student's papers if a failing grade has been assigned.
h. A student may not chew gum in class.
i. Any student in possession of a weapon will be automatically and immediately suspended.
j. No student may speak without being recognized by the teacher.
k. Everyone must sit in his or her assigned seat.
l. Boys must have their hair neatly combed.
m. Textbooks must be covered.
n. Fourth-graders have to pass a writing sample to be promoted to fifth grade.
o. A student may not go to the water fountain during class.
p. When the bell rings, students will sit quietly and wait for the teacher's instructions.
q. A student who fails the final exam fails the course.
r. The school day will not be started with a prayer over the P.A. system.

Part III Student Resources

FOR EACH CHAPTER

- Learning Objectives
- Study Guide
- Sample Chapter Quiz
- Answers to Chapter Quizzes

ARTICLE REVIEW FORM

STUDENT RESOURCES

The chapter study guides and quizzes in this section are designed to provide the student with a quick method for checking their comprehension of the key points in each of the chapters and to give your students feedback on their mastery of the chapter material.

Many student users of this text are in their first or second year of college and are inexperienced with college-level material and the demands of their new, independent status. Study guides and practice quizzes may provide them with the help to get the most out of the text and your course.

These study guides and quizzes, along with the generic quiz answer sheet at the beginning of this section, can be photocopied directly and given to the students. The quiz answers are on pages 261–268 of this manual. Answers to the study guide questions have not been provided since all of them are clearly evident in the text in approximately the same order as the study guide presents them. The purpose of the study guides is to provide the student guidance, not to become a graded assignment.

QUIZ ANSWER SHEET

Name ______________________________

Course ______________________________

Instructor ______________________________

Date ______________________________

Chapter ______________________________

Multiple Choice

1. ______
2. ______
3. ______
4. ______
5. ______
6. ______
7. ______
8. ______
9. ______
10. ______

Short Answers

Chapter 1 Why Teach?

Learning Objectives

After studying the chapter, students will be able to

- identify several personal motivations for wanting to become a teacher.
- identify and discuss common motivations for people wanting to teach.
- identify the most common reasons teachers give for leaving the profession.
- identify and explain both extrinsic and intrinsic rewards in teaching.
- list and explain sources of useful experience regarding teaching.
- explain a potential difficulty faced by teachers whose primary motivation is to teach a particular content or subject matter.
- explain the potential difficulty of using teaching as a means to work out one's own problems.
- explain how teachers can aid in the renewal of society through their teaching.
- apply the concepts introduced to their own perspective on teaching.
- think, speak, and write with greater clarity and insight about why they are considering (or not considering) a career in teaching.

Chapter 1 Why Teach?

Study Guide

Completing this study guide will help you prepare for the major topic areas on an exam; however, it does not cover every piece of information found in the chapter or the test questions.

1. Name several of the most common motives for becoming a teacher.

2. Describe the reasons teachers most often give for wanting to leave the profession.

3. Name the extrinsic rewards of a career in teaching.

4. Name the possible intrinsic rewards of a teaching career.

5. List and describe three alternative kinds of sources of information on a career in teaching.

6. Describe the drawbacks of using media representations as sources of vicarious experiences.

Chapter 1 Why Teach?

Sample Chapter Quiz

A. Read each of the following questions, and write the letter of the best answer in the appropriate space on your answer sheet.

1. Working as an aide or volunteer in a school is one of the best ways to
   a. test your interest in and aptitude for teaching.
   b. get sound advice about a range of career choices.
   c. learn about subject areas such as history or math.
   d. earn money for college expenses.

2. The extrinsic reward of teaching is primarily
   a. the high salary.
   b. the power of the position.
   c. the work schedule, which allows for a lot of flexibility.
   d. the prestige of being a teacher.

3. Which of these reasons was *not* a major motivation to leave teaching?
   a. Salary
   b. Respect
   c. Control over work
   d. Chance for promotion

4. Using the classroom as an avenue for solving your personal problems will most likely
   a. be successful.
   b. make you less effective.
   c. earn you the respect of your students.
   d. help you make connections with the students.

5. Teachers can help in renewing society by
   a. working on political campaigns during election years.
   b. having students do service projects as part of their classwork.
   c. going with the students to register to vote.
   d. teaching critical pedagogy in the class.

6. The work schedule in teaching that allows for personal time is a(n)
   a. monetary reward.
   b. status symbol.
   c. extrinsic reward.
   d. intrinsic reward.

7. Among the motivations for teaching given by those at work in the profession, which was the least cited response?
   a. "I want to make a good salary."
   b. "I enjoy working with children."
   c. "I think teaching is important and honorable work."
   d. "I want to make a contribution to the community."

8. One way of jeopardizing your effectiveness as a teacher is
   a. to be enthusiastic about your content or subject matter.
   b. to use teaching as a way of meeting your personal needs.
   c. to advise students after school about their education.
   d. to maintain a formal tone in your classroom.

9. Melinda has a particular fondness for geography and does more of it in her elementary class than any other subject. If she continues to focus so narrowly on geography, what might happen?
   a. The students can lose interest and become disengaged.
   b. Students will win state geography bees.
   c. She will burn out.
   d. She will become disengaged.

10. One way to predict what we will accomplish as teachers is to ask ourselves this question:
    a. "What subjects most interest me?"
    b. "What are my personal skills?"
    c. "What do my trusted advisors say to me about teaching?"
    d. "Why should I teach?"

B. Answer each of the following questions briefly in complete sentences.

1. Identify three ways that you could explore if teaching is right for you.

2. What are intrinsic rewards? How do they apply to teaching?

Chapter 2 What Is a School?

Learning Objectives

After studying the chapter, students will be able to

- distinguish between education and schooling.
- describe the purposes of schooling.
- apply and analyze a school's formal statement of purpose.
- explain, apply, and analyze the school models described in the text: worker trainer, college prep, social panacea, social escalator, shopping mall, family, human potential developer, acculturator.
- describe how schools function as representatives and transmitters of culture.
- identify, explain, and discuss some elements of American dominant culture evidenced in schools.
- describe how schools could operate as vehicles for social reconstruction.
- describe some of the similarities and differences among schools.
- list and explain some of the features of schools that are effective with respect to academic outcomes and those that are considered effective on the basis of more holistic outcomes.

Chapter 2 What Is a School?

Study Guide

Completing this study guide will help you prepare for the major topic areas on an exam; however, it does not cover every piece of information found in the chapter or the test questions.

1. Define and contrast these terms:
   - Education
   - Schooling

2. Describe or give an example of each of the following models:
   - Trainer of good worker
   - Preparer for college
   - Shopping mall
   - Social escalator
   - Social panacea
   - Developer of human potential
   - Acculturator
   - Family

3. Give an example of schools functioning as:
   - Representatives of culture
   - Transmitters of culture

4. Distinguish between the focuses of the three types of reconstruction.

5. What are the characteristics that most schools have in common?

6. Describe the characteristics of effective schools presented in either the academic outcome or holistic point of view in the chapter.

Chapter 2 What Is a School?

Sample Chapter Quiz

A. Read each of the following questions, and write the letter of the best answer in the appropriate space on your answer sheet.

1. Schooling is most generally defined as
   a. a process of human growth that leads to greater self-control.
   b. an informal arrangement made for the benefit of students of all ages.
   c. a specific, formalized process.
   d. an experience over a set period of time spent in an institution.

2. When a student is able to exist productively in a rule-bound system and can read, write, and compute, it is probably the result of his or her
   a. schooling.
   b. vocational training.
   c. education, defined broadly.
   d. directed study.

3. The formal statement of a school's purpose
   a. details the curriculum theory espoused by the school and the preferred instructional methods.
   b. helps newcomers to the school understand the daily running of the school.
   c. reveals what the school and/or community believes are the school's appropriate functions.
   d. details the curriculum theory of the school, helps newcomers understand the daily running of the school, and reveals what the school believes is its appropriate function.

4. Which of these is *not* a motivating factor to use schools as institutions for reconstruction?
   a. Inadequacy of the democratic system to direct schools
   b. Threats from hostile countries or terrorists
   c. Interdependent world economy
   d. Large number of immigrants

5. A curriculum designed to teach people how to be effective students, able to master complex academic content, is characteristic of schools of the
   a. college preparatory type.
   b. trainer of good worker type.
   c. human development type.
   d. acculturator type.

6. Which of the following is *not* a characteristic that is the same in the majority of public schools?
   a. Number of hours in the day
   b. Amount of funding per pupil
   c. Number of days in the school year
   d. Pupil-teacher ratio

7. In one high school, students are given freedom to choose from a broad selection of courses in the fine arts, sciences, literature, vocational areas, and athletics. This high school probably represents the
   a. shopping mall model.
   b. college prep model.
   c. acculturator model.
   d. factory model.

8. The human development type of school might choose for its model a person who
   a. is most notable for his or her unfailing curiosity, evident in continuous learning.
   b. learns discipline early and becomes successful as a business owner.
   c. is famous for his or her success in formal education settings.
   d. is famous for his or her solid work habits and enviable employment record.

9. A society's culture is its
   a. educational organizations.
   b. system of values and beliefs.
   c. informal art and craft forms.
   d. political structures.

10. A school that has high "holistic" outcomes in schooling is characterized by
    a. competitiveness, extensive extracurricular activities, and teachers with advanced degrees.
    b. a healthy budget, adequate facilities, and good communications.
    c. coherence, vital teacher subgroups, and consistent discipline.
    d. high teacher expectations, small classes, and an innovative curriculum.

B. Answer each of the following questions briefly in complete sentences.

1. Explain the concept of a school as a social panacea. To what degree do you think this model is appropriate for schools?

2. Why has "cultural transmission" been a recognized element of our schools? What are the arguments supporting the cultural transmission role for schools?

Chapter 3 What Is Life in Schools Like?

Learning Objectives

After studying the chapter, students will be able to

- explain how the school serves a socialization function through the explicit and implicit curricula.
- explain why students in elementary classrooms learn to deny desire, delay gratification, cope with interruptions, and work through distractions.
- describe the range of educational experiences for middle-grade students, based on the grade configuration of the school, the size of the school, the administration's and teachers' orientations, the goals of the school, and the staffing patterns.
- explain how conflicting goals of the high school require numerous elective courses that often strain the resources of the institution.
- explain how the instructional practices in high schools have remained largely unchanged over the past century.
- explain how secondary students experience high school differently from each other, based on tracking, the courses in which they enroll, the feedback they receive from teachers, and the tacit agreements they make with their teachers.
- describe the nature and role of peer groups and adolescent subculture in shaping the attitudes and behaviors of secondary students.
- explain how teachers' expectations of students are formed and how they affect teachers' interactional patterns with students.

Chapter 3 What Is Life in Schools Like?

Study Guide

Completing this study guide will help you prepare for the major topic areas on an exam; however, it does not cover every piece of information found in the chapter or the test questions.

1. Explain how the implicit (informal) curriculum contributes to the socialization of the student.

2. What is the explicit curriculum? Give an example.

3. Name and describe the common experiences of elementary students.

4. Describe the effects of ability grouping on several categories of students.

5. Name and describe the common characteristics of high schools.

6. What are four of the areas for improving the quality of American high schools suggested in *Breaking Ranks: Changing an American Institution*?

7. Compare and contrast how teachers behave toward "low" and "high" students.

8. Distinguish between the jocks and burnouts; discuss the peer group behavior and orientation toward school of each group.

9. Which student characteristics influence teacher expectations?

Chapter 3 What Is Life in Schools Like?

Sample Chapter Quiz

A. Read each of the following questions, and write the letter of the best answer in the appropriate space on your answer sheet.

1. By the end of the first year, a student knows how to behave in class, on the playground, and in the lunchroom, and as a result is well liked by the teachers. This appropriate behavior is probably a result of successful
   a. socialization.
   b. achievement.
   c. peer-group influence.
   d. immersion in an interactive environment.

2. Jackson's study of elementary classrooms found that
   a. students learn to be aggressive and loud.
   b. students learn to wait and repress desires.
   c. teachers learn to wait and take turns.
   d. teachers are loud and repressive.

3. Ability grouping, a common practice in U.S. schools, tends to
   a. favor the high-ability children.
   b. favor the low-ability children.
   c. facilitate learning for non-English speakers.
   d. have no effect on most students' learning.

4. One difference between a science exam graded on a curve and a science fair where all entries are displayed prominently is that the exam promotes
   a. competitiveness and the fair promotes personal initiative.
   b. learning and the fair promotes activity.
   c. cooperation and the fair promotes competitiveness.
   d. compliance and the fair promotes cooperation.

5. Eckert's study found that teens either belonged to or identified with a social group within the school. One function of this group seems to be to
   a. give students a sense of belonging so they can be more successful in school.
   b. prepare teens for the social classes that exist in mainstream society.
   c. facilitate communication between teens and their parents.
   d. help the teens find jobs.

6. Boyer's study of modern high schools showed that a major problem that most experience is
   a. an accumulation of contradictory purposes.
   b. the absence of written goals.
   c. the inability to offer relevant courses.
   d. an unwillingness to provide something for everyone.

7. One way to implement Cuban's recommendations for improving secondary education would be
   a. to revise secondary curricula to include more courses responsive to student interests.
   b. to retrain teachers to use small groups, cooperative learning, and student-interest projects more effectively.
   c. to retrain principals to use leadership that makes schools more attractive to students.
   d. to retrain teachers to use teacher-centered methods more effectively and compensate for the extra work demanded by the reforms.

8. In *The Shopping Mall High School,* which group of students was described as neglected?
   a. Gifted athletes
   b. Underachievers
   c. Special needs students
   d. Average students

9. Which one of the following was *not* suggested as a way to improve quality in American high schools?
   a. More variety
   b. Personalization
   c. Flexible scheduling
   d. More technology

10. After an eight-year study of the way teachers teach, what does John Goodlad conclude about classroom instructional practices?
    a. Most teaching strategies were inefficient in conveying information to the students.
    b. The majority of classroom practices that were observed reinforced the status quo.
    c. Over the eight-year period, teachers showed the tendency to include more student-centered activities.
    d. The amount of time spent by students on particular instructional activities was constant across grade level.

B. Answer each of the following questions briefly in complete sentences.

1. Why is it important for teachers to understand the peer groups in their high schools?

2. What changes can be noticed in the organization and instructional practices in high schools over the past one hundred years?

Chapter 4 Who Are Today's Students?

Learning Objectives

After studying the chapter, students will be able to

- explain the concepts of cultural diversity and cultural pluralism, and their implications in the classroom.
- describe the demographic trends of U.S. minorities and describe how ethnic and cultural differences between public school teachers and students may foster misunderstanding.
- identify and explain William Glasser's control theory and describe how this theory can influence a teacher's behavior with students.
- explain Howard Gardner's theory of multiple intelligences and relate that theory to teaching.
- describe the concept of learning styles and their potential influence on teachers.
- discuss the opposing positions in the debate on multicultural education.
- describe the salient elements of the IDEA, including the key terms *appropriate public education* and *least-restrictive environment.*
- describe the term *gifted and talented* as applied to students, and explain how gifted and talented students are identified and educated.
- explain the impact of the *Lau* v. *Nichols* Supreme Court decision on bilingual education.
- describe the models of bilingual education.
- describe the work of Dr. James Comer in the school intervention project of New Haven, Connecticut.

Chapter 4 Who Are Today's Students?

Study Guide

Completing this study guide will help you prepare for the major topic areas on an exam; however, it does not cover every piece of information found in the chapter or the test questions.

1. List at least four different *categories* of student diversity in the classroom.

2. Define cultural pluralism.

3. According to Willam Glasser's control theory, what are an individual's basic needs?

4. What are the eight areas in Howard Gardner's multiple intelligences?

5. Explain the rationale behind James Comer's school intervention program.

6. Describe or give an example of each of the following models of bilingual education: transitional, immersion, submersion, English as a second language. What does LEP stand for?

7. Describe PL94-142-IDEA and its major provisions.

8. Distinguish between the practices of inclusion and mainstreaming.

9. Why is cultural and economic diversity a special challenge for most teachers?

Chapter 4 Who Are Today's Students?

Sample Chapter Quiz

A. Read each of the following questions, and write the letter of the best answer in the appropriate space on your answer sheet.

1. The anticipated student population trend for the next ten years is
   a. significant increases in all populations.
   b. an increase in the white population while the minority population remains stable.
   c. an increase in the minority population while the white population remains stable or declines.
   d. zero growth for any population.

2. Before laws regarding bilingual education were passed, the most frequent model for teaching non-English-speaking students was likely to have been
   a. immersion.
   b. submersion
   c. transition.
   d. ESL.

3. Mrs. Blazer has been strongly influenced by William Glasser's control theory. Unlike most teachers, she never puts "happy face" stickers on her students' work or provides them with other rewards like bonus points for work well done. Why would she avoid such practices?
   a. Because they exert a form of control on students by encouraging them to desire external rewards
   b. Because the external rewards such as stickers have no intrinsic relationship to the work itself
   c. Because she wants students to develop their own internal standards for judging the quality of their work
   d. Because she believes the competition spurred by handing out stickers encourages her students to exert psychological control over each other

4. What previous legislation does IDEA build on?
   a. PL 94-142, which established special education for students with disabilities
   b. The *Lau Remedies* for non-English-speaking students
   c. The Head Start program, an early intervention program
   d. Title I for disadvantaged children

5. Dominic is a basketball player, and he has the ability to run quickly, jump high into the air, and easily make a basket from the three-point range. Which of the following identifies Dominic's ability as a form of intelligence?
   a. John Goodlad
   b. Howard Gardner
   c. Jean Piaget
   d. Erik Erickson

6. Which way of implementing learning-style theory in classrooms would be the most educationally sound?
   a. Test the students in the classroom, and then individually determine their learning styles.
   b. Design monthly units featuring a particular learning style, and emphasize it with your class.
   c. Have teachers identify their learning styles, and then have them teach in the ways in which they feel most comfortable.
   d. Integrate the learning-style theory in as many activities and lessons as possible so that all students would have the opportunity to perform well.

7. Generally, white women constitute the majority of teachers. In the near future, teaching will
   a. gain a significant increase in the number of female minority teachers.
   b. attract more men to the profession; nearly 40 percent of the teaching force will be men within the next twenty years.
   c. continue to be a profession where white women will be the majority.
   d. see a marked decrease in the dominance of white women in the field.

8. The goal of multicultural education is to
   a. reduce prejudice and foster tolerance for other cultures.
   b. academically support ethnic minority students.
   c. provide a nurturing environment for children who have been abused.
   d. teach students to speak other languages.

9. The decision of *Lau* v. *Nichols* provided for
   a. the free and appropriate education of children with disabilities.
   b. the creation and maintenance of programs for the gifted and talented.
   c. the early intervention for education of children with special needs who are between three and five years old.
   d. the establishment of bilingual education programs.

10. Inclusion refers to
    a. including students with disabilities in the regular classroom.
    b. including students with disabilities in after school sports.
    c. including non-English speakers in the regular classroom.
    d. including parents in their child(ren)'s education.

B. Answer each of the following questions briefly in complete sentences.

1. Why do some educators oppose multicultural education in the schools?

2. How will the changing student population affect teaching?

Chapter 5 What Social Problems and Tension Points Affect Today's Students?

Learning Objectives

After studying the chapter, students will be able to

- identify the impact of poverty, homelessness, and child abuse on children's classroom behavior and learning.
- describe the structures of U.S. families today, identifying the difficulties that single parents and working parents face in raising children.
- describe the impact that alcohol abuse, drug abuse, and suicide have had on students in recent years.
- describe the problems of school violence and vandalism, and summarize some of the aspects that contribute to student aggression.
- discuss some of the things that schools, principals, and teachers can do to reduce the incidence of school violence.
- understand the reasons for students dropping out and discuss successful preventive measures.
- explain the effect of *Brown* v. *Board of Education of Topeka* on American education.
- describe the methods used to bring about school desegregation based on race, especially busing and magnet schools, and their effectiveness in achieving integration.
- explain how gender bias leads to unequal educational opportunities for females and how federal legislation, in particular Title IX, seeks to reduce these inequalities.

Chapter 5 What Social Problems and Tension Points Affect Today's Students?

Study Guide

Completing this study guide will help you prepare for the major topic areas on an exam; however, it does not cover every piece of information found in the chapter or the test questions.

1. What does the term *at risk* refer to?

2. Name the major social problems affecting education.

3. Describe the ruling in *Brown* v. *Board of Education* and its effect on schools.

4. Compare and contrast de facto and de jure segregation.

5. Describe several examples of compensatory education.

6. List the general provisions of Title IX and give an example of each.

7. What are some of the things that principals and teachers can do to reduce the incidence of violence.

8. List the major reasons students give for dropping out.

9. Describe the role magnet schools play in desegregation.

10. What evidence is there that gender bias exists in schools, and what are the educational effects for girls of this gender bias?

Chapter 5 What Social Problems and Tension Points Affect Today's Students?

Sample Chapter Quiz

A. Read each of the following questions, and write the letter of the best answer in the appropriate space on your answer sheet.

1. Since the 1954 Supreme Court decision, urban schools have a growing minority population and a declining white population. One of the reasons for this trend is that
   a. housing costs have increased substantially in urban areas but not in suburban areas.
   b. white families are moving out of urban areas into suburban areas.
   c. the birth rate for teen mothers is declining.
   d. minorities are dissatisfied with the education their children receive in the urban areas.

2. The major reason that magnet schools have been able to play a positive role in the integration of schools is that
   a. they are usually situated at the juncture between a white and a minority neighborhood.
   b. they focus on developing the empathic nature of the students so that the students understand other racial groups better.
   c. they have taken an active role in community service, and residents become impressed with the way students of different races work together.
   d. parents are able to choose to send their child to the school, unlike forced integration.

3. A basal reader has fifty stories about people. Thirty-five of the stories involve males having adventures in which they always succeed. Fifteen of the stories are about females who have either of two roles: a "damsel in distress" or a parent in a two-parent family. The stories featuring females are mysteries, romances, or stories about families. This text might be called sexist because
   a. male role models are successful in their pursuits.
   b. the stories concerning males involve adventure.
   c. the stories are about females who are shown as weak or able to succeed only in partnerships.
   d. the stories featuring women emphasize mysteries or stories about families.

4. Compensatory education is primarily aimed at
   a. all underachieving kindergartners.
   b. disadvantaged students.
   c. most academically deficient middle school students and disadvantaged high schoolers.
   d. female students who have been victims of sexual discrimination.

5. Ms. Juniper suspects that one of the students in class is being abused at home. When she asks the student about it, he first denies it, then reluctantly tells her the truth, but begs her not to say anything or he'll "really get in trouble." What should Ms. Juniper do?
   a. Report it to the proper authority right away.
   b. Respect the boy's wishes and not say anything.
   c. Go to see the boy's father and tell him to stop or she will have to report him to the police.
   d. Wait a while to see if he continues to be abused.

6. The practice of gender bias in any school activity that is funded in part or wholly by federal dollars is forbidden by provisions of
   a. Chapter I of the ESEA.
   b. *Brown* v. *Board of Education.*
   c. Title IX of the Educational Amendment Act.
   d. Title I.

7. The highest percentage of poverty-stricken people in America live
   a. in isolated towns.
   b. in inner cities.
   c. in remote rural areas.
   d. in suburbs.

8. Ivan always seemed to be a perfectly normal high schooler. Suddenly, his teacher noticed that he began changing. She noticed that he distanced himself more and more from people; it seemed as if he lacked the capacity to care about anyone, even himself. Noticing this abrupt change to extreme emotional coldness, his teacher became concerned that he was
   a. abusing alcohol.
   b. smoking marijuana.
   c. taking barbiturates.
   d. taking crack.

9. Which of the following is the largest factor in the growing number of children living with a single parent?
   a. Teen mothers
   b. Deaths
   c. Divorce
   d. Working parents

10. Research seems to indicate that high school principals can help reduce violence and vandalism in schools by
    a. maintaining a stern, watchful eye and punishing misbehavior consistently.
    b. being a good friend to all students.
    c. cultivating the support of student leaders for programs to subdue troublemakers.
    d. establishing high expectations for student behavior and performance.

B. Answer each of the following questions briefly in complete sentences.

1. Why is it important to provide a stable class for an abused child?

2. Why have schools not been very successful in reducing poverty?

Chapter 6 What Makes a Teacher Effective?

Learning Objectives

After studying the chapter, students will be able to

- describe the teacher's role as a decision maker.
- explain how teachers' attitudes toward themselves, their students, their colleagues and other adults, and their subject matter affect teaching.
- identify and explain attitudes that can foster effective teaching and those that can hinder it.
- describe how knowledge of a discipline, the disciplinary knowledge covered in the curriculum, and pedagogical content knowledge contribute to effective teaching.
- identify and explain the characteristics of effective teachers.
- describe what reflective teaching is.
- describe what a constructivist view of learning is.
- identify and explain the implications of recent cognitive research on teaching and learning.
- explain the relationship between academically engaged time and learning.
- define Jacob Kounin's terms (*with-it-ness, smoothness,* and *momentum*) in terms of their meaning in classroom management.
- summarize guidelines for effective classroom management.
- explain how questioning, wait-time, and planning contribute to teaching effectiveness.

Chapter 6 What Makes a Teacher Effective?

Study Guide

Completing this study guide will help you prepare for the major topic areas on an exam; however, it does not cover every piece of information found in the chapter or the test questions.

1. Name at least three alternative methods for examining your own instructional effectiveness.

2. List and give an example of each of the three categories of decisions that teachers make.

3. Describe the process of reflective teaching.

4. Explain the constructivist theory of learning.

5. Define and give an example of academically engaged time.

6. Describe and give an example of each of the following: *with-it-ness, smoothness, momentum* from Jacob Kounin's research.

7. Explain the advantages of using wait-time.

8. How does a self-fulfilling prophecy affect the relationship between a student and a teacher?

9. Distinguish between a theory and a theory-in-use.

Chapter 6 What Makes a Teacher Effective?

Sample Chapter Quiz

A. Read each of the following questions, and write the letter of the best answer in the appropriate space on your answer sheet.

1. Angel Herrara is a sixth-grade teacher. She spends many days during August visiting the school library, reviewing material, and creating lessons for her class in September. During this time, Carolyn makes
   a. planning decisions.
   b. reflective decisions.
   c. interactive decisions.
   d. prescriptive decisions.

2. Teacher A argues that professional training ought to focus mainly on practical skills, because beginners desperately need those from the first day. Teacher B responds that theoretical knowledge about learning and human behavior is more essential. Which teacher does the text support?
   a. Teacher A
   b. Teacher B
   c. Both teachers
   d. Neither teacher

3. Dana was in the middle of teaching a lesson he had worked hard preparing when he realized that many students did not understand it. He immediately changed the direction of the lesson to help them understand. In this instance, Dana made a(n)
   a. management decision.
   b. reflective decision.
   c. interactive decision.
   d. prescriptive decision.

4. According to the text, one reason for studying theoretical knowledge is that it
   a. equips the teacher to interpret the complexities of the classroom.
   b. has been shown to discipline the teacher's mind to make learning easier.
   c. is part of the rites of passage of teacher education.
   d. enables a teacher to cover more material with students.

5. According to research on teaching, which teacher is most likely to stimulate students to high achievement?
   a. One who is well educated in a subject
   b. One who is consistent in discipline
   c. One who is enthusiastic about a subject
   d. One who is unyielding

6. The explanation that people use to justify one course of action over another is called
   a. a theory-in-use.
   b. a theory.
   c. a discipline.
   d. knowledge about knowledge.

7. When the principal comes in unannounced to ask the teacher a question, she notices that several students are creating a model together. Other students are reading science books, and the rest are writing. They all seem immersed in their task. These students are demonstrating
   a. cooperative learning.
   b. classroom management.
   c. group process.
   d. academic engaged time.

8. Which of the following teacher behaviors is properly classified as classroom management?
   a. Using a student team learning approach
   b. Defining routines for the use of class supplies
   c. Having a spelling bee to make spelling more interesting
   d. Assigning a timed test in math

9. The three major categories of decisions that teachers make in the course of instructing are
   a. planning, management, and environment.
   b. planning, implementing, and evaluating.
   c. instructional, management, and evaluating.
   d. planning, environment, and instructional.

10. Every morning during math, your class seems to go haywire. At most other times, the students are not a problem. What do "Kevin and Jim's Management Rules" tell you to do first?
    a. Go straight to your mentor for help.
    b. Check your instruction.
    c. Try a threat of calling home.
    d. Ask a colleague to come in and observe the class to give you some pointers.

B. Answer each of the following questions briefly in complete sentences.

1. In what ways is theoretical knowledge vital for an effective teacher? Explain.

2. What are the defining characteristics of a reflective teacher?

Chapter 7 What Should Teachers Know About Technology and Its Impact on Schools?

Learning Objectives

After studying the chapter, students will be able to

- describe some of the events in the historical evolution of the audiovisual and computer technologies used in the classroom.
- identify the sources of pressure on schools to use more technology.
- discuss a variety of ways that technology can be used to assist student learning.
- summarize how technology changes the teacher's role in instruction and contributes to the teacher's productivity.
- explain several ways computers may be "deployed" for use within a school.
- debate the issues surrounding the use of computers in education.
- analyze the equity issues regarding equal access to technology for disadvantaged students and girls.
- use computer terminology with greater understanding.

Chapter 7 What Should Teachers Know About Technology and Its Impact on Schools?

Study Guide

Completing this study guide will help you prepare for the major topic areas on an exam; however, it does not cover every piece of information found in the chapter or the test questions.

1. Identify the sources of pressure on schools to incorporate more technology.

2. Distinguish between activities to learn about the computer and activities using the computer to learn.

3. List and give examples of how computer technology can serve as a cognitive tool.

4. List and give examples of how computer technology can serve as a communication tool.

5. List and give examples of different kinds of instructional uses of technology.

6. Describe the ways technology can change how teachers do their job (consider communication, instruction, and productivity).

7. Identify the pros and cons of each of the three common ways of deploying computers for student use within a school.

8. Give examples of the factors that contribute to the inequities of computer technology between students of affluent and disadvantaged socioeconomic classes.

9. Describe the ways in which boys and girls use computer technology differently.

10. Describe several different ways computers are used as assistive technology for students with special needs.

Chapter 7 What Should Teachers Know About Technology and Its Impact on Schools?

Sample Chapter Quiz

A. Read each of the following questions, and write the letter of the best answer in the appropriate space on your answer sheet.

1. The sources of pressure on schools to increase their use of technology tools include
   a. parents and teachers.
   b. students and legislators.
   c. businesses and citizens.
   d. all of the above.

2. When Jan Schmidt, a third-grade teacher, uses e-mail to schedule a conference with Maria's father, she is using the computer as a
   a. cognitive tool.
   b. tool to facilitate instruction.
   c. communication tool.
   d. resource for students with special needs.

3. A database is most often used for
   a. sorting.
   b. recording.
   c. analyzing.
   d. editing.

4. In the classroom the most commonly used computer tools are
   a. communication tools.
   b. instructional facilitation tools.
   c. cognitive tools.
   d. tools for individuals with special needs.

5. A search engine is
   a. a Web site.
   b. a large database.
   c. the Internet.
   d. an icon.

6. The educational advantages of using technology to assist students with special needs are
   a. unlimited patience.
   b. undivided attention.
   c. enhanced communication.
   d. all of the above.

7. The impact of educational technology is most influenced by
   a. student acceptance.
   b. how teachers use it.
   c. community interest.
   d. business demand for it.

8. In 1997 the national average student-to-computer ratio was
   a. 5 to 1.
   b. 9 to 1.
   c. 3 to 1.
   d. 12 to 1.

9. The text, graphics, and links that appear simultaneously on the display screen are called a
   a. Web site.
   b. byte.
   c. Web page.
   d. master page.

10. Which arrangement of computers is a more expensive investment for schools?
    a. Single-computer classroom
    b. Computer labs
    c. Classroom clusters
    d. All three require equal investments.

B. Answer each of the following questions briefly in complete sentences.

1. Describe at least three ways that educational technology affects teaching today; give examples.

2. Identify the major contributors to unequal access to computers for students across schools or districts.

Chapter 8 What Is Taught?

Learning Objectives

After studying this chapter, students will be able to

- define the formal and informal curriculum and differentiate between the two, giving specific examples.
- explain how shifting purposes have affected school curriculum throughout American history.
- describe recent trends in curriculum reform.
- discuss international comparisons of achievement.
- summarize debates about curricular changes in language arts, science, math, social studies, foreign languages, art, physical education, and vocational studies.
- explain the relationship between textbook adoption practices, textbook content, and a national curriculum.
- describe several instructional approaches—interdisciplinary teaching, cooperative learning, critical thinking, writing across the curriculum, and block scheduling.

Chapter 8 What Is Taught?

Study Guide

Completing this study guide will help you prepare for the major topic areas on an exam; however, it does not cover every piece of information found in the chapter or the test questions.

1. Compare and contrast child/society-centered and subject-centered curriculum focuses.

2. Give a concise description of the curriculum trends in each of the following subject areas:

   - Language Arts and English
   - Mathematics
   - Science
   - Social Studies
   - Foreign Languages
   - The Arts
   - Physical Education, Health, and Recreation
   - Elective courses
   - Vocational courses

3. Summarize American students' achievement in comparison to student achievement in other developed countries. What are some of the possible reasons for this achievement discrepancy?

4. Why are textbooks considered such a powerful force in curriculum?

5. Describe the main advantage of the following innovative instructional approaches:

   - Interdisciplinary curriculum
   - Cooperative learning
   - Critical thinking and problem solving
   - Writing across the curriculum
   - Block scheduling

6. In your own words, explain the contrasting views on each of the following controversies:

   - Multicultural curriculum versus core curriculum
   - Cultural literacy
   - Outcomes-based education

7. Define the following terms:

   - Structure of the discipline approach
   - Spiral curriculum
   - Back-to-basics movement
   - Whole language

Chapter 8 What Is Taught?

Sample Chapter Quiz

A. Read each of the following questions, and write the letter of the best answer in the appropriate space on your answer sheet.

1. The mission of the schools from colonial times to the present has
   a. remained unchanged.
   b. changed to respond to the values of the society.
   c. remained basically the same with some peaks and valleys.
   d. changed to respond to the changes to Europe.

2. The renewed interest in education in the late 1950s and 1960s was instigated by
   a. the launch of *Sputnik*.
   b. the Korean conflict.
   c. the Vietnam War.
   d. the death of Eisenhower.

3. A student listens to an editorial response on the TV news in which the speaker charges that a city politician is acting like Macbeth. The student immediately knows by the reference to Macbeth that the city politician is trying to usurp power, according to the speaker. The student is able to make that connection because
   a. of her critical thinking skills.
   b. of her powers of memorization.
   c. she is culturally literate.
   d. she has had courses in British history.

4. Studies of effective ways to teach writing have led to the belief that
   a. writing is most efficiently taught within the regular language arts program.
   b. writing is best learned in the context of a course focused only on writing.
   c. writing cannot be taught directly but can be learned only with practice and feedback.
   d. writing achievement as well as content area mastery is enhanced when writing instruction is spread over several content areas.

5. A teacher who uses a social studies or science lesson to show students how to find and evaluate evidence is teaching
   a. mastery of content knowledge.
   b. critical thinking.
   c. Socratic dialogue.
   d. data analysis.

6. Outcomes-based education seeks to improve education by
   a. integrating the arts into the regular curriculum.
   b. specifying the skills and knowledge that students should possess at each grade level.
   c. instituting standardized tests at all grades.
   d. developing critical thinking skills.

7. Many new, hands-on elementary science programs require the teacher to assume the role of
   a. information provider.
   b. examiner.
   c. problem solver.
   d. research director.

8. Successful cooperative learning strategies include
   a. group goals and individual work.
   b. individual goals and group accountability.
   c. group goals and individual accountability.
   d. homogeneous grouping and individual accountability.

9. An important reason for emphasizing reading in the curriculum is that
   a. most people like to read, once they become skilled.
   b. reading is not very hard to teach.
   c. success in reading raises students' pride.
   d. success in reading contributes to success in all areas of curriculum.

10. A curriculum arranged so that at each new level the student re-encounters familiar concepts in more complex forms is called the
    a. discovery curriculum.
    b. spiral curriculum.
    c. saber-tooth curriculum.
    d. developmental curriculum.

B. Answer each of the following questions briefly in complete sentences.

1. Explain the differences between instruction based on core curriculum and multicultural curriculum with regard to goals and content.

2. How does interdisciplinary teaching lead to enhanced learning?

Chapter 9 How Are Schools Governed, Influenced, and Financed?

Learning Objectives

After studying the chapter, students will be able to

- describe and identify the contributions to public education from the state and local districts.
- identify and explain the influence that the state legislature and governor's office have upon educational policy.
- define the source of authority and particular responsibilities of the state board of education, the chief state school officer, the state department of education, the local school board and superintendent, and the school principal.
- describe the demographic data relating to school superintendents, principals, and school board members and explain the significance of those data.
- describe some ways school officials exercise informal influence in education.
- identify and explain the historical influence business has had upon public education.
- describe the current business interest in public schooling and analyze its effects.
- explain the strengths and shortcomings of standardized tests as measures of school effectiveness.
- explain the implications of several court cases regarding state and local funding of education, including the *Serrano* case and cases in Kentucky, Texas, and New Jersey, and the alternative plan to finance public education in Michigan.
- describe the typical pattern of school funding by local, state, and federal agencies, and explain the relationships among the local economy, tax structure, and the quality of education.
- describe the trends in federal support of education from the 1960s through the 1990s.

Chapter 9 How Are Schools Governed, Influenced, and Financed?

Study Guide

Completing this study guide will help you prepare for the major topic areas on an exam; however, it does not cover every piece of information found in the chapter or the test questions.

1. Describe the relationship between the state board of education, the state department of education, and the chief state school officer.

2. Describe the role of the district superintendent of schools.

3. Identify and describe six groups or types of constituencies that influence the decisions made in education.

4. Indicate the three levels of governance that contribute to school funding, the relative amounts they contribute, and their source for these funds.

5. Give an example of privatization in education.

6. Distinguish between the appropriate uses for categorical grants and block grants.

7. Define site-based decision making and give an example.

8. To which level of government is the legal responsibility for the governance of schools delegated, and what legal document states this?

9. Describe several ways in which business influences education.

10. Compare and contrast the pros and cons of year-round schools.

11. List the allowable areas for federal funds to private schools.

Chapter 9 How Are Schools Governed, Influenced, and Financed?

Sample Chapter Quiz

A. Read each of the following questions, and write the letter of the best answer in the appropriate space on your answer sheet.

1. Control of schools was awarded to the individual states by the
   a. Tenth Amendment to the U.S. Constitution.
   b. Fourteenth Amendment to the U.S. Constitution.
   c. Twenty-First Amendment to the U.S. Constitution.
   d. First Amendment to the U.S. Constitution.

2. In practice, which body is most responsible for carrying out the majority of educational policies?
   a. The federal government
   b. The state legislature
   c. The state department of education
   d. The local school board

3. State authorities usually delegate to local school boards the responsibility for
   a. certifying or licensing teachers.
   b. setting guidelines for elementary education.
   c. setting policy and administering schools.
   d. advising teacher-training institutions on professional programs.

4. Talia Lopez is meeting with the teacher education faculty at Shelburne State College to discuss the new changes in teacher licensure and how they will affect the teacher education program at this state college. Based upon this description, Ms. Lopez most likely represents
   a. the state department of education.
   b. the state board of education.
   c. the governor's office.
   d. the U.S. Department of Education.

5. A prospective math teacher has interviewed for a teaching position at the Longmeadow Middle School. Who makes the final decision about her employment?
   a. The mathematics supervisor
   b. The Longmeadow school principal
   c. The district superintendent
   d. The local board of education

6. Bob Moorehead was the district superintendent of a small city's public school system for twenty years. Bob's longevity in this nontenured position was most likely due to
   a. his ability to assess student achievement.
   b. his ability to resolve conflicts among groups that make competing claims on the schools.
   c. his ability to rejuvenate the faculty through his strong program in staff development.
   d. his ability to restrict spending and to manage finances creatively.

7. During this century, the local school board has shifted to the local school superintendent responsibilities such as
   a. certifying qualified teacher applicants.
   b. determining priorities for the district.
   c. selecting and promoting personnel.
   d. setting educational policy.

8. Professional educators exercise formal control in schools through
   a. daily decision making about program implementation.
   b. policy-setting powers shared by school boards.
   c. activities of professional associations.
   d. input and decision making about school finances.

9. Education budgets are funded through contributions from federal, state, and local agencies, with the amount from each varying from state to state. Which agencies *never* contribute the greatest proportion of funds?
   a. Federal agencies
   b. State agencies
   c. Local agencies
   d. County agencies

10. The court decision ruling that a child is entitled to an education of the quality most reflective of the state's wealth is the
   a. U.S. Supreme Court's *Lau* decision.
   b. Michigan Supreme Court's *Kalamazoo* decision.
   c. California Supreme Court's *Serrano* decision.
   d. U.S. Supreme Court's *Serrano* decision.

B. Answer each of the following questions briefly in complete sentences.

1. Which organization, the state board of education or the state department of education, will most likely have a more direct impact on the life of a prospective teacher?

2. Why have so many state systems for financing education been declared unconstitutional?

Chapter 10 What Are the Philosophical Foundations of American Education?

Learning Objectives

After studying this chapter, students will be able to

- describe the role of philosophical knowledge in clarifying questions of educational decision making in policy and practice.
- explain how four branches of philosophy—metaphysics, epistemology, logic, and axiology—relate to the work of the teacher.
- describe and distinguish among four philosophies of education—perennialism, progressivism, essentialism, and existentialism—and explain the implications of each for schooling.
- identify the key contributions of John Dewey to U.S. education.
- apply the information they have learned about educational philosophy to analyze existing school curricula.
- begin to formulate and articulate their personal philosophy.

Chapter 10 What Are the Philosophical Foundations of American Education?

Study Guide

Completing this study guide will help you prepare for the major topic areas on an exam; however, it does not cover every piece of information found in the chapter or the test questions.

1. Define the word *philosophy*.

2. List and define the four branches of philosophical study.

3. Compare and contrast inductive and deductive reasoning.

4. List and describe the characteristics of the four educational philosophies. Be able to recognize examples of each (goals, methods, teacher role, student role, key ideas, etc.).

5. Describe the fields of aesthetics and ethics.

6. Who is John Dewey, and with which educational philosophy is he most closely associated?

7. What is an eclectic philosophy, and what are the hazards associated with it?

Chapter 10 What Are the Philosophical Foundations of American Education?

Sample Chapter Quiz

A. Read each of the following questions, and write the letter of the best answer in the appropriate space on your answer sheet.

1. Philosophers try to find answers to fundamental questions about existence by using
   a. historical patterns.
   b. human experience.
   c. intuition.
   d. reasoning.

2. An advanced placement biology class is discussing if physicians should transplant tissue and organs from aborted fetuses to patients diagnosed with various diseases. The discussion centers on the physician's conduct in performing such procedures. This discussion is focusing on
   a. aesthetics.
   b. epistemology.
   c. ethics.
   d. logic.

3. Asked why she taught history, Mrs. Wong replied that the study of history revealed the universality of human nature and that by studying the constancy of human nature, we could best learn how to approach contemporary issues. She is a(n)
   a. existentialist.
   b. progressive.
   c. perennialist.
   d. agnostic.

4. When students study Latin and also learn about the Roman virtues and Roman art, part of their instruction is in
   a. aesthetics.
   b. axiology.
   c. logic.
   d. metaphysics.

5. Making choices about whether meaning comes from collective wisdom or from the individual's context probably represents which aspect of a teacher's philosophy?
   a. Axiological
   b. Epistemological
   c. Metaphysical
   d. Phenomenological

6. A group of teachers met to decide if a newly created standardized test of mathematics should be administered to the students in their school. One teacher was opposed to administering the test because she claimed the test could *not* demonstrate how the students knew the mathematical concepts. Her concerns were of a(n) __________ nature.
   a. aesthetic
   b. epistemological
   c. ethical
   d. metaphysical
7. Which of the following is most representative of a perennialist curriculum?
   a. *The Odyssey,* by Homer, *Introduction to European History,* and *Biology: The Science of Living Things*
   b. *The Grapes of Wrath,* by John Steinbeck, *The Elements of Keyboarding,* and *Money Management for the '90's*
   c. *The Joy Luck Club,* by Amy Tan, Bruce Catton's volumes on the Civil War, and *Introduction to Psychology*
   d. *A Catcher in the Rye,* by J. D. Salinger, *Introduction to Mechanical Drawing,* and *Geometry*
8. In the essentialist school of education, the worth of any knowledge is measured by
   a. the stimulation and curiosity it provokes on the students' part.
   b. the degree to which an individual needs that knowledge to be a productive member of society.
   c. its potential to be verified, observed, and proven to be the truth.
   d. its usefulness in helping someone in his or her quest for personal meaning.
9. In a progressivist school, which of the following would most likely be evident?
   a. A flexible curriculum, allowing for a diversity of educational experiences and reflecting that knowledge is always being redefined
   b. An emphasis on the problem-solving capacities of the students
   c. An emphasis on students' self-discipline to sustain and propel them through the rigors of academic work
   d. A flexible curriculum, reflecting that knowledge is always being defined, and an emphasis on the problem-solving capacities of the students
10. A teacher is leading a class in a discussion about the responsibility of children to parents. During the discussion, the students freely explain their positions. The teacher emphasizes that there are no right or wrong answers, but that the students should use the discussion to clarify their own values. This exercise is an activity derived from
    a. behaviorism.
    b. essentialism.
    c. existentialism.
    d. progressivism.

B. Answer each of the following questions briefly in complete sentences.

1. Why is essentialism considered an "American" philosophy? What facets of it indicate that it reflects America?
2. Why is it important to understand the philosophy of education?

Chapter 11 What Is the History of American Education?

Learning Objectives

After studying the chapter, students will be able to

- identify, explain, and analyze the six key forces that have shaped the history of American education: local control of schools, universal education, public education, comprehensive education, secular education, and the changing ideas of the basics.
- identify and describe the purposes of the various types of elementary schooling available during the colonial period and be able to associate particular types of schooling with the geographical region in which it was most common.
- identify and describe the purposes of various types of secondary schooling available, from the colonial period through the present.
- locate on a time continuum the introduction of the following major developments in U.S. education: grammar schools, public (common) schools, academies, kindergarten, and secondary schools.
- identify, explain, and apply the educational ideas and methods of several key European educators.
- identify, explain, and apply the educational ideas and methods of several key American educators.
- articulate the major arguments supporting and opposing the establishment of common schools in the United States.
- define and explain the impact that several key rulings or laws have had upon expanding education: the Old Deluder Satan Act, the Northwest Land Ordinances, the *Kalamazoo* case, the Morrill Acts, *Plessy* v. *Ferguson*, and *Brown* v. *Board of Education.*
- explain and apply the general principles of the Progressive Education Association.
- describe the evolution of education for women, for African Americans, for Hispanic Americans, for Asian Americans, and for Native Americans.

Chapter 11 What Is the History of American Education?

Study Guide

Completing this study guide will help you prepare for the major topic areas on an exam; however, it does not cover every piece of information found in the chapter or the test questions.

1. List and describe the six themes in American education.

2. Describe the location, time period, and characteristics of dame schools, town schools, moving schools, district schools, and common schools.

3. Identify the European educators that have made significant contributions to American education and briefly describe each of their contributions.

4. Describe the significant changes in education that have taken place since World War II.

5. Describe Latin grammar schools, English grammar schools, and academies. Distinguish between their purposes.

6. Identify the significant characteristics of true middle schools.

7. For women and for each group of minority students in American schools, briefly describe the historical evolution of their participation in the American school system.

8. Indicate how the ruling in each of the following legal cases affected education in the United States: Old Deluder Satan Act, the *Kalamazoo* case, *Plessy* v. *Ferguson,* and *Brown* v. *Board of Education.*

9. Indicate the percentage of students who attend private schools and analyze the significance of this option in the United States.

10. List the pros and cons of establishing common schools.

Chapter 11 What Is the History of American Education?

Sample Chapter Quiz

A. Read each of the following questions, and write the letter of the best answer in the appropriate space on your answer sheet.

1. Private, family-based education, generally relying on tutors, was characteristic of colonial
   a. New England.
   b. mid-Atlantic communities.
   c. communities of the South.
   d. agricultural centers.

2. Common schools were founded on the belief that
   a. democracy required a well-educated citizenry.
   b. all students needed to have a moral education.
   c. students needed to develop workplace skills in school.
   d. all students had a right to a free education.

3. The purpose of the Old Deluder Satan Act, passed in Massachusetts in 1647, was to
   a. encourage religious instruction in the schools.
   b. require parents to educate their children.
   c. set up a system of secular schools.
   d. set aside land for schools in every township.

4. Friedrich Froebel is best known for
   a. developing kindergarten.
   b. developing a hands-on approach to science.
   c. initiating bilingual education in the United States.
   d. proposing writing across the curriculum.

5. Horace Mann argued in favor of the common school because he believed that
   a. the common school would help forge a national identity.
   b. all people should receive a religious education in the schools.
   c. the common school would train better workers.
   d. common schools would allow for greater harmony of thought and ideals.

6. One reason why the science of teaching began to develop in the early 1900s was that
   a. the application of psychology to education began to provide a basis for that work.
   b. laws were passed requiring that work.
   c. teachers began to get more curious.
   d. school administrators required more skills.

7. The main difference between the Latin and English grammar schools in the 1700s was that
   a. Latin schools were for boys and English schools were for girls.
   b. Latin schools were just early, primitive forms of English schools.
   c. Latin schools prepared students for college and English schools prepared them for work.
   d. Latin schools had higher status but did not differ from English schools in goals or curriculum.

8. The Progressive Education Association maintained that schools should help to
   a. train teachers.
   b. develop the students' interests in working.
   c. make the connection between school and the real world.
   d. end poverty and homelessness.

9. The Morrill Acts of 1862 and 1890 provided for the establishment of
   a. multicultural education.
   b. the common school.
   c. colleges to educate African Americans.
   d. segregated but equal schools.

10. Female academies to teach women how to be intelligent and productive companions for men or to be qualified teachers were established in the 1800s by
    a. Willa Cather, Laura Ingalls, and Catherine Stowe.
    b. Catherine Beecher, Emma Willard, and Mary Lyon.
    c. Harriet Beecher Stowe and Maria Montessori.
    d. Jane Addams, Mary Lyon, and Dorothea Dix.

B. Answer each of the following questions briefly in complete sentences.

1. Describe the impact that one of the following people had on American education: Horace Mann, W. E. B. Du Bois, or Noah Webster.

2. Although religious instruction was considered an essential part of early American education, its prominence in the curriculum gradually diminished. When did it first begin to take a less prominent role in the curriculum, and why?

Chapter 12 What Are Ethical and Legal Issues Facing Teachers?

Learning Objectives

After studying the chapter, students will be able to

- distinguish between ethics and the law and explain the proper province of each.
- list, explain, and apply the six dimensions of ethical teaching, as defined by Kenneth Howe.
- give examples of some ethical problems that teachers commonly face and explain how to think about resolving them.
- define due process, liability, assault, and battery as they relate to teaching.
- explain in general terms the laws relating to copyright, self-defense, religion in the classroom, lifestyle choices, and academic freedom.
- describe the rights of students regarding privacy, corporal punishment, access to public education, and access to their own school records.

Chapter 12 What Are Ethical and Legal Issues Facing Teachers?

Study Guide

Completing this study guide will help you prepare for the major topic areas on an exam; however, it does not cover every piece of information found in the chapter or the test questions.

1. Explain the difference between "the law" and ethics.

2. What are the six dimensions of ethical teaching?

3. Define the following terms:
   - Due process
   - Tenure
   - Liability
   - Academic freedom
   - *In loco parentis*

4. What does the Buckley Amendment establish?

5. How do a school administrator's search and seizure rights differ from those of a law enforcement officer?

6. What guidelines would you give to a new teacher based on recent Supreme Court rulings on teachers' rights regarding personal appearance, right to free speech, and personal sexual behavior?

7. What are a licensed teacher's responsibilities regarding the reporting of child abuse?

8. Briefly summarize copyright provisions for print, video, and software resources.

9. Describe the three guidelines teachers should keep in mind when dealing with student behavior that might lead to suspension or expulsion.

10. Describe three or four basic guidelines for the interface between religion and education.

11. Give examples of how students' rights may be abridged by their status as students as they have been decided in cases such as Tinker, Bethel/Fraser, and Hazelwood/Kuhlmeier.

Chapter 12 What Are Ethical and Legal Issues Facing Teachers?

Sample Chapter Quiz

A. Read each of the following questions, and write the letter of the best answer in the appropriate space on your answer sheet.

1. A teacher is notified on the day before school begins that no contract will be offered to him for that year. On hearing the teacher's objection, the principal announces that the teacher may plead the case for employment at the end of the school board meeting that night, at about 11 P.M. What violation of rights has been suffered by the teacher?
   a. Violation of the everyday ethics of teaching
   b. Violation of Fourteenth Amendment rights
   c. Violation of professional courtesy
   d. Violation of the right to due process

2. The case that resulted in a decision to permit teachers to discuss the theory of evolution in science classes was the
   a. *Scopes* case.
   b. *Nichols* case.
   c. *Pickering* case.
   d. *Kalamazoo* case.

3. In a public elementary or secondary school setting, *academic freedom* refers to a teacher's right to
   a. select any published course textbook that seems appropriate.
   b. use any reading in class that bears on the general subject of the course.
   c. select any published course textbook that seems appropriate, and use any reading in class that bears on the general subject of the course.
   d. use a reading for class if it is age-appropriate and directly relevant to the goals of the course curriculum.

4. The Family Educational Rights and Privacy Act, also known as the Buckley Amendment, guarantees the right of
   a. students to see teachers' personnel files.
   b. parents to see school files kept on their own children.
   c. teachers to see the files of students in the whole family.
   d. parents to see personnel files of their children's teachers.

5. Under current copyright laws, a teacher may
   a. copy a published article for use in preparing for class.
   b. tape off-the-air copies of special broadcasts for student viewing the next day.
   c. copy a published article for use in preparing for class and tape off-the-air copies of special broadcasts for student viewing the next day.
   d. neither copy a published article for use in preparing for class nor tape off-the-air copies of special broadcasts for student viewing the next day.

6. The rights protected under due process include
   a. the right to timely notice of dismissal.
   b. the right to wear one's hair in any style.
   c. the right to take public positions on policy.
   d. the right to take public positions on policy and the right to wear one's hair in any style.

7. A student accuses a teacher of having used profanity when she reprimanded him in the hall. The teacher is guaranteed by the Supreme Court decision in *Goldberg* v. *Kelly* (1970) that when this incident comes under investigation,
   a. she will have an impartial decision maker in the investigation.
   b. she will have an impartial decision maker in the investigation, and she may cross-examine witnesses.
   c. the school district will pay her legal fees.
   d. she may cross-examine witnesses.

8. Knowledge of the professional code of morality is particularly helpful for cases in which the teacher
   a. must decide whether to sign the contract offered for the following year.
   b. is asked to drive some students to a math contest.
   c. suspects that one of the children in class is bullying another.
   d. suspects that one of the children in class is abused at home.

9. A teacher should understand the professional code of morality that applies to education because
   a. teachers must help children learn about the place of moral codes in society.
   b. teachers have a special role in the lives of children.
   c. teachers must protect themselves from unjust court actions.
   d. teachers must help children learn about the place of moral codes in society, and they have a special role in the lives of children.

10. A tenured teacher is dismissed from her teaching position. According to the text, for which of the following reason(s) could a tenured teacher legally be dismissed?
    a. She had not demonstrated professional growth during the past several school years.
    b. She had written a letter to the editor of the local newspaper sharply criticizing the policies of the school board.
    c. There was a reduction in force in the school district.
    d. She had not demonstrated professional growth during the past several school years, and she had written a letter to the editor of the local newspaper sharply criticizing the policies of the school board.

B. Answer each of the following questions briefly in complete sentences.

1. What is the distinction between ethics and law in teaching? Give an example demonstrating each.

2. What is meant by the "everyday ethics of teaching"? Provide some examples.

Chapter 13 How Should Education Be Reformed?

Learning Objectives

After studying the chapter, students will be able to

- recognize the complexity of educational reform in the United States.
- identify and describe seven elements that are essential to true and lasting school reform.
- explain national efforts to bring about educational reform.
- describe state reform efforts, identifying common elements found in these efforts.
- identify successful state efforts to bring about educational reform.
- explain the constraining factors that restrict local reform efforts.

Chapter 13 How Should Education Be Reformed?

Study Guide

Completing this study guide will help you prepare for the major topic areas on an exam; however, it does not cover every piece of information found in the chapter or the test questions.

1. Identify and give an example of the three main aims of education.

2. List and describe the seven elements of education reform.

3. Explain the constructivist theory of learning.

4. Compare and contrast authentic assessment with the traditional model of assessment.

5. Describe the components of character education.

6. How are school choice, charter schools, site-based decision making, and vouchers related?

7. Explain the genesis and significance of the *A Nation at Risk* report.

8. What are five common components of state reform efforts?

9. List and give an example of each of the three initiatives to improve teacher quality.

10. Identity the five principles suggested to guide reform.

Chapter 13 How Should Education Be Reformed?

Sample Chapter Quiz

A. Read each of the following questions, and write the letter of the best answer in the appropriate space on your answer sheet.

1. The complexity of achieving educational reform is accentuated by the
   a. disagreement over universal education.
   b. lack of financial resources for private education.
   c. debate over class size.
   d. relative autonomy that schools enjoy.

2. Ryan and Cooper identify seven essential elements of true school reform. Which of the following is *not* one of these elements?
   a. Excellence
   b. Consensus
   c. Community
   d. Choice

3. In the call-to-excellence movements, students are expected to
   a. feel good about themselves.
   b. appreciate the importance of education.
   c. achieve high levels of academic performance.
   d. speak more than one language fluently.

4. Reformers advocate for smaller school because students
   a. feel a sense of belonging and become more engaged in their work.
   b. can get lost in the crowd and feel isolated.
   c. can see the chalkboard and hear the teacher better.
   d. do not have to walk as far to get from one class to the next.

5. Charter schools are seen as a way to reform schools because they
   a. offer an alternative type of education in a public school.
   b. are run by the state department of education.
   c. have a lower student-teacher ratio.
   d. require students to clean the school.

6. Joe's school requires that he complete twenty hours of community service in order to graduate. This requirement reflects a commitment to
   a. basic skills testing.
   b. teaching students life skills.
   c. improving the local economy.
   d. character education.

7. The most recent wave of educational reform efforts began with
   a. Desert Storm.
   b. Woodstock II.
   c. *A Nation at Risk.*
   d. the end of the Vietnam War.

8. Common among state reform proposals are
   a. higher teacher salaries and easier licensure criteria.
   b. fewer graduation requirements and longer school years.
   c. stricter graduation requirements and higher teacher salaries.
   d. longer school days and larger class sizes.

9. State reform efforts have been largely characterized by
   a. grassroots efforts coming from the teachers.
   b. top-down reform from state legislatures.
   c. collaborative efforts of teachers and administrators.
   d. federal mandates.

10. Local reform efforts have been
    a. limited because of scarcity of resources.
    b. driving the reform movement.
    c. nonexistent because of a lack of interest on the part of the teachers.
    d. most effective in bringing about change.

B. Answer each of the following questions briefly in complete sentences.

1. Why do Ryan and Cooper maintain that change is a slow process?

2. How does Goals 2000 reflect a commitment to reform education?

Chapter 14 What Are Your Job Options in Education?

Learning Objectives

After studying the chapter, students will be able to

- describe the current and projected job market in education.
- explain factors that affect the supply and demand of teaching positions.
- identify and explain effective job search strategies.
- describe the purpose of both traditional-route and alternative-route licensure.
- identify competencies and areas of specialized knowledge that may enhance their employment opportunities.
- identify other occupations for which they may be qualified on completion of a teacher education program.

Chapter 14 What Are Your Job Options in Education?

Study Guide

Completing this study guide will help you prepare for the major topic areas on an exam; however, it does not cover every piece of information found in the chapter or the test questions.

1. What are the major factors influencing the demand for new teachers?

2. What is the beginning teacher salary and the average teacher salary?

   National:

   Beginning ____________________

   Average ____________________

   Your state:

   Beginning ____________________

   Average ____________________

3. Describe the purpose and procedures for alternative licensure.

4. What are the advantages and disadvantages of teaching in a private school?

5. What are some other job options open to teachers besides classroom instruction?

6. What are the components of a successful job search?

7. Licensure requirements are enacted by states to accomplish what purpose?

8. Why is there a shortage of minority teachers?

9. Why is it important to have minority teachers (for white students as well as minority students)?

10. What are the advantages of substitute teaching while you are looking for a full-time position?

11. Distinguish between the terms *licensure* and *certification*.

Chapter 14 What Are Your Job Options in Education?

Sample Chapter Quiz

A. Read each of the following questions, and write the letter of the best answer in the appropriate space on your answer sheet.

1. According to the text, the strategy most likely to prepare a prospective teacher for a successful job search is
   a. specializing in physics and chemistry.
   b. moving to a community where teachers are in great demand.
   c. planning to work in a private school.
   d. acquiring exceptional competence, knowledge, and experience during preservice training.

2. General reports on the demand for teachers are limited in their usefulness for individual teachers because
   a. the figures are often incorrect, since it is difficult to predict with accuracy the number of teaching positions available.
   b. they may not specify the demand for a particular teaching area in which the prospective teacher is interested.
   c. such reports are difficult to interpret.
   d. the time it takes to collect and publish data makes some of the information dated.

3. The expected teacher shortage of the 1990s never materialized because
   a. not as many teachers retired as expected.
   b. not as many new students were enrolled as expected.
   c. not as many new teachers are looking for jobs as expected.
   d. schools had to make cutbacks and restricted hiring.

4. Which of the following plays a significant role in determining if a school district hires new teachers?
   a. Student enrollment
   b. National economy
   c. Number of alternative-route teaching candidates in the area
   d. Size and space of the physical plant

5. A public school teacher's salary is determined by his or her years of experience and
   a. any additional coaching or advising.
   b. the grade level taught.
   c. the level of education.
   d. the quality of teaching.

6. The shortage of minority teachers is problematic because
   a. minority students do not have enough positive minority role models.
   b. white students do not have enough positive white role models.
   c. educated minorities are going into other, higher-paying fields.
   d. many teachers are expected to retire in the next ten years.

7. Alternative teaching licensure programs are based on the premise that
   a. subject-matter knowledge alone is sufficient to teach.
   b. competency in teaching requires more field experience than does subject-based knowledge.
   c. this route to certification is less costly and more efficient than traditional teacher education programs.
   d. the state needs to have greater control over who becomes certified to teach.

8. States establish licensure requirements in order to
   a. attract the best to teaching.
   b. maintain authority over teachers.
   c. collect licensure fees.
   d. ensure that teachers meet a minimum standard of excellence.

9. Alternate licensure programs become popular when
   a. there is a shortage of teachers.
   b. there are salary negotiations for teachers.
   c. tests scores decline.
   d. the economy is slow.

10. An effective job search includes
    a. an academic rating of public schools.
    b. an individually typed cover letter for each school district.
    c. the names and addresses of current superintendents of area schools.
    d. the application to a very limited number of schools, thereby concentrating one's efforts.

B. Answer each of the following questions briefly in complete sentences.

1. How can prospective teaching candidates most effectively use data on expected teacher demand?

2. How can prospective teachers best prepare themselves for a job search?

Chapter 15 What Can the New Teacher Expect?

Learning Objectives

After studying the chapter, students will be able to

- define and discuss the culture shock experienced by first-year teachers.
- identify and explain the role of the principal and the principal's relationship to the teacher.
- identify and explain supervisors' roles in the school.
- summarize the authors' recommendations for the first day of teaching.
- identify the most reliable indicator of a teacher's success with students.
- describe the impact that other teachers can have on the first-year teacher's experience.
- describe and analyze the potential difficulties inherent in parent-teacher communication.
- identify and analyze the change that many first-year teachers undergo in their attitude toward children.
- explain and analyze the concept of "social distance" between teacher and student.
- identify and apply the practical teaching tips the authors supply for surviving the first year of teaching.

Chapter 15 What Can the New Teacher Expect?

Study Guide

Completing this study guide will help you prepare for the major topic areas on an exam; however, it does not cover every piece of information found in the chapter or the test questions.

1. Give a brief description of at least six of the nine roles principals play.

2. What kinds of help can new teachers expect from principals or supervisors?

3. According to the authors, what accounts for the very idealistic views of children and classrooms that most new teachers have when they begin teaching?

4. List and describe the reasons new teachers may experience discipline problems according to the authors.

5. What are the two extremes of behavior new teachers may adopt when trying to establish appropriate social distance? Describe the problem with this.

6. Identify and give an example of each of the five reasons for parent-teacher problems.

7. What are the seven recommendations the authors make for surviving the first years of teaching?

8. List the authors' six recommendations for getting off to a good start on the first day of school.

9. What are the authors' seven additional rules for surviving the first year of teaching?

Chapter 15 What Can the New Teacher Expect?

Sample Chapter Quiz

A. Read each of the following questions, and write the letter of the best answer in the appropriate space on your answer sheet.

1. The feeling of dislocation people experience when they initially encounter a foreign culture is called
   a. alienation.
   b. ennui.
   c. anxiety.
   d. culture shock.

2. The principal's role is to act as a liaison between the central office administration and his or her school. This is done by
   a. guiding teachers in achieving the district's curriculum goals.
   b. being the scapegoat for parental disgruntlement.
   c. frequently visiting the teachers in their classrooms.
   d. keeping abreast of current research and reform efforts.

3. A supervisor can help a new teacher because he or she
   a. can give the new teacher professional and pedagogical advice.
   b. can invite the new teacher to lunch.
   c. can give the new teacher job postings from other districts.
   d. can evaluate the new teacher officially.

4. Beginning teachers can look to colleagues in the school for
   a. support, ideas, and information.
   b. support, friendship, and role models.
   c. little practical help, but strong moral support.
   d. information about the school climate and students, and theoretical ideas about pedagogy.

5. After a typical first year, in which both victories and disasters abounded, two new teachers decide to grade their own performance. To what evidence should they give the greatest weight?
   a. Student achievement gains, considered in light of reasonable expectations
   b. Gains in evaluation ratings from the teachers' first to last formal administrative observations
   c. The number of students who indicated by word or action that they liked the teachers
   d. The number of supportive comments received by parents

6. From the start of preservice training to the end of the first year of teaching, how does the attitude of most new teachers change?
   a. At first they find children upsetting, but in the end they get more comfortable.
   b. At first they think children are really interesting, and by the end of that first year they are even more positive.
   c. At first they think children are cruel, but they come to appreciate their virtues.
   d. At first they think children are special, but in the end they think children are cruel.

7. Kayla is concerned about her knowledge of Spanish as she begins teaching middle school. However, after the first month, she realizes that a greater concern is
   a. classroom management.
   b. her salary.
   c. the workload.
   d. her unfriendly colleagues.

8. The recommendations made by the text for the teacher's first day include
   a. assigning some sort of homework activity, for those who teach above grade 2.
   b. acknowledging to students that the teacher "intends to make them work"—let the students know that the teacher is serious.
   c. learning and using the children's names.
   d. learning and using the children's names, and assigning some sort of homework activity for students above grade 2.

9. A frequent factor in the ineffectiveness of parent-teacher communication is that
   a. American parents believe that teachers are low-status people.
   b. teachers do not believe that parent involvement is necessary in children's education.
   c. parents and teachers have a different view of the strengths and weaknesses of the child.
   d. parents disagree with the curriculum being taught and refuse to talk with the teachers.

10. One of the most important reasons to maintain the social distance between student and teacher is that
    a. once the teacher loses that distance, it becomes increasingly difficult to assume authority again in the class.
    b. it is inappropriate for a teacher and student to have a warm relationship.
    c. that is the traditional way students and teachers have interacted.
    d. too many people would misinterpret informality between student and teacher.

B. Answer each of the following questions briefly in complete sentences.

1. Explain the role of the principal in a school.

2. According to most research, what is the first-year teacher's biggest challenge?

Chapter 16 What Does It Mean to Be a Professional?

Learning Objectives

After studying the chapter, students will be able to

- trace the major developments in the history of teaching and teacher education from the colonial period to the present.
- identify the defining characteristics of a profession.
- identify and describe arguments that support the position that teaching is a profession and those that support the contention that it is not.
- discuss the role of the two major professional organizations in education, the National Education Association and the American Federation of Teachers.
- explain continuous learning opportunities available to teachers.

Chapter 16 What Does It Mean to Be a Professional?

Study Guide

Completing this study guide will help you prepare for the major topic areas on an exam; however, it does not cover every piece of information found in the chapter or the test questions.

1. Briefly describe the historical development of teacher education.

2. List the criteria that must be satisfied for teaching to be considered a profession and indicate which of these criteria teaching meets.

3. Compare and contrast the characteristics of the NEA and the AFT.

4. Describe what the National Board for Professional Teaching Standards is and how it could affect your career in teaching.

5. List and give examples of the types of continuing education opportunities for teachers.

6. Explain what a "normal" school was and what the name *normal* refers to.

Chapter 16 What Does It Mean to Be a Professional?

Sample Chapter Quiz

A. Read each of the following questions, and write the letter of the best answer in the appropriate space on your answer sheet.

1. Changes in teacher education over the past two hundred years have led to
   a. a principal focus on pedagogy over subject-matter knowledge.
   b. more in-depth subject-matter knowledge and pedagogical training.
   c. more demands on teachers and longer school days.
   d. higher salaries but lower qualifications.

2. One contributing factor to explain the influx of women into teaching in the nineteenth century was
   a. the vulgarization of schooling, creating a need for many teachers.
   b. the paucity of men because of the war.
   c. the teaching superiority of women.
   d. the better moral fiber of women.

3. At normal schools, the students learned
   a. the ordinary values, or norms, of society.
   b. the norms, or rules, of teaching.
   c. the usual, or normal, college subjects.
   d. the norms of childhood behavior.

4. To be defined as a professional, a worker must
   a. provide an essential service, relying on intellectual skills.
   b. have considerable autonomy and be accountable for the consequences of work.
   c. provide an essential service, relying on intellectual skills, and have considerable autonomy and accountability for work.
   d. provide an essential service, relying on either intellectual or craftsman skills, with extensive accountability for work.

5. One could argue that teaching is *not* a profession because
   a. teachers have limited power.
   b. teachers do not provide an essential skill.
   c. teaching does not particularly require intellectual skill.
   d. teachers do not earn high salaries.

6. Why is there a need for continuous education for teachers?
   a. Universities are very expensive now.
   b. Teachers do not know how to teach very well when they finish college.
   c. The needs of the students are constantly changing.
   d. Teachers need a break from the classroom.

7. The National Board of Professional Teaching Standards is developing a board certification for teachers in order to
   a. make it easier to become a teacher.
   b. establish a baseline of effective teaching.
   c. relieve the states of the burden of licensure.
   d. create a career ladder for administrators.

8. The teacher organization that represents about three out of four public elementary and secondary teachers and that takes a relatively conservative stand on school reform issues is the
   a. National Education Association.
   b. American Federation of Teachers.
   c. Association for Curriculum and Development.
   d. American Educational Research Association.

9. A difference between the AFT and the NEA is that the NEA
   a. is much older than the AFT.
   b. is more progressive than the AFT.
   c. is more concerned with teacher autonomy and the AFT is concerned with national issues.
   d. has always been more aggressive in pursuing teachers' benefits and salaries.

10. Ryan and Cooper contend that teaching is a semiprofession because
   a. new teachers coming in are more professional than the ones currently teaching.
   b. Congress will pass legislation soon on the status of teaching.
   c. it is continually changing and developing more professional-like characteristics.
   d. teachers frequently take part in professional development activities.

B. Answer each of the following questions briefly in complete sentences.

1. If you were to join a teachers' association, which one would it be, the NEA or AFT? Support your answers with reference to the work of both organizations.

2. Why was the shift from teacher training to teacher education in the 1950s an important one?

Answers to Chapter Quizzes

CHAPTER 1 Why Teach?

A. Multiple Choice

1. a	6. c
2. c	7. b
3. d	8. b
4. b	9. a
5. a	10. d

B. Suggested Answers to Questions

1. The ways in which a person can explore whether teaching is a suitable match for him or her is through real experience, vicarious experience, reflection, and counsel. Real experience entails working with students in a school or school-like setting. Vicarious experience is gained from reading books, talking to other teachers, and watching movies. Reflection entails carefully thinking about why you want to be a teacher and what you hope to accomplish. Counsel is the considered advice from those whom know you.

2. An intrinsic reward is something that exists within the work itself. For example, the pleasure of working with children is an intrinsic reward of teaching; working closely with children is an integral part of a teacher's job. Other intrinsic rewards in teaching include the performance of an important social service, the contribution to one's community, working in a collegial atmosphere, and the teaching itself.

CHAPTER 2 What Is a School?

A. Multiple Choice

1. c	6. b
2. a	7. a
3. c	8. a
4. a	9. b
5. a	10. c

B. Suggested Answers to Questions

1. A school as a social panacea sees the school as doing whatever is necessary to relieve the social problems of society. If students are threatened with AIDS, then the school should provide AIDS instruction. If the community has a problem with widespread alcohol abuse,

then the schools should provide instruction or training in resisting substance abuse. The school as an institution is used as a vehicle for combating social ills and problems.

2. Many would argue that cultural transmission is a vital element of public schools, for it is through cultural transmission that the country is able to forge some unity and some sense of purpose in its people. Furthermore, supporters of cultural transmission would argue that it was particularly vital that schools acted as transmitters of culture when our country was accepting millions of immigrants during the early twentieth century. Otherwise, the country would have splintered into various different ethnic groups without any common bond. Similar arguments appear now. In addition, many people who support cultural transmission feel that a society will not endure unless the values, beliefs, and practices are passed down from one generation to another.

CHAPTER 3 What Is Life in Schools Like?

A. Multiple Choice

1. a
2. b
3. a
4. a
5. b
6. a
7. d
8. d
9. a
10. b

B. Suggested Answers to Questions

1. These groups are not just cliques, as described by Eckert, but cultural categories. They define or reflect to a great degree the student's perspective on the world. Understanding these groups as representatives of a cultural view is an important step for teachers to take toward understanding the world of the adolescent. Also, public schools haven't been consistently effective in bringing alienated subcultures into greater participation in the school. There are thousands of students whom teachers do not reach.

2. Most studies show that little has changed in either the organizational patterns or the instructional practices in most high schools in the recent past.

CHAPTER 4 Who Are Today's Students?

A. Multiple Choice

1. c
2. b
3. c
4. a
5. b
6. d
7. c
8. a
9. d
10. a

B. Suggested Answers to Questions

1. Educators who oppose multicultural education in schools do so because they are concerned that a focus on multiculturalism will destroy any sense of common tradition, values, and beliefs in the American society. They recommend that cultural pluralism be limited.

2. Because the student population is expected to become more diverse while the teaching population remains heavily white female, the two groups (minority students and white teachers) may have difficulty relating to one another, thus limiting the effectiveness of the learning environment.

CHAPTER 5 What Social Problems and Tension Points Affect Today's Students?

A. Multiple Choice

1. b	6. c
2. d	7. c
3. c	8. d
4. b	9. c
5. a	10. d

B. Suggested Answers to Questions

1. Children who have been abused need to be able, more than anything else, to learn to trust people again. For that reason, it is vital that a teacher be a positive, trustworthy role model. The teacher should set the tone for the class, and much of the teacher's time should be spent in creating an environment in which children can expect or trust certain things to happen. That doesn't mean that the teacher can never change the routine of the day; rather, it means that children will know that the teacher will maintain a consistently fair atmosphere in the class. Also, the teacher should take care that he or she follows through on things said to students so that students will know that the teacher is to be trusted.

2. Although many educators and social scientists saw education as a way out of poverty, schools are middle-class institutions with middle-class values and look down on the poor, who may not share these same values. These poor students become more and more disengaged with school and are not very successful. The cycle of poverty remains.

CHAPTER 6 What Makes a Teacher Effective?

A. Multiple Choice

1. a	6. a
2. b	7. d
3. c	8. b
4. a	9. d
5. c	10. b

B. Suggested Answers to Questions

1. Theoretical knowledge gives one the ability to interpret situations, solve problems, and avoid pat solutions to problems in the classroom.

2. A reflective teacher is one who has developed the attitudes and skills to become a lifelong student of teaching. A reflective teacher examines his or her teaching practices and asks questions like "What am I doing and why?" "How can I meet my students' needs better?"

CHAPTER 7 What Should Teachers Know About Technology and Its Impact on Schools?

A. Multiple Choice

1. d	6. d
2. c	7. b
3. a	8. b
4. c	9. c
5. b	10. c

B. Suggested Answers to Questions

1. Answers should include references to using the computer for communication, for instruction, for presentation, to enhance productivity, and so on.

2. Answers could include lack of funding in low socioeconomic areas, inadequate electrical systems, lack of access to the Internet, and poorly trained teachers.

CHAPTER 8 What Is Taught?

A. Multiple Choice

1. b	6. b
2. a	7. c
3. c	8. c
4. d	9. d
5. b	10. b

B. Suggested Answers to Questions

1. A core curriculum presents a shared understanding of our national culture, history, and traditions: a Eurocentric curriculum. A multicultural curriculum involves cultural pluralism. The curriculum should reflect the contributions and experiences of American people of all ethnic backgrounds.

2. Interdisciplinary teaching allows students to experience coherence in the curriculum and connections to real-world situations. They see that all knowledge is related, so that what they learn in one subject is reinforced in another.

CHAPTER 9 How Are Schools Governed, Influenced, and Financed?

A. Multiple Choice

1. a	6. b
2. d	7. d
3. c	8. a
4. a	9. a
5. d	10. c

B. Suggested Answers to Questions

1. Because the state department of education's responsibilities include the accreditation of college and university educational certification programs, as well as certifying teachers, it is more likely that they will have a greater direct impact on the life of a prospective teacher.

2. Many school systems depend on local property taxes to raise funds to run the schools, so the wealthier towns have more money to run their schools than the less affluent towns. Therefore, the children who live in wealthier towns have better educational opportunities, and those in the less affluent towns receive unequal educational opportunities, which is in conflict with state constitutions that guarantee equal educational opportunities.

CHAPTER 10 What Are the Philosophical Foundations of American Education?

A. Multiple Choice

1. d	6. b
2. c	7. a
3. c	8. b
4. b	9. d
5. c	10. c

B. Suggested Answers to Questions

1. Essentialism is a highly pragmatic philosophy of education. It looks to what one will need to function in society and includes those skills and subjects in the curriculum. In that respect, it is closely linked to the demands of the market, because functioning in society is typically understood to be working and contributing to the country.

2. Understanding the philosophy of education transforms a teacher from being merely a skilled or technical deliverer of information to being a professional educator. With the understanding of different philosophies of education, a teacher will know more clearly his or her goals, his or her methods for teaching, and the reasons behind all the decisions he or she will make. The teacher will also be able to spot more easily any inconsistencies in practice.

CHAPTER 11 What Is the History of American Education?

A. Multiple Choice

1. c
2. a
3. b
4. a
5. a
6. a
7. c
8. c
9. c
10. b

B. Suggested Answers to Questions

1. See text for brief biographies.
2. Some type of religious instruction, whether it was reading the Lord's Prayer or learning moral and religious values from a primer, made up much of early American education. During the early to mid-nineteenth century, however, the emphasis on religious instruction diminished as the demand for students skilled in practical trades or possessing functional knowledge for life after school drove the formal curriculum. More emphasis was placed on practical subjects and less on religious instruction.

CHAPTER 12 What Are Ethical and Legal Issues Facing Teachers?

A. Multiple Choice

1. d
2. a
3. d
4. b
5. c
6. a
7. b
8. c
9. d
10. c

B. Suggested Answers to Questions

1. Ethics is the code of morality followed by a particular group of people. For professional groups, there is frequently a code of ethics that the professionals agree to follow. The National Education Association, for example, has a code of ethics for educators. The laws are agreed-on rules that a community must follow. The law is part of the system of rules governing the community. Examples of ethics and law in teaching will vary, but the examples should be clear indications of ethics or law. Examples of an ethical act by a teacher are encouraging a discouraged student to do the best he or she can on an activity and treating each child fairly. Examples of laws are the laws regarding reporting suspected child abuse and regarding the procedures for search and seizure of students' lockers.
2. The everyday ethics of teaching, according to the authors, involve teaching every day in the manner in which it ought to be done. That means doing the job to the best of one's professional ability. Every day, a teacher has to make hundreds of small ethical decisions, and if a teacher is observing the everyday ethics of teaching he or she will approach each of

these decisions in a consistent, thoughtful manner with goodwill. Some examples includes not taking a "sick" day unless one really is ill; spending time carefully responding to students' work and returning work within a reasonable time; putting care into the daily planning of lessons; treating all students fairly; and not gossiping about colleagues, students, or administrators.

CHAPTER 13 How Should Education Be Reformed?

A. Multiple Choice

1. d
2. b
3. c
4. a
5. a
6. d
7. c
8. c
9. b
10. a

B. Suggested Answers to Questions

1. Ryan and Cooper explain their position by noting the size of American education, which involves 15,000 centers of decision and 50 million people, and influences from many quarters of society. More important, it has a standard operating procedure that is very hard and slow to alter.

2. Goals 2000 grew out of America 2000, a statement on American education developed by the country's governors at the education summit in 1989. Because the states have control over educational practices, a national commitment to improving education had to come from the governors. The six goals in America 2000 were adopted by the governors, who pledged their commitment to achieving these goals.

CHAPTER 14 What Are Your Job Options in Education?

A. Multiple Choice

1. a
2. d
3. d
4. a
5. c
6. a
7. a
8. d
9. a
10. b

B. Suggested Answers to Questions

1. Prospective teachers may use published data to provide them with some information on general trends, such as geographical areas or subject specialties in which there will be an expected demand. Yet prospective teachers should also recognize that such reports can change rapidly and may vary according to a variety of factors.

2. First, prospective teachers should attempt to get the most thorough training and extensive education that they can. When looking for a job, they should prepare a job file that includes their college transcript, several letters of recommendation, a résumé, and individually written and typed letters to school districts.

CHAPTER 15 What Can the New Teacher Expect?

A. Multiple Choice

1. d	6. d
2. a	7. a
3. a	8. c
4. a	9. c
5. a	10. a

B. Suggested Answers to Questions

1. Principals play a number of different roles in the school. They are the liaison between the teachers and the superintendent; they are reward dispensers; they act as buffers between angry parents and teachers. They can be helpers and evaluators of teachers. Because they play so many different roles, it is not unusual for them to be in conflict.

2. One of the best ways to prepare prospective teachers for their experience in schools is to prepare them with a number of field experiences and have them read accounts of first-year teachers to learn about the difficult change in perspective. Knowing about teachers' somewhat negative feelings toward students at the end of the year will serve to prepare the prospective teachers.

CHAPTER 16 What Does It Mean to Be a Professional?

A. Multiple Choice

1. b	6. c
2. a	7. b
3. b	8. a
4. c	9. a
5. a	10. c

B. Suggested Answers to Questions

1. Answers will vary.

2. The shift from teacher training to teacher education gave recognition to the concept of pedagogy and the need for teachers to study pedagogy rather than just the subject matter.

Note to Instructors: This form is provided for use by students who are reviewing *Kaleidoscope* articles as part of their foundations course.

Article Review Form

Feel free to photocopy this page and use it to help you review each article you read in this edition of *Kaleidoscope.*

Name: ______________________ Date: ____________ Article no.: ________

Title: ____________________________ Author's name: ______________

In your own words, briefly state the main idea of the article:

____

____

____

____

With what points or arguments made by the author(s) do you agree or disagree:

Agree:

____

____

____

Disagree:

____

____

____

What did you learn from the article that you think is (1) important, (2) interesting, and (3) unclear?

(1) ____

(2) ____

(3) ____

List any new terms or concepts you found in the article, and briefly define them:

____

____

____

____

____

____

Part IV Assessment Materials

FOR EACH CHAPTER

- Multiple-Choice Items with Answer Key
- Short-Answer Questions with Suggested Answers
- Essay Questions
- Alternative Assessment Ideas
    - Independent Reading
    - Reflective Papers
    - Journal Writing

Chapter 1 *Why Teach?*

Multiple-Choice Items

Read each item carefully. On the appropriate line, write the letter of the choice that represents the best answer.

d _____ 1. Denise, a medical sales representative, is considering a career switch to teaching. She is bright, outgoing, and likes the high pay she has earned in sales. Yet she has felt drawn to teaching because of the positive contribution she could make to students' lives. If she makes the career switch, which reward is Denise *least* likely to experience in teaching?

a. a lively intellectual atmosphere with colleagues and students
b. a work schedule offering generous personal time
c. the satisfaction of contributing positively to others' lives
d. a salary that rivals other professional salaries

c _____ 2. Telly, the president of the senior class at State U., thinks he would enjoy teaching history and civics, because he has always taken a prominent role in student government and finds politics fascinating. If Telly decides to become a teacher, which of the following of Telly's interests would *least* likely be satisfied in a teaching career?

a. his pleasure in working with other people
b. the opportunity to learn more about history and civics
c. his attraction to status
d. the opportunity to help create change in people's lives

b _____ 3. Juan, a talented young artist, has already had some of his watercolors displayed at showings. In addition to painting, he also enjoys teaching painting to young children. He feels strongly that art should be part of every child's education. If Juan decides to become an art teacher, which of the following extrinsic rewards will he most certainly experience?
a. the status and recognition of being an accomplished teacher
b. a generous work schedule, providing him time to paint
c. a secure and high salary
d. the sense of power that he will be able to change curriculum

c _____ 4. Tai is a college sophomore with numerous interests. Teaching has always appealed to her, yet she is not sure if teaching will be the most satisfying career. Which of the following is the best indication that Tai would find satisfaction in teaching?
a. She feels a strong desire to contribute to society and wants a secure salary.
b. She wants recognition for her work, and she enjoys working with people.
c. She wants to perform an important social service, and she enjoys intellectual stimulation.
d. She wants to work with others and wants a work schedule with ample personal time.

d _____ 5. Of the following extrinsic rewards, which is most closely associated with teaching?
a. a competitive salary
b. high status and prestige
c. power over one's subordinates and working associates
d. a work schedule allowing generous time for oneself

b _____ 6. What is the best indication that you will be satisfied teaching?
a. listening to your parents, friends, and others who know you well who think that teaching would be a good career for you
b. being attracted to performing an important social service
c. knowing that children usually like you very much
d. enjoying the power and influence you can have upon others

d _____ 7. Intrinsic rewards in teaching include
a. the close work with young people, the actual teaching, and the power in the career.
b. performing a significant social service and the flexible work schedule.
c. the salary, the actual teaching, and the status.
d. the actual teaching and satisfaction from the performance of an important social service.

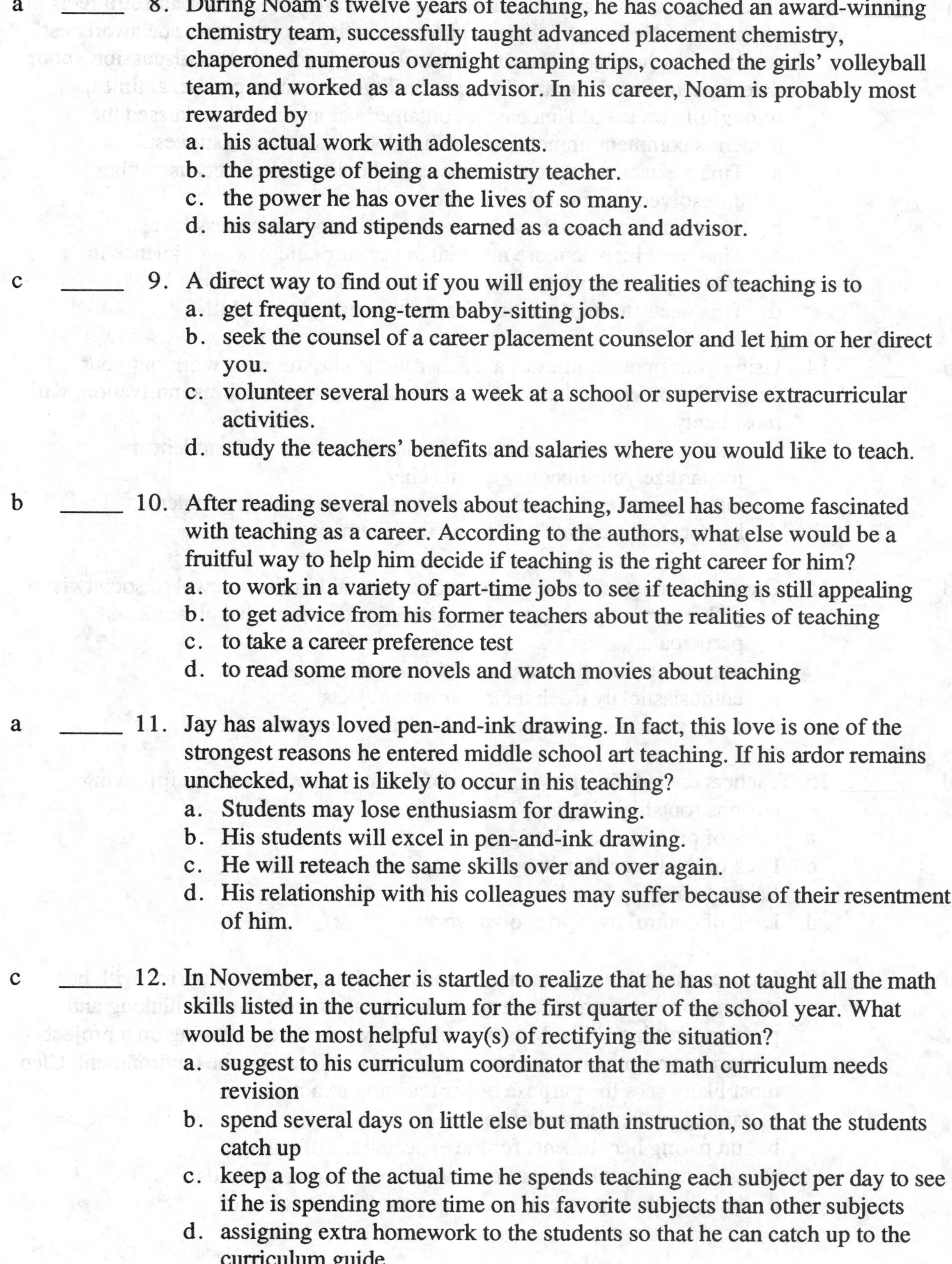

a ______ 8. During Noam's twelve years of teaching, he has coached an award-winning chemistry team, successfully taught advanced placement chemistry, chaperoned numerous overnight camping trips, coached the girls' volleyball team, and worked as a class advisor. In his career, Noam is probably most rewarded by
a. his actual work with adolescents.
b. the prestige of being a chemistry teacher.
c. the power he has over the lives of so many.
d. his salary and stipends earned as a coach and advisor.

c ______ 9. A direct way to find out if you will enjoy the realities of teaching is to
a. get frequent, long-term baby-sitting jobs.
b. seek the counsel of a career placement counselor and let him or her direct you.
c. volunteer several hours a week at a school or supervise extracurricular activities.
d. study the teachers' benefits and salaries where you would like to teach.

b ______ 10. After reading several novels about teaching, Jameel has become fascinated with teaching as a career. According to the authors, what else would be a fruitful way to help him decide if teaching is the right career for him?
a. to work in a variety of part-time jobs to see if teaching is still appealing
b. to get advice from his former teachers about the realities of teaching
c. to take a career preference test
d. to read some more novels and watch movies about teaching

a ______ 11. Jay has always loved pen-and-ink drawing. In fact, this love is one of the strongest reasons he entered middle school art teaching. If his ardor remains unchecked, what is likely to occur in his teaching?
a. Students may lose enthusiasm for drawing.
b. His students will excel in pen-and-ink drawing.
c. He will reteach the same skills over and over again.
d. His relationship with his colleagues may suffer because of their resentment of him.

c ______ 12. In November, a teacher is startled to realize that he has not taught all the math skills listed in the curriculum for the first quarter of the school year. What would be the most helpful way(s) of rectifying the situation?
a. suggest to his curriculum coordinator that the math curriculum needs revision
b. spend several days on little else but math instruction, so that the students catch up
c. keep a log of the actual time he spends teaching each subject per day to see if he is spending more time on his favorite subjects than other subjects
d. assigning extra homework to the students so that he can catch up to the curriculum guide

a _____ 13. Tina suffered a vicious assault when she was a college senior and still feels the aftereffects. Now, several years later, she actively organizes rape awareness seminars for her high school students. During a recent class discussion about date rape, one student raised the possibility that people can be, at times, wrongfully accused. Tina barely contained her anger and dismissed the student's comment immediately. What does this scenario suggest?

a. Tina's effectiveness as a teacher may be diminished because of her unresolved personal problems.
b. Tina must continue to work to raise students' awareness levels.
c. Tina must include more material in her curriculum about violence in contemporary society.
d. Tina needs to improve her classroom management skills.

b _____ 14. Using your opportunities as a teacher in the classroom to work out your personal problems, whether it is a conscious or unconscious motivation, will most likely

a. enable you to communicate more honestly with your students.
b. jeopardize your integrity as a teacher.
c. allow you to encourage students to get help for their problems.
d. hinder your students' academic achievement.

d _____ 15. One of the most effective ways teachers can aid in the renewal of society is to

a. pick a service project for their classes and require that all students participate.
b. work on political campaigns with fellow teachers.
c. enthusiastically teach their favorite subjects.
d. teach students to become involved and informed citizens.

d _____ 16. Teachers considering leaving the profession gave which of the following reasons (outside of salary)?

a. Lack of professional prestige
b. Lack of intellectual challenge
c. Lack of vacation benefits
d. Lack of control over your own work

a _____ 17. Cleo, an earth science teacher, spends considerable time working with her students on environmental projects that demand their critical-thinking and problem-solving skills. Most recently, they have been working on a project exploring groundwater contamination and its effects on the environment. Cleo most likely sees the purpose of her teaching as a means of

a. aiding in the renewal of society.
b. preparing her students for the expectations of college.
c. gaining recognition for her innovative teaching methods.
d. helping students memorize important facts in science.

b _____ 18. One way to predict what we might accomplish as teachers is to ask ourselves this question:
a. What subjects most interest me?
b. Why should I teach?
c. What are the extrinsic and intrinsic rewards in teaching?
d. What are my personal skills?

c _____ 19. According to the authors of this text, the question "Why teach?" is important because our answer is a good indicator of
a. what kind of institution is best for our training.
b. what subjects we will teach.
c. what we will accomplish as teachers.
d. whether we will be effective teachers.

Short-Answer Questions

Respond to each of the following questions briefly, but specifically, in complete sentences.

20. In most respects, teaching ranks rather low in all extrinsic rewards except for one. Which extrinsic reward is it, and how can teachers use it best?

(suggested answer) The one extrinsic reward most noted in teaching is the work schedule. Because of the frequent vacations throughout the school year and during the summer, teaching offers a work schedule that allows the teacher more time at his or her disposal than most other professions. Professional development and planning ahead for the next school year are two constructive ways to use the time.

21. One way of deciding if a teaching career is for you is through vicarious experience. Although very helpful, vicarious experience also has its limitations in helping you decide if teaching is for you. Name and explain the strengths and limitations of using vicarious experience in your decision to become a teacher.

(suggested answer) Vicarious experience can help by providing you with experience you may not have had. Therefore, reading a book or watching a movie about teachers may show you intriguing aspects of the profession. However, one must also remember that the vicarious experience you gain from reading a book or watching a movie may not always be completely realistic. In literature, movies, and other art forms, particular facets are emphasized to create interest, so the actual book or movie may not be factually correct in every detail.

22. In one of the short narratives in the text, Julia recognized that her deep interest in science was both an advantage and a disadvantage. Describe the advantages and disadvantages and their effects as well as how Julia could change her instruction to solve her problems.

(Answers will vary.)

23. In the text, Fred repeatedly asks for "low-achieving" classes in history because he has a strong commitment to helping those students become involved, reflective citizens. He strongly believes that preparing those students to become participating citizens is vital for the renewal of society. In the teaching field you are considering, what could you do in your classes to enhance students' abilities in active citizenship? How does that relate to the renewal of society?

    (suggested answer) Answers will vary, but ideas should clearly demonstrate how a teaching strategy or activity helps enhance students' critical thinking. Also, educating students to become active, reflective citizens aids in the renewal of society because participating citizens are fundamental for the maintenance of a democracy. Active citizens can successfully work toward the improvement of society.

Essay Questions

Read each of the following questions, and respond by composing an organized essay that includes an introduction, fully developed paragraph(s), and a conclusion.

24. Many would argue that the rewards of a task are what propel people to become actively engaged in their work. Rewards, both intrinsic and extrinsic, reside in all occupations to some degree or another. What are the extrinsic rewards of an occupation, and to what degree would you claim that teaching supplies those extrinsic rewards? What are the intrinsic rewards associated with teaching? Identify and explain them.

    (suggested answer) The extrinsic rewards are salary, status, power, and work schedule. Teaching does not typically reward teachers with high salaries; however, some could argue that teachers' salaries are improving in certain geographical areas, based on the attention to education and the increased expectations for teachers. In the United States, teaching has never been considered a high-status job, perhaps partly because of the lack of power a teacher has in comparison to other professions. A teacher's work schedule, with its frequent vacations, is the strongest extrinsic reward.

    The intrinsic rewards in teaching are teaching itself, working with students, working in a collegial atmosphere, and performing a vital social service.

25. One teacher recalled that he decided to go into teaching because of a daydream he had. He imagined teaching biology to students and having them really interested in him and what he was teaching them. He also imagined himself acting as a counselor and mentor to his students. Other than that pleasant daydream, he had little opportunity to test out his attraction to teaching. For someone attracted to teaching, what are some useful sources of experience to help in the career choice? Analyze three types of useful experience, explaining the benefits of each.

    (suggested answer) The authors contend that actual work with children and adolescents is a very useful way of determining if one would be happy as a teacher. Several possibilities

exist for prospective teachers to test out. They are baby-sitting, working as a camp counselor, working at the Y or other club as an instructor, serving as an assistant coach for Little League or other athletic team, either assisting or working as a religious teacher at a church or temple, serving as a Big Brother or Big Sister, working at a preschool, day care center, or the like, and tutoring a younger student. With each possibility selected, the answer should demonstrate how that particular experience adds to one's useful knowledge of teaching. For example, tutoring or baby-sitting usually involves only one or two children, whereas coaching a Little League team requires work with many children. Another distinction is that tutoring, coaching, or instructing involves actual teaching whereas baby-sitting or serving as a Big Brother or Sister may not involve direct teaching.

Alternative Assessment Ideas

The following activities are suggestions for student portfolio activities. They are a means of providing alternative assessment of the students' capabilities.

Independent Reading

Read and respond to any of the following selections from Ryan/Cooper, *Kaleidoscope: Readings in Education* (Houghton Mifflin, 1998). You may want to use the Article Review Form on page 269.

Csikszentmihalyi and McCormack—"The Influence of Teachers"

Fried—"The Heart of the Matter"

Metzger—"Calling in the Cosmos"

Reflective Papers

Choose one of the following topics to write a reflective paper (2–5 pages). The purpose of the paper is to help you assimilate new knowledge by blending it with your previous knowledge and experiences.

1. Many people who choose to teach have vivid, warm memories of one (or several) teachers. Choose one memorable teacher from your schooling and write a descriptive paper about him or her. What made that teacher memorable to you? Are there any key events that made you remember this teacher? From your perspective, what made him or her such a good teacher?

2. Conversely, many people choose to teach, in part, because they had a terrible teacher at one point in their education. Choose a teacher who made a negative impression on you and write a description of this person. How did that teacher behave with students? What was his or her teaching style? Why do you have negative memories of that teacher? From your perspective, what were some of the person's attributes that made him or her a poor teacher?

3. Select any of the real teacher story books listed in "Additional Resources for Instructors" or others approved by the instructor. Analyze the teacher's motive for entering teaching, his or her philosophy, and the theme(s) reflected in the story. Include your reaction to the story.

Journal Writing

Suggestions for journal topics for students' selection:

1. Articulate your own reasons for becoming a teacher as you understand them.
2. Indicate your thoughts and feelings after observing in a classroom like one in which you will teach.
3. Describe the characteristics of your own most significant teacher.

Chapter 2 What Is a School?

Multiple-Choice Items

Read each item carefully. On the appropriate line, write the letter of the choice that represents the best answer.

d ____ 1. Which of the following statements best exemplifies the definition of education presented in the text?
   a. "After I finish that one biology course, I'll have all the education I'll need to be a medical doctor."
   b. "I never was very interested in schooling and education. I prefer to teach myself things I'm interested in."
   c. "I completed my education in 1989. Since then, I've been working for J & K Associates."
   d. "I'm a newspaper reporter by trade, but over the past few years, I've learned carpentry and I am perfecting my skills."

b ____ 2. Which of the following is the best definition of education, according to the text? Education is
   a. technical proficiency in skills and knowledge that allows one to maneuver throughout the world.
   b. a continual growth process whereby a person gains greater understanding of himself or herself and the world.
   c. extensive knowledge of several discrete areas that allows one to become a productive member of society.
   d. a formal process of instruction and learning by which one learns to read, write, compute, problem-solve, and think critically about issues.

c _____ 3. Schooling is most generally defined as
a. a process of human growth that leads to greater self-control.
b. a formal arrangement designed so that students will achieve their creative potential.
c. a specific, formalized process aimed mostly at the young.
d. an experience over a set period of time spent in an institution.

a _____ 4. When a student is able to exist productively in a rule-bound system and can read, write, and compute, it is probably the result of his or her
a. schooling.
b. vocational training.
c. self-discipline.
d. directed study.

d _____ 5. Which of the following people would find the school's formal statement of purpose most useful for his or her task at hand?
a. a new teacher seeking information on the best approach for teaching a unit in social studies
b. a new union representative, curious about the community's financial support of its public schools
c. a parent moving into the community, curious about what her daughter will be doing next year in the fourth grade
d. the principal encouraging the teachers to strive to meet the ideals held by the school and community regarding education

c _____ 6. Which of the following statements would most likely be found in a formal statement of a school's purpose?
a. "By the end of kindergarten, students will be able to match letters with sounds and will have completed several journals of their original writing composed with invented spelling."
b. "Teachers are expected to be in their classrooms thirty minutes before the beginning of school and remain thirty minutes after the last bus has left in the afternoon."
c. "It is important that all students achieve success; therefore, each student will follow a course program specifically designed to help him or her become a productive, contributing member of the community."
d. "All teachers are encouraged to enroll in staff development seminars; therefore, three times a year the school will provide a selection of workshops and seminars for teachers."

b _____ 7. "The biggest mistake our schools ever made was in encouraging these kids to become 'individuals.' They need to learn how to work with each other efficiently and to take pride in the work that they do. I urge the board to move toward the redesign of our schools' mission," commented one school board member. This school board member is advocating the model of schools as

a. acculturators.
b. trainer of workers.
c. shopping malls.
d. social panaceas.

d _____ 8. The "product" of schools run on the trainer model is students who

a. become craftspeople.
b. work quickly.
c. fit into dominant U.S. culture.
d. become good workers.

b _____ 9. A typical student in her high school, Keisha is enrolled in physics, trigonometry, Spanish IV, English, and U.S. history. Her school would most likely be described by the model of school as

a. social escalator.
b. preparer for college.
c. acculturator.
d. trainer of workers.

c _____ 10. Which of the following best typifies the view of a school board member who sees schools' purpose as preparing students for college?

a. "How many electives will the high school be able to offer in the fall?"
b. "Are the teachers prepared to meet the different learning styles of the students so they can succeed?"
c. "Wouldn't it make sense to add another hour to the school day so students can enroll in another academic course?"
d. "How are our school's graduates doing in their chosen paths? What can we do to strengthen their skills?"

b _____ 11. Although Donna is a bright and creative student, her teacher is concerned because Donna forgets to follow the standard procedure for completing and preparing her work. Donna's school most likely represents which of the following models?

a. trainer type
b. bureaucracy type
c. social escalator type
d. college prep type

c _____ 12. The goal of schools in the bureaucracy model is to produce students who
a. thrive working in an office with numerous coworkers.
b. think independently.
c. work productively in a rule-bound system.
d. assume leadership within an organization.

a _____ 13. Russ Williams is a teacher in a "shopping mall" high school. Which of the following best typifies how he teaches?
a. He provides students with numerous activities from which to choose. He grades their work easily, so that they will continue to come to class and be cooperative with him.
b. He stresses cooperative learning groups and group tutoring, believing that peers engage each other's interest better than an adult.
c. He assigns frequent, rigorous assignments. He pushes the students to achieve excellence and praises them for industriousness.
d. He designs individual activities for each student that help the student achieve his or her potential in that area.

c _____ 14. Hildi has selected her courses for the academic year, but she finds, after one week, that two of the courses do not interest her. She plans a meeting with her guidance counselor to rearrange her schedule. If this school is accurately represented by the "shopping mall" model, her guidance counselor will most likely
a. provide her with a series of forms to fill out and steps to complete so that her registration will be accurate.
b. tell her that it is a poor habit to switch courses so early in the year; she should learn to work hard and develop good work habits for her future.
c. show her the course listings of numerous other courses available at the times she requested and sign her drop-add sheet to expedite the process.
d. encourage her to take courses that will best further her goals.

b _____ 15. Ben Franklin, with his great range of talents and notable curiosity, might well be a role model for which type of school?
a. college prep type
b. human development type
c. social escalator type
d. acculturator type

a _____ 16. Which of the following programs would be well suited to a human development model of a school?

a. an individual reading program designed to stimulate a lifelong interest in reading
b. a career education course designed to inform high school students of the careers available and the requirements for each one
c. a math program designed to boost every student's math scores on standardized tests by 15 to 20 percent
d. a personal keyboarding and computer course designed to help students strengthen their skills on the computer

d _____ 17. Sophie Kao urges her working-class students to learn all they can and to work hard, for if they do well in school, they will have wider choices concerning where and how they want to live. Sophie is promoting the vision of a school as

a. a preparer for college.
b. a source of human development.
c. a social panacea.
d. a social escalator.

a _____ 18. Horace Mann ardently believed that education provided the means for people to rise out of poverty and to live a more personally satisfying life. He most likely would have agreed with the model of a school as

a. a social escalator.
b. a shopping mall.
c. a bureaucracy.
d. a preparer for college.

b _____ 19. A city is distressed by the number of unwed teen-age pregnancies handled by the local hospital. City officials loudly proclaim that the schools are not doing their jobs because they are not teaching students about sexual restraint or, at least, reliable birth control methods. Their vision of school is one of

a. an acculturator.
b. a social panacea.
c. a social escalator.
d. a source for human development.

a _____ 20. The parents and school board of Williamsport are having a heated debate about sex education and condom distribution in schools. Although one group is vehemently opposed to condom distribution, a slightly larger group, "Citizens for Informed Education," argues that the schools must provide students with adequate and up-to-date information to make informed choices about their sexual lives. "Citizens for Informed Education" would support the notion of a school as

a. social panacea.
b. family.
c. acculturator.
d. human developer.

c _____ 21. During the early 1900s, America accepted millions of immigrants from various countries. The model that best represents the model of schooling demonstrated by the schools of the time would be
a. the trainer model.
b. the human development model.
c. the acculturator model.
d. the social panacea model.

a _____ 22. The acculturator model of schools is best explained by
a. the statement that schools should direct their attention to helping students accept the values of and blend into the dominant culture of the society.
b. the statement that schools should provide students with courses that will enable them to become cultured: courses in music, art, and literature.
c. the statement that schools should emphasize the benefits of democracy and capitalism.
d. the statement that schools' major purpose is to help students advance out of their social and economic class if they are needy and to maintain their class status if they are affluent.

d _____ 23. Several teachers are having a team meeting. They discuss whether Jimmy, one of their students, is getting enough positive reinforcement during class and how he is adjusting to his new reading buddy. These teachers support the notion of school as
a. acculturator.
b. trainer.
c. bureaucracy.
d. family.

b _____ 24. Principal Alma Juliana described the work of Howell Elementary School to a member of the press: "Most of our students don't live with both parents, and their grandparents, aunts, and uncles often are scattered in different parts of the country. They don't have roots the way we did growing up. We need to teach them how to act, how to treat each other, how to care for one another. And we need to discipline them when they make mistakes." Alma's comments demonstrates what model of schooling?
a. school as bureaucracy
b. school as family
c. school as developer of human potential
d. school as social panacea

c _____ 25. The system of norms and standards that a society develops over the course of many generations and that influences everyday behavior is called
a. education.
b. schooling.
c. culture.
d. religion.

b _____ 26. A description of a society's culture includes
a. its wedding customs and ceremonies celebrating a baby's birth.
b. its world views and the social rules designed to sustain the community.
c. the traditional housing structures and the living space designs.
d. its social customs, its world views, and its traditional housing structures.

a _____ 27. Reid Conrad firmly believes that the purpose of schools is to transmit dominant American culture. What might he do in class to further his educational goals?
a. Emphasize the benefits of competition and consistently reward students who perform better than their classmates.
b. Take his students on field trips to museums, theaters, and music halls.
c. Frequently tell students that they must create their own meaning and must search for their purpose in life.
d. Emphasize cooperative learning and peer tutoring.

b _____ 28. One drawback of using schools as vehicles for cultural transmission is that
a. time limitations will prevent students from studying all the important works necessary for them to understand the culture.
b. students may then not be able to recognize the merits of any other culture but the dominant culture of their society.
c. teachers cannot both prepare students to go to college and impart the benefit of the culture to the students.
d. schools have achieved limited success in cultural transmission.

c _____ 29. Heidi demonstrates fervent support of the dominant culture's belief that one must always strive to get ahead. When she meets people from another country, she scorns them for their lack of ambition. Which of the following would best explain Heidi's attitude?
a. being taught in a school that models itself on social reconstructionism
b. being taught in a school that follows a trainer model
c. being taught in a school that narrowly interprets its role as a cultural transmitter
d. being taught in a school that advocates economic reconstructionism

c _____ 30. John believes that schools can help students become actively involved in alleviating the problem of homelessness. John personifies the view of
a. cultural transmission.
b. human development education.
c. social reconstructionism.
d. the acculturator model of schooling.

a _____ 31. The goal of an educator who is a democratic reconstructionist would be
a. to have all students be vigorous participants in the government, working to improve social conditions.
b. to have all students register to vote when they are of legal age.
c. to have all students support all of the actions of a democratically elected government.
d. to have all students register to vote, to have all students become vigorous participants in the government, to improve social conditions, and to have all students support all of the actions of a democratically elected government.

d _____ 32. Which of the following would a democratic reconstructionist support?
a. student involvement in local government with the expressed intention of maintaining the security and the stability of the status quo
b. the perspective that social problems are best solved by government officials whom citizens select
c. students singlemindedly preparing for their own individual success
d. the notion that change happens most effectively when citizens are actively involved as change agents

c _____ 33. Lou Parker harshly criticizes public schools, claiming that they reinforce the inequities that exist in the current system. Furthermore, he claims that the values taught by public schools are the values of IBM, Dow Chemical, Exxon, and the other corporations that dominate America. Lou is most likely a
a. supporter of cultural transmission in schools.
b. supporter of schools as developers of human potential.
c. supporter of the economic reconstructionist conception of schooling.
d. supporter of schools as the social panacea for society.

b _____ 34. How would it be difficult for someone who advocates the economic reconstructionist theory of schools to be a public school teacher? He or she would
a. be dismayed by the other teachers' reluctance to transmit the values of the dominant culture to students.
b. see schools as serving, through their very nature, the economic powers that are the reason for social and economic inequity.
c. be disheartened by students' general apathy for working to improve society.
d. be disturbed by the lack of knowledge demonstrated about economic systems exhibited in general by the teachers and administrators.

a _____ 35. Among the characteristics of schools with records of great success in academics are
a. high teacher expectations, strong instructional leadership, and orderly environments.
b. strict rule enforcements, high levels of funding, and enthusiastic teachers.
c. low-key teacher ambitions, a cooperative administration, and good textbooks.
d. supportive parents, strict rules, and few extracurricular activities.

d _____ 36. Schools with high academic success are characterized by
a. strict rule enforcement and involved parents.
b. a variety of course offerings and teachers with advanced degrees.
c. current textbooks and ample new materials.
d. pleasant environments and strong instructional leadership.

b _____ 37. One way that a well-run extracurricular program contributes to all-around school success is by
a. offering students a respite from the academic grind.
b. promoting the development of pro-social behavior.
c. showcasing and appreciating the talents of the athletically gifted.
d. providing opportunities for students to improve their health.

c _____ 38. Wynne's study of school effectiveness indicates that coherence, good communication, vital teacher subgroups, pervasive student incentives, consistent discipline, and appealing extracurricular activities are associated with
a. unusual success in basic skill development.
b. very high scores on the College Board Entrance Examinations.
c. strength in "holistic" outcomes of schooling.
d. low teacher turnover.

Short-Answer Questions

Respond to each of the following questions briefly, but specifically, in complete sentences.

39. What are the limitations of assigning a model for any school?

(suggested answer) Although learning about particular models of schools can be very helpful to understand various types of schools and the pressures and expectations they meet, a model does not capture every complexity or nuance of a school. Schools could, in fact, match the requirements of several models. The power of a model lies in its ability to make sense of what we perceive; however, we must analyze and assess the school and then see how well the model describes what we see. A model is helpful in organizing our perceptions, not replacing them.

40. Describe two characteristics of a school that is unusually effective in promoting development of basic skills.

(suggested answer) High expectations of student success, high task orientation, lots of academic engaged time, good behavior management, strong instructional leadership from the principal, effective collaboration with parents, safe and orderly school environment. Students should identify and describe two of these criteria clearly.

41. Describe two characteristics of a school that is unusually effective by a holistic measure.

(suggested answer) Coherence, good communications, vital teacher subgroups; variety of student incentives; clear, consistent enforcement of rules; constructive extracurricular activities.

Essay Questions

Read each of the following questions, and respond by composing an organized essay that includes an introduction, fully developed paragraph(s), and a conclusion.

42. Explain the distinction made in this chapter between *education* and *schooling*. Give some examples of each. Describe the limitations of schooling, and explain its advantage over less formal education for some purposes.

(suggested answer) The broad term *education* refers to the process of human growth by which one gains greater control over oneself and one's world. Education involves mind, body, and relations with others and with the world. Its end is learning. The term *schooling* refers to the specific, formal process by which one gains certain limited bits of knowledge. Schooling is more reliable in transmitting essential content and skills than is education, which is less formal. Education can include many experiences that lead to learning. Schooling usually involves enrolling for credit and following the course set by a teacher.

43. Analyze the model or models of schooling that were prevalent in the high school you attended. Cite specific examples to demonstrate how a model or models accurately describe your school.

(Answers will vary.)

44. Explain the concepts of schools as transmitters of culture and as a means of both democratic and economic reconstruction. Which theory of schools most adequately fulfills your concept of the purpose of schools? Why?

(suggested answer) The view of schools as transmitters of culture would argue that schools exist to advance society by ensuring that the young know and appreciate the dominant values of their society's culture. Their perspective should be that the dominant values are positive, enabling the society to survive and prosper. The aim of schools as transmitters of

culture should be that students become active and creative participants in the dominant culture of the existing society.

Democratic reconstructionists believe that the solution to serious social ills lies in an aroused and skilled citizenry. The goal of the democratic reconstructionist is to prepare students to participate responsibly in creating positive social change in society.

Economic reconstructionists are very suspicious of public education as it exists now. They see schools as traditionally serving those economic forces that are already in power. They see schools as extensions of corporate America, reflecting and reproducing the dominant economic values with little chance of social change.

(Answers on which theory best fulfills the purpose of schooling will vary.)

Alternative Assessment Ideas

The following activities are suggestions for student portfolio activities. They are a means of providing alternative assessment of the students' capabilities.

Independent Reading

Read and respond to any of the following selections from Ryan/Cooper, *Kaleidoscope: Readings in Education* (Houghton Mifflin, 1998). You may want to use the Article Review Form on page 269.

Johnson and Immerwahr—"First Things First"

Powell—"Being Unspecial in the Shopping Mall High School"

Squires and Kranyik—"The Comer Program"

Wynne—"Looking at Good Schools"

Reflective Papers

Choose one of the following topics to write a reflective paper (2–5 pages). The purpose of the paper is to help you assimilate new knowledge by blending it with your previous knowledge and experiences.

1. Consider your own school experience. Which types and to what degree did your school(s) exemplify the models presented in the text? As a student, how did the purposes of the school become evident to you?

2. Based upon your observation of your field-site school (or another school where you have had experience), write what could be the school's formal statement of purpose. Consider the range of functions the school serves as you prepare this statement.

3. Schools, historically, have transmitted the dominant culture of society. Describe several instances of cultural transmission in your own schooling or in the school where you observe. Analyze your own reflections.

Journal Writing

Suggestions for journal topics for students' selection:

1. Describe the school model that best illustrates one of the schools you've attended in the past.
2. Describe the model that is closest to the school you are working in.
3. Pick the model you would feel most comfortable teaching in and explain why.

Chapter 3 What Is Life in Schools Like?

Multiple-Choice Items

Read each item carefully. On the appropriate line, write the letter of the choice that represents the best answer.

b _____ 1. Socialization is an important element of schooling. As a result of socialization, children learn how to
- a. succeed academically.
- b. become acceptable members of society.
- c. pursue their own interests.
- d. become more popular.

a _____ 2. Generally, in U.S. society, self-reliance is highly valued. How do schools instill that trait in their students?
- a. through socialization
- b. through using conflict-resolution techniques
- c. through providing interactive learning environments
- d. through ability grouping

d _____ 3. Randy, a fourteen-year-old boy, has progressed successfully through school. Which of the following would demonstrate Randy's successful socialization in school?
- a. He knows the importance of playing by the rules and being a "team player."
- b. He knows how to get along with his teachers.
- c. He knows how to dress in the latest style and what songs are the biggest hits.
- d. He is a "team player" and gets along well with his teachers.

a _____ 4. Which of the following is a way of socializing students?
   a. A teacher reads a story to her class about a boy who learns to work hard and try his best.
   b. Teachers teach a unit on making friends.
   c. The teacher praises a student who has followed the teacher's directions.
   d. Schools provide ample extracurricular activities.

d _____ 5. The residents and the faculty of the small town of Unity value honesty, hard work, and conscientiousness. How might the school participate in the children's socialization into the town's culture?
   a. It praises, in front of the class, students who are naturally bright.
   b. It rewards perfect attendance at the end of the year.
   c. It has a homework policy.
   d. It includes a biographical unit on "People of Integrity" in the fifth-grade social studies curriculum.

b _____ 6. Debra Bonanno, a varsity swimmer, is aware of how each course grade affects her cumulative average, and is preparing to take several advanced placement exams for college credit. She has been named by the faculty as the outstanding girl in the senior class. The teachers were particularly impressed by Debra's cheerfulness and helpful nature. According to Elliot Eisner's work on schools, it is quite likely that through her socialization in schools Debra
   a. learned self-acceptance and perseverance.
   b. internalized the values of compliance and competition.
   c. adopted the values of conscientiousness and creativity.
   d. adopted the values of intellectual curiosity and personal initiative.

c _____ 7. A fourth-grade girl, Maria, carefully prepares all the papers she turns in to Mrs. Baxter, her teacher. Maria writes neatly and always puts a complete heading on her paper. She also frequently volunteers to water the class's plants. Maria has most likely learned how to
   a. be well liked by her peers.
   b. take personal initiative.
   c. please the teacher.
   d. cooperate with people.

a _____ 8. In his study, Philip Jackson noted that teachers engage in hundreds of interchanges a day. He found that most of these interchanges were
   a. the teacher directing and controlling the discussion.
   b. the teacher sharing responsibility for the flow of the discussion with selected students.
   c. the teacher speaking to colleagues and administrators.
   d. the teacher seeking information from the students.

a _____ 9. The teacher behaviors that Philip Jackson described were in response to the teachers' work conditions. These conditions are characterized by
- a. limited resources and high student-teacher ratios.
- b. one-on-one tutoring situations.
- c. low student-teacher ratios.
- d. repressive administrative environments.

a _____ 10. What could one reasonably conclude from Jackson's observations of elementary classrooms?
- a. The structure of the elementary classroom requires students to develop self-restraint and patience.
- b. Elementary classrooms are structured to fulfill the needs of every child.
- c. Classrooms are designed to make children resourceful with their time.
- d. The elementary classroom structure caters to precocious children, generally ignoring the particular needs of the other children.

b _____ 11. Based on Jackson's observations, which of the following descriptions indicates a student who will be the most likely to successfully maneuver through elementary school?
- a. Kim talks frequently during class and finishes all of her work quickly.
- b. Bobby is able to resume silent reading quickly after a public address announcement and is able to work alone in a noisy classroom.
- c. Courtney has numerous friendships with her classmates, and she likes her teacher very much.
- d. Raphael resists all of the teacher's efforts to help. He likes to get his work done by himself, no matter how long it takes.

a _____ 12. Ability grouping, a common practice in American elementary schools, entails homogeneous grouping of students for instruction. This practice
- a. favors high-achieving students to the detriment of low achievers.
- b. is a common practice in most countries around the world.
- c. is most frequently done in social studies and science.
- d. fosters cooperation and friendship among students.

c _____ 13. Despite innovative instructional techniques that encourage a more student-centered approach to education, much of the instruction in elementary schools remains teacher-directed. Evidence of this can be seen in classrooms where
- a. students are required to put together a portfolio of their work for the year.
- b. teachers implement writing across the curriculum.
- c. students are rarely given responsibility for any decisions in class.
- d. teachers integrate computers and technology into their lessons.

d _____ 14. A consistent similarity that emerges from schools teaching students in the middle grades is that
   a. teachers work in teams, sharing the same body of students.
   b. those who teach students in grades between 5 and 8 emphasize their students' personal growth and developmental issues.
   c. staffing for schools serving students in the middle grades is overwhelmingly departmentalized.
   d. few consistent similarities exist; the schools vary widely based on the grades included in the school and the goals of the administration.

b _____ 15. The Brandon school district has a middle school that includes grades 6, 7, and 8. The Lamington school district has no middle school. Rather, they house their seventh- and eighth-graders in a junior–senior high (grades 7–12). In what way will the emphasis of the principal of the Brandon Middle School and the principal of the Lamington Junior–Senior High School differ from one another in their goals for the seventh and eighth grades?
   a. The Lamington principal is more likely to ask the teachers to stress critical-thinking skills and abstract reasoning than the Brandon principal.
   b. The Lamington principal is more likely to ask teachers to stress critical-thinking skills, whereas the Brandon principal is more likely to stress the need for units on resisting peer pressure.
   c. The Lamington principal is more likely to stress mastery of subject matter and competency in basic skills.
   d. The Brandon principal is more likely to stress the need for units on resisting peer pressure and developing self-confidence than the Lamington principal.

c _____ 16. Which of the following students' experiences support Ernest Boyer's findings about life in high schools?
   a. Barbara entered high school placed in the general studies track. However, after her sophomore year, she was able to switch rather easily into the college preparatory track upon the advice and encouragement of several of her teachers.
   b. Keisha is in the academic track at high school and wants to go to college. She consults with her friends about which courses to take rather than consulting with her guidance counselor or a teacher.
   c. Ellen is in the general studies track. Her teachers are well equipped to teach but are uninterested in the students in the general-level courses.
   d. Despite low scores on the achievement test, Juanita is encouraged by her teachers to pursue the academic track.

b _____ 17. Which of the following statements captures the findings of Ernest Boyer's research on high schools?

a. Despite small problems, high schools generally have and follow a clear vision of their purpose.
b. In the efforts to be all things to all people, high schools are burdened by many contradictory goals.
c. High schools have streamlined their objectives since earlier times; however, their ability to translate those objectives into real instructional practices is weak.
d. High schools in affluent areas have clear visions shared by both the administrators and the faculty alike.

a _____ 18. According to Larry Cuban's analysis of high schools, which of the following practices is likely to remain the same in the future?

a. the amount of time teachers teach through the lecture method and directed question and answer
b. the heavy use of cooperative learning and peer tutoring
c. tracking students by academic ability
d. the strong emphasis on sports to the neglect of academic achievement

c _____ 19. If Larry Cuban's recommendations were followed, which of the following would occur?

a. Instruction in schools would emphasize student-centered classrooms over teacher-centered ones.
b. Class sizes would be reduced to near fifteen, with no more than twenty students.
c. Research would focus on ways of strengthening teacher-centered instruction.
d. Instruction in schools would emphasize student-centered classrooms, and class sizes would be reduced to near fifteen.

d _____ 20. In Penny Eckert's study *Jocks and Burnouts,* what function does belonging to a group serve in the life of the adolescent?

a. Belonging to a group helps the student be more successful in school.
b. Groups are a channel through which the teen's values are clarified and defined.
c. Membership in a group facilitates communication between the student and his or her school, family, and community.
d. Belonging to a group serves as a training ground for the roles teens will assume as adults.

c ____ 21. How does the use of space, such as the school cafeteria, symbolize the burnouts' relationship to the school as an institution?

a. It symbolizes their grudging acceptance because they use it only when necessary.
b. Their use of the cafeteria demonstrates their acceptance of the school as a social institution.
c. Their avoidance of the cafeteria demonstrates their rejection of the school as an institution and as the mainstream culture.
d. Their use of the cafeteria shows their acceptance of the school as an institution of authority.

b ____ 22. What is the most likely conclusion to explain why jocks adapt and succeed in school more often than burnouts?

a. Jocks are more conscientious workers and are generally better-prepared students than burnouts.
b. Jocks are more comfortable in school because it reflects the same values of their middle-class background. The burnouts feel alien in a school that represents middle-class interests and concerns.
c. The jocks are strongly motivated to succeed in the real world. They learn at a young age how to use egalitarian social networks of friends to get help studying, locating a job, or meeting other needs. Their interpersonal skills enable them to succeed in school. The burnouts do not have the same drive to succeed or the same system of working with people.
d. The jocks succeed in school because they are conscientious, strongly motivated to succeed in the real world, and very comfortable in the school's world.

a ____ 23. Studies of peer relationships among adolescents show that

a. high school has become a social system with its own set of values and activities.
b. adolescent relationships with adults are more important than with other adolescents.
c. more and more adolescents live in dormitories.
d. the values of adolescents are the same as those of their parents.

b ____ 24. According to Steinberg, which one of the following is *not* a factor in poor achievement in high school?

a. going through the motions
b. role model of siblings
c. lack of parent involvement
d. working more than 15 hours a week

c _____ 25. You are an observer in Leonard Filipone's algebra class. Leonard teaches for about 20 minutes out of a 55-minute period. While he teaches, he writes on the board and calculates, pausing periodically to ask if the students understand. The students sit quietly, but few take notes or seem engaged. When Leonard puts his chalk down, a student calls out, "We can work on our homework now, right?" Leonard gives them about six problems for homework, and the students quietly do their homework for the rest of the period. At the end of the period, the students file out of the class, several of them saying friendly good-byes to Leonard. What can you conclude from this observation?

a. The class was probably a basic-level class that could not handle a heavy workload.
b. Leonard runs an orderly, quiet classroom, which demonstrates his teaching ability.
c. Leonard and his students probably have an unspoken agreement that if he doesn't work them too hard, they won't misbehave.
d. Leonard has serious problems in his teaching because of his own laziness.

b _____ 26. According to *The Shopping Mall High School,* how do many teachers deal with classroom management?

a. They strictly monitor their classes, ruling their classes with an iron fist.
b. They make tacit agreements with their students that neither will push the other too hard.
c. They have little classroom management. The students rule the classes.
d. They provide, for the most part, engaging lessons with plenty of student involvement so that there is little time for students to become bored or distracted.

a _____ 27. Andy is a B– or C+ student. He is fairly interested in school, yet he is not strong in any one subject. He does the work assigned, but knows he could do better. In many respects, he is the typical average student. According to the authors of *The Shopping Mall High School*, the school's treatment of Andy can be described as

a. passive indifference. Andy does not demand or require a lot of attention. Therefore, the school lets Andy choose his own courses.
b. warm regard. They see students like Andy as the foundation of the school. What Andy lacks in academic ability, he makes up for in being a "good kid."
c. strong encouragement. They know that Andy has not distinguished himself academically, but they know that many "average" students are quite bright and just need to be encouraged.
d. cool disregard. They know Andy could do better if he wanted. If he doesn't want to work hard, then so be it.

b _____ 28. According to the authors of *The Shopping Mall High School,* average high school students
a. are encouraged to achieve.
b. enjoy a variety of school options.
c. are ignored and poorly served.
d. embody the lively spirit of the "mall."

d _____ 29. Colbie is soon entering first grade. Which of the following will most likely *not* affect the academic expectations her teachers will have for her?
a. She is a pretty little girl.
b. Her kindergarten teacher has written a positive report in Colbie's folder.
c. She is extremely polite to other children and adults.
d. Her parents think she is gifted.

b _____ 30. How do teachers' expectations influence students' achievement?
a. Students somehow perceive how the teacher feels and act accordingly.
b. In subtle—often unconscious—ways, teachers "teach" good students differently than they teach "bad" students.
c. Teachers consciously work harder with the slower students.
d. When teachers indicate, in subtle and clear ways, that they don't think the students will succeed, the students try especially hard to succeed to prove them wrong.

c _____ 31. Which of the following was suggested in the report *Breaking Ranks: Changing an American Institution* to improve the quality of high schools?
a. lower pupil-teacher ratios
b. personalization
c. a larger variety of choices
d. accelerated pace

c _____ 32. You are an observer in a sixth-grade classroom. You notice Tony, sitting in the back of the room, because every time he raises his hand the teacher calls on someone else. When she finally does call on him, she waits only several seconds for a response from him before she calls on the next student. As the class begins to work on individual projects, the teacher works her way around the room, pausing frequently to talk to individual students. As she passes Tony's desk, she merely says, "Everything OK, Tony? Good," and walks away. Later in the day, Tony stands up to sharpen a pencil, and the teacher becomes exasperated with him. Given your observations of the teacher's interactions with Tony in class, you would most likely expect Tony to be
a. a gifted and talented student.
b. a bright but unmotivated student.
c. a low achiever.
d. a student whose native language is not English.

b _____ 33. Andre is a high school junior who works at a local fast-food restaurant. He is an above-average student who aspires to go to college; however, his family situation makes his attending somewhat questionable. He and his four younger siblings live with their mother, whose job barely covers monthly expenses. Andre has been working 12 hours a week and maintaining good grades. Now with college looming, he wants to ask to work more hours a week. Based on the findings of Bennett and Lecompte, what would be likely to happen if Andre worked 25 hours a week?

a. There would be no difference in his school performance.
b. He wouldn't have time for his homework, and his grades would suffer.
c. He would have enough time to read extensively, and his grades would improve.
d. He would be more tired but would be able to maintain his grades.

Short-Answer Questions

Respond to each of the following questions briefly, but specifically, in complete sentences.

34. The author of *The Shopping Mall High School* concludes that "average" students are basically left to their own devices in high schools. They are benignly ignored, apparently, by both the teachers and the administration. If this is, in fact, a common phenomenon among high schools, what does this mean for the quality of education that these students are receiving?

(suggested answer) The quality of education is most likely mediocre. Teachers negotiate with these students a peaceful coexistence in which each group causes little difficulty for the other. These students then are not receiving a challenging or demanding education and are consequently not learning to their potential. The potential for a large segment of the population to be minimally educated with little motivation or drive is significant.

35. What have Fordham and Ogbu found to be the effect of peer pressure on high-achieving African Americans?

(suggested answer) Fordham and Ogbu studied a predominantly black high school in Washington, D.C., and found that students were expected to conform to the norms of the collective identity of African Americans, which included mediocre academic results. Students achieving high academic performance were considered to be adhering to the cultural values of the white society and were referred to as "acting white." The pressure not to succeed was very strong.

36. Why does Larry Cuban support teacher-centered instruction? What does he suggest for improving education?

(suggested answer) Cuban analyzed the instructional methods from 1890 to 1980 and found little change in the emphasis on teacher-centered instruction. Teachers consistently

favored lecture, directed questions and answers, and other teacher-centered instructional techniques. Cuban says the structure of the school—including such things as the number of students in classes, the format or structure of the report card, and the relative lack of power teachers have to change that structure—reveals an important underlying reason why student-centered instruction will never dominate. Therefore, he says, more real gains would be made in classroom teaching if efforts were made to improve teacher-centered instruction.

Essay Questions

Read each of the following questions, and respond by composing an organized essay that includes an introduction, fully developed paragraph(s), and a conclusion.

37. Schools have been defined as socialization agents that can teach children to be compliant, competitive, creative, cooperative, or curious. Define *socialization*, and give examples of school routines or practices that might nurture the development of the traits just listed.

    (suggested answer) Socialization is the general process of social learning whereby a person learns what must be known in order to be an acceptable member of society and learns what rules must be followed and how to follow them. Compliance can be nurtured by offering rewards to children who follow rules and don't "make waves" and by excessive fuss over ordinary orderly behavior. Competitiveness is nurtured by grading or recognition systems that honor students at the top only, rather than all who meet the standard of excellence. Creativity is nurtured in activities that call for divergent thinking and brainstorming. Cooperation is nurtured by reward systems or task structures that are most productive when students help each other. Curiosity is nurtured by lessons that end with questions, by research activities, and by attention to critical thinking.

38. Teachers form expectations based on several perceptions of students and then, often unconsciously, act according to their expectations. Explain at least three of the factors mentioned in the text that influence the formation of teachers' expectations. List three practices teachers use more with children for whom they have low expectations.

    (suggested answer) Teachers form expectations on the basis of students' physical attractiveness, cumulative folder information, race, social class, and classroom conduct. Teachers discourage low achievers by giving them insufficient time to answer, criticizing them often, praising them seldom, demanding less of them, seating them farther away, and interacting with them less often.

39. Penelope Eckert describes as jocks and burnouts the two adolescent subcultures she finds in her study of high schools. Each group distinguishes itself through the clothes the members wear, the territory in the building they occupy, and their relationship to the school as an institution. You may not have used the terms *jocks* or *burnouts* in your high school, but your high school most likely had particular subcultures. Describe the dominant groups

in your high school. What were their names? How did they distinguish themselves, and, finally, what was their relationship toward the school as an institution?

(Answers will vary.)

Alternative Assessment Ideas

The following activities are suggestions for student portfolio activities. They are a means of providing alternative assessment of the students' capabilities.

Independent Reading

Read and respond to any of the following selections from Ryan/Cooper, *Kaleidoscope: Readings in Education* (Houghton Mifflin, 1998). You may want to use the Article Review Form on page 269.

Canady and Rettig—"The Power of Innovative Scheduling"

Combs—"Affective Education or None at All"

Marsh and Raywid—"How to Make Detracking Work"

Resnick and Nolan—"Where in the World Are World-Class Standards?"

Shanker—"Developing a Common Curriculum"

Reflective Papers

Choose one of the following topics to write a reflective paper (2–5 pages). The purpose of the paper is to help you assimilate new knowledge by blending it with your previous knowledge and experiences.

1. Think back on your own high school experiences. Which social group did you belong to or relate to most closely? How did your affiliation with this peer culture affect your experience? Your academic performance? Your social interactions? If you could relive your high school years, would you choose to belong to the same group or a different one? Explain.

2. Tracking is a hotly debated issue, with both proponents and opponents presenting convincing arguments to defend their position. Think about your own views of tracking. What do you see to be the advantages of tracking? What are the disadvantages? Under what circumstances do you think tracking would be beneficial?

3. In *Jocks and Burnouts,* Penelope Eckert suggests a relationship between peer groups and socioeconomic status. Based on your experiences, do you believe there is a correlation between the two? How would you explain this relationship? What, if anything, could be done to break the cycle of socioeconomic standing?

Journal Writing

Suggestions for journal topics for students' selection:

1. Name one common practice in schools that you would like to change and describe *how* you would change it.

2. Describe how the routine, methods, or organization in an elementary classroom could be altered to change the students' experience.

3. Describe what track or peer subgroup you think you were a part of in high school and what gives you this impression.

Chapter 4 Who Are Today's Students?

Multiple-Choice Items

Read each item carefully. On the appropriate line, write the letter of the choice that represents the best answer.

c _____ 1. Takuya and his family came to the United States one year ago when his father was transferred here from Tokyo. Takuya, who is eight years old, was enrolled in the third grade in the local elementary school. He spoke no English, so he was given some one-on-one tutoring to help him learn English during his first school year there. When school began again in September, Takuya's teacher recommended that he be fully mainstreamed since his English proficiency was so good. Takuya's success may be explained by

a. his love of American food.
b. the strong attachment he felt for his teacher.
c. the value that Asians place on education.
d. his birth date.

d _____ 2. Melinda is a first-year teacher in a culturally diverse classroom. After a few months, she notices that she infrequently sees the parents of her Hispanic American students even though she speaks Spanish quite well and has communicated that to parents by sending home letters written in both English and Spanish. What does Melinda need to understand about these parents?

a. They probably don't like her because she is a female.
b. They probably are embarrassed that their Spanish isn't very correct.
c. They probably don't want their child going to an English-speaking school.
d. They probably are not used to being involved in the school life of their children.

a _____ 3. The Allen Elementary School is in the midst of revising its curricula. Some community members are asking that the school pay more attention to cultural pluralism. What would the residents like to see in the curriculum?

a. more attention given to the contributions of nonwhite, non-Europeans to the development of the United States
b. a two-pronged curriculum with two social studies texts, one written from an Anglo perspective and one from an African-American perspective
c. new emphasis on anthropology as part of the social studies curriculum
d. greater focus on classical literature

d _____ 4. If cultural pluralism were part of a U.S. school, how would that affect a group of immigrant students from Portugal?

a. They would mingle together during school, but teachers would encourage them to become Americanized and make U.S. friends.
b. The school they attended would hold a "Portugal" month with banners and posters of Portugal in the hallways.
c. The teachers would treat the Portuguese students warmly and would make sure that the U.S. students treated the Portuguese students nicely, too.
d. The Portuguese would be encouraged to treasure their culture, and teachers would provide ways for the U.S. students to learn about life in Portugal.

c _____ 5. How could one describe the anticipated *proportional* population trends among the various ethnic groups?

a. The populations of Asian Americans, Hispanics, and whites will rapidly increase. African Americans will experience a slight decline in growth.
b. Whites and African Americans will experience steady growth, Asian Americans will experience rapid growth, and Hispanics will experience a decline in growth.
c. Asian Americans, Hispanics, and African Americans will make significant gains in growth; whites will experience a decline in growth.
d. African Americans and Hispanics will make large gains in their populations; whites and Asian Americans will experience rapid declines in their growth.

d _____ 6. The United States is undergoing some significant population changes. By the year 2000, it is expected that 38 percent of all children will be

a. African American.
b. Hispanic and Native American.
c. Asian American and Indian.
d. African American, Hispanic, and Asian American.

b _____ 7. Which of the following is the most commonly used criterion for identifying gifted students?

a. academic record
b. individual intelligence test scores
c. group intelligence test scores
d. standardized achievement test scores

c _____ 8. Regular teachers who are effective in teaching children with disabilities
- a. have students with disabilities work together in pairs.
- b. find one teaching strategy that is most effective and stick with it.
- c. are open to the idea of including students with disabilities.
- d. stand back and let the special education teacher manage the disabled student's program.

c _____ 9. The reason gifted students receive most or all of their education in regular classrooms is that
- a. the philosophy favors mixed-ability grouping.
- b. gifted funding is restricted to use in regular classrooms.
- c. parents object to elitist programs.
- d. appropriate curriculum and material resources to separate them don't exist.

d _____ 10. Which student group is probably underrepresented because of current gifted identification practices?
- a. girls
- b. Asian students
- c. white males
- d. economically disadvantaged minority students.

c _____ 11. Which of the following best explains William Glasser's control theory?
- a. People in positions of authority typically have a strong need to control those around them.
- b. People have inherent desires to control other people, yet the fully mature adult has resolved issues of control and accepted others as autonomous beings.
- c. Personal empowerment and full psychological development are attained when a person controls how he or she chooses to react to ideas and events.
- d. In order to learn, people must think that they will soon have control, or mastery, of a concept or skill.

d _____ 12. According to William Glasser's control theory, why would a person feel discontented or be unsatisfied with his or her life?
- a. He or she lacks the power to control people and events in his or her life.
- b. He or she has basic needs unmet.
- c. He or she does not yet know how to attain personal empowerment.
- d. He or she has basic needs unmet and does not have the capacity to attain personal empowerment.

c _____ 13. Ms. O'Neill, a sixth-grade teacher, knows that Song feels proud of herself when she can construct something. Therefore, Ms. O'Neill provides Song with many opportunities to make models, draw pictures, and create objects. After Song has completed one of her creations, Ms. O'Neill can tell that she has fulfilled her needs for power, or self-esteem, and fun. O'Neill's classroom practices are clearly influenced by

a. Maslow's hierarchy of needs.
b. Gardner's theory of multiple intelligence.
c. Glasser's control theory.
d. the Comer model.

b _____ 14. Lynn Kaiser is an outstanding sales broker in real estate. She can immediately strike up a conversation with anyone, and half of her clients are repeat clients. She frequently remembers small details about her clients, such as their favorite color or their birthday, which makes them feel special. According to Howard Gardner's theory, what strong intellectual capacity does Lynn possess?

a. intrapersonal
b. interpersonal
c. linguistic
d. kinesthetic

c _____ 15. If Howard Gardner's theory of multiple intelligence took hold in public schools, what would be a close approximation of the educational practices he would advocate?

a. Students would be tested to determine the breadth and range of their multiple intelligences; then they would follow an individually determined course of study.
b. Students would enroll in courses that would maximize their strongest type of intelligence. Gradually, they would focus almost entirely on their strongest abilities.
c. Students would work as apprentices to sharpen or enrich a particular type of intelligence.
d. Traditional academic courses would be eliminated, and schools would design each new course so that it targeted a particular intelligence.

d _____ 16. Bonnie learns most easily when she can see something written down, such as instructions for an assignment or instructions for assembling a bicycle. In which of the following situations would Bonnie find it the most difficult to learn?

a. a tutorial session for biology
b. a small cooperative learning group to complete a science project
c. a reenactment of a discovery of a famous invention
d. a large-group lecture in biology

b _____ 17. What does IDEA establish?
a. the right of non-English-speaking children to instruction in their native language
b. the right of children with disabilities to a free, appropriate public education
c. the right of children to a public education based on the wealth of the state, not the wealth of the community
d. the right of families and students to examine the administrative records kept on the student

b _____ 18. IDEA mandates special services for students who
a. dislike school.
b. have any kind of physical or mental disability.
c. have a low socioeconomic status.
d. cannot speak English.

a _____ 19. The Americans with Disabilities Act (ADA) protects the rights of individuals with disabilities in society. Because of this act,
a. handicap facilities must be provided in all public places.
b. people with disabilities qualify for free medical care.
c. people with disabilities qualify for free dental care.
d. handicap facilities are not necessary in churches.

d _____ 20. Which of the following would fit into the newer definition of giftedness?
a. a ten-year-old who can add a series of three-digit numbers in her head
b. a twelve-year-old who can hit a three-point throw in basketball 95 percent of the time
c. an eight-year-old who can read at a tenth-grade level
d. All of the above would be considered gifted.

a _____ 21. Why have gifted and talented programs met with resistance from many Americans?
a. Having a gifted and talented program, to some, implies a superiority or an elitism that does not favorably impress many Americans.
b. Too many children have been identified as "gifted" or "talented," so the phrase has lost its currency.
c. The programs have not had any discernible effect on the students.
d. Because of the structure of the gifted and talented programs, they disrupt the running of the school.

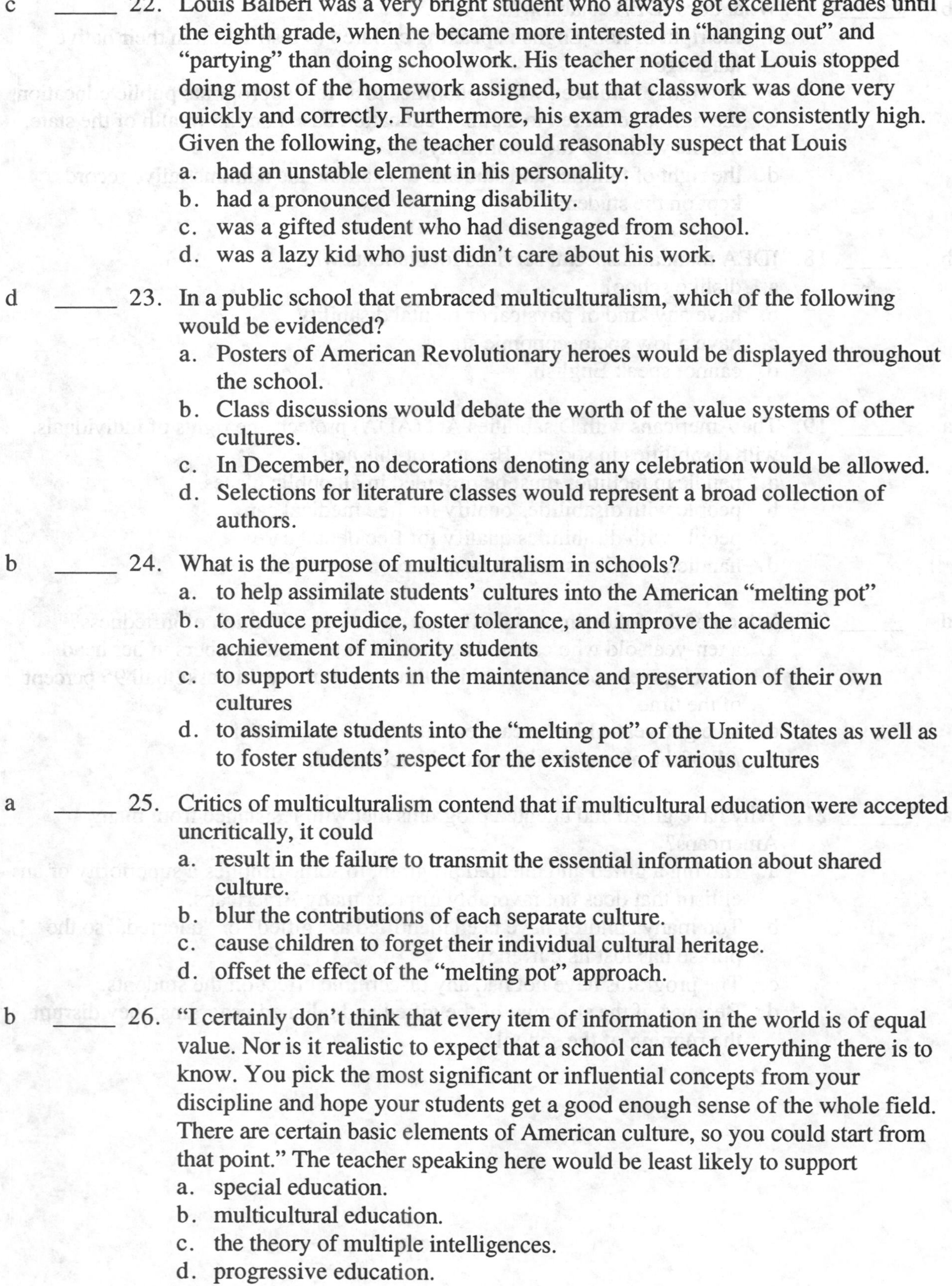

c _____ 22. Louis Balberi was a very bright student who always got excellent grades until the eighth grade, when he became more interested in "hanging out" and "partying" than doing schoolwork. His teacher noticed that Louis stopped doing most of the homework assigned, but that classwork was done very quickly and correctly. Furthermore, his exam grades were consistently high. Given the following, the teacher could reasonably suspect that Louis

a. had an unstable element in his personality.
b. had a pronounced learning disability.
c. was a gifted student who had disengaged from school.
d. was a lazy kid who just didn't care about his work.

d _____ 23. In a public school that embraced multiculturalism, which of the following would be evidenced?

a. Posters of American Revolutionary heroes would be displayed throughout the school.
b. Class discussions would debate the worth of the value systems of other cultures.
c. In December, no decorations denoting any celebration would be allowed.
d. Selections for literature classes would represent a broad collection of authors.

b _____ 24. What is the purpose of multiculturalism in schools?

a. to help assimilate students' cultures into the American "melting pot"
b. to reduce prejudice, foster tolerance, and improve the academic achievement of minority students
c. to support students in the maintenance and preservation of their own cultures
d. to assimilate students into the "melting pot" of the United States as well as to foster students' respect for the existence of various cultures

a _____ 25. Critics of multiculturalism contend that if multicultural education were accepted uncritically, it could

a. result in the failure to transmit the essential information about shared culture.
b. blur the contributions of each separate culture.
c. cause children to forget their individual cultural heritage.
d. offset the effect of the "melting pot" approach.

b _____ 26. "I certainly don't think that every item of information in the world is of equal value. Nor is it realistic to expect that a school can teach everything there is to know. You pick the most significant or influential concepts from your discipline and hope your students get a good enough sense of the whole field. There are certain basic elements of American culture, so you could start from that point." The teacher speaking here would be least likely to support

a. special education.
b. multicultural education.
c. the theory of multiple intelligences.
d. progressive education.

c _____ 27. Congress passed the Bilingual Education Act in 1968 in order to
a. develop fluency in another language by all Americans.
b. encourage foreigners to visit the United States.
c. cope with the large number of students who did not speak English.
d. promote linguistic awareness in all students.

c _____ 28. One result of the *Lau* v. *Nichols* decision might be seen in which of the following cases?
a. A Vietnamese child is taught entirely in English with English textbooks in order to speed the process of assimilation.
b. A Spanish-speaking child is sent to a school where only Spanish is spoken so that she can learn basic skills.
c. A German-speaking child is given textbooks and basic skill instruction in German and English until he or she is fluent enough in English.
d. The experiences of the Vietnamese child, the Spanish-speaking child, and the German-speaking child all demonstrate the influence of the decision.

b _____ 29. How did the *Lau* remedies affect public education?
a. They concluded that non-English-speaking children would best learn from submersion in English-speaking classrooms; therefore, schools felt little impact.
b. They required that non-English-speaking students be taught academic subjects in their native language until their command of English allowed them to benefit from English instruction.
c. They required schools to limit the amount of time any student could spend in a bilingual education program.
d. They provided for intensive language education programs for children in the elementary grades. They made little provision for students in secondary schools.

a _____ 30. Juan is a non-English-speaking student who has recently enrolled in a public school in the United States. He has been placed in a classroom with some other native English speakers and some non-English-speaking students. Although he is encouraged to practice English, when he gets stuck he can speak Spanish to his teacher, because she is fluent in Spanish. However, she will only answer him using English. The model for this type of instruction is
a. immersion.
b. submersion.
c. transition.
d. ESL.

b _____ 31. Amber, a three-year-old, was born with mild cerebral palsy, which reduced her motor coordination on her left side and delayed her speech development. Her parents want her to receive special therapy, but have been told by the school system in their town that nothing is available for her. Based on the Education of the Handicapped Act Amendments (PL 99-457), what should Amber's parents do?

a. seek a private school that could provide services for Amber and cover the costs themselves
b. remind the school system that it is required to provide Amber with free appropriate education from age three on
c. ask for federal government assistance to cover Amber's education in a private school
d. keep Amber at home until she is five and eligible to be enrolled in a public kindergarten

c _____ 32. Mr. and Mrs. Wells are meeting with their daughter's teacher to discuss her individualized education plan (IEP) for the next school year. Their daughter, Donna, has a learning disability that affects her reading skills. When Mr. and Mrs. Wells review Donna's IEP, they should expect to find

a. information on how Donna compares to the rest of the students in the class.
b. a complete list of curricular materials that will be used with Donna.
c. the services that will be provided by the school for Donna during the upcoming year and an assessment plan.
d. the maximum potential level that Donna will achieve as an adult.

a _____ 33. An individualized education plan (IEP) is a document required for special education students. Which of the following elements must be included in it?

a. criteria for evaluating student progress
b. the student's personality profile
c. the student's learning style inventory
d. the mean score of same-age students on the school-authorized standardized test (such as the CAT or Iowa tests)
e. a plan for the student's education for the next two years

c _____ 34. *Inclusion* of students with disabilities refers to

a. including those students in schoolwide activities.
b. including the study of a wide range of subject areas in the special education curriculum.
c. educating those students to the maximum extent possible in the regular classroom.
d. pairing those students up with regular education students.

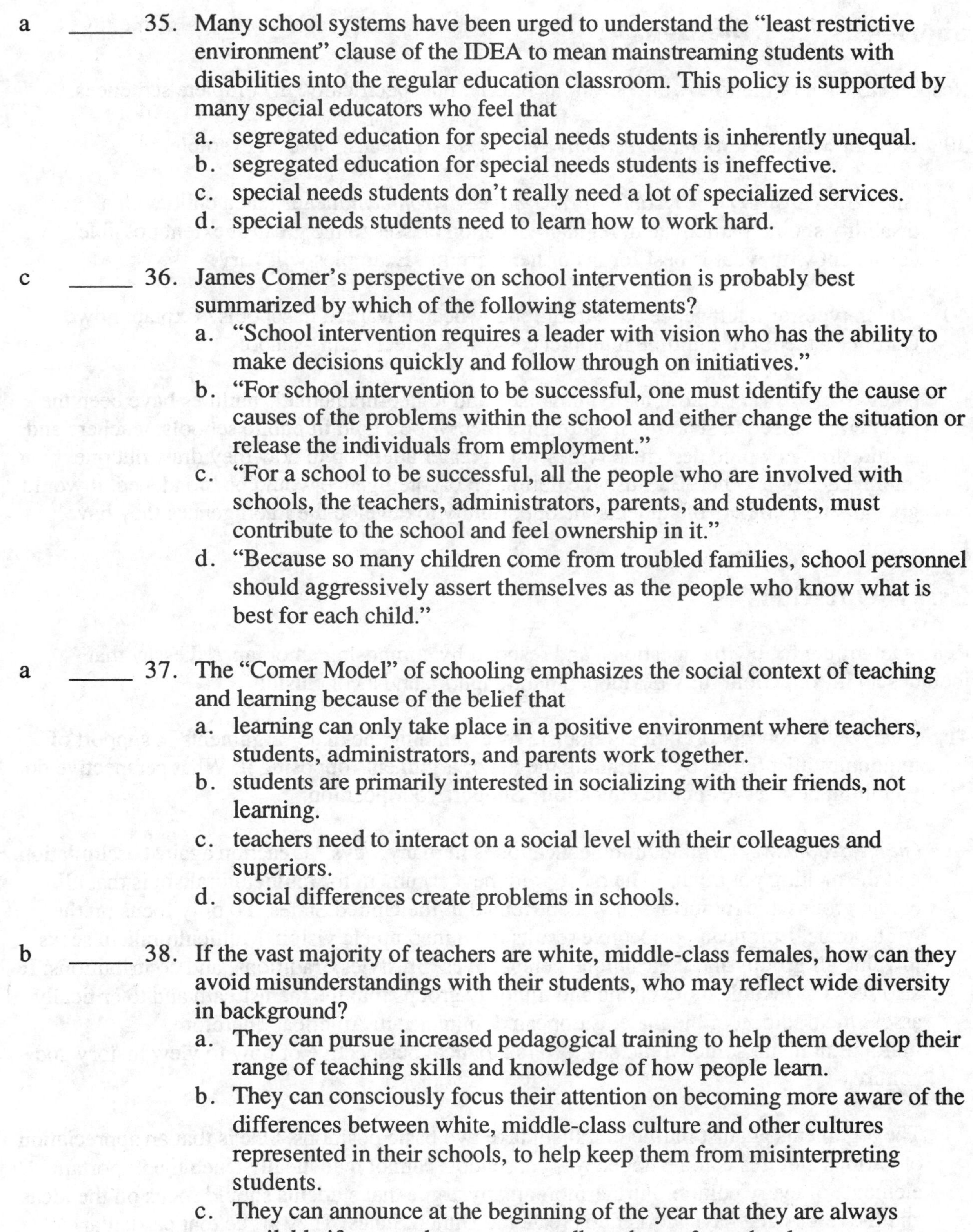

a _____ 35. Many school systems have been urged to understand the "least restrictive environment" clause of the IDEA to mean mainstreaming students with disabilities into the regular education classroom. This policy is supported by many special educators who feel that

a. segregated education for special needs students is inherently unequal.
b. segregated education for special needs students is ineffective.
c. special needs students don't really need a lot of specialized services.
d. special needs students need to learn how to work hard.

c _____ 36. James Comer's perspective on school intervention is probably best summarized by which of the following statements?

a. "School intervention requires a leader with vision who has the ability to make decisions quickly and follow through on initiatives."
b. "For school intervention to be successful, one must identify the cause or causes of the problems within the school and either change the situation or release the individuals from employment."
c. "For a school to be successful, all the people who are involved with schools, the teachers, administrators, parents, and students, must contribute to the school and feel ownership in it."
d. "Because so many children come from troubled families, school personnel should aggressively assert themselves as the people who know what is best for each child."

a _____ 37. The "Comer Model" of schooling emphasizes the social context of teaching and learning because of the belief that

a. learning can only take place in a positive environment where teachers, students, administrators, and parents work together.
b. students are primarily interested in socializing with their friends, not learning.
c. teachers need to interact on a social level with their colleagues and superiors.
d. social differences create problems in schools.

b _____ 38. If the vast majority of teachers are white, middle-class females, how can they avoid misunderstandings with their students, who may reflect wide diversity in background?

a. They can pursue increased pedagogical training to help them develop their range of teaching skills and knowledge of how people learn.
b. They can consciously focus their attention on becoming more aware of the differences between white, middle-class culture and other cultures represented in their schools, to help keep them from misinterpreting students.
c. They can announce at the beginning of the year that they are always available if any student wants to talk to them after school.
d. They can take courses concerning the major cultures of the world.

Short-Answer Questions

Respond to each of the following questions briefly, but specifically, in complete sentences.

39. Explain what the term *least restrictive environment* means. Give an example.

    (suggested answer) The term *least restrictive environment* means that a child with a disability should participate in regular education classes to the greatest extent possible consistent with what is best for his or her learning. Examples will vary.

40. Which types of intelligence have traditionally been rewarded in schools? Explain how Gardner's theory of multiple intelligences would affect public schools.

    (suggested answer) Traditionally, linguistic and logico-mathematic abilities have been the most emphasized in schools. If Gardner's theory took hold in public schools, teachers and administrators would design activities with greater attention to how they draw out one intelligence or another. Because the definition of intelligence would be broadened, it would give greater numbers of students the opportunity to develop the intelligences they have.

Essay Questions

Read each of the following questions, and respond by composing an organized essay that includes an introduction, fully developed paragraph(s), and a conclusion.

41. Analyze the concept of multiculturalism by examining the major arguments in support of multiculturalism, then by examining the major arguments opposing it. What perspective do you think best serves public education? Support your position.

    (suggested answer) Multicultural education is in many ways "a reaction against assimilation and the melting pot myth." The most prominent argument for multiculturalism is that all ethnic groups and minorities have contributed to the United States. To only focus on the white, male, European perspective results in an incomplete vision. Multiculturalism seeks to value all groups and their unique perspectives, lifestyles, traditions, and contributions. It also seeks to include more ethnic and minority groups into the mainstream and to critically assess the tradition of the male, European dominance in America. Therefore, multiculturalism, some would say, offers a radical perspective of how to view history and culture.

    The arguments against multiculturalism take two basic positions. One is that an appreciation of various cultures is to be hoped for, yet schools cannot realistically teach the important elements of every culture. Furthermore, many argue that students should focus on the ideas and the forces that have worked to create the United States. They argue that particular people, particular events, and particular ideas do have greater importance than others. If we focus on multiculturalism to its extreme, some fear, we will lose our commonalities as Americans. The other major argument against multiculturalism is based on the perceived relativism of multiculturalism. Some argue against multiculturalism on a moral basis, claiming that the values of a particular group do not necessarily make something moral.

42. The debate over full inclusion of special needs students continues to rage. Discuss the issue by presenting the major arguments from both sides of the debate.

    (suggested answer) Students should identify and explain the arguments in favor of full inclusion such as greater social interaction and learning to function in a "real world" environment, as well as the arguments against inclusion, which revolve around adequate services for special needs students.

Alternative Assessment Ideas

The following activities are suggestions for student portfolio activities. They are a means of providing alternative assessment of the students' capabilities.

Independent Reading

Read and respond to any of the following selections from Ryan/Cooper, *Kaleidoscope: Readings in Education* (Houghton Mifflin, 1998). You may want to use the Article Review Form on page 269.

Giangreco—"What Do I Do Now?"

Minicucci et al.—"School Reform and Student Diversity"

Ravitch—"Multiculturalism"

Shanker—"Where We Stand on the Rush to Inclusion"

Reflective Papers

Choose one of the following topics to write a reflective paper (2–5 pages). The purpose of the paper is to help you assimilate new knowledge by blending it with your previous knowledge and experiences.

1. After completing a learning style inventory, how do you feel about the results? How well do you feel the inventory matched you? Did you learn anything about yourself that rang true, although you may not have realized it before? Based on your learning style, which methods of learning are most comfortable for you?

2. Think about your position on full inclusion of special needs students in the classroom. How would you feel about it as a regular classroom teacher? What particular challenges do you imagine that such an environment would present to you?

3. How did your perceptions of poor and homeless people differ from what you read about in this chapter? Given the information that the chapter presents and your own experience, what solutions do you see as being effective to fight poverty and homelessness?

Journal Writing

Suggestions for journal topics for students' selection:

1. As a student, what particular disabilities have you experienced with a peer in your classes?

2. Which type of disability would you find most challenging to adapt for? What can you do to prepare for this?

3. Which area of Howard Gardner's multiple intelligences do you feel is your area of strength? Explain why and give an example.

Chapter 5 What Social Problems and Tension Points Affect Today's Students?

Multiple-Choice Items

Read each item carefully. On the appropriate line, write the letter of the choice that represents the best answer.

d _____ 1. Which of the following statements is a common, but *false,* assumption about poverty in America?
- a. Children in poverty are undernourished.
- b. Most of the poor people in America live in semirural towns.
- c. Half of all heads of poor households are employed.
- d. The majority of poor people in the United States are minorities.

d _____ 2. Perry is a student in your class, and you know he is homeless. What potential problems might Perry face in light of his living situation?
- a. His parent(s) may not participate at school.
- b. He may not be allowed to attend school without a permanent address.
- c. His teacher may not know how to meet his particular needs.
- d. He may have trouble making friends because of poor personal hygiene, and may frequently miss school because of transportation difficulties.

b _____ 3. Jenna is seventeen years old, the mother of an infant, and a full-time employee at a small manufacturing company. What else is likely true about Jenna's life?
- a. She is making progress advancing in her company.
- b. She lives below the poverty line.
- c. She is enrolled part-time in college.
- d. She and her child are physically healthy.

a _____ 4. Why are teen-age mothers particularly vulnerable to poverty?
   a. They do not usually have marketable skills or a trade.
   b. They usually demonstrate a lack of commitment to any job.
   c. They usually expect that social service agencies will be able to meet their needs.
   d. They don't set attainable goals.

a _____ 5. The psychological effects of abuse on a child can lead to
   a. serious learning difficulties for the child.
   b. a dislike for school.
   c. free breakfast and lunch in school.
   d. more study hall time.

c _____ 6. Darla LeMan suspects that her student Sheila is being abused at home. After she reports her suspicion to the principal, how can Darla best serve Sheila's needs?
   a. offer Sheila extra attention by spending time with her after school
   b. informally stop by Sheila's home to visit with Sheila and her family
   c. provide a stable class environment to foster student learning
   d. uphold very high standards for Sheila and her work so that Sheila knows that Darla believes in her

b _____ 7. Which of the following is uppermost among a teacher's responsibilities toward a child who is disadvantaged, neglected, or abused?
   a. giving the child lots of attention and affection
   b. offering the haven of a well-run, orderly classroom
   c. maintaining a cool but fair approach to help the child learn independence and feel a sense of accomplishment when he or she completes work
   d. showing the child that you care, perhaps by buying the child a toy or an ice-cream cone

c _____ 8. It is the third week of September, and you are just beginning to know your first-grade students. One child, Marcus, stands out in your mind. He has not made friends with any playmates so far, and he rarely talks to the other children. Yesterday, during play time, after playing with a cardboard puzzle for several minutes, he stomped on it. Later, he told you he got mad at it because "it wasn't all fitting in." During the past several days, he has had several such outbursts, usually when things get busy in the class, such as lining up for lunch or recess, or marching to music. Given his behavior, you think he may
   a. have dyslexia.
   b. have a low IQ.
   c. be suffering from abuse.
   d. be homeless.

d _____ 9. The U.S. family structure is changing. Today, it would not be unusual to find
a. a single-parent family.
b. a blended family with children from previous marriages.
c. children living with grandparents or other relatives.
d. All of the above are quite likely.

c _____ 10. Gayle Singleton is a divorced mother of two children who works at a local shipping company. If she is representative of most divorced mothers, what is the most significant problem she is facing?
a. deep feelings of depression after her marriage ended
b. the relocation of her family, including finding a new home and a new school for her children
c. the financial strain of supporting her family on limited income
d. harassment from her ex-husband

d _____ 11. Over 60 percent of all children live in homes where the only parent or both parents work. What significance does that have for teachers?
a. Many teachers will have difficulty contacting parents.
b. Teachers should be aware that parents' work schedules may prevent them from taking a more visible role in their child's education.
c. Parents are now generally expecting teachers to monitor children much more closely than the parents will.
d. Teachers will have difficulty contacting parents and should be aware that parents' work schedules may prevent them from taking a more visible role in their child's schooling.

a _____ 12. A teacher notices that Victor, a student in her class, has been acting differently. He has quit the hockey team and stopped spending time with his friends. When she asks Victor about it, he withdraws. The teacher feels that she has seen a happy, popular, attractive boy become a disheveled-looking loner. She raises the issue with a guidance counselor, who thinks Victor may have a drug or alcohol problem. The guidance counselor and teacher should also consider, given Victor's behavior, that he
a. is contemplating suicide.
b. has abused a child.
c. may just be going through a stage of adolescent development.
d. has joined a gang.

d _____ 13. A teacher has serious concerns, based on a student's behavior, that the student is contemplating suicide, and one day the student admits that the possibility has occurred to him. The teacher should
a. have a long talk with the student, telling him why he should want to live.
b. tell the student that he or she will always be available if the student needs to talk.
c. call the student's parents.
d. contact the school psychologist or guidance counselor and explain the situation.

b ______ 14. Relief from a high incidence of school violence and vandalism seems to come directly from programs that
a. strictly enforce rules and punish offenders.
b. establish a firm, fair, and consistent system.
c. generously and publicly reward compliant student behavior.
d. do all of the above.

c ______ 15. Mrs. Wasserberg is the principal of Kenmont High School, located in an urban area. She has managed to develop ways for all staff members to have positive and productive interactions with students, while maintaining order. Such an atmosphere in a school, according to research, helps reduce which of the following problems?
a. teenage pregnancy
b. child abuse
c. violence and vandalism in schools
d. teenage suicide

a ______ 16. The national drop-out rate during the 1970s, 1980s, and early 1990s has
a. remained steady.
b. sharply increased in the 1970s, leveled in the early 1980s, and declined in the late 1980s and early 1990s.
c. gradually, steadily increased over the years.
d. sharply increased.

d ______ 17. Youth join gangs
a. to belong to and identify with a group.
b. for companionship and camaraderie.
c. because they feel ignored.
d. because of all of the above.

c ______ 18. To minimize the influence of gangs, educators can
a. hire more security personnel.
b. ignore minor activity.
c. establish programs that stress positive youth involvement.
d. investigate the use of metal detectors and dogs.

b ______ 19. What is the most-cited reason for students dropping out of school?
a. pregnancy
b. poor grades
c. dislike of school
d. employment opportunities

b _____ 20. Equality of educational opportunity was defined as equal allocation of resources *until* the U.S. Supreme Court ruled on which of the following cases?
a. *Swan* v. *Charlotte-Mecklenburg*
b. *Brown* v. *Board of Education*
c. *Wolman* v. *Walter*
d. *Lau* v. *Nichols*

d _____ 21. After the *Brown* v. *Board of Education* decision, what new component was added to considerations of whether educational opportunities offered to all children were equal?
a. the amount spent on teachers' salaries
b. the class size
c. the quality of the textbooks provided
d. the measurable effect of schooling

c _____ 22. Although the 1954 Supreme Court decision ended *de jure* school segregation, *de facto* segregation continued because of
a. widespread refusal to obey the law.
b. federal regulations.
c. neighborhood housing patterns.
d. unequal distribution of magnet schools.

c _____ 23. Cross-region busing was an attempt to integrate metropolitan regions in response to
a. white flight, in which many white families moved out of urban cities into the metropolitan areas.
b. magnets schools, which were built primarily in urban areas.
c. federal court orders to desegregate public schools.
d. recent waves of immigrants settling in metropolitan areas.

d _____ 24. The impact of housing patterns on school desegregation is somewhat offset by
a. busing children to achieve balance.
b. creating magnet schools to attract racially balanced student groups.
c. parents who voluntarily transfer schools.
d. busing children to achieve balance and creating magnet schools to attract racially balanced groups.

b _____ 25. Compensatory education was designed to overcome learning deficiencies in students who
a. do not speak English as a first language.
b. are from a disadvantaged socioeconomic background.
c. have developmentally delayed speech.
d. are not very smart.

a _____ 26. Critics have charged that compensatory education programs are ineffective because students served by the programs
- a. show no increase in their IQ scores.
- b. are still placed in special education classes with the same frequency as before the program.
- c. take longer than originally planned to move out of their bilingual classrooms and into English-speaking classes.
- d. have a higher suicide rate than those who are not served by the programs.

a _____ 27. Kindergarten and first-grade teachers would probably support Head Start programs because
- a. they help children get ready to begin school.
- b. they provide children with playmates.
- c. they help to connect school and home.
- d. they provide nourishment for children.

b _____ 28. The educator who advocated using structured environments with supplies and equipment that give children the learning opportunities they needed while they engaged in "free play" was
- a. Herbert Kohl.
- b. Maria Montessori.
- c. Jonathon Kozol.
- d. Johann Pestalozzi.

c _____ 29. What might be found in a classroom designed according to Montessori's methods?
- a. dozens of storybooks and puzzles
- b. colorful workbooks with carefully sequenced lessons in math and reading
- c. a child-sized kitchen and dining area with appropriate supplies and equipment
- d. small desks with old-fashioned inkwells and little drawers for children's toys

b _____ 30. Magnet schools are
- a. private schools that receive public support because they resolve some problems of segregation.
- b. public schools with high-quality, special-interest, cost-effective programs.
- c. private schools that attract minority and white students and are inexpensive.
- d. expensive public schools.

a _____ 31. Magnet schools were initially designed to do which of the following?
- a. contribute to the desegregation of schools in urban areas
- b. provide musically and artistically talented students with a school tailored to their talents
- c. provide a rich academic environment for children at risk
- d. fill the need for public schools that demand rigorous academic work from their students and have high expectations for their academic success

a _____ 32. Mrs. Li's son shows a strong interest for and aptitude in science. He is enrolled at P.S. 101 in Manhattan, where he is doing superior work; however, Mrs. Li is not satisfied with the science facilities at her son's school, and she doesn't have enough money to send him to a private school. What other options would she have?
a. She can arrange for her son to go to a magnet school.
b. She can send her son to a school in another neighborhood with better science facilities.
c. She can ask the school district to provide a science tutor for her son.
d. She can move out of the city to a rural school.

b _____ 33. Ms. Bradley, a high school math teacher, teaches a trigonometry class with thirteen boys and eight girls. One day, she was in the middle of a lesson reviewing answers to a test when her overhead projector malfunctioned. Looking up, she asked, "Do any of you boys know how to fix this machine?" One boy, Ed, came up and quickly fixed the projector. Which of the following indicates sexist behavior on Ms. Bradley's part?
a. She teaches a class dominated by males.
b. She asked only if one of the boys could fix the machine.
c. She is unable to fix the machine herself.
d. She uses an overhead projector in her class.

d _____ 34. Features that indicate gender bias in a history textbook include
a. descriptions of common occupations held only by men.
b. women mentioned infrequently, usually with reference to their husbands or fathers.
c. generic use of masculine pronouns.
d. all of the above.

c _____ 35. How have different social expectations affected behaviors of boys and girls?
a. Boys are ruder whereas girls are more polite and courteous.
b. Girls tend to be more aggressive now than they were twenty years ago.
c. Boys are expected to be aggressive and independent, whereas girls are expected to be passive conformists.
d. Boys aren't as noisy as they were ten years ago.

b _____ 36. A recent report by the American Association of University Women contends that schools are not meeting girls' needs because
a. boys are always making trouble in class and girls are not.
b. boys get more attention from teachers and have higher expectations placed on them.
c. girls always have to clean up in the classroom and boys do not.
d. girls are not allowed to use the computers in the classroom.

a ______ 37. Melissa, a seventh-grader at East Highwater Middle School, is afraid to go to her locker because every time she does, a group of boys is standing around making lewd comments to her. Melissa's grades are beginning to suffer. Melissa's case is an example of
a. sexual harassment.
b. gender bias.
c. sexual preferential treatment.
d. gender stereotyping.

b ______ 38. The National Insurance Company is looking to hire high school students to do data entry work during the summer months. The positions require knowledge of computers and minimal typing skills. Because the company is located near a depressed urban area, the company is actively recruiting urban teenagers. Unfortunately, the company has not been able to fill the positions. This is probably because the high school students
a. are not interested in working.
b. do not have access to computers at school or at home and are not computer literate.
c. would rather work at a fast-food restaurant.
d. do not have enough time to work.

b ______ 39. Interpretation of the implications of Title IX means that
a. females must be offered equal educational opportunities in institutions that receive any federal dollars.
b. females must be offered equal opportunities for participation in a program that is funded by federal dollars.
c. females must be permitted to play on any team that is fielded at federal expense.
d. educational achievement awards of students must be equally distributed between males and females.

b ______ 40. Sex education is a very controversial topic. However, most people would agree on which of the following?
a. School is the appropriate institution to offer sex education.
b. Young people need information about sex.
c. Students should receive only factual information about sex.
d. Young people can learn enough about sex from television.

c ______ 41. It is unlikely that the debate over sex education will be resolved soon because sex education is
a. too costly for most school systems.
b. too complex for most students to understand.
c. linked to people's religious and moral beliefs, which represent a wide range of views.
d. tied to people's socioeconomic standing.

a _____ 42. The Tyler school system would like to implement a sex education course in seventh and eighth grade, but administrators have met with considerable resistance from the community. What statistics should the central administration present to the community to convince them of the need for the course?

a. Ten thousand adolescents under the age of fifteen give birth annually.
b. Sex education courses have not been shown to either increase or reduce teen sexual activity.
c. Sex education programs are rarely long enough to be effective.
d. Fourteen and one-half percent of the U.S. population lives below the poverty line.

Short-Answer Questions

Respond to each of the following questions briefly, but specifically, in complete sentences.

43. Explain the difference between *de jure* and *de facto* segregation, and explain why one is easier to eliminate than the other.

(suggested answer) De jure segregation is governed by law, whereas *de facto* segregation is governed by practices and habits. *De jure* segregation was eliminated by the Supreme Court decision of 1954, which made it unconstitutional. *De facto* segregation still exists because the law cannot govern where people choose to live. *De jure* segregation is easier to eliminate because it requires new laws or legislation. *De facto* segregation requires that people change their living habits or ways of thinking, which is much more difficult to do.

44. Some people criticize the presence of magnet schools, claiming that they siphon off the best students from the neighborhood schools and that the existence of magnet schools, in effect, minimizes the attention and resources neighborhood schools should get to improve the education of all students. How do you respond to this criticism? Are magnet schools, on the whole, positive or negative contributions to public education?

(Answers will vary.)

45. Education has been proposed as a solution to poverty, yet despite numerous programs and great expense, the vicious cycle of poverty remains. Discuss the reasons why schooling does not seem to be an effective solution to poverty.

(suggested answer) Students should recognize that schools are a middle-class concept with middle-class values that are in conflict with the circumstances of the poor. Consequently, economically disadvantaged youth often feel alienated in schools and do not succeed academically.

Essay Questions

Read each of the following questions, and respond by composing an organized essay that includes an introduction, fully developed paragraph(s), and a conclusion.

46. Compensatory education attempts to overcome learning deficiencies of economically disadvantaged children. In light of the middle-class values of schools and the mediocre results of compensatory education programs to date, argue a position either in favor of or opposed to maintaining these federally funded programs in the schools. If you favor eliminating the programs, what would you propose in their place? You must support your position with specific information.

    (*suggested answer*) Answers will vary. Students must support their position with information, statistics, or facts from the book or from other sources.

47. Consider the following quote by Neil Postman: "If you heap upon the school all of the problems that the family, the church, the political system, and the economy cannot solve, the school becomes a kind of well-financed garbage dump, from which very little can be expected except the unsweet odor of failure." To what degree does this statement represent public schools? What do you see as the role of the public school in solving or ameliorating social problems?

    (Answers will vary.)

Alternative Assessment Ideas

The following activities are suggestions for student portfolio activities. They are a means of providing alternative assessment of the students' capabilities.

Independent Reading

Read and respond to any of the following selections from Ryan/Cooper, *Kaleidoscope: Readings in Education* (Houghton Mifflin, 1998). You may want to use the Article Review Form on page 269.

Barr—"Who Is This Child?"

Edelman—"Defending America's Children"

Eitzen—"Problem Students"

Reflective Papers

Choose one of the following topics to write a reflective paper (2–5 pages). The purpose of the paper is to help you assimilate new knowledge by blending it with your previous knowledge and experiences.

1. Think about your high school experience. What was the ethnic and racial composition of the student body? How did the different groups interact? How did the makeup of the school community affect your experience there?

2. Do you remember a time when you realized that a friend (or a classmate) was "different" from you, that is, when it became clear to you that this friend (or classmate) was being treated differently because of his or her race, ethnic background, or socioeconomic status? Tell about the experience and how it affected you.

3. Have you ever had the opportunity to work with economically disadvantaged youth—for example, in a soup kitchen, a homeless shelter, or a boys and girls club? Describe the experience.

Journal Writing

Suggestions for journal topics for students' selection:

1. What do you feel will be the most significant social challenge that you will face as a teacher?

2. Pick one of the social challenges and give as many ideas as you can for how a teacher could address its effects in his or her classroom.

3. How would you feel about teaching sex education? Why?

Chapter 6 What Makes a Teacher Effective?

Multiple-Choice Items

Read each item carefully. On the appropriate line, write the letter of the choice that represents the best answer.

c ____ 1. Before starting a new unit, Sally White reviews her notes on students, refers to written goals for them, and collects materials that she will need for her class. During this process, what kind of decisions is Sally making?
   a. planning
   b. evaluating
   c. instructing
   d. managing

a ____ 2. After giving her class several algebra problems to work on individually, Melina observed that half the students were stuck. She called the class's attention and asked them to work on their algebra problems in pairs so they could help each other. What kind of decision did Melina make?
   a. adopting
   b. evaluating
   c. planning
   d. implementing

d ____ 3. When teachers choose a student to respond, pause to permit questions, and add more examples of a concept to reinforce learning, the type of decision they are making is
   a. planning.
   b. managing.
   c. implementing.
   d. evaluating.

c _____ 4. Which of the following is the best description of reflective teaching?
- a. teaching that mirrors the culture in which the teacher is working
- b. teaching that puts current theoretical research into classroom practice
- c. teaching that incorporates a teacher's self-examination and self-evaluation
- d. teaching that responds to the interests and needs of the students

a _____ 5. Which of the following teachers best exemplifies the behavior of a reflective teacher?
- a. Keshia reviews her lessons each day after teaching and keeps a teaching journal.
- b. Anselm talks frequently to veteran teachers to see how they teach particular topics.
- c. Darnell uses commercially prepared instructional materials when he begins a unit.
- d. Tina prepares detailed thematic units demonstrating the most recent research on different learning styles.

b _____ 6. A teacher's attitude toward students plays an obvious role in influencing teacher behavior. Which other attitude also plays an important role?
- a. a teacher's attitude toward his or her teacher education program
- b. a teacher's attitude toward his or her colleagues
- c. a teacher's attitude toward professional associations
- d. a teacher's attitude toward his or her own parents

c _____ 7. Teaching is significantly affected by the teacher's attitude toward
- a. work, toward learning, and toward the practice of habits.
- b. being a professional and toward being a good staff member.
- c. other teachers and parents and toward the subject.
- d. training, toward the status of teachers, and toward oneself.

d _____ 8. An essential part of understanding and dealing with the feelings of students is
- a. watching students' behavior out of class.
- b. taking courses in adolescent psychology.
- c. studying students' records and talking to their previous teachers.
- d. knowing and understanding one's own feelings.

b _____ 9. How does accepting one's own feelings of anger help a teacher?
- a. She cannot rid herself of unhealthy emotions if she doesn't accept them.
- b. It can help her understand how a student's anger can affect his or her learning.
- c. It enables her to control the anger of her students.
- d. She can draw on it for energy and inspiration in her work with students.

b _____ 10. Psychologist Carl Rogers identified "valuing" as an essential attitude for a teacher to be successful. "Valuing" is best described by which of the following?

a. the teacher valuing herself or himself as a professional, setting and meeting high expectations
b. the teacher valuing the learners, for both their positive and negative characteristics
c. the teacher valuing the interests of both parents and specific children as a guide in curriculum design
d. the teacher valuing the input of colleagues and administrators for curriculum and instruction

c _____ 11. Brian, frustrated by his math worksheet, tears the paper in half. Which of the teacher's following responses would best characterize what psychologist Carl Rogers calls "empathic understanding"?

a. "Joanna, why don't you sit with Brian and help him with his math worksheet? He needs your help."
b. "Brian, tearing your math worksheet is not a constructive way to solve your problems."
c. "You were working on those problems for some time without getting many done. Why don't you show me where you got stuck?"
d. "Math was always my worst subject, too. Finally, I just realized I was better at other things."

b _____ 12. Sasha, an extremely bright teacher, often collaborates with other teachers in interdisciplinary projects. At times, she will teasingly joke with other teachers to "see if they can do better." With administrators, her manner changes. She challenges them at faculty meetings, demanding explanations for their actions. Which characteristic of Sasha most likely contributes to her positive relationship with her colleagues?

a. her level of intelligence
b. her collaborative approach to teaching
c. her enthusiasm for competition with other teachers
d. her strength to challenge the administration

d _____ 13. Effective teachers demonstrate certain traits in their dealings with peers, administrators, and parents. What are those traits?

a. intellectual rigor, fair-mindedness, and competitiveness
b. vision, cooperation, and innovativeness in problem solving
c. creativity, competence, and control of students
d. cooperation, collaboration, and acceptance of others

a _____ 14. Which of the following will impede a teacher's effectiveness?

a. a tendency to seek recognition from teaching peers
b. a desire to maintain exacting standards
c. an interest in collaborating on long-term curricular projects
d. an inclination toward becoming personally invested in one's students

b ____ 15. Joe is a high-energy teacher who works constantly. As he plans lessons, Joe compares his to those of other teachers and works to make his stronger and more engaging for his students. He is friendly to everyone and is noted for his quick wit and sometimes sarcastic sense of humor. Joe's peers don't particularly like him. What is the most probable reason why?

a. He works too hard and is too efficient.
b. He is competitive with his peers.
c. He does not maintain a professional distance from his colleagues.
d. He has a sense of humor that borders on sarcasm.

c ____ 16. During an Open House night, Tyrone Green met with parents of his Algebra I students. He briefly mentioned some of the fundamental concepts in Algebra I and spent most of his time explaining his techniques for teaching Algebra I to ninth-graders. What kind of knowledge did Tyrone use to explain how he taught algebra?

a. discipline content knowledge
b. curriculum content knowledge
c. pedagogical content knowledge
d. theory-in-use knowledge

c ____ 17. David Kornfeld, a college senior majoring in history, was concerned that his knowledge of history would be insufficient to teach high school. He was considering enrolling in more American history courses to prepare himself for the classroom. According to research about teacher effectiveness, what is most likely a better use of David's time as he prepares to teach?

a. developing tests in American history for his use with students
b. studying history from an interdisciplinary perspective so he could draw upon those other areas in his teaching
c. reading and reviewing the curriculum to determine what is covered in the course
d. learning alternative strategies for facilitating a group process in the classroom

b ____ 18. Isabel Alvarez teaches high school English. Before the students hand a paper in, she schedules class time for them to read and respond to other classmates' papers. When they ask why she schedules class time to do this, she tells them that their writing should be read by many people. How else could her explanation be described?

a. as her theory of composition
b. as her theory-in-use
c. as common sense
d. as pedagogical content knowledge

c _____ 19. A theory-in-use is best described as
a. a hypothesis designed to bring generalizable facts, concepts, or scientific laws into systematic connection.
b. a commonsense idea proven throughout repeated experiences.
c. an explanation used to justify action.
d. a practical solution to a theoretical problem.

d _____ 20. A panel of educators is asked to review a new "fifth-year" teacher training program that focuses almost exclusively on presentation and evaluation methods, or "practical" skills. One shortcoming the panel might expect to find in the program is that its graduates
a. will lack adequate content knowledge (for example, in history or math).
b. will be unable to use some of the more innovative methodologies they learn in their school settings.
c. will resist using some of the methodologies to which they have been exposed.
d. will lack the theoretical knowledge that would help them interpret the complexities of the classroom.

c _____ 21. Gigi Underwood's class has been doing a hands-on unit on World War I. First, the students were enthusiastically responding. Yesterday, Gigi noticed that the class's interest seemed to be flagging. Which of the following would be most helpful to help Gigi interpret the situation?
a. her own common sense
b. discipline knowledge
c. theoretical knowledge
d. curriculum content knowledge

b _____ 22. Which of the following statements from teachers best exemplifies a constructivist view of learning?
a. "Sometimes, to understand a concept, the students just have to discipline themselves enough to memorize fundamental principles."
b. "I ask the students to explain what they already know about an idea, and then I help them relate new information to their prior knowledge."
c. "I like to build in plenty of time for students to practice skills, so I supply lots of additional exercises for them."
d. "I assume the students know very little about the subject, so I move quite slowly with them, providing them with the essential concepts of the discipline."

c _____ 23. In Mr. Nillson's classroom, all of the following activities occur. Which one is most representative of a constructivist view of learning?
a. Small groups of students engage in a choral reading of a story.
b. Students work individually on worksheets at their desks.
c. Students work in pairs, discussing how best to put together a model.
d. One student leads the others in an energetic "quiz-show" activity.

a _____ 24. Which of the following would be most consistent with recent cognitive research on teaching and learning?

a. Ask students to talk about how they complete a task and structure cooperative learning experiences for students.

b. Establish high expectations for all students and structure frequent competitive activities for all students.

c. Arrange for students to have cognitive apprenticeships and teach students mnemonic devices to help improve their memory.

d. Observe students as they work through problems and prevent students from attempting problems that are beyond their ability.

d _____ 25. Janice Mafucci would like to help her composition students develop intellectually. Based upon current cognitive research, which of the following activities are most likely to help Janice meet her goal?

a. Present students with direct guidelines on how to structure essays.

b. Meet with students individually to point out errors in their writing.

c. Provide students with numerous opportunities to rewrite papers without handing papers in for a grade.

d. Ask students to keep a learning log in which they reflect upon their composing process.

a _____ 26. Lois and Charlotte are considered successful teachers. Lois revises her units each year, working to improve them, whereas Charlotte rarely teaches the same unit twice. Lois is able to cover much material with her class by adhering to lesson plans, whereas Charlotte will alter her lesson plan if she thinks it is necessary. Which teacher demonstrates the behavior of an effective teacher?

a. Charlotte, because she will modify her lessons if she thinks it's necessary

b. Lois, because she is able to teach her students a large amount of material by adhering to her plans

c. Charlotte, because she never teaches the same unit twice

d. Lois, because she teaches a unit over again to a different group of students

c _____ 27. Julie prepared an extensive unit on the nesting habits of swallows for her second-grade class. She included a variety of activities, including showing a documentary film. Her students fidgeted during the film, paying little attention to it. According to research on effective teaching, what should Julie do the next time?

a. Show the film over several days to cut down on students' restlessness.

b. Present the students with several questions before the film to focus their attention.

c. Reassess whether that particular film is suited for her second-graders.

d. Eliminate showing films altogether, opting for more active student learning.

c _____ 28. A teacher smoothly makes transitions from one activity to another so that no time is wasted, she clearly explains what she wants her students to do during activities, and she sets up a system by which they can quickly and quietly have their work checked by her before moving on to the next activity. These tasks of the teacher all fall under the description of
a. teaching methodology.
b. academic engaged time.
c. classroom management.
d. preactive decision making.

b _____ 29. Raoul Fernandes is able to create a purposeful learning environment in his class through behaviors that focus on instruction and help him run the classroom smoothly. This skill can best be described as
a. preactive decisions.
b. classroom management.
c. momentum.
d. engaged time.

c _____ 30. When the principal comes in unannounced to ask the teacher a question, she notices that several students are creating a model. Other students are reading science books, several others are writing, and one or two are clustered around a computer, working on an instructional program. They all appear immersed in their tasks. These students demonstrate
a. cooperative learning.
b. classroom management.
c. academic engaged time.
d. authentic assessment.

d _____ 31. Which of the following best describes the concept of "academic engagement"?
a. Students work quietly on tasks without any break in their involvement, mastering skills.
b. Students work sequentially through more varied and complex material.
c. Students show a high degree of interest and demonstrate independence in pursuing new tasks.
d. Students work on activities relevant to the teacher's goals and work with a high degree of success.

c _____ 32. A student was overheard saying to his friend, "There's no way I would act up in her class. She acts like she knows what's going to happen before it happens. Ted tried to fool her, but she got him right away. You can't pull anything on her." According to Kounin, this teacher has
a. realness.
b. smoothness.
c. "with-it-ness."
d. pedagogical content knowledge.

b _____ 33. In Liz's class, some students worked quickly through tasks and sat with nothing to do. Liz often had to stop other students in the middle of their work to clarify the assignment. As a result, the class usually took much longer than Liz planned to complete their work. What elements of classroom management does Liz lack, according to Jacob Kounin's ideas?
a. with-it-ness and realness
b. smoothness and momentum
c. clarity and appropriateness
d. planning and consistency

c _____ 34. Ms. Salama frequently scans her classroom to see how students are working, she varies the type and difficulty of questions she asks students, and she reinforces the expectations she has for them. All of her behaviors best match which of the following terms?
a. reflective teaching
b. interactive decision making
c. classroom management
d. theory-in-use

a _____ 35. Mike Hsu, a sixth-grade teacher, is having difficulty with Benny, one of his students. Benny finishes his tasks quickly and then distracts other students. According to Jim and Kevin's suggestions for classroom management, what should Mike do?
a. Use assertive discipline to control Benny's behavior.
b. Review his teaching to see if it is appropriate for Benny.
c. Pair Benny with a student who needs assistance.
d. Design activities to boost Benny's self-esteem.

c _____ 36. Which of the following is consistent with the tone of "Kevin and Jim's Suggestions for Classroom Discipline"?
a. Be discreet about your problems. Don't tell anyone until you have tried everything.
b. Make polite but firm corrections to individuals publicly so everyone gets the benefit of the instructions.
c. Confront student misbehavior immediately. Don't let things slide.
d. Make unilateral decisions about the kinds of disciplinary action a student needs. The administration should support you as a professional.

c _____ 37. Although Noam's math students are bright and interested, their responses to his questions are minimal. Which is the best suggestion for Noam to improve the length and quality of his students' responses?
a. Have them practice giving oral reports.
b. Have them write their own questions to ask and answer.
c. Wait longer between asking a question and calling for a response.
d. Tell them that their final grade will also include "contribution to class."

d _____ 38. To use questions effectively, teachers should
a. ask abstract questions.
b. ask long questions.
c. call a student's name before asking the question.
d. probe students' responses.

c _____ 39. According to research, what typically happens when teachers increase their wait-time when questioning students?
a. The momentum of the class lesson slows down, and advanced students lose their concentration.
b. The teachers' questions change from being primarily recall questions to questions that require higher-order thinking.
c. The students provide lengthier responses without being asked.
d. The students' attitude about the subject improves, and they are more willing to follow the teachers' lead.

Short-Answer Questions

Respond to each of the following questions briefly, but specifically, in complete sentences.

40. Describe a situation that would exemplify a constructivist view of learning. Explain how it demonstrates constructivism.

(suggested answer) The students' examples will vary. However, the example should clearly show a person engaged in building knowledge or constructing meaning for himself or herself, rather than passively receiving knowledge. Typical examples might include group problem solving, cooperative learning, and think-aloud protocols.

41. Why are such practices as think-aloud problem solving and cooperative learning groups suggested by current educational research? What do they provide for students that many traditional paper-and-pencil assignments lack?

(suggested answer) Problem solving and cooperative learning groups stress activities that foster learners' capacities for using prior knowledge in their assimilation and utilization of new knowledge. Current cognitive research demonstrates that learners build upon prior knowledge and existing schema to incorporate new knowledge. Such activities also foster learners' own awareness of their own thinking. Traditional paper-and-pencil assignments usually do not foster that kind of learner awareness, nor have they traditionally asked learners to build upon what they already know when learning new material.

42. Using the text, identify four questions that teachers can ask themselves to gauge their classroom management skills. What implications do those four questions have for gauging the teacher's behavior and the class's behavior?

(Answers will vary.) The list of questions includes the following:

a. Can you see all students from any place in any room in which you instruct or work?
b. Are students who frequently need your help or assistance seated where you can easily monitor and reach them?
c. Do some students frequently bother others who sit near them?
d. Are your major class procedures being followed without constant prompting and reminders?
e. Are you spending as much time going over directions and procedures now as at the beginning of the year?
f. Do students sometimes claim that they didn't know an assignment was due or what its requirements were?
g. Do many of your students fail to complete assignments or not turn them in at all?
h. Do you reward good student behavior, including effort, in a variety of ways?
i. Do you find yourself assessing penalties more and more often and rewarding students less than you previously did?
j. Do you tend to notice misbehavior only after it involves several students?
k. Do you sometimes have the feeling that some students are misbehaving simply to gain your attention?
l. Do you often discover that students have not understood your presentations and that they therefore cannot complete assignments correctly?
m. Are transitions from one activity to another taking a long time?
n. Are a few of your students so far behind the class that you have just given up on them?

43. Drawing from your experiences as a student or from the classroom, give an example of a theory-in-use. If the person in the example had had greater theoretical knowledge, how would the theory-in-use fare?

(Answers will vary.)

Essay Questions

Read each of the following questions, and respond by composing an organized essay that includes an introduction, fully developed paragraph(s), and a conclusion.

44. List five characteristics of effective teachers and give an example of each.

(suggested answer) Effective teachers ask higher- and lower-order questions appropriately, reinforce desired student behavior, diagnose students' needs, vary teaching to sustain interest, recognize and use cues about student engagement, use necessary equipment, judge the utility of materials, set behavioral objectives, connect new knowledge to prior learning, structure lessons clearly and pace them rapidly, communicate high expectations, provide safety and order, and foster conviviality. Examples will vary.

45. List five of Kevin and Jim's rules of management. Explain each.

(suggested answer) Kevin and Jim's rules for classroom management are when students misbehave, check teaching; make sure everyone knows the rules; monitor the class regularly; squelch flagrant misbehavior quickly; correct in private; don't make empty threats; don't put hands on a child in anger; think through problems; get help; have a back-up; and make sure your rules are consistent with the school's. Examples will vary.

46. Teachers used to be noted for having good "disciplinary skills." Now researchers talk about teachers' "classroom management styles." Explain how the concept of classroom management differs from discipline.

    (suggested answer) Discipline usually implies keeping order and control of students. It has a much more limited scope than classroom management because it focuses on ensuring that students behave appropriately. Classroom management, on the other hand, is broader in scope. It includes maintaining an appropriate and orderly environment for student learning, but it also includes a wider variety of related activities. Much emphasis in classroom management is on a teacher's instructional skills—developing developmentally appropriate lessons, asking a wide variety of questions, and understanding students' needs—in addition to a teacher's ability to help regulate student behavior. Classroom management also has a fairly wide variety of approaches, including such approaches as assertive discipline, or building the socioemotional climate of the classroom.

47. Identify and explain the attitudes that can foster and those that can impede effective teachers.

    (suggested answer) Effective teachers demonstrate collaborative, cooperative, accepting attitudes toward others. Resentment toward authority, competition for recognition, and prejudicial or superior attitudes impede a teacher's effectiveness.

Alternative Assessment Ideas

The following activities are suggestions for student portfolio activities. They are a means of providing alternative assessment of the students' capabilities.

Independent Reading

Read and respond to any of the following selections from Ryan/Cooper, *Kaleidoscope: Readings in Education* (Houghton Mifflin, 1998). You may want to use the Article Review Form on page 269.

Clifford—"Students Need Challenge"

Csikszentmihalyi and McCormack—"The Influence of Teachers"

Dodd—"Engaging Students"

Ducharme—"The Great Teacher Question"

Haberman—"Selecting 'Star' Teachers"

Strong, Silver, and Robinson—"What Do Students Really Want?"

Reflective Papers

Choose one of the following topics to write a reflective paper (2–5 pages). The purpose of the paper is to help you assimilate new knowledge by blending it with your previous knowledge and experiences.

1. Recall your own experience as a student. Choose one teacher who made a positive impact on you. Write a short description of that teacher, showing what he or she typically did to impress you. Then analyze your recollections and description. To what extent did that teacher manifest the behaviors and attitudes of an effective teacher?

2. Recent cognitive research suggests that teachers should provide meaningful problem-solving experiences for learners. Assume the perspective of either a teacher or a student. Based upon that point of view, describe what you think would constitute a meaningful problem-solving experience.

3. In the text, Carol Landis had a number of unexamined theories-in-use that determined how she interacted with her students. Reflect upon your own assumptions about learning and teaching. Identify and list several of your own theories-in-use. What does each one reveal about some of your notions about education, about being a teacher, or about how teaching and learning should occur?

Journal Writing

Suggestions for journal topics for students' selection:

1. In your opinion, what is the *single* most important characteristic of an effective teacher?

2. Who was your most effective teacher? Why?

Chapter 7 What Should Teachers Know About Technology and Its Impact on Schools?

Multiple-Choice Items

Read each item carefully. On the appropriate line, write the letter of the choice that represents the best answer.

b _____ 1. When did technology that helped teachers use pictures in the classroom first become available?
a. 1880–1890
b. 1910–1920
c. 1930–1940
d. 1950–1960

d _____ 2. According to the text, what was one of the earliest technological devices used in classrooms?
a. filmstrip
b. television
c. radio
d. blackboard

c _____ 3. When a new technology is first introduced in the classroom, it is often proclaimed that
a. the materials will be too expensive.
b. students won't have to work in order to learn.
c. it will be the end of instruction as we now know it.
d. teachers will automatically know how to use it.

a _____ 4. According to the text, why has educational television *not* had a larger impact?
a. inadequate funding
b. poor teacher training
c. ineffective marketing
d. fear of new ideas

b _____ 5. Which one of these is *not* one of the stages of technology maturity? Technology
a. is applied to tasks we already do.
b. makes the tasks unnecessary.
c. is used to improve the tasks we do.
d. is used to do tasks that were not possible before.

b _____ 6. All of these are examples of using the computer as a cognitive tool *except*
a. word processor
b. drill and practice
c. database
d. spreadsheet

c _____ 7. When Li Chiu uses her computer to combine text, graphics, and a video to complete her eighth-grade science project presentation, she is using her computer as a
a. cognitive tool.
b. facilitator of instruction.
c. communication tool.
d. resource to compensate for her disability.

b _____ 8. When Mrs. Sanchez creates a multimedia project to individualize for her gifted and talented students, she is using her computer as a
a. cognitive tool.
b. facilitator of instruction.
c. communication tool.
d. poor substitute for her personal attention.

b _____ 9. Students who use word processors are more likely to
a. finish the assignment more quickly.
b. make more substantial revisions.
c. include more errors.
d. learn less about proofreading and editing.

a _____ 10. Which of the following tools would be useful to make a forecast or a prediction?
a. spreadsheet
b. database
c. word processor
d. calculator

a _____ 11. Which of the following was *not* created specifically to facilitate instruction?
a. World Wide Web
b. drill-and-practice software
c. simulation software
d. interactive multimedia

c _____ 12. One of the reasons drill-and-practice software in the 1970s and 1980s had relatively little impact on classroom instruction was because it was
a. too expensive.
b. ineffective.
c. perceived as a threat by teachers.
d. a panacea for student learning.

c _____ 13. The Berkeley public school district has just invested a considerable sum of money on computers for classroom use. If the administration and the faculty want to encourage widespread, habitual use of computers by the students, they should ensure
a. a one-to-one ratio of computer to student.
b. that students are rewarded with "computer time."
c. that the students have adequate access to computers during and after class.
d. that each student has a computer at home.

d _____ 14. Teachers will be able to use computers effectively only if
a. they receive proper training in their use.
b. they have on-site support.
c. each teacher has adequate access to appropriate hardware and software.
d. all of the above.

b _____ 15. Equity concerns regarding the integration of technology revolve around
a. the rapidity with which technology advances, making most hardware obsolete within three years.
b. the potential for increased disparities between rich schools and poor schools.
c. the lack of space in many schools for technology hardware.
d. the difficulty of finding qualified maintenance personnel.

d _____ 16. Sandra Wilkinsburg, a middle school social studies teacher in the Northeast, would like to teach a unit on the climatic regions of the world, with particular emphasis on tropical regions. How could new technologies enhance her instruction?
a. Students could access data banks from different libraries to find out about the flora and fauna of different regions.
b. Students could communicate through electronic mail with students in tropical regions to get firsthand information.
c. Students could work on a computer simulation of different climatic regions to understand the effect of natural and man-made factors on the environment.
d. All of the above would enhance her unit.

d _____ 17. The use of new technology in the classroom, which includes the computer, CD-ROMs, and multimedia, can enhance the curriculum by
a. accessing data banks from diverse sources.
b. creating simulations to solve real-life problems.
c. linking students in different states or countries to one another.
d. doing all of the above.

c _____ 18. Carr High School, located in a remote region of New Hampshire, has several students who are ready to enroll in calculus and others who wish to take Latin, but there aren't any teachers who can teach either course. Based upon the most recent advances in education, which proposal would be the best solution for Carr High School's problem?
a. an individualized correspondence course for each student
b. to tell students that they should postpone taking such courses until they enroll in college
c. to institute a distance education program whereby the students can enroll in calculus and Latin
d. to bus the students to other schools that do offer such courses

b _____ 19. What is the most significant benefit for instituting distance education within a school district?
a. Establishing and maintaining a program is less expensive than paying a teacher.
b. It provides a way to provide educational equity between rural and poorer students and those who come from larger, more affluent districts.
c. At-risk students who are enrolled in distance education programs demonstrate greater academic achievement than those who are not participants.
d. Distance education programs have proved to stimulate student productivity and time on task.

b ______ 20. Tutorial software can be used for all of the following *except*
a. presentation of a new skill or concept.
b. drill and practice.
c. evaluation of the learner's understanding.
d. check for understanding.

d ______ 21. Simulation software's advantages include all of the following *except*
a. management of information.
b. reaction to student input.
c. immediate feedback for the students.
d. substitution for the teacher as mentor of the instruction.

c ______ 22. The most efficient way to find something on the Internet is to
a. "surf."
b. locate a good home page.
c. use a search engine.
d. use a hard copy index.

b ______ 23. One of the main problems with using the Internet in schools is that
a. it's too expensive.
b. it contains some incorrect or inappropriate information.
c. it's too hard for students to learn to use.
d. it's not readily available.

d ______ 24. Distance education provides for all of the following *except*
a. overcoming problems of budget, size, and location.
b. using two-way audio and video interaction.
c. offering upper division or advanced placement courses.
d. flexibility of time.

a ______ 25. Which of the following is *not* a common type of computer deployment in schools?
a. a computer for each student
b. computer labs
c. single-computer classrooms
d. classroom computer clusters

b ______ 26. The provision of assistive technology in the classroom for students with special needs is mandated by
a. ADA—Aid for Disabled Americans.
b. IDEA—Individuals with Disabilities Act.
c. the Bill of Rights.
d. Goals 2000.

a _____ 27. One problem with using computers in instruction is that
a. many teachers focus their activities on learning about computers rather than using computers to learn.
b. teachers must move from whole-class instruction toward smaller group projects.
c. teachers must view themselves as coaches or facilitators.
d. classrooms evolve into cooperative rather than competitive social structures.

d _____ 28. Test generators, lesson-planning software, and outline and concept mapping tools are examples of
a. teacher-generated software.
b. teacher communication tools.
c. teacher instructional tools.
d. teacher productivity tools.

a _____ 29. A disadvantage to organizing the computers in a school into a computer lab is that
a. labs do not lend themselves to cooperative learning activities.
b. labs do not provide open table space.
c. labs foster instruction about technology.
d. all of the above are true.

d _____ 30. The optimum student-to-computer ratio in schools is thought to be
a. 10 to 1.
b. 9 to 1.
c. 1 to 1.
d. 3 to 1.

d _____ 31. Mrs. Brown teaches in an inner-city school district. Each of the classrooms in her school has one computer for student use. The equal opportunity issue in this school may be related to
a. inadequate funding.
b. inadequate electrical systems and network wiring.
c. inadequate access to the Internet.
d. all of the above.

b _____ 32. Which of the following is *not* a characteristic of teachers who use computers effectively?
a. They have received formal training.
b. They use computers for drill and practice.
c. They have a social network of computer-using teachers.
d. They use computers for consequential activities.

c _____ 33. In regard to gender differences in the use of computer technology, which of the following statements is true?
a. Girls are *more* likely to participate in out-of-school computer programs.
b. Families of boys are *less* likely to have computers at home.
c. Girls use computers *less* frequently in high school.
d. Boys are *less* likely to choose computer electives.

d _____ 34. Which of the following is evidence of the disparity in the quality of educational technology between affluent and disadvantaged students?
a. Affluent students are more likely to have a computer at home.
b. Disadvantaged students are more likely to be using computers for drill and practice.
c. White students are more likely than minority students to have a computer at home.
d. All of the above.

a _____ 35. In a technology-assisted classroom, the role of the teacher
a. is expanded and involves more higher-level evaluation of performance and more coaching of student learning.
b. changes minimally. The teacher will still be the dispenser of information, directing the students' learning.
c. becomes obsolete. The students can learn better on their own with the technology available.
d. is reduced to technology maintenance. The teacher ensures that the hardware is functional.

b _____ 36. Joey was born with a birth defect that left him unable to use his vocal cords and consequently to speak. Yet Joey has successfully completed his high school studies and looks forward to a challenging college career. How has assistive technology helped Joey communicate in class?
a. He has a full-time interpreter who speaks for him.
b. He makes use of a voice output device that produces synthesized sound.
c. He uses a voice input device to translate spoken words to written text.
d. He uses an adaptive word processing program to write his papers.

b _____ 37. Which of the following is *not* an example of assistive technology?
a. remote control units
b. Internet
c. ramps
d. computer to enhance communication

Short-Answer Questions

Respond to each of the following questions briefly, but specifically, in complete sentences.

38. Briefly identify and explain a benefit of as well as an obstacle to installing educational technology within classrooms.

    (suggested answer) The benefits that can be gained by using educational technology are many, including the benefits of distance education, interactive video software, individualized instruction, and greater access to educational information. The biggest obstacle for bringing educational technology into the classroom is the sometimes prohibitive cost of starting up programs with technology: the costs of computers, software, printers, CD-ROMs, and the like.

39. Choose one of the three ways that computers can be distributed in a school. Describe the advantages and disadvantages of this arrangement and tell why you prefer it.

    (suggested answer) Computer labs are one way. Advantages are that all students can use computers simultaneously, labs are best for teaching about the computer, and they facilitate demonstration. However, they are not useful for cooperative or interdisciplinary learning because of the lack of table space. Access is sometimes limited.

    Single-computer classrooms are another way. They are good for record keeping and can be used to facilitate cooperative groups. However, there is limited opportunity for each student.

    Classroom clusters are a third way. They encourage education *with* technology. This is the most flexible use of computers. However, they are costly, they require more printers, and they are not very useful for training *how* to use technology.

Essay Questions

Read each of the following questions, and respond by composing an organized essay that includes an introduction, fully developed paragraph(s), and a conclusion.

40. Clearly describe a specific topic or subject area and then indicate *all* of the ways you could use educational technology with your students to support and enhance effective instruction and learning.

    (suggested answer) Answers will vary. Look for the widest variety of applications suggested in the text.

41. Pick one of the controversial issues surrounding the use of technology in education. Clearly state *all* points of view on the issue and then give your own opinion and support it.

(suggested answer) Answers will vary depending on the issue selected—gender, expense, or equal opportunity.

42. The equity issues surrounding educational technology regarding gender and socioeconomic status create many problems for educators. Clearly describe one of these issues (gender, or economic advantage) and your solution for the problem.

    (Answers will vary.)

Alternative Assessment Ideas

The following activities are suggestions for student portfolio activities. They are a means of providing alternative assessment of the students' capabilities.

Independent Reading

Read and respond to any of the following selections from Ryan/Cooper, *Kaleidoscope: Readings in Education* (Houghton Mifflin, 1998). You may want to use the Article Review Form on page 269.

Hancock and Betts—"From the Lagging to the Leading Edge"

Levin and Thurston—"Educational Electronic Networks"

Mather—"Exploring the Internet Safely"

Milone and Salpeter—"Technology and Equity Issues"

Postman—"Making a Living, Making a Life"

Reflective Papers

Choose one of the following topics to write a reflective paper (2–5 pages). The purpose of the paper is to help you assimilate new knowledge by blending it with your previous knowledge and experiences.

1. Trace the development of one type of audio, visual, or computer technology in its use in the public schools. Include information on its purpose(s), advantages, and disadvantages, and any information regarding the documentation of the effectiveness of its use.

2. Research the gender (or socioeconomic) differences in the use of computer technology. Include information on programs designed to remedy this inequity and give your own ideas about solutions.

3. Investigate the literature predicting the future of technology in education. Form your own opinion about the probabilities of these predictions coming true and support it with past or present examples.

Journal Writing

Suggestions for journal topics for students' selection:

1. Think about your own education. At what grade level did you first encounter computers, CD-ROMs, or the Internet at school or in your classroom?

2. If you had the opportunity to take a course or all the courses in your degree program over the Internet, would you? Why or why not?

3. How is technology used at your field-site school? Consider equipment and software, student opportunities, and teacher abilities.

Chapter 8 What Is Taught?

Multiple-Choice Items

Read each item carefully. On the appropriate line, write the letter of the choice that represents the best answer.

b _____ 1. Which of the following curriculum emphases existed during the 1600s, 1700s, and 1800s?
a. cultivation of American loyalty
b. moral development and moral values
c. acquisition of a foreign language
d. self-adjustment

d _____ 2. During the colonial period, a school's curriculum would typically include
a. candle-making, weaving, arithmetic, and writing.
b. writing, knowledge necessary for trade, and arithmetic.
c. arithmetic, religious instruction, and citizenship.
d. reading, Bible teaching, and arithmetic.

c _____ 3. During the Revolutionary War era, schools emphasized literacy primarily to
a. prepare students for work.
b. enable students to recite Bible passages.
c. prepare students to maintain the democratic government.
d. enable students to read for pleasure.

a _____ 4. Based on the curricular trends in the mid- to late 1800s, which selection would a student be most likely to find in a reader?
a. a tale extolling the virtue of a hard-working girl
b. a short account of the life of Sir Isaac Newton
c. an analysis of the War of 1812
d. a daring adventure story of a pirate designed to maintain student interest

b _____ 5. The missions entrusted to schools from colonial times to the present have
a. remained constant as the nation pursued timeless democratic ideals.
b. changed as the nation has changed.
c. been essentially stable with occasional major upheavals.
d. changed often in response to new educational discoveries made in Europe.

d _____ 6. Through the history of American education, the public's understanding of the schools' mission has always included
a. moral education.
b. skills in trade.
c. conservative republican values.
d. none of the concepts cited here.

c _____ 7. As a reaction to the earlier curricular emphases in schools, progressive educators of the 1920s, 1930s, and 1940s emphasized which of the following in their curriculum?
a. foreign language
b. computational skills
c. self-adjustment
d. rote memorization

a _____ 8. The event that contributed to a swing from progressive and child-centered education in the United States to a more discipline-centered approach was the
a. launch of the Soviet satellite *Sputnik.*
b. passage of the National Defense Education Act.
c. *Brown* v. *Board of Education* decision.
d. death of John Dewey.

b _____ 9. In the late 1950s and early 1960s, the U.S. public placed renewed emphasis on the school curriculum because
a. there was a sudden increase in school-age children.
b. the public was concerned over the apparent U.S. lag in science and technology.
c. the federal government provided millions of dollars in support for education and research.
d. the dominant educational philosophy shifted from existentialism to progressivism.

b _____ 10. Jerome Bruner advocated teaching the "structure of a discipline," by which he meant the discipline's
a. history.
b. basic concepts and methods of inquiry.
c. most famous ideas and scholars.
d. relationship to other disciplines.

c _____ 11. The goal of using the discovery method, based on teaching the structure of a discipline, is to help students
a. learn factual material efficiently.
b. improve reading skill while adding to their content knowledge.
c. learn how to learn.
d. learn factual materials efficiently and improve reading skills.

a _____ 12. In the lessons of the spiral curriculum, as students move to new levels, they encounter
a. familiar concepts in more complex forms.
b. information about circular shapes.
c. planned repetition of content.
d. simplified versions of familiar concepts.
e. a greater focus on the interdisciplinary nature of concepts.

d _____ 13. Which of the following would most likely be included in a school's curriculum that espoused Bruner's theory of the spiral curriculum?
a. providing instruction in earth science for grade 9, biology for grade 10, and chemistry for grade 11
b. learning about the ecosystem in science class, the history of the debate between developers and environmentalists in social studies, and researching and writing about an environmental issue in language arts
c. teaching about how human digestion works in one grade and continuing to teach that concept the next year until all students demonstrate understanding of the concept
d. in lower elementary grades, the observation of the life cycle of a plant; in upper elementary grades, the performance experiments on the effect light and dark have on plants; in high school, the study of the chemical process of photosynthesis

a _____ 14. In the text, E. D. Hirsch defines cultural literacy as being
a. knowledgeable of the historical events and notable persons of a culture.
b. familiar with the ways people from other cultures act.
c. acquainted with the background knowledge authors assume readers have.
d. well versed in all of the choices listed here.

c _____ 15. A culturally literate person in the United States
a. speaks English and one other language fluently.
b. moves into new and culturally different environments easily and graciously.
c. recognizes and understands the reference to Calypso from *The Odyssey* in a magazine article she is reading.
d. has attended a liberal arts college and has taken courses emphasizing multiculturalism.

a _____ 16. The prosperity of the 1960s brought about extensive curricular changes in schools because
a. the middle class perceived education as the "key to success" and wanted their children to receive the best education possible.
b. schools were still recovering from wartime destruction.
c. students were calling for greater freedom and flexibility in the curriculum.
d. parents wanted their children to study the classics.

b _____ 17. Why did the back-to-basics group push for the return to a "basic" curriculum?
a. They believed that schools did not have the financial resources to support a wide range of programs.
b. They believed that schools should prepare students to work hard and persevere at difficult tasks.
c. They believed that students were being exposed to topics and concepts that only a small percentage would actually need.
d. They vehemently opposed any inclusion of multiculturalism in the curriculum.

d _____ 18. Which of the following curricular topics would a proponent of a back-to-basics curriculum support?
a. a unit on the vanishing rain forest
b. a course in consumer economics
c. the history of science and technology
d. the study of Latin or Greek

b _____ 19. The calls for national curriculum standards are a response to
a. a perceived need for greater teacher autonomy in the classroom.
b. a perceived need to have a more centralized system of curricula.
c. the burgeoning national debt.
d. a desire to maintain the decentralized system of education.

c _____ 20. A series of activities that includes reading and analyzing a book, writing and performing a play based on the book, and creating a set of poems on the themes of the book is probably part of a program in
a. drama.
b. fine arts.
c. language arts.
d. speech.

d _____ 21. Goals 2000: Educate America Act responds to calls for reform in American education by
a. mandating a national curriculum for all schools.
b. centralizing the decision-making authority for education.
c. re-establishing the authority of the states over education.
d. setting national goals that all schools strive to achieve.

c _____ 22. Outcomes-based education seeks to standardize student learning by
a. identifying topics to be covered at each grade level.
b. focusing on the affective and cognitive development of the students.
c. specifying what skills and knowledge students should possess at each level.
d. giving standardized tests at every grade level.

a _____ 23. In many states, curricular reform consists of
a. providing a comprehensive curriculum framework from which teachers can develop learning activities.
b. providing a comprehensive curriculum guide with specific goals, objectives, and learning activities.
c. adopting a skills-based approach to education.
d. integrating the arts into the basic curriculum.

c _____ 24. Current trends in math instruction are likely to lead to graduates who are able to
a. add long columns of numbers accurately in their heads.
b. explain math theories and concepts with insight and ease.
c. use mathematical reasoning to solve real problems that confront them.
d. find exact answers speedily by referring to texts and tables.

a _____ 25. Based on the newer trends in math instruction, which of the following will most likely occur in math classes?
a. an increased use of calculators and computers in class
b. greater emphasis on drill and practice to reduce errors
c. an increased emphasis on computational skills
d. an increased number of math courses offered at the high school level

b _____ 26. The dominant subject in the social studies curriculum at both elementary and secondary levels has been
a. geography.
b. history.
c. world cultures.
d. sociology.

a _____ 27. In the mid-1980s, instruction in foreign language in secondary schools
a. experienced a modest upswing after years of decline.
b. continued on the downward trend.
c. experienced a downturn after years of gain.
d. maintained a stable enrollment.

b _____ 28. Foreign language departments have sought to attract more students by
a. making more use of language labs.
b. expanding their course offerings and integrating the study of language with the study of culture.
c. using the audiolingual approach.
d. decreasing the course requirements for most language classes.

c _____ 29. In the past, school programs in the arts have focused on the creation of art forms, but recently they have attended more to
a. individual performance.
b. drama, music, and dance.
c. aesthetic perceptions and cultural meanings.
d. art history.

c _____ 30. Given recent trends in art education at the elementary and secondary levels, the course that is most likely to be offered now is
a. oil painting.
b. modern dance.
c. art appreciation.
d. dramatic storytelling.

a _____ 31. Physical education programs try to meet biological, psychological, and social needs of the students by emphasizing
a. cooperative team sports.
b. competitive team sports.
c. information on the history of sports.
d. minimal physical exertion.

c _____ 32. The SCANS report argues that in order for all high school graduates to be prepared for the world of work, they need to
a. go to a vocationally oriented high school.
b. do extensive part-time work as an apprentice in a school-sponsored program.
c. develop higher sets of competencies and a foundation of skills.
d. receive on-the-job training.

b _____ 33. In addition to using technology and emphasizing problem solving, mathematics instruction is moving toward
a. back-to-basics arithmetic.
b. blending of the traditional subject-matter areas—algebra, geometry, etc.
c. compartmentalization of subject areas.
d. more skill drills.

d _____ 34. Successful cooperative learning strategies include the following:
a. group goals, even distribution of labor, and equal opportunities for participation.
b. equal opportunities for success, heterogeneous grouping, and individual goals.
c. homogeneous grouping, individual accountability, and goals.
d. group goals, individual accountability, and equal opportunities for success.

b _____ 35. In the 1980s, a number of reports were published that examined the state of American education. These reports
a. harshly criticized the public schools and public school boards for their lack of vision and purpose.
b. advocated far-reaching school reform to streamline the curriculum.
c. hailed the curriculum, which was designed to serve the needs of all students.
d. developed a national standardized exam to assess a high school graduate's knowledge.

b _____ 36. Leslie Taylor is a twelve-year teaching veteran. She has taught seventh grade and has recently moved to fifth grade. She is concerned about the lack of active involvement the students have in their science lessons and the simplistic memorization that the science materials seem to emphasize. Leslie would be encouraged by
a. the work of E. D. Hirsch.
b. Project 2061 and the work of Jerome Bruner.
c. the work of Mortimer Adler.
d. the advocates of the core curriculum.

a _____ 37. Proponents of interdisciplinary teaching contend that such an approach helps students
a. see how different disciplines are interrelated.
b. memorize facts and figures.
c. become better readers and writers.
d. develop oral communication skills.

c _____ 38. If Project 2061, sponsored by the American Association for the Advancement of Science, came to fruition, which of the following would occur?
a. A core science curriculum would be instituted for all high school students.
b. Finer distinctions would be made between the scientific disciplines, and the use of interactive videos in elementary and high school science classes would be widespread.
c. Elementary science education would actively engage children in the scientific processes of experiments.
d. All of the above.

b _____ 39. According to the text, which is the greatest problem impeding the social studies curriculum?
a. the traditional Eurocentric emphasis in the social studies curriculum
b. the lack of coherence and the randomness of approaches in the social studies curriculum
c. the lack of change in the social studies curriculum over the past few decades
d. the emphasis on the memorization of facts rather than on historical analysis of events

d _____ 40. The National Assessment of Educational Progress (NAEP) assigns the following achievement levels:
a. satisfactory, very good, excellent.
b. failing, passing, outstanding.
c. slow progress, average progress, fast progress.
d. basic, proficient, advanced.

c _____ 41. A physical education teacher wants to help students avoid lower back injuries. In which of the following activities would she engage the class?
a. low-impact aerobics
b. weight training
c. stretching and abdominal exercises
d. cooperative team sports

d _____ 42. A teacher in New England is planning a social studies unit on the Revolutionary War. According to the text, which of the following typically has the largest influence on the teacher's planning?
a. teacher-made materials (notes, worksheets, activities)
b. accessibility to various historical sites (Bunker Hill, Lexington, Concord, and so on)
c. a district curriculum guide
d. the textbook

b _____ 43. If a teacher's goal were to foster critical thinking in his students, which of the following activities would he most likely include for his art class?
a. a listing of the characteristics of impressionism
b. a project researching and evaluating the art of Andrew Wyeth
c. a unit in acrylic painting in which the students would paint a still life
d. an essay requiring students to describe the art of the Romantic age

d _____ 44. Which of these activities are part of the school's curriculum?
a. bake-sale fund-raisers for the sophomore dance
b. a districtwide track meet at the school's track
c. driver ed instruction given after school
d. All of these activities are part of the school's curriculum.

a _____ 45. A school's curriculum could best be defined as
a. all of the organized and planned experiences of students for which the school assumes responsibility.
b. a scope and sequence plan for the subjects to be learned by students from grades K–12.
c. the written document in which the school outlines its goals for the school district for the next decade.
d. an explanation of the minimum skills in each of the required subject areas for students in grades K–12.

c _____ 46. U.S. schools responded to the rapid changes in U.S. society during the early 1900s by
a. emphasizing the worth of the classical curriculum.
b. emphasizing foreign language acquisition.
c. de-emphasizing the traditional curriculum of the past.
d. de-emphasizing the need for individual achievement.

a _____ 47. Until the Soviet Union launched *Sputnik* in 1957 and created a clamor in the United States for discipline-centered education, public school education had been growing more focused on
a. the child.
b. the classics of art and literature.
c. the community.
d. transcendent ideas from ancient cultures.

b _____ 48. During the late 1950s and early 1960s, the public became concerned that U.S. public schools
a. were not preeminent in the basic disciplines of reading, writing, and arithmetic.
b. were unable to prepare students to deal with the country's increased need for science, math, and technology.
c. were overemphasizing the need for math and science at the expense of other disciplines.
d. were teaching students different math and science curricula based on the students' abilities.

c _____ 49. The educational reports of the 1980s were similar in that they
a. criticized the federal, state, and local governments for their lack of financial support for public education.
b. praised teachers for being dedicated, scholarly professionals who were unrecognized by the public.
c. criticized schools for their inadequacy in educating U.S. students.
d. praised schools for their success in teaching math and science, but castigated them for their failure to teach reading and writing.

c _____ 50. Which of the following states' students score as high on the NAEP test as the students in some of the highest-scoring countries?
a. Mississippi, Louisiana, Arkansas
b. California, Texas, Florida
c. Iowa, Minnesota, North Dakota
d. Illinois, New York, Michigan

a _____ 51. In which area do American students surpass their international peers?
a. self-concept in mathematics
b. achievement in science
c. verbal skills
d. history, geography, and civics

b _____ 52. In a junior high language arts class, a group of teachers decide to put aside the textbook for a while and work with their students on *To Kill a Mockingbird.* Which component of their program is probably best served by this adjustment?
a. instruction in reading local dialects
b. expansion of cultural knowledge gained from literature
c. improvement in vocabulary building skills
d. general improvement in reading comprehension

b _____ 53. According to the recent assessments cited in the text, U.S. students performed
a. below average in both math and science.
b. above average in math but below average in science.
c. above average in both math and science.
d. below average in math but above average in science.

a _____ 54. According to the text, which would very likely be demonstrated in a high school biology class?
a. students' memorization of orders, classes, and phyla indicated by their completion of charts
b. students' demonstration of the principles of both chemistry and biology through experiments on the life cycle of corn plants
c. the design and construction of biology experiments by teams of students
d. all of the above

c _____ 55. The dominance of history in the social studies curriculum at both elementary and secondary levels is evidenced by the fact that
a. it is almost always taught by highly skilled teachers.
b. it usually represents the most profound ideas and significant events of our past.
c. it is the most commonly offered course.
d. history tests are usually harder than tests in other social studies disciplines.

a ____ 56. Social studies is not considered a discipline because
- a. it draws from a number of disciplines, such as psychology, sociology, and anthropology.
- b. the curriculum of social studies courses has changed over the past ten years.
- c. there is no college major in social studies.
- d. it does not have the objective standards of math and science.

d ____ 57. Among the trends in the social studies curriculum in the recent past are
- a. an emphasis on enabling students to develop an analytical perspective of the human condition.
- b. the addition of courses in geography, civics, and global studies.
- c. an acknowledgment of the diversity of U.S. people and their experiences.
- d. all of the above.

a ____ 58. In assessments made during the 1980s, educators discovered that, after years of decline, instruction in foreign language was
- a. experiencing a modest upswing.
- b. at its lowest ebb and unlikely to recover, despite the widespread perception that the world is "shrinking."
- c. holding steady.
- d. in the midst of a remarkably strong upswing in response to improved world trade.

d ____ 59. According to the recent trends in foreign language instruction, which of the following would one expect to see in foreign language classes?
- a. students making frequent use of a language lab
- b. students speaking French to give directions to a school activity to their classmates
- c. students translating *Don Quixote* from Spanish into English
- d. all of the above

a ____ 60. Students in a physical education class spend the greatest amount of time either riding a stationary bicycle or jogging. Their teacher has most likely planned that lesson to meet which of the following goals?
- a. cardiorespiratory efficiency of students
- b. increasing body strength
- c. skills development of students
- d. cardiorespiratory efficiency of students and increasing body strength

a _____ 61. Which activity most closely reflects the new trends in physical education instruction?
a. a team of students developing their own set of rules for a game they have modified
b. a playoff game in basketball between two teams who have the highest winning record of all the teams in the class
c. repetitive sets of drills to build students' coordination and skills
d. all of the above

d _____ 62. A health education unit on AIDS directed toward adolescents would focus on
a. lectures on the effects of teen pregnancy.
b. how to identify symptoms of AIDS.
c. how to resist peer pressure and information on avoiding risk of infection.
d. lectures on the dangers of sexual activity and how to resist peer pressure.

d _____ 63. Which of the following is *not* a contributing factor to U.S. students scoring lower in mathematics than their international counterparts?
a. lower expectations of students
b. students working
c. more time in nonacademic activities
d. less sophisticated texts and instructional materials

a _____ 64. After extensive research on long-term job prospects in the community, a student decides to work toward a career in carpentry and cabinetmaking. According to the text, which of the following will provide the best foundation for this kind of work?
a. developing excellent skills in reading, writing, and math
b. working after school, on weekends, and during vacations to develop a good work history and good work habits
c. enrolling in the local vocational technical school, where the student can take numerous courses in woodworking
d. developing excellent basic skills and enrolling in the local vocational technical school

d _____ 65. For both teachers and students, most of the content in any lesson is taken from
a. district curriculum guides.
b. research reports on each subject.
c. school scope-and-sequence charts.
d. textbooks, manuals, worksheets, and tests.

b _____ 66. Profit incentives in the textbook publishing business can lead to decisions about content, making the curriculum
a. liberal.
b. conservative.
c. inclusive.
d. reactionary.

d ______ 67. In general, educational writers comment that textbooks
a. provide sufficient depth of coverage.
b. are written in a lively, varied style.
c. typically pique students' interest and stimulate student learning.
d. match none of the descriptions given here.

a ______ 68. Which of the following would be a likely cause for rejecting a social studies textbook for adoption?
a. a critical portrait of the U.S. treatment of Japanese Americans during World War II
b. an uninteresting style of writing
c. too many excerpts of original documents, letters, or diaries
d. too much cultural information

b ______ 69. Block scheduling is a more efficient use of time because it reduces
a. the number of courses students take during high school.
b. passing time between classes.
c. the hours in the school day.
d. homework time.

c ______ 70. In order to avoid the problem of the smart student in a group doing all the work, cooperative learning strategies
a. focus on group accountability.
b. develop a sense of community within the group.
c. are organized and highly structured methods that involve individual assignments.
d. entail specific, clearly articulated steps to complete an activity.

a ______ 71. Socratic questioning, problem solving, identifying biases or assumptions, weighing evidence, and studying philosophy are among the many activities of a curriculum in
a. critical thinking.
b. perennialist issues.
c. discovery learning.
d. mastery learning.

b ______ 72. The primary purpose of using writing across the curriculum is to
a. focus on new, creative ways for students to express themselves.
b. facilitate the student's exploration of relationships between concepts and connections between ideas.
c. demonstrate the student's mastery of key concepts in the discipline.
d. strengthen the student's communication skills by emphasizing grammar, syntax, and usage.

c _____ 73. Evidence suggests that the use of writing activities in other curricular areas
a. enhances writing skills but adds nothing to the mastery of the other areas.
b. enhances achievement in the other areas without changing skills in writing.
c. enhances writing skills as well as achievement in other areas.
d. does not change achievement in either writing or the other areas but adds interest to both.

a _____ 74. The first-grade teachers at the Rainbow School are interested in implementing a whole language approach in their classes. They have met with opposition from some of the parents. How can they defend their position?
a. Whole language incorporates the learning of all language skills in an environment that is relevant and meaningful to the students.
b. Whole language starts with single words, then progresses to sentences and paragraphs.
c. Whole language stresses drill and practice.
d. Whole language is more structured than the current approach.

b _____ 75. "The Saber-Tooth Curriculum" is a parable demonstrating which education philosophy?
a. existentialism
b. perennialism
c. essentialism
d. behaviorism

c _____ 76. Which of the following school-level actions represents a type of problem highlighted by the parable "The Saber-Tooth Curriculum"?
a. dropping the French course to make room for a course in modern Japanese
b. adding a Latin course
c. refusing to make room for one course in modern Japanese by dropping one of the two sections of underenrolled sections of Latin
d. adding courses in ancient Egyptian art

Short-Answer Questions

Respond to each of the following questions briefly, but specifically, in complete sentences.

77. Since 1987, when E. D. Hirsch published his work on cultural literacy, the concept has generated much attention. Briefly explain Hirsch's major argument for cultural literacy.

(suggested answer) Hirsch argues that cultural literacy is the ability to recognize and understand the central ideas, stories, characters, events, and scientific knowledge of a culture. It is necessary for a person to understand references to these ideas that authors assume readers know because without knowing those allusions, the person will not understand fully the society in which he or she lives, and as a result may have limited participation in it. Hirsch also argues that schools should teach cultural literacy to develop a shared national framework and unity.

78. How did the launching of the Soviet *Sputnik* affect the U.S. public's perception of U.S. education?

    (suggested answer) The U.S. public saw the launching of *Sputnik* as a harbinger of diminishing U.S. power in the world. They felt threatened that the Soviets would have made such advanced strides in science and aerospace technology. The United States was shocked out of its complacent assumption that U.S. schools were the best and demanded that schools respond to the challenges of preparing students to live in a highly scientific, technological world.

79. Choose one of the innovative instructional approaches and explain how it seeks to improve student learning.

    Answers will vary, but should include elements of the following:

    a. *Interdisciplinary teaching:* Students become aware of the interrelatedness of disciplines and see learning and school as a coherent unit rather than fragmented pieces. Student learning is enhanced because students are hearing the same message in different subjects; in this way their knowledge is reinforced.
    b. *Cooperative learning:* Students see learning as a social process and appreciate the abilities of their peers. Students take charge of their own learning and have greater motivation to do well. Individual accountability ensures that all members of the group participate.
    c. *Critical learning and problem solving:* Students learn to evaluate the worth of ideas before making a decision. The focus on critically evaluating ideas helps make students better thinkers. Students appreciate their own learning strategies.
    d. *Writing across the curriculum:* Students come to see writing as a tool for learning, not as a skill to be mastered. Through writing, students can learn more in the disciplines, focusing on expanding their knowledge.

80. To what degree is U.S. education influenced by the perceptions held by those people outside of schools? Pick one instance cited from the book and explain its significance on the curriculum.

    Answers will vary. Possible examples include the public's perception after *Sputnik* that the United States was losing power and the resulting changes in the math and science curriculum. Another example is the perceptions held by particular conservative interest groups in Texas who then influenced textbook adoption.

81. Goals 2000: Educate America Act was based on America 2000, a document drawn up in 1989 by American governors, who identified six national goals for education to be accomplished by the year 2000. Goals 2000 maintained the six goals of America 2000 and then added a seventh. Name and explain the one goal you think will be the most difficult to accomplish.

    Answers will vary. The educational goals are as follows:

a. All U.S. children will start school ready to learn.
b. The high school graduation rate will increase to at least 90 percent.
c. U.S. students will leave grades 4, 8, and 12 having demonstrated competency in challenging subject matter, including English, mathematics, science, history, geography, and civics and government; every school in the nation will ensure that all students learn to use their minds well, so they may be prepared for responsible citizenship, further learning, and productive employment in our modern economy.
d. U.S. students will be first in the world in science and mathematics achievement.
e. Every adult American will be literate and will have the knowledge and skills necessary to compete in a global economy and to exercise the rights and responsibilities of citizenship.
f. Every school will be free of drugs and violence and will offer a disciplined environment conducive to learning.
g. Our nation's teaching force will have access to programs for the continued improvement of their professional skills and the opportunity to acquire the knowledge and skills needed to instruct and prepare all American students for the next century.

82. In what ways does the physical education curricula of the 1980s and 1990s differ from that of the 1960s?

(suggested answer) The 1960s stressed competitive sports and physical fitness. Now there is more emphasis on cooperative sports, lifelong sports, and attitudinal goals. Physical fitness is now only one goal of several in the physical fitness curriculum.

83. Why must art educators struggle to retain art's place in the curriculum?

(suggested answer) Art educators have to struggle against two impediments to the maintenance of art courses in schools. First, art has been de-emphasized by some of the curriculum reform reports, which place much more emphasis on math, science, and English, thus diminishing art's place in the curriculum. Secondly, art educators lack agreement on a rationale for arts education in the public schools.

84. How has the attention given to multiculturalism affected the way foreign languages are taught?

(suggested answer) Because of the greater attention now given to the various cultures from which languages evolve, the text suggests that foreign language is now taught by focusing on cultural foundations and encouraging cultural sensitivity. Therefore, foreign language classes expect students not only to speak, read, and write the language, but to demonstrate an understanding of the various cultures that use a particular language.

Essay Questions

Read each of the following questions, and respond by composing an organized essay that includes an introduction, fully developed paragraph(s), and a conclusion.

85. Trace the major curricular emphases from the early 1900s to the present, including the curriculum emphases and the dominant educational philosophies. Why did major educational shifts occur? How did the public use the schools to meet society's needs at any given time?

Answers should include the major curricular trends noted concisely in Table 8.1, "Curriculum Trends in American Education," in the textbook.

86. Robert Maynard Hutchins once wrote, "The best education for the best is the best education for all." If you, as an educator, were to use this statement as the overriding principle for creating the curriculum for a school, select two or three of the theories, trends, or projects discussed in the text and explain why you would include those in your curriculum.

(Answers will vary.)

Alternative Assessment Ideas

The following activities are suggestions for student portfolio activities. They are a means of providing alternative assessment of the students' capabilities.

Independent Reading

Read and respond to any of the following selections from Ryan/Cooper, *Kaleidoscope: Readings in Education* (Houghton Mifflin, 1998). You may want to use the Article Review Form on page 269.

Beane—"Curriculum Integration and the Disciplines of Knowledge"

Glasser—"The Quality School Curriculum"

Guskey—"Making the Grade"

Hirsch—"The Core Knowledge Curriculum"

Noddings—"Teaching Themes of Care"

Peddiwell—"The Saber-Tooth Curriculum"

Resnick and Nolan—"Where in the World Are World-Class Standards?"

Ryan—"Mining the Values in the Curriculum"

Slavin—"Cooperative Learning and the Cooperative School"

Sternberg—"Investing in Creativity"

Reflective Papers

Choose one of the following topics to write a reflective paper (2–5 pages). The purpose of the paper is to help you assimilate new knowledge by blending it with your previous knowledge and experiences.

1. Think back on your own high school experiences and discuss instructional approaches used in your math, science, or English classes (choose one). How would you characterize them based on what you have read in this chapter? How effective were these approaches in helping you learn? How could these approaches have been improved to enhance your learning?

2. As you observe in your field site, what instructional strategies do you see being implemented? With what degree of success? Do the students respond differently to these strategies? With what results?

3. Review the curricular changes that have taken place since the 1950s and speculate on the curricular changes that will be implemented in the next twenty years. How will your teaching be affected?

Journal Writing

Suggestions for journal topics for students' selection:

1. What seems to be the curriculum philosophy at your field placement school?

2. What do you believe is the greatest challenge to developing and maintaining a strong curriculum?

3. What are your thoughts and feelings about any one of the controversial curriculum issues addressed in this chapter?

4. Describe the curriculum philosophy that seemed to be in effect when you were in high school (identify your year of graduation).

Chapter 9 How Are Schools Governed, Influenced, and Financed?

Multiple-Choice Items

Read each item carefully. On the appropriate line, write the letter of the choice that represents the best answer.

b _____ 1. What effect did the Tenth Amendment to the U.S. Constitution have upon public education?
- a. The state department of education was established.
- b. Legal responsibility for school governance was reserved for the state.
- c. Responsibility for the majority of funding for public education was assumed by the federal government.
- d. Equal educational opportunity was guaranteed for all.

b _____ 2. Control of educational policy decisions and administration is delegated to
- a. the federal government by the states.
- b. local school boards by the states.
- c. local superintendents by the federal government.
- d. states by the local school boards.

c _____ 3. Which of these bodies makes law and is considered the most influential in setting up educational policy?
- a. the local school board
- b. the state department of education
- c. the state legislature
- d. the state board of education

c _____ 4. Which of the following best describes the role that state legislatures play in public education?
a. They are responsible for teacher certification and the accreditation of schools.
b. They communicate the mission of public education to the citizens of the state.
c. They write and pass laws concerning public education.
d. They determine public expenditures for education and establish state standards.

d _____ 5. The state of Illinois wants to establish a policy regarding its public education in the twenty-first century. Illinois wants to create a broad-based policy outlining its priorities and establishing its goals for the state's students. Which agency would issue this policy?
a. the state department of education
b. the federal Department of Education
c. the local school boards
d. the state board of education

a _____ 6. New Jersey's citizens are arguing for expanded computer technology and instruction within public schools. If that change is implemented, which agency is responsible for identifying and reinforcing the minimum standards for computer literacy within the public schools?
a. the state board of education
b. the state department of education
c. the state legislature
d. the local school board

c _____ 7. On assuming the position of chief state school officer, Mr. Cooperman would expect to
a. set policy and determine rules for school districts.
b. appoint local school board members.
c. function as executive officer for the state board of education.
d. appoint state board of education members.

a _____ 8. Organizing programs of study, supervising elementary and secondary education programs, and applying school finance laws are all tasks of
a. the chief state school officer.
b. the state department of education.
c. the federal Department of Education.
d. the school principal.

d _____ 9. The school district in Shamokin Dam is starting a federally funded educational program. Which of the following would administer and distribute those funds to the school district?
a. U.S. Department of Education
b. state board of education
c. office of the state superintendent
d. state department of education

a _____ 10. The agency that administers and distributes state and federal funds, certifies or licenses teachers, and accredits professional training programs is the
a. state department of education.
b. state board of education.
c. office of the state superintendent.
d. local school board.

c _____ 11. Heidi Pfluger is interviewing for a teaching position in the Florham Park school system. According to school management and organization, which of the following is the hiring authority?
a. the building principal
b. the assistant superintendent of instruction
c. the local school board
d. the school superintendent

b _____ 12. The official state officers who hire school personnel, determine policy, evaluate local programs and personnel, and monitor schools' conformity to state guidelines are
a. school principals.
b. members of local boards of education.
c. state department of education specialists.
d. members of the state board of education.

c _____ 13. The typical holder of this position is white, male, and college educated, and has a salaried managerial job unrelated to the position. The position is
a. district curriculum specialist.
b. department chairperson.
c. local school board member.
d. consultant from the state department of education.

c _____ 14. Which of the following people is most representative of the typical school board member?
a. Loretta Padovani, a white, 68-year-old retired bookkeeper with grandchildren in the public schools
b. Carla Wilson, African American, 40 years old, with a master's degree in nursing, is a nurse practitioner at a large hospital
c. John Baxter, white, 51 years old, who has an M.B.A. and is an executive at a computer software company
d. Joe Eichler, white, 44 years old, a high school graduate who works in a tool and die factory

d _____ 15. Brian Bomberger spends part of his work time interviewing and promoting personnel. He ensures that there are adequate funds to run school facilities through his planning and administration of the budget, and he also is responsible for administering curriculum and instruction. What is Brian's occupation?
a. chief state school officer
b. curriculum coordinator
c. school principal
d. district superintendent

a _____ 16. Which of the following would be included in the district superintendent's responsibilities?
a. the administration of curriculum and instruction
b. the approval of school sites
c. the scheduling of students and classes
d. the certification/licensure of teachers

b _____ 17. Susan Breiner has just completed interviewing two prospective faculty members, has sent in a large teaching supply order, has proofread the new school discipline policy written by a team of teachers, and has reviewed the school budget for the next academic year. Based upon those activities, what is Susan?
a. a department chairperson
b. a school principal
c. the assistant superintendent of personnel
d. the superintendent of schools

c _____ 18. Nicholas Kallas is the principal of the Marion T. Bedwell Elementary School. Which of the following would most typically fall within his job responsibilities?
a. promoting a classroom teacher to assistant principal
b. writing and implementing new administrative policy for the district
c. making teaching assignments for each academic year
d. formally hiring new teachers

b _____ 19. During recent presidential elections, hundreds of thousands of educators have been mobilized to support a particular party platform and the candidate endorsed by that party. Which organization has been instrumental in influencing the educators to support a particular candidate?

a. the National Association of School Boards
b. the National Education Association
c. the Association of Teacher Educators
d. the national Parent Teacher Association

a _____ 20. How have the AFT and NEA earned such power over schools?

a. They have gradually become a powerful voice in the collective bargaining between teachers and school boards.
b. They have created innovative instructional strategies that have been adopted by numerous school districts.
c. They have managed to persuade educators and school boards of their philosophy of education.
d. They have been foremost in advocating for technological advances in classroom instruction.

d _____ 21. Patrice Grayson, the head of a particular group associated with the Carlisle Elementary School, works primarily to establish open communication between the administrators, faculty, staff, and community. What organization does Patrice head?

a. the National Education Association
b. the administrative association
c. the state board of education
d. the parent-teacher organization

c _____ 22. Mary Ellen DuPree, a teacher at Belleville High School, also volunteers as the drama coach. The school musical selected this year, *Little Shop of Horrors,* has generated widespread student involvement; however, because of the tight school budget Mary Ellen has not been able to get the necessary costumes or props for the show. Which of the following would be the most likely or most able to provide her with the help she needs for the school play?

a. the district superintendent
b. the assistant superintendent for curriculum and instruction
c. the parent-teacher organization
d. the local school board

b _____ 23. Which of the following most typically describes the relationship between a superintendent of schools and the local school board?

a. one of overt hostility and antagonism
b. one of conflict, laden with political overtones
c. one of benign indifference
d. one of mutual respect and cooperation

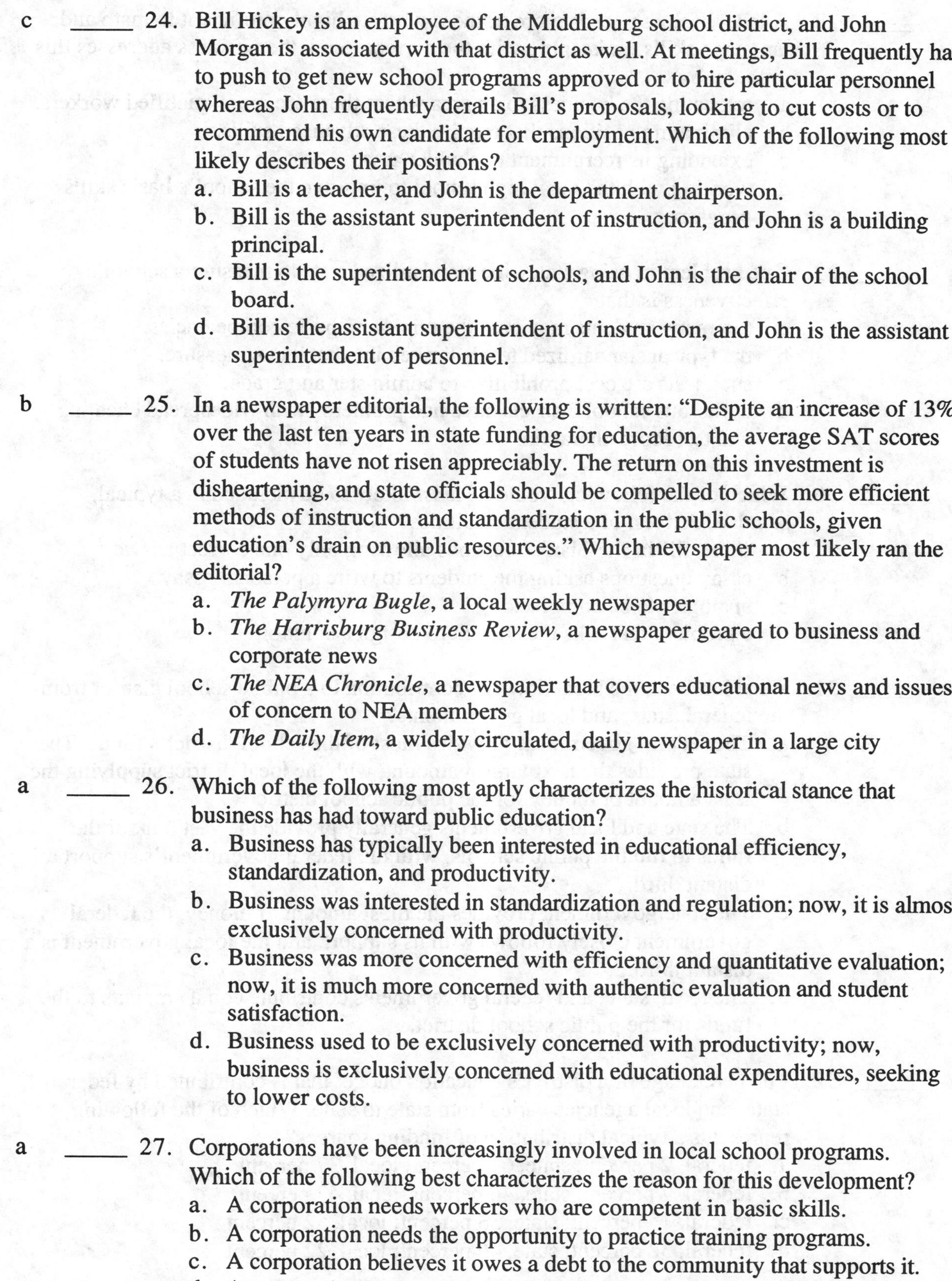

c _____ 24. Bill Hickey is an employee of the Middleburg school district, and John Morgan is associated with that district as well. At meetings, Bill frequently has to push to get new school programs approved or to hire particular personnel whereas John frequently derails Bill's proposals, looking to cut costs or to recommend his own candidate for employment. Which of the following most likely describes their positions?

a. Bill is a teacher, and John is the department chairperson.
b. Bill is the assistant superintendent of instruction, and John is a building principal.
c. Bill is the superintendent of schools, and John is the chair of the school board.
d. Bill is the assistant superintendent of instruction, and John is the assistant superintendent of personnel.

b _____ 25. In a newspaper editorial, the following is written: "Despite an increase of 13% over the last ten years in state funding for education, the average SAT scores of students have not risen appreciably. The return on this investment is disheartening, and state officials should be compelled to seek more efficient methods of instruction and standardization in the public schools, given education's drain on public resources." Which newspaper most likely ran the editorial?

a. *The Palymyra Bugle*, a local weekly newspaper
b. *The Harrisburg Business Review*, a newspaper geared to business and corporate news
c. *The NEA Chronicle*, a newspaper that covers educational news and issues of concern to NEA members
d. *The Daily Item*, a widely circulated, daily newspaper in a large city

a _____ 26. Which of the following most aptly characterizes the historical stance that business has had toward public education?

a. Business has typically been interested in educational efficiency, standardization, and productivity.
b. Business was interested in standardization and regulation; now, it is almost exclusively concerned with productivity.
c. Business was more concerned with efficiency and quantitative evaluation; now, it is much more concerned with authentic evaluation and student satisfaction.
d. Business used to be exclusively concerned with productivity; now, business is exclusively concerned with educational expenditures, seeking to lower costs.

a _____ 27. Corporations have been increasingly involved in local school programs. Which of the following best characterizes the reason for this development?

a. A corporation needs workers who are competent in basic skills.
b. A corporation needs the opportunity to practice training programs.
c. A corporation believes it owes a debt to the community that supports it.
d. A corporation can collect state school funds for participating in education.

d _____ 28. A local business needs more trainees who are highly proficient in math and language skills. In keeping with the current trend, the business addresses this problem by

a. relocating the business to an area where there are more qualified workers.
b. eliminating positions that require these advanced skills.
c. extending its recruitment to a wider area.
d. working with the local high school to improve the school's basic skills program.

b _____ 29. One problem in using statewide standardized tests to measure a school's effectiveness is that

a. too many students may pass the minimum basic competencies.
b. the typical standardized test is limited in what it can measure.
c. such tests are cost prohibitive to administer and grade.
d. numerous school districts have had problems with widespread cheating and test score alteration.

d _____ 30. Which of the following would be *least* likely to be included in a typical, standardized test of a student's abilities?

a. short, fill-in-the-blank questions allowing only one correct answer
b. essay questions asking the students to write a personal essay
c. analogies to be completed
d. a problem that asks the student to design a solution

b _____ 31. What has been the breakdown of contribution to a public school district from the federal, state, and local governments?

a. The federal government provides most of the school district's funds. The state provides the next largest amount, with the local district supplying the least amount of money for the public school district.
b. The state and local governments generally provide the vast bulk of the funds to run the public schools, with the federal government's support a distant third.
c. The state government provides the most amount of money, the federal government closely follows with its support, and the local government is a distant third.
d. The local, state, and federal governments contribute equal amounts to the funds for the public school district.

b _____ 32. The percentage of a district's education budget that is contributed by federal, state, and local agencies varies from state to state. Which of the following represents a typical distribution of funding sources?

a. federal, 2 percent; state, 61 percent; local, 37 percent
b. federal, 7 percent; state, 46 percent; local, 47 percent
c. federal, 15 percent; state, 33 percent; local, 52 percent
d. federal, 32 percent; state, 46 percent; local, 22 percent

c _____ 33. Local districts rely primarily on property taxes to fund schools. Which revenue is most commonly used by the state for support of education?
a. "sin" taxes from cigarettes and alcohol
b. property taxes
c. sales and income taxes
d. vehicle taxes

a _____ 34. Wichita Falls is a small city containing several retail malls, several corporations, and numerous neighborhoods. Assuming that Wichita Falls is a typical school district, which of the following is its primary source of funds for public education?
a. property taxes
b. sales taxes
c. corporate taxes
d. income taxes

d _____ 35. St. Michael's Elementary School, a parochial school, is receiving some funding from taxes. Which of the following does that funding most likely support?
a. tuition aid for students
b. teachers' salaries
c. building maintenance and improvement
d. school lunch programs

b _____ 36. For particular items, the courts have allowed tax money to support private schools. Which of the following costs can receive tax money?
a. overhead costs of the buildings and faculty tuition reimbursement for graduate work
b. transportation and milk costs
c. after-school programs and physical education costs
d. technological improvements (computers, printers, software, interactive videos)

c _____ 37. In the *Serrano* v. *Priest* and *Serrano II* decisions, the Supreme Court of California determined that according to the laws of the state, the quality of a child's education must reflect the wealth of the
a. local school district.
b. child's family, which has the first responsibility for its members.
c. state.
d. nation, for the U.S. Constitution guarantees equal protection for all citizens.

b _____ 38. In Billburn, a foundering industrial city with a shrinking tax base, the average per-pupil expenditures amount to about $4,100 annually. Yet Bracton, a nearby affluent town, spends nearly $10,000 annually per pupil. A Billburn parent contests this situation in the courts. After the *Serrano* v. *Priest* court decision, the parent would most likely use which of the following arguments?

a. The per-pupil cost of every student in the state needs to be exactly equal; otherwise, it is a violation of the Constitution.
b. To finance schools primarily on local property taxes is unconstitutional.
c. To ensure equality, Bracton should send tax revenues to Billburn to equalize the per-pupil expenditures.
d. The Constitution states explicitly that education is a protected right, and Billburn's students are being denied educational opportunity.

b _____ 39. How has federal funding to education changed from the 1970s through the 1990s?

a. Funding has increased and has been issued almost exclusively in categorical aid.
b. Funding has decreased, shifting from categorical aid to block grants.
c. Funding has increased, shifting from block grants to categorical aid.
d. Funding has decreased and has emphasized categorical aid.

a _____ 40. Which statement best reflects recent changes in federal contributions to education?

a. States have greater freedom with less money than in the 1970s.
b. States have less freedom with less money than in the 1970s.
c. States have greater freedom with more money than in the 1970s.
d. States have less freedom with more money than in the 1970s.

c _____ 41. Jersey City, a struggling city, has applied for federal aid. All of its aid, several million dollars, comes in the form of a block grant. Which scenario most typifies the way in which Jersey City can use those federal funds?

a. Jersey City can spend the money only on those programs identified by the federal agency as being most important to Jersey City's schools.
b. Part of the money will be spent on federally designated areas under strict regulation. The rest of it can be spent according to Jersey City's decision.
c. Jersey City administrators and state officials will decide where best to spend the money, identifying areas of highest priority.
d. The teachers and principals of Jersey City schools will identify what needs additional funds and will be allocated equal sums of money.

c _____ 42. The national average per-pupil expenditure from all sources in 1995 to 1996 was

a. $6,500.
b. $8,300.
c. $5,600.
d. $4,500.

c _____ 43. Della is a twelve-year-old student at risk. Because of her problems with absenteeism and summer lag, many educators believe that one of the following would be most helpful in her academic achievement. Which one is it?

a. placing her in a separate, intensive educational setting
b. increased monitoring and testing of her competency in basic skills
c. year-round school attendance
d. enrolling her in a vocational training program

c ____ 44. Most proponents of year-round schooling agree that the strongest reason for instituting it is

a. to ease school budget problems.
b. the flexibility and variety possible in the curriculum.
c. the expected increase in student learning and the prevention of "summer slippage."
d. to make more efficient use of their school facilities.

b ____ 45. All of the following have been documented as advantages of privatization *except*

a. more individualized instruction.
b. academic improvement.
c. cleaner buildings.
d. greater access to computers.

Short-Answer Questions

Respond to each of the following questions briefly, but specifically, in complete sentences.

46. Why might one say that the school district superintendent's job is precarious? What are the potential difficulties in the position?

(suggested answer) Since the superintendent does not have tenure, he or she may lose his or her position at any time that he or she loses the confidence of the school board. In addition to having the knowledge, experience, and expertise required for running a district's schools, the superintendent must have finely polished interpersonal skills. Much of his or her time will be spent either in conflict resolution between groups who have competing claims, or in diplomatically trying to answer demands that may be very difficult or impossible. He or she must also possess strong leadership to direct the schools forward, without getting mired in the politics that frequently engulf school systems.

47. Why are the demographics of a typical school board member important? What are the implications of those demographics to the running of public schools?

(suggested answer) The typical school board member is a white, middle-aged, college-educated male who is working in a managerial or professional position and who is middle class or upper middle class. The demographics are important because if the overwhelming

number of school members fit this profile, then the particular interests associated with this demographic group may be more well attended to than other interests. For example, the school boards may pay greater attention to college preparatory education than to vocational education; they may adopt a favorable attitude toward greater business involvement in the public schools; they may emphasize the values of the dominant middle class. Such representation may not be problematic; however, it is important to recognize that if any particular demographic group is overwhelmingly represented on school boards, the concerns of that group usually take precedence over others' concerns.

48. Many would argue that a principal is the single most important person for ensuring the success of a particular school. Explain how this could be true.

    (suggested answer) Principals are responsible for management, supervision, and inspection of the school and its operation. Although they have numerous formal responsibilities, their informal tasks are also vital to the well-being of a school. Namely, effective schools have principals who are strong leaders. They can grasp the vision of the school and articulate this vision to others, like faculty, within the school. They can also guide the faculty and students toward achievement.

49. Oakdell is a town with a sizable portion of its residents living on fixed incomes. Explain why Oakdell potentially could have difficulty passing school budgets from year to year.

    (suggested answer) Because public schools are funded in large part from local property taxes, a community with large numbers of residents on fixed incomes may resist any increase in the school budgets from year to year because they may not be able to afford increases in their property taxes.

Essay Questions

Read each of the following questions, and respond by composing an organized essay that includes an introduction, fully developed paragraph(s), and a conclusion.

50. Assess the involvement of the corporate world in public education. Is greater business involvement in public education a benefit, a disadvantage, or a mixed benefit to public education? Explain.

    Answers will vary, but they should give logical, well-supported reasons and clear examples.

51. Define and explain the relationships among the state board of education, the state superintendent, the state department of education, the local school boards, and the local superintendent.

    (suggested answer) The state board of education is the chief educational policy-making agency in the state. Its chief executive officer is the state superintendent, who carries out its

directives through the work of the state department of education. The state department oversees operations, providing technical assistance, certifying teachers, and developing programs. The local school board is the local arm of the state, responsible for seeing that state requirements are carried out at the local level. The local superintendent is the executive officer of the local board. At each level down, agents have acquired informal control by virtue of being closer to the schools, where policy is translated into programs.

52. Explain the relative contributions of the federal, state, and local communities to schools, and tell how state and local funds are raised. Describe the implications of the *Serrano* decision for equity of educational opportunity.

    (suggested answer) The federal government provides the least amount, about 6 percent of the total budget on average, with a high of 17 percent (in Mississippi). On average, the state and local communities each now contribute about half of the remainder. States raise money by income and corporate taxes, excise taxes, and lotteries. Local governments usually raise funds by means of a property tax. *Serrano* resulted in some states' reapportioning funds to various districts to equalize per-pupil expenditures. If a state has an "equal protection" clause in its constitution, the amount spent on each pupil in the state must be roughly the same, reflecting the state's wealth, not the local community's. Not every state is affected by *Serrano* because not every state has an "equal protection" clause that includes education.

Alternative Assessment Ideas

The following activities are suggestions for student portfolio activities. They are a means of providing alternative assessment of the students' capabilities.

Independent Reading

Read and respond to any of the following selections from Ryan/Cooper, *Kaleidoscope: Readings in Education* (Houghton Mifflin, 1998). You may want to use the Article Review Form on page 269.

David—"The Who, What, and Why of Site-Based Management"

LoVette—"You Ask, 'Why Have School Costs Increased So Greatly?'"

Reflective Papers

Choose one of the following topics to write a reflective paper (2–5 pages). The purpose of the paper is to help you assimilate new knowledge by blending it with your previous knowledge and experiences.

1. Recent press reports have focused on Channel One and Whittle Communications' involvement with public schools. Present your understanding of the issues involved and explain your position.

2. Consider yourself both as a student and as a prospective teacher and describe your views on year-round schooling. If you are observing in a school now, consider the impact year-round schooling would have on your school setting.

3. In many respects, local control is guaranteed over public schools as long as property taxes fund such a large percentage of the school budget. Any attempt to equalize educational spending across districts, some argue, diminishes local control and ultimately parents' freedom to select schooling for their own child. Others vehemently disagree, claiming that the per-pupil spending disparity among school districts is grossly unfair; therefore, the funding of schools needs to be dramatically changed. What do you think?

Journal Writing

Suggestions for journal topics for students' selection:

1. Describe how you think the inequities in school funding could be resolved.

2. What do you think is the relationship between school funding and student achievement? Why?

3. Outside of teacher, in which of the governing roles (legislator, principal, superintendent, school board member) would you most like to serve? Why?

Chapter 10 What Are the Philosophical Foundations of American Education?

Multiple-Choice Items

Read each item carefully. On the appropriate line, write the letter of the choice that represents the best answer.

a _____ 1. What is a philosopher's primary mode of inquiry?
   a. through reason and argument
   b. through the analysis of historical patterns
   c. through intuition
   d. through experimentation and data gathering

b _____ 2. Which of the following is most representative of the type of question a philosopher pursues?
   a. "Would waging a war against that particular country be economically viable?"
   b. "How do I know that what appears true actually is?"
   c. "What were the ramifications of the Enlightenment upon people's thinking?"
   d. "Where are the physical boundaries of the universe?"

b _____ 3. During a music class, a student comments that Muddy Waters remains the most influential blues musician of the twentieth century. The teacher asks, "How do you know that?" The teacher's question elicits the student's understanding of
   a. axiology.
   b. epistemology.
   c. ethics.
   d. logic.

d _____ 4. A metaphysician is a philosopher who is most concerned with questions such as
a. "What are appropriate ways of knowing?"
b. "Which object is the most beautiful?"
c. "How is reasoning done most effectively?"
d. "Does life have meaning?"

c _____ 5. A veteran teacher considers his thirty-year career and asks himself, "Has my career had a core purpose?" What kind of philosophical question is this?
a. aesthetic
b. epistemological
c. metaphysical
d. ethical

d _____ 6. A young child asks his teacher, "How can love be real if you don't ever see it?" Which branch of philosophy has that child's question tapped into?
a. axiology
b. epistemology
c. logic
d. metaphysics

a _____ 7. An art teacher is prompting his Sculpture I students to identify the elements of beauty that exist in Michelangelo's *David.* This activity is focusing on developing students' comprehension of
a. aesthetics.
b. ethics.
c. logic.
d. metaphysics.

c _____ 8. Two historians debate the merits of a recent historical analysis. One claims it is the definitive account of that period; the other argues that the historical period could be legitimately analyzed through several other perspectives equally as well. What kind of philosophical discussion are these historians having?
a. axiological
b. logical
c. epistemological
d. metaphysical

d _____ 9. Mr. Nguyen, an algebra teacher, emphasizes the epistemological aspects of mathematics to his students. Which of the following kind of questions is he most likely to ask students?
a. "When are you likely to use algebra?"
b. "What is the purpose of the quadratic equation?"
c. "If I know $b = c$, then what is the value of a?"
d. "Explain how you know that $x = 12$."

c _____ 10. The study of axiology provides one with an understanding of
a. the way knowledge is apprehended.
b. the nature of humankind.
c. the values people hold concerning beauty and conduct.
d. the elements of reasoning.

c _____ 11. Maria is studying the relationship between medieval ethical virtues and the painting and sculpture of the time. What branch of philosophy deals with the subjects of Maria's study?
a. positivism
b. metaphysics
c. axiology
d. aesthetics

a _____ 12. Several people watch a popular music video on TV. After it is over, several people think the video is deeply symbolic, beautiful, and emotionally gripping. Others argue it is hackneyed, technically flawed, and simplistic. From which of the following branches of philosophy does this draw?
a. aesthetics
b. metaphysics
c. epistemology
d. logic

d _____ 13. At Bowker High School, students take many required courses, including Latin, history, humanities, mathematics, and science. The students study those disciplines as a way of developing their intellect and discovering the universal truths of humankind. Bowker High's philosophy of education is derived from
a. asceticism.
b. essentialism.
c. existentialism.
d. perennialism.

c _____ 14. Two kindergartners are fighting over a Power Ranger toy. Ms. Hernandez tells the children gently, "Brian, you promised Ali you would share that toy with her. It's not fair to Ali if you go back on your promise." Ms. Hernandez is giving the children a simple lesson in which of the following?
a. aesthetics
b. axiology
c. ethics
d. logic

b ______ 15. A student completing a project on bird identification knows that insect-eating birds have narrow, pointed bills. One day, her mother and she look out the window and see a bird they don't recognize with a narrow bill. The mother exclaims, "What an unusual bird. I've never seen any bird like that all through this snowy winter." The daughter replies, "You wouldn't. That bird must migrate to warmer climates during the winter." Which of the following is the girl using?

a. metaphorical thinking
b. inductive reasoning
c. correctional thinking
d. deductive reasoning

c ______ 16. When a long-term heavy smoker was sixty-five, she was fitted for dentures. Months later, she was diagnosed with throat cancer. Her neighbor explained, "I don't want to have my denture fitting now. Getting dentures gave my neighbor throat cancer!" A background in one area of philosophy would have helped the neighbor come to a stronger conclusion. Which one would be of most help?

a. aesthetics
b. ethics
c. logic
d. metaphysics

c ______ 17. Two teachers were discussing their students' lives. Mr. Chagas commented, "These kids have so many more complexities to their lives, so many more pressures that we need to modify the curriculum to meet their needs." Mrs. Montero disagreed: "Kids have always had complexities and pressures in their lives. Fundamental issues in human existence do not change." Based upon Mrs. Montero's comment, which of the following schools of thought would she most likely support?

a. progressivism
b. behaviorism
c. perennialism
d. emotivism

c ______ 18. A frustrated faculty member stated at a department meeting, "We have one female author in the curriculum! Shakespeare, Sophocles, Dickens, Homer! When are we going to acknowledge that other people have contributed to the universe of knowledge? When are we going to provide a broader framework for our students?" This teacher would be *least supportive* of which of the following educational philosophies?

a. essentialism
b. existentialism
c. perennialism
d. progressivism

b _____ 19. A candidate interviewing for the superintendent of school's position told school board members, "The fundamental purpose of education is to help people develop their intellect. Therefore, if I am hired, I will eliminate the self-esteem and peer pressure workshops, the courses in careers, personal banking, and auto tech." This candidate follows which one of these educational philosophies?
a. progressivism
b. perennialism
c. existentialism
d. essentialism

c _____ 20. A teacher education class is discussing the duties of a teacher and the principles that should guide a teacher's conduct with students. This class's discussion concerns which of the following?
a. metaphysics
b. epistemology
c. ethics
d. axiology

d _____ 21. The Oak Valley school board is conducting a very heated board meeting in which board members and residents are debating the educational goals of the school district. One parent, an essentialist, stands up and asserts that
a. the school district should shy away from all the group emphasis on teaching methods, for that does not allow the individual student to truly learn the meaning of his or her existence.
b. the school needs to focus on stimulating the students' natural curiosity and eagerness to learn, which it is stifling by emphasizing the study of traditional disciplines.
c. the school's current emphasis on "relevance" for students is completely misguided; students will benefit most from the self-discipline and the intellectual growth that studying the classics fosters.
d. the school board will best serve the needs of the students and of the community if it emphasizes the subject areas that will most help the students become functioning, productive members of society.

c _____ 22. Mrs. Svensen, the school principal, explained to parents that because human nature does not change, students can discover rich truths through studying biographies of significant people from history. What educational philosophy is Mrs. Svensen supporting?
a. existentialism
b. humanism
c. perennialism
d. progressivism

b _____ 23. Laurent High School's written curriculum includes the following: Students will strengthen their reasoning abilities; students will develop their critical inquiry abilities; students will develop their analytic abilities. Given those statements, which educational philosophy most closely matches the curriculum?

a. progressivism
b. perennialism
c. humanism
d. behaviorism

c _____ 24. Which of the following best depicts a classroom of a progressive teacher?

a. Students are sitting quietly reading the *Odyssey,* while the teacher writes key passages on the chalkboard for the students to memorize.
b. A list of computer assignments for math and writing is on the board for the students to complete; students are clustered around computer terminals, and the teacher is explaining the commands for several of the most common functions of the computer.
c. A group of students are working cooperatively on a student-initiated project to discover how gears operate; the teacher acts as a facilitator for their experimentation.
d. The teacher and a student meet individually to decide on which topics could best help a student discover the meaning within his life.

d _____ 25. Which of the following best depicts an existentialist teacher's classroom?

a. Some students work together on a scale model of the Globe Theater, and others work on sewing costumes for a play they will perform.
b. Students in a French class chorally read a passage from their textbook, and the teacher corrects the pronunciation of several students.
c. Students work individually on worksheets or exercises to help reinforce their skills in computation.
d. A student, after checking in the school and local library, draws up a reading list and meets with the teacher to inform her of his course of study for the semester.

c _____ 26. Which of the following would most closely represent a progressive's philosophy of education?

a. Human nature is static, and knowledge is absolute; therefore, people will learn by imitating the practice of our wise ancestors.
b. Human nature is constant, but new knowledge is constantly being discovered; therefore, people must learn from the past and present.
c. Human nature is ever changing; therefore, people must continually rediscover and redefine knowledge and its application.
d. Human nature is an illusion; there is no reality outside the individual; therefore, the individual must make meaning for himself or herself.

d _____ 27. John Dewey, an educator of the twentieth century, was most noted for his work on
a. essentialism.
b. existentialism.
c. perennialism.
d. progressivism.

c _____ 28. The social studies department at a high school noted that the students' achievement, by and large, was mediocre. One teacher told the others: "The students' achievement will probably always be mediocre if they have no impelling desire to learn what is in the curriculum. We need to examine our curriculum for possible revision." How would this teacher describe herself?
a. as a conceptual empiricist
b. as an essentialist
c. as a progressivist
d. as a perennialist

c _____ 29. Mrs. Conrad never writes up rigid lesson plans because she knows that rigidly set plans will not sustain a child's interest and curiosity. Rather, she records what children do and how they progress. She meets with each child frequently to discuss his or her interests in learning and to agree on what activity the child will start next to explore those interests. She considers herself a facilitator in the children's learning. Mrs. Conrad would probably describe herself as a(n)
a. behaviorist.
b. perennialist.
c. progressivist.
d. essentialist.

d _____ 30. Which knowledge is of the most importance to progressivists?
a. that which represents the best of human thought and action
b. knowledge that enables humans to make economic and technological progress in the world
c. knowledge that assists people in understanding social conventions
d. that which reflects the needs and interests of the learner

a _____ 31. Which of the following statements best represents progressive thought?
a. Human nature is fluid, changing through time and different conditions.
b. The essence of humanity is determined by existence.
c. The nature of humanity remains constant over time.
d. The core aspects of human nature have changed slightly over the course of human history.

c _____ 32. A new teacher spoke up at a department meeting. "I've examined the curriculum," he stated, "and I notice that although much of the traditional curriculum is worthwhile, we don't seem to include enough courses that will help these students function in the real world." Which of the following educational philosophies best reflects this teacher's concerns?
a. liberal humanism
b. perennialism
c. essentialism
d. existentialism

a _____ 33. According to the essentialists, the central element of reality is
a. the mind, which distinguishes humans from animals.
b. recognition of the different ways of knowing.
c. the ability to observe the spiritual world.
d. awareness of human consciousness.

c _____ 34. According to existentialists, a person's relationship to existence is a matter of
a. chance.
b. divine determination.
c. personal choice.
d. social expectations.

a _____ 35. Mr. Sharif thinks that there is a core body of knowledge that most students can master, that this core knowledge is important for students to become productive members of society, and that students can best learn this knowledge through a problem-solving approach to learning, motivated by their own curiosity. His philosophy of education is that of a(n)
a. eclectic.
b. essentialist.
c. existentialist.
d. perennialist.

a _____ 36. A school board that was strongly committed to essentialism would be most supportive of which of the following?
a. a core curriculum
b. student input on the creation of new courses
c. the inclusion of Latin and Greek courses
d. viewing the teacher as facilitator, not expert

b _____ 37. Alma is meeting with her guidance counselor to select courses. She tells her counselor, " I know that course would be interesting, but will it help me get a job or help prepare me for college?" Alma is probably supportive of which of the following philosophies?
a. eclecticism
b. essentialism
c. existentialism
d. progressivism

c _____ 38. Mrs. Boxleitner tells her students at the beginning of the year: "You need to find out who you are and what's important for you. You need to be able to make choices about your life and live with those choices. Don't look to me to provide you with answers. You need to think about these things yourselves." Mrs. Boxleitner represents which of the following philosophies?

a. perennialism
b. essentialism
c. existentialism
d. progressivism

d _____ 39. A school board that was strongly committed to existentialism would be most supportive of which of the following?

a. the "Great Books" approach for teaching
b. reading and writing groups differentiated by student ability
c. cooperative learning groups
d. a student's unrestricted choice of subjects

c _____ 40. Which of the following statements best reflects existentialism?

a. Individuals naturally drift toward others in order to learn.
b. Individuals learn best by adapting wisdom from the past to their own lives.
c. Individuals must create meaning for themselves by themselves.
d. Individuals can only hope to thrive by learning what is necessary to prosper in their society.

d _____ 41. In a literature class, the students discuss if the Prince's banishment of Romeo was just or unjust. Their discussion is directed toward

a. aesthetics.
b. metaphysics.
c. logic.
d. ethics.

b _____ 42. Which of the following might be found in either an existentialist or a progressivist school?

a. character education
b. individualized instruction
c. instruction in citizenship
d. cooperative learning

d _____ 43. John Dewey thought that ideas

a. were divinely inspired, allowing us to transcend the confines of our temporal existence.
b. should be passed on from one generation to the other so the younger generation could learn the wisdom from the past.
c. were important in and of themselves, without any link to action.
d. were instruments that enabled people to solve problems.

c _____ 44. Which of the following activities or practices would John Dewey most likely support?
a. the inculcation of patriotic sentiments to promote citizenship
b. frequent testing of students to encourage high competition among them
c. the widespread use of the scientific method, which shows students how to think
d. the memorization of passages from literature, and of scientific and mathematical equations

a _____ 45. A private school would like to have a beautiful statue on its front lawn. The school trustees invite several artists to submit sketches of the proposed statue, and the faculty and students will decide on which statue they prefer for the school. As members of the school community look at each sketch, they are most likely basing their decision for the statue on
a. aesthetics.
b. epistemology.
c. metaphysics.
d. logic.

c _____ 46. A town resident writes a letter to the local paper, harshly criticizing the public schools and their method of educating the students. She claims the schools do not recognize the inherent freedom of each individual to determine the meaning of his or her life but rather unnecessarily emphasize group learning and the "usefulness" of knowledge. This woman most likely ascribes to
a. behaviorism.
b. essentialism.
c. existentialism.
d. progressivism.

d _____ 47. Which hypothetical teaching situation would John Dewey be most likely to support?
a. teaching geometry by studying the lives of Greek mathematicians
b. teaching geometry by making up songs and stories the students enjoy
c. teaching geometry by giving many examples of its uses
d. teaching geometry by explaining principles when the need arises as the students build a tree house

a _____ 48. Essentialists believe that knowing reality requires the ability to
a. observe and measure the physical world accurately.
b. use essential skills to make progress.
c. interact democratically in learning situations.
d. make personal decisions about the nature of one's relationship to the world.

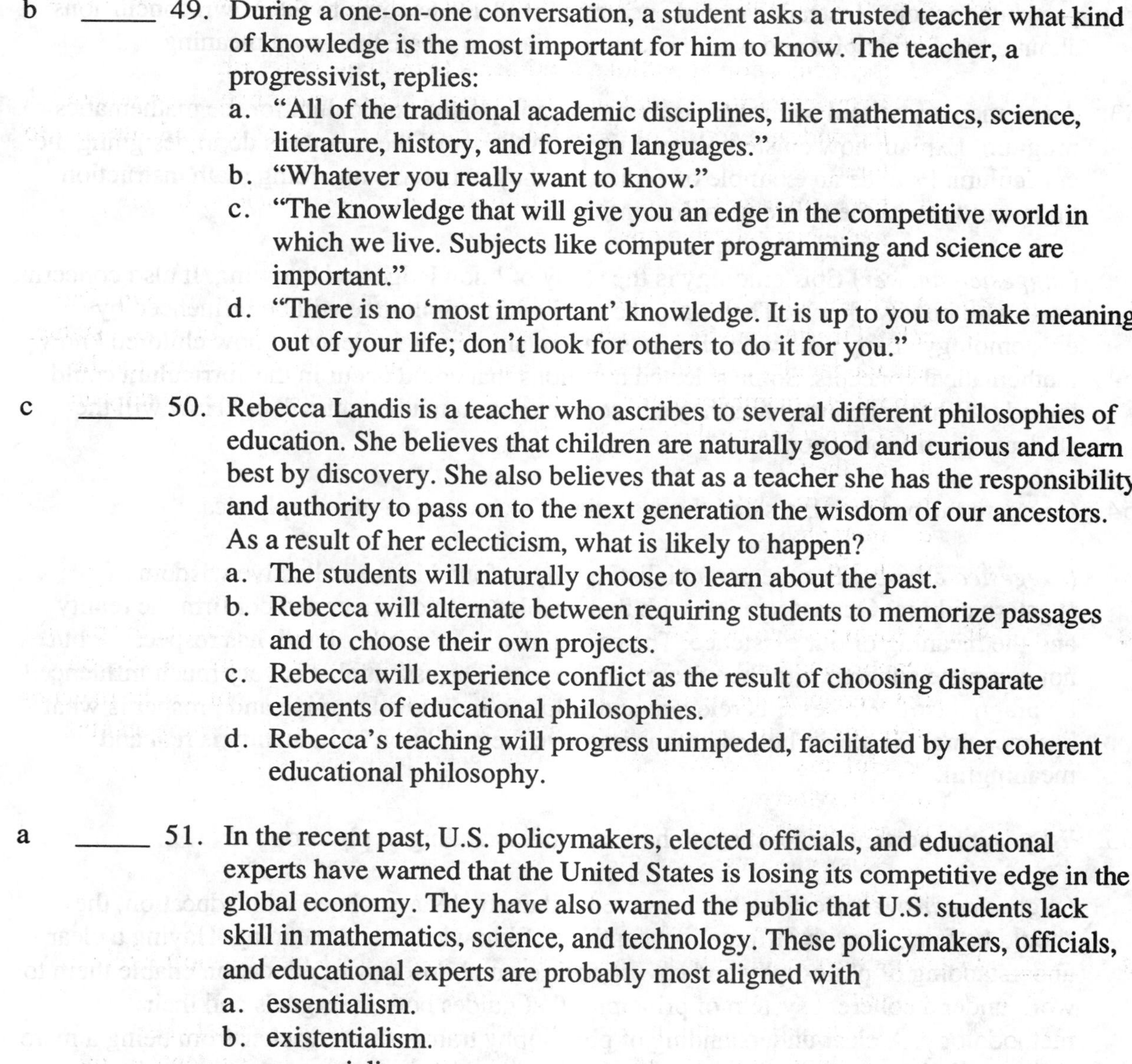

b _____ 49. During a one-on-one conversation, a student asks a trusted teacher what kind of knowledge is the most important for him to know. The teacher, a progressivist, replies:

a. "All of the traditional academic disciplines, like mathematics, science, literature, history, and foreign languages."
b. "Whatever you really want to know."
c. "The knowledge that will give you an edge in the competitive world in which we live. Subjects like computer programming and science are important."
d. "There is no 'most important' knowledge. It is up to you to make meaning out of your life; don't look for others to do it for you."

c _____ 50. Rebecca Landis is a teacher who ascribes to several different philosophies of education. She believes that children are naturally good and curious and learn best by discovery. She also believes that as a teacher she has the responsibility and authority to pass on to the next generation the wisdom of our ancestors. As a result of her eclecticism, what is likely to happen?

a. The students will naturally choose to learn about the past.
b. Rebecca will alternate between requiring students to memorize passages and to choose their own projects.
c. Rebecca will experience conflict as the result of choosing disparate elements of educational philosophies.
d. Rebecca's teaching will progress unimpeded, facilitated by her coherent educational philosophy.

a _____ 51. In the recent past, U.S. policymakers, elected officials, and educational experts have warned that the United States is losing its competitive edge in the global economy. They have also warned the public that U.S. students lack skill in mathematics, science, and technology. These policymakers, officials, and educational experts are probably most aligned with

a. essentialism.
b. existentialism.
c. perennialism.
d. progressivism.

Short-Answer Questions

Respond to each of the following questions briefly, but specifically, in complete sentences.

52. You are an existentialist teacher, and in your curriculum you are expected to teach ethics to your high school students. How would you respond to this element of the curriculum?

(suggested answer) Since existentialists believe that existence precedes essence and that the individual is ultimately free, I would be reluctant to impose a predetermined code of ethics onto the students. I would refrain from identifying the "rightness" or "wrongness" of

particular actions. Instead, I would encourage students to come to their own conclusions about ethical principles and would encourage them to create their own meaning.

53. An elementary school committee is designing an updated curriculum for the mathematics program. Explain how epistemology will affect the work the members do in designing the curriculum. Provide an example of a question they may have regarding math instruction that would reveal the epistemological influence.

    (suggested answer) Epistemology is the study of knowledge and knowing. It also concerns itself with how we know. Therefore, the curriculum committee will be influenced by epistemology at any time when it wants an explanation or evidence of how children know mathematical concepts. Some selected questions that could occur in the curriculum could include "What constitutes fourth-grade competency in mathematics?" or "How will the students learn subtraction?"

54. Compare the perennialist's and the essentialist's conception of metaphysics.

    (suggested answer) For the perennialist, reality is found in the collective wisdom of Western culture. Our association with that enables us to discover and confirm the reality and the meaning of our existence. The essentialist, on the other hand, has respect for but not complete adherence to the wisdom of the past. The essentialist is very much influenced by pragmatism. Whatever is relevant and helps an individual survive and prosper is what has meaning. Whatever helps humans improve the condition of humanity is real and meaningful.

55. Why is it important for teachers to have an understanding of philosophy?

    (suggested answer) Because teachers are fundamentally associated with education, they should be familiar with different conceptions of knowledge and meaning. Having a clear understanding of philosophy and having their own philosophy of education enable them to work under a coherent system of principles that guides both their goals and their methodology. A clear understanding of philosophy transforms a teacher from being a mere skilled technician to being a professional.

Essay Questions

Read each of the following questions, and respond by composing an organized essay that includes an introduction, fully developed paragraph(s), and a conclusion.

56. Explain the differences among the four schools of philosophy with regard to the role of the teacher and the role of the student. For each philosophy—perennialism, progressivism, essentialism, and existentialism—answer these two questions: What is the role of the teacher? What is the role of the student?

    (suggested answer) Answers are summarized in Table 10.1 of the textbook.

57. Two of the philosophies discussed were somewhat distorted in popular practice. Dewey's progressivism was sometimes twisted in ways that reduced its real value. Existentialism, on the other hand, was trimmed of some of its bleaker ideas and made into a greater force for personal growth. Briefly explain the important elements of Dewey's educational philosophy, and note some of the abuses eventually perpetrated in its name. Also explain the principal concepts of Sartre's version of existentialism and describe the simpler forms that came down to schools.

    (suggested answer) Dewey said that school should be instructive participation in life, not preparation for life, and that school should be a microcosm of democratic society in which students learn the skills of citizenship. Dewey's curriculum was built around the activities and occupations of adult life. Corruptions of Dewey's philosophy hold that content is virtually unimportant, that only process counts. Sartre and his followers believed that we live an alien, pointless life, whose only meaning is that which people make themselves, or is not very much. To the existentialists, life is a quest for meaning. In the absence of preexisting relationships with the world, people are entirely free. Ultimately, educators seized on the existential focus on self-determination and self-definition. Activities deriving from the human potential movement, values clarification, and individualized learning experiences are examples of experiences that build on the notion of self-creation.

58. Consider the school in which you now observe. If you are not currently observing in a school, consider your high school. What is the dominant educational philosophy of the school? To answer that question, describe the role of the teacher, the choice of curriculum, and the goals set for the students.

    (suggested answer) Answers will vary; however, the answer should match its description of teacher's role, curriculum, and student expectations with one of the educational philosophies presented in the chapter.

Alternative Assessment Ideas

The following activities are suggestions for student portfolio activities. They are a means of providing alternative assessment of the students' capabilities.

Independent Reading

Read and respond to any of the following selections from Ryan/Cooper, *Kaleidoscope: Readings in Education* (Houghton Mifflin, 1998). You may want to use the Article Review Form on page 269.

Adler—"The Paideia Proposal"

Betts—"What's All the Noise About?"

Boyer—"The Educated Person"

Dewey—"My Pedagogic Creed"

Hutchins—"The Basis of Education"

Postman—"Making a Living, Making a Life"

Rogers—"Personal Thoughts on Teaching and Learning"

Skinner—"The Free and Happy Student"

Reflective Papers

Choose one of the following topics to write a reflective paper (2–5 pages). The purpose of the paper is to help you assimilate new knowledge by blending it with your previous knowledge and experiences.

1. Select any current controversy in education and demonstrate how philosophical differences inform the analysis of the issue.

2. Imagine you have been named superintendent of schools in a brand-new school district. Everything—from buildings to faculty to students—is new to this school district. You have been hired because of your vision for education, including your educational philosophy. What would your guiding philosophy be for this new school district? Describe and give examples of how it would be carried out.

3. Imagine you are interviewing now for a teaching position. One part of your interview includes writing your educational philosophy as a teacher. Describe your educational philosophy and how you see it influencing your work with students.

4. As you observe in your field-site school, think about the educational undergirding of what you observe. Based upon the activities, lessons, and interactions between students and teachers and teachers and colleagues, what educational philosophy emerges? What seems to be the general conception of what knowledge is and how it is best acquired?

Journal Writing

Suggestions for journal topics for students' selection:

1. Indicate which of the four philosophies of education seems closest to your own and tell what in your life may have contributed to developing your philosophy.

2. Tell what philosophy you think your instructor holds most strongly and describe what evidence you have for this.

3. Pick one person or group of people (state legislators, the president of the United States, a political party, parents, yuppies, etc.) and indicate which philosophy they seem to be acting from and why you think so.

Chapter 11 What Is the History of American Education?

Multiple-Choice Items

Read each item carefully. On the appropriate line, write the letter of the choice that represents the best answer.

c _____ 1. In the late 1600s, who would most likely have been a student in an elementary school?
a. a white female
b. a white male and white female of the middle class
c. a white, upper-class male
d. a male of any race

c _____ 2. Since colonial times in this country, formal education of some kind has almost always been available to
a. immigrants from England.
b. immigrants from various countries.
c. middle-class and upper-class white males.
d. white males and females of any class.

b _____ 3. How were dame schools organized?
a. An unmarried woman would travel from village to village conducting lessons in reading, writing, and religion.
b. A housewife would teach children basic literacy and household skills in her home.
c. Several women joined to form a cooperative school that taught reading, writing, and arithmetic.
d. Female teachers taught young women in a boarding school domestic arts, French, music, and art to prepare them for marriage.

a _____ 4. What was the purpose of a dame school?
 a. to teach basic literacy, religion, and some household skills to children
 b. to supplement the public education provided through teaching religion
 c. to prepare girls to be homemakers
 d. to provide boys with rudimentary education in reading, writing, and Latin

a _____ 5. During colonial times, where would a community-controlled, religiously oriented school most likely be found?
 a. Massachusetts
 b. Georgia
 c. New Jersey
 d. Virginia

d _____ 6. During the colonial period, which type of formal education was most typical in New England?
 a. secular public schools attended in large part by one ethnic type
 b. individual tutors hired to work with one or two families in a home
 c. private religious schools supported by tuition
 d. tax-supported public schools with a religious orientation

d _____ 7. Residents of a small village in Massachusetts in 1651 decide that they need a school for their children. Given the era, what is the most likely reason the parents feel they need a school?
 a. They want their children to learn to become good citizens.
 b. They want their children to learn the skills necessary for trade.
 c. They feel their colony will not prosper unless the children can read, write, and do arithmetic.
 d. They want their children to read and understand the Bible.

d _____ 8. Why did Massachusetts colonists pass the Old Deluder Satan Act?
 a. They wanted to eradicate all signs of satanic influence from the colony.
 b. They wanted to ensure that religion would be taught in all schools so that children would not be tempted into doing the devil's work.
 c. They wanted to guarantee the religious education of non-Christians so they would convert to Puritanism.
 d. They wanted to ensure that all children would learn how to read and be able to understand the teachings of the Bible.

c _____ 9. Which of the following were the predominant forms of elementary schooling in New England during the colonial period?
 a. private venture schools, dame schools, and religious schools
 b. private academies, individual tutors, and Quaker schools
 c. town schools, moving schools, and district schools
 d. Latin schools, dame schools, and individual tutors

b ______ 10. Why did New England moving schools come into existence?
   a. Before villages became firmly established, residents moved the location of the school periodically to determine the most convenient site for all.
   b. Moving schools, through traveling schoolteachers, allowed children in outlying areas to be educated.
   c. Moving schools allowed several villages to share the cost of schooling by paying for a schoolmaster to work several months in each town.
   d. Because of shifting populations, the district schools could not rely on steady enrollment.

b ______ 11. For over two hundred years, adults believed that when a student experienced academic difficulty, he or she
   a. was simply "dimwitted" with little chance of improvement.
   b. was morally lax and had been tempted by the work of the devil.
   c. needed more encouragement from the teacher to do better.
   d. would understand the subject if he or she concentrated more on memorization.

c ______ 12. Why was corporal punishment an accepted practice in American schools for over two hundred years?
   a. Adults believed the threat of physical punishment helped youngsters develop the powers of concentration.
   b. It was commonly believed that a teacher's authoritative behavior added to his or her effectiveness.
   c. Students easily fell under the devil's influence and needed corporal punishment to deter them from misbehavior.
   d. Adults disregarded the feelings of children and thought they needed to be trained like animals.

b ______ 13. How did the Southern Anglican population differ in their conception of a common education from the Puritan New Englanders?
   a. They believed that children could not learn when they were grouped together, but needed to be taught individually.
   b. They did not believe that everyone had a religious obligation to learn to read.
   c. Most of the families in the South were affluent enough to hire private tutors and governesses, so there was no need for public education.
   d. They believed that the Puritan-influenced schools were far too bleak and harsh for children.

c ______ 14. It is during the colonial times, and a child has just been born to a Southern plantation family. How would he most likely be educated?
   a. through a small local school run by the Anglican church
   b. through a tax-supported community school
   c. at home with traveling scholars or local ministers
   d. in a boarding school in a large Southern town

a _____ 15. The settlers in the Middle Colonies represented numerous ethnic and religious groups and wanted their children educated about their own faith and heritage. What kinds of schools were established as a result of this need?
a. private venture schools
b. private academies
c. land-grant schools
d. common schools

b _____ 16. What is the best description of private venture schools?
a. schools formed so different ethnic groups could be instilled with American democratic values and learn reading, writing, and arithmetic
b. schools designed to educate children within the tenets of their faith and to provide an elementary education for them
c. schools that prepared young men to enter commerce and trade
d. small, community-run and financed schools designed to teach reading, writing, vocational skills, and religion

c _____ 17. What change did the Northwest Ordinances of 1785 and 1787 effect?
a. All townships were required to hire a teacher for the children.
b. All households would be taxed to support and sustain public high schools within their district.
c. Each township was required to set aside land for the maintenance of public schools.
d. Each township was required to institute public elementary/secondary schools and agricultural colleges on parcels of tax-supported public land.

a _____ 18. Why were the Northwest Ordinances of 1785 and 1787 so significant in the history of American education?
a. It was the first time the federal government became involved in establishing laws advancing public education.
b. The ordinances provided the land to establish secondary schools and required both sexes to be educated there.
c. The federal government ensured that states would continue to have complete local control over schooling by supporting their right to determine what kind of education they would provide.
d. They required that all schools receiving tax monies, including those in outlying rural areas, enforce compulsory school attendance laws.

a _____ 19. It is during the early 1800s, and at a town meeting a prominent man is arguing that the proposed school will bring about unity for a new nation and economic growth through increased productivity. For what is this man arguing?
a. the establishment of common schools
b. the founding of religiously oriented, private schools
c. free education for white men and women through high school
d. the establishment of a Latin academy in the town

b _____ 20. Which of the following ideas was promoted for the establishment of common schools?
a. equal educational access for upper-class men and women
b. the need for a literate citizenry to maintain a democracy
c. the need for strong instruction in religion and morals for U.S. youth
d. the importance of vocational training for those who could not afford further schooling

c _____ 21. One obstacle for establishing common schools was economic. Which of the following best exemplifies the economic argument against common schools?
a. The number of teachers needed for the establishment of common schools would cost too much for residents to support.
b. There appeared to be no feasible, economically viable way to build and maintain the necessary school buildings.
c. People should be held responsible for paying only for their own children's education, not for others' children.
d. Paying for instructional materials and teachers' salaries would unduly burden taxpayers.

d _____ 22. For parents who enrolled their child in a private venture school, what is the likely reason they would be opposed to common schools?
a. The numbers of students would prevent individual attention for their child.
b. Their child would be required to follow the common academic curriculum given to all students.
c. Common schools would not provide their child with the necessary background to succeed in trade.
d. Their child would not be instructed in the tenets of his or her faith or about his or her own ethnic heritage.

a _____ 23. For what educational innovation is Friedrich Froebel, a German educator, best known?
a. developing the first kindergarten
b. designing a system by which to teach blind children
c. instituting grade levels for students
d. writing the curriculum that became the standard high school curriculum

c _____ 24. Why did Froebel emphasize play for kindergarteners?
a. He believed they were too young to do anything but play.
b. He believed play would help children expend their excess energy and be able to concentrate on intellectual activities.
c. He believed play allowed children to express themselves and develop their own abilities.
d. He thought that most teachers were best at teaching children how to play.

b ______ 25. During the mid-1800s a schoolteacher helps her students learn by giving them spoons to count. Also, she demonstrates affection toward all her students, never showing disapproval of them. Which of the following educators has influenced her?
  a. Horace Mann
  b. Johann Pestalozzi
  c. Friedrich Froebel
  d. John Dewey

a ______ 26. Johann Pestalozzi worked hard and experienced many discouraging failures before experiencing the rewards of being a respected educator. Why did many of his contemporaries scoff at his educational philosophy?
  a. He believed that the teacher should demonstrate respect and affection for each student.
  b. He believed most children learned best through memorization and drill.
  c. He thought the only subjects that should be included in elementary school were art and music.
  d. He contended that the only real learning that occurred happened when students focused on abstract learning.

a ______ 27. Today, many of Horace Mann's ideas about education are commonly accepted. Which of the following ideas of Mann were considered radical during his day?
  a. that teachers should not hit students; that education was a means of social mobility
  b. that religious education belonged in public schools; that teachers should be highly educated
  c. that formal education should focus on practical as well as academic skills; that cooperative learning was highly effective
  d. that schools should admit both sexes; that a core curriculum should be provided for all students

c ______ 28. Which of the following best describes Horace Mann's advocacy of common schools?
  a. He thought common schools were the only way to forge national unity.
  b. He thought that common schools would be easier to control and regulate, ensuring some consistency in students' education.
  c. He believed that common schools would provide an education for all, and that was the best means for social mobility.
  d. He thought that common schools would turn out a literate work force, especially important for worker productivity and worker loyalty.

b _____ 29. A new school in the early part of the twentieth century builds its curriculum on its students' natural development and natural interests. Teachers act as guides for student discovery, rather than as presenters of information. This school is carrying out the principles of which of the following groups?
a. The National Education Association
b. The Progressive Education Association
c. The Committee of Ten
d. The Association of Middle Schools

d _____ 30. Which of the following would be a likely occurrence in a school following the principles of the Progressive Education Association?
a. students individually reciting their lessons at the teacher's desk
b. students progressing through a highly organized, sequential mathematics curriculum written by the teachers
c. students working on projects in ability level groupings
d. a school trip for students to explore vernal pools

c _____ 31. During the 1700s, if a boy wanted to prepare for college, the best choice of preparation would have been
a. an English grammar school.
b. an academy.
c. a Latin grammar school.
d. a common school.

d _____ 32. It is 1763, and Thomas Smith is attending an English grammar school. What is the primary purpose of Thomas's schooling?
a. to prepare him for college
b. to prepare him for the ministry
c. to teach him the humanities
d. to prepare him for commerce and trade

b _____ 33. A young woman living in the Middle Colonies during the 1700s is attending a secondary school. Given the types of secondary schooling available at that time for women, which of the following schools would she attend?
a. a Latin grammar school
b. a private venture school
c. a public high school
d. a female academy

c _____ 34. Molly Fiske, a young woman living during the colonial period, is pursuing a secondary education. Which of the following best describes her likely course of study?
a. bookkeeping, natural sciences, writing, and reading
b. reading, writing, and arithmetic
c. geography, French, the three R's, and music
d. foreign languages, engineering, Latin, and geometry

b _____ 35. One distinctly American feature of the secondary academies that flourished in the mid-1800s was their
a. admission of all students without regard to religion, race, sex, or social class.
b. curriculum covering both classical and commercial subjects.
c. adherence to an essentially Puritan morality.
d. democratic faculty structure.

c _____ 36. During the 1800s, which type of secondary school had a curriculum that included both classical and commercial subjects?
a. Latin schools
b. English schools
c. academies
d. district schools

c _____ 37. What was the significance of Emma Willard, Mary Lyon, and Catharine Beecher in the history of American education?
a. They were the first women to graduate from an academy.
b. They started a grassroots movement protesting the exclusion of women from Latin schools.
c. They each started a female academy.
d. They were the first graduates of a normal school.

a _____ 38. What would a young woman expect to learn at a female academy?
a. how to be an intelligent companion for her husband or how to be a teacher
b. the traditional subjects of a Latin school, including reading, Latin, writing, rhetoric, and mathematics
c. the fundamentals of commerce and trade
d. how to raise children, along with advanced mathematics, science, philosophy, and languages

d _____ 39. Why was the ruling of the *Kalamazoo* case in Michigan significant in American educational history?
a. It stated that all Americans are entitled to a free, public education.
b. It stated that males and females must be taught in the same schools.
c. It stated that church and state must remain separate in public schools.
d. It stated that school districts can levy taxes to support high schools.

b _____ 40. Which of the following was the underlying argument for the *Kalamazoo* case ruling in 1874?

a. Public high schools were necessary to ensure employment of the middle class.
b. Providing a free elementary education but a secondary education to only those who could afford tuition was inherently unequal.
c. Establishing public high schools would foster national unity and loyalty in the same way common schools did.
d. Instituting public high schools would allow greater economic opportunity for the working class and the middle class, as well as recent immigrants.

a _____ 41. Why were junior high schools developed during the twentieth century?

a. to introduce new subjects of study and to attend to the needs of adolescents
b. to extend the basic skills instruction that elementary schools offered to prepare college-oriented students for the rigors of high school
c. to implement team teaching and a core curriculum, and to foster the special learning needs of adolescent students
d. to start to offer courses of study that would stream students into either a vocational or academic track during high school

c _____ 42. What is the distinction between junior high schools and middle schools?

a. Junior highs typically place students in teams where they follow a core academic program whereas middle schools typically track their students on the basis of ability.
b. Junior highs usually put more emphasis on the adolescents' emotional and cognitive development than the middle schools do.
c. Junior highs typically place greater emphasis on academic and athletic competition than middle schools do.
d. Junior highs usually offer a greater and wider range of courses suited to adolescents than middle schools do.

c _____ 43. Which of the following is characteristic of a middle school?

a. strong emphasis on competition in sports and academics
b. great emphasis on skills proficiency for students and the consistent use of one teacher for all subjects for students
c. interdisciplinary team teaching and a curriculum that focuses on students' personal development
d. multiage grouping and highly competitive sports teams

d _____ 44. During a typical school day, a student spends one block working on a history/literature project. Two of the teachers on his team see what he's doing and ask him to present it to the other students. Then, in the afternoon, he and his cooperative learning group work on their math problems, helping each other. Given this typical day, what kind of school does this student most likely attend?
a. a private college preparatory school
b. a junior high
c. a public high school
d. a middle school

b _____ 45. How much change has occurred in the instructional practices of high schools during the last century?
a. no change at all
b. relatively little change
c. substantial change
d. highly dramatic, radical change

c _____ 46. Why have high schools demonstrated minimal changes in their instructional practices over the last one hundred years?
a. Public high schools have always done a highly satisfactory job of educating students, so little change was needed.
b. Teachers are usually poorly educated, and are thus unable and unwilling to make any changes in their instruction.
c. Because high schools are organized by department and tend to be isolated from one another, it makes schoolwide instructional change difficult.
d. Changes in teaching practices are usually opposed by the community, making most high schools reluctant to change instructional practices.

b _____ 47. What percentage of the school-age population attends private schools?
a. 2 to 4 percent
b. 10 to 15 percent
c. 20 to 25 percent
d. 40 to 45 percent

c _____ 48. Historically, private education has met the needs of various groups of people. Which of the following groups have most often been served by private institutions throughout American education history?
a. African-American separatists and Episcopalians
b. women and Anglo-Americans
c. the wealthy and Roman Catholics
d. Eastern European immigrants and the upper middle class

b _____ 49. When an African American was educated before the Civil War, who typically taught him or her?
a. a business member or a clergy member
b. a clergy member or an abolitionist
c. an abolitionist or a plantation owner
d. a plantation owner or a Puritan

c _____ 50. Which of the following was a prevalent reason for educating African Americans before the Civil War?
a. to stir up slave discontent and to encourage rebellion
b. to teach African Americans how to be diligent, loyal workers
c. to convert African Americans to Christianity
d. to help teach African Americans new trades

d _____ 51. It is the early 1900s, and a young black man dreams of becoming a success. He doesn't want to just have a skilled job, though. He dreams of an education, of becoming an intellectual leader. He sees advanced education as the way for African Americans to make real progress in a white world. This young man's beliefs are most closely associated with the ideas of
a. Booker T. Washington.
b. Horace Mann.
c. Catharine Beecher.
d. W. E. B. Du Bois.

a _____ 52. Booker T. Washington, founder of the Tuskegee Institute, believed that
a. African Americans should view education as a way to learn practical skills.
b. there must be an intellectually rigorous program for the "talented tenth" who would make up the bulk of African-American leaders.
c. if African Americans learned the classics, they could ease the tensions between blacks and whites.
d. the only real hope for African-American advancement was repatriation to Africa.

b _____ 53. It is 1900, and a land-grant college for agriculture is just opening. Which of the following would apply to the college in order for it to receive federal money?
a. If sufficient interest is demonstrated by African Americans in attending an agricultural college, the land-grant college is responsible for establishing it. Otherwise, it is under no legal obligation to provide that kind of facility for African Americans.
b. The college would be prohibited from discriminating against African Americans unless a separate agriculture college for African Americans existed.
c. The college would be required to admit certain percentages of each ethnic and racial group that applied.
d. The college would be prohibited from discrimination of any kind.

c _____ 54. Why were the Morrill Acts of 1862 and 1890 important in the history of American education?
- a. They established that separate but equal public facilities must exist, ensuring an education for African Americans.
- b. They established that equal educational opportunity must be provided for women as well as men.
- c. They paved the way for establishing collegiate education for African Americans.
- d. They supported the rights of the states in maintaining local control of the public education system.

c _____ 55. According to the case of *Plessy* v. *Ferguson* (1896),
- a. separate facilities for minorities were inherently unequal.
- b. separate schools for black students were inherently unequal, but other facilities might be separate.
- c. separate but equal facilities for minorities were constitutionally acceptable.
- d. separate facilities were consistently equal, despite claims to the contrary.

a _____ 56. According to *Brown* v. *Board of Education of Topeka* (1954),
- a. separate facilities for minorities are inherently unequal and therefore constitutionally unacceptable.
- b. the determination of whether separate facilities for minorities are equal is the right of each state.
- c. separate facilities for minorities are ordinarily found to be equal.
- d. separate facilities represent a viable choice for those districts who want to maintain cultural heritage and identity.

c _____ 57. Which of the following best explains the underlying reason that whites initially wanted to teach Native Americans?
- a. The whites' goal was for greater social harmony and cultural understanding through educating Native Americans.
- b. The whites believed that Native Americans would coexist more easily with whites if they knew how to read and write.
- c. The whites wanted to teach Native Americans how to read and write so they could convert to Christianity.
- d. The whites saw Native Americans as a potential labor force and wanted to teach them basic literacy so they could be employed.

c _____ 58. Once the federal government assumed control for Native Americans' education, the government had a particular goal. Which of the following best identifies the goal that the federal government had for Native Americans?
- a. maintaining their cultural identity and practices
- b. improving upon the basic standard of living for Native Americans
- c. aiding Native Americans in their assimilation into white American culture
- d. fostering the education of a talented minority who would then become the liaisons between the white American government and the Native American nations

d _____ 59. During the 1970s, the federal government made changes in the Native American schools. Which of the following were included in those changes?
a. curricular changes, emphasizing a college preparatory course of study rather than vocational skills
b. establishing mentoring programs for Native American high school graduates to work with Native American high school students
c. identifying minimum competencies that Native American students would be expected to achieve before graduation
d. adding culturally relevant material to the subjects and skills taught

b _____ 60. Current public education for Native Americans is threatened by a number of problems. Which of the following are the most direct problems affecting the public education of Native Americans today?
a. crime, violence in schools, and a breakdown in the family structure
b. poverty, absenteeism, and a high drop-out rate
c. isolation, loneliness, and lack of respect for teachers
d. lack of cultural cohesion, acting out in schools, and friction between students and teachers

d _____ 61. Historically, a common stereotype existed that Hispanic-American children were intellectually less capable than Anglo-American children. Which of the following best describes how standardized testing compounded that misconception?
a. It demonstrated that Hispanic-American children's Spanish grammar was less logical than Anglo-American children's English grammar.
b. Many standardized tests included advanced cognitive skills that many Hispanic-American children could not perform.
c. The time limit on standardized tests was rigid, not allowing Spanish-speaking children sufficient time to complete the tasks, and their scores suffered.
d. Standardized tests like the I.Q. test were culturally biased, asking questions that would be common knowledge for Anglo-American children but unfamiliar to Hispanic-American children.

a _____ 62. Which of the following supplies the best description of the goals for bilingual education?
a. Non-native English-speaking children could learn content in their native language while gradually developing English fluency, and eventually joining English-only classes.
b. Non-native English-speaking children would learn content in their native tongue and would develop pride in their ethnic heritage.
c. Non-native English-speaking children would be taught a culturally appropriate curriculum and would not be required to join English-speaking students.
d. Non-native English-speaking children would attend some classes in English and some in their native tongue, hastening their assimilation into Anglo-American culture.

d _____ 63. What is typically lacking in Asian Americans' approach to education?
a. industriousness
b. a sense of honor for students' work
c. attention at home to the academic work of the child
d. the active, visible participation of the parents in the child's school

b _____ 64. What is a disadvantage for Asian Americans in being perceived as the "model minority"?
a. No agencies are willing to assist in housing or education because they believe that Asian Americans can succeed on their own.
b. It minimizes the needs Asian Americans have for English language instruction and multicultural education.
c. It may become more difficult for them to blend in with other groups.
d. They may assimilate too quickly into the mainstream culture, quickly losing their cultural identity.

Short-Answer Questions

Respond to each of the following questions briefly, but specifically, in complete sentences.

65. Identify and explain two of the characteristics of middle schools. Why are these particular characteristics considered important in middle school education?

(suggested answer) Answers will vary. A correct answer will identify two of the following characteristics and explain how each one supports the middle school philosophy of dealing with adolescents' particular emotional and developmental needs. The following are the characteristics of a middle school: 1) incorporating the questions and concerns of students into the curriculum; 2) interdisciplinary team organization; 3) long-term teacher-student relationships, including a teacher-advisor for each student; 4) core academic program for each learner; 5) extended range of teaching strategies, including use of cooperative learning activities; 6) school transition programs; 7) flexible scheduling; 8) exploratory activities and courses.

66. Explain the difference between universal education and comprehensive education in the history of American education.

(suggested answer) Universal education is the concept that all people have a right to be educated. Early in American history, only upper-class white males were educated. Gradually, during the 1800s, the common school was instituted, in which white children of town residents could obtain a grammar school education. During different stages of American history, universal education became more inclusive of groups of people previously excluded: women, African Americans, Native Americans, and the disabled. A comprehensive education is an education that includes both the traditional curriculum for college preparation and training for trades. The need for comprehensive education was first seen during the nineteenth century, and the comprehensive high school was founded to address the needs of students requiring job training and college preparatory studies.

67. How did the educational philosophies of European educators Friedrich Froebel and Johann Pestalozzi contrast with the prevalent U.S. view toward the student and learning?

    (suggested answer) Both Froebel and Pestalozzi had student-centered educational philosophies. Froebel, who founded the kindergarten, believed children learned best through play and through their own interest in activities such as art, music, science, and language. Pestalozzi had similar ideas about children, believing that they learned best when they received unconditional love and acceptance from the adult or teacher. Both men highlighted the positive nature of the child. The American practice of education, on the contrary, did not focus on the needs or interests of the child. The concept of self-discipline and morality was stressed most heavily in schools. The common belief that children would succumb to the temptations of the devil held for close to 250 years and was used to justify the harsh atmosphere in many of the nation's schoolrooms.

68. What role did the academies play in American education?

    (suggested answer) Some would call the academies the precursors of the comprehensive high school. Through the 1700s, Latin grammar schools were run to teach young men the classical subjects that they would need to continue their education in college. English grammar schools focused on more practical skills and subjects, preparing their students to work in commerce and trade. Academies sprang up during the second half of the eighteenth century. They combined elements of the Latin and English grammar school. The instruction was conducted in English, not Latin, but classical subjects were also offered in the curriculum. Gradually, as academies grew, they began to emphasize a college preparatory curriculum but held to the ideal of a utilitarian curriculum.

69. The 1896 *Plessy* v. *Ferguson* decision was overturned by *Brown* v. *Board of Education of Topeka* in 1954. The effects of the *Brown* decision were far-reaching, although much work remains to be done in establishing equality of educational opportunity. Explain the basic nature of each decision, and tell how the *Brown* decision affected U.S. education.

    (suggested answer) Plessy v. *Ferguson* said that operating separate facilities for members of different ethnic groups was not inherently unconstitutional as long as the facilities were equal. The *Brown* decision said that separate facilities could not help being unequal and that operating separate school systems for black students ensured their unequal treatment for a variety of reasons. As a result of *Brown,* school districts all over the country were obliged to come up with plans to desegregate school populations and to demonstrate equality of treatment. A common strategy was to bus black students to white schools. The problem of ensuring equality of educational opportunity has not yet been solved.

Essay Questions

Read each of the following questions, and respond by composing an organized essay that includes an introduction, fully developed paragraph(s), and a conclusion.

70. Education in New England, the Middle Colonies, and the South took three different forms. Each form of education reflected the beliefs and the social organization of the area in which it predominated. Describe the differences among the predominant forms of education in each of these three areas. Explain the features of community life that seemed to influence education to develop as it did in each area.

(suggested answer) New England: Settled by Puritans who lived in compact communities and believed that everyone should be able to read and interpret the Bible. The Puritans first had town schools, one in each town of fifty families or more, then moving schools, which went to remote farmlands. District schools were finally established in each township. Schools were funded by the town treasury and included moral instruction according to Puritan ideas because in terms of religion the population was fairly homogeneous. *Middle Colonies:* Settled by a variety of religious and ethnic groups, each of which valued separate education. Promoted private venture schools licensed by civil government but funded by parents, not by taxes. Religious training was offered, but differed among schools, according to the religion of those sponsoring each school. *South:* Settled by Anglican Englishmen of the upper class who established large plantations and settlements quite distant from each other. They did not believe in a religious imperative to learn to read. Southerners hired tutors to educate children. Schools might be established by government authority but run by a corporation that collected tuition and administered the school.

71. During the 1700s, secondary education in the colonies included both the Latin grammar school and the English grammar school. Compare the curricula and goals for each type of school. Then explain to what degree their influences are felt in contemporary secondary education curricula.

(suggested answer) The Latin schools, designed for young men who intended to attend college, offered classical subjects of study, heavily emphasizing Latin, Greek, and Hebrew. The knowledge that the students learned was solely to prepare them for further study, and no attention was given to practical skills. The English schools, on the other hand, served young men and some young women by providing them with a more practical education. The students continued with reading, writing, and arithmetic but also studied subjects that would help them in their future work: bookkeeping, navigation. At times, the students were also taught subjects that helped them socialize: music and art.

In contemporary secondary education, the influence of the Latin schools is still seen. Private college preparatory ("prep") schools are the modern-day counterpart of the Latin schools. Furthermore, public high schools also show the influence of Latin schools in their college preparatory curriculum and in advanced placement course selections, those courses designed to earn college credits for those who score high on the exams. The English school influence is seen in the more practical course selections offered by contemporary high schools. Some high schools continue to offer bookkeeping; other examples of courses might be courses such as keyboarding, computer classes, or business English.

72. Some would argue that the history of American education has been the history of education for the middle-class to upper-class white male. Identify three significant changes in the

history of American education that expanded educational opportunities for others. Explain the impact that each of these changes had upon the education of Americans.

(suggested answer) Answers will vary. However, some of the changes that may be included are the advent of the common schools and public high schools; the opening of female academies; the *Kalamazoo* case; the Morrill Acts; *Brown* v. *Board of Education of Topeka;* the inclusion of Native Americans within public education; the beginning of bilingual education and special education; and the education of the gifted and disadvantaged.

73. In the beginning of the chapter, the authors identified six major forces in American educational history: local control, universal education, public education, comprehensive education, secular education, and the changing ideas of the basics. Many of the contemporary educational problems or issues emanate from these forces. Select two contemporary education issues or problems, and briefly explain them. Then describe how each one is associated with one of the major forces of American education.

(suggested answer) Answers will vary. The answers should show an identification of an issue and a clear link with one of the educational forces. An example might be the current debate of school choice and its tie to public education and/or secular education. Another example might be multicultural education and its link to the changing ideas of the basics.

Alternative Assessment Ideas

There are no specific readings from *Kaleidoscope: Readings in Education* for this chapter. However, you may want to assign the following activity.

Independent Reading

Select three recent articles (those written within the past five years) on any of the following topics. You may choose three within the same topic or vary your selections.

- the common school
- the education of American women
- secular education
- comprehensive high schools
- the education of minorities
- the history of the curriculum

Reflective Papers

Choose one of the following topics to write a reflective paper (2–5 pages). The purpose of the paper is to help you assimilate new knowledge by blending it with your previous knowledge and experiences.

1. Considering your background (race, gender, ethnicity), imagine that you are living in the 1700s, 1800s, or early 1900s in a particular region of the United States. Write about the kind of education you probably would have received. What would have been the kinds of

knowledge you would have been expected to possess? Compare that to your own education.

2. Think about your own education up to this point. What has been your educational history in terms of the kinds of schools you've attended and the curriculum you've followed? To what degree can you see elements of the chapter's topics reflected within your own education?

3. The history of American education can be viewed from a number of different perspectives. As discussed in the text, one underlying reason that public schools came about was that many believed public education would build national unity and increase economic productivity. From that vantage point, education's purpose is primarily for the common economic good of the society. At other points in the text, the authors indicate that many people believed that the purpose of education was for humanitarian reasons: so the individual would be enriched. Think about those vantage points and respond. What do you see as important considerations for either or both of those positions? What do you see as the primary purpose of education?

4. Visit two schools in your area—one built within the last ten years and the oldest one that you can find that is still in use. Compare the differences in the architectural form and function and link these to historical changes in education.

5. If you're working at a field-site school, consider its organization, curriculum, and educational philosophy. To what degree can you identify certain themes present in your school that were discussed in the history chapter? For example, your school might be rewriting its math curriculum. What kinds of questions are being asked? Are teachers concerned about which students enroll in upper-level mathematics? Are they discussing what minimum competencies all students should have? Are they trying to identify the skills necessary for college entrance? All those questions are linked to the historical themes presented in the text. See if you can identify and discuss similar concerns that you can trace back in time.

Journal Writing

Suggestions for journal topics for students' selection:

1. Discuss a current school practice you consider to be the result of a historical relic (like an agrarian calendar).

2. Select a period in the history of education and tell why you would or would not want to be a teacher during this period.

3. Predict what will have changed about today's schools by the year 2020.

Chapter 12 What Are Ethical and Legal Issues Facing Teachers?

Multiple-Choice Items

Read each item carefully. On the appropriate line, write the letter of the choice that represents the best answer.

c _____ 1. When people determine the conduct that people ought to exhibit, they are discussing which of the following?
a. law
b. due process
c. ethics
d. psychology

c _____ 2. A system of rules that members of a community, state, or nation must follow is called
a. ethics.
b. due process.
c. the law.
d. a cultural code.

a _____ 3. Sara spoke sharply to one of her students. Later, she regretted her action because she felt she did not act as she ought to have. Sara's deliberations about her behavior primarily concern which of the following?
a. ethics
b. due process
c. fair use
d. developmental psychology

b _____ 4. Which of the following is the best distinction between ethics and law?
a. Ethics is based upon religion whereas the law is not.
b. Law is primarily concerned with what people are required to do whereas ethics is concerned with what people ought to do.
c. Ethics is a system of rules articulated to guide human conduct whereas the law suggests what people should do.
d. Law deals with human rights whereas ethics rarely does.

c _____ 5. Gene Kruczek listens attentively to his students and understands when they feel upset or anxious. Which of the following characteristics of ethical teaching identified by Kenneth Howe is exemplified by Gene?
a. moral deliberation
b. knowledge
c. empathy
d. moral insight

b _____ 6. Howe's six dimensions of professional codes of morality include
a. appreciation for moral deliberation and sincerity in purpose.
b. knowledge and courage.
c. subject-matter knowledge and sympathy.
d. reasoning and integrity.

c _____ 7. A student who has lied in the past tells you that his math teacher has been drinking alcohol while in school. You know the student has never liked that teacher, but you also know that your colleague has acted erratically lately. Which of Howe's characteristics of ethical teaching would best help you resolve this situation?
a. empathy and sincerity in purpose
b. interpersonal skills and sympathy
c. knowledge and moral deliberation
d. reasoning and conviction

c _____ 8. Mayumi Ikebe responds to students' papers with suggestions and encouragement. She carefully plans each lesson, even though sometimes she could take shortcuts. In this aspect, she demonstrates
a. minimum teaching competency.
b. adherence to the NEA code of ethics.
c. the everyday ethics of teaching.
d. the legal obligations of a teacher.

a _____ 9. Which of the following best represents the "everyday ethics of teaching"?
   a. While teaching *The Scarlet Letter,* Teacher A asks the class, "What does this novel demonstrate about honesty?"
   b. Teacher B designs and constructs colorful bulletin boards that relate to topics under study.
   c. Teacher C is extremely careful never to show anger at any time while she is in school.
   d. Teacher D joins a charitable organization and encourages his students to join as well.

b _____ 10. Duane teaches in an industrial city where residents are concerned about groundwater contamination. Duane is elected president of a citizens' environmental group that is controversial with some in the city. Near the end of the school year, Duane's principal quietly tells him that he will not be offered a third-year teacher's contract because of his reputation as a "radical environmentalist." Which of this teacher's rights has been violated?
   a. the everyday ethics of teaching
   b. the right to substantive due process
   c. the right to a teaching contract
   d. the right to procedural due process

c _____ 11. When the principal greeted a kindergartner at recess, the child smiled and told him his teacher had some white powder on her desk. The principal, fearing a teacher was abusing drugs, ran to the classroom and demanded to search her handbag. When the superintendent learned of this incident, he severely reprimanded the principal. What was the superintendent's reason?
   a. The principal violated the teacher's right to substantive due process.
   b. The principal would be held liable for any potential injury or overdose the teacher suffered on school grounds.
   c. The principal disregarded the teacher's right to procedural due process.
   d. The principal exceeded the reasonable force guidelines.

d _____ 12. A veteran teacher is suspected of drinking on the job. The principal tells this to the teacher and apprises him of the process that will be followed concerning his hearing, retaining an attorney, and other facts. The teacher asks if he will be given the name of his accusers. According to the laws concerning procedural due process, how will the principal answer?
   a. To prevent any possibility of retaliation, their identities will remain hidden.
   b. The accusers' names will be provided if a preliminary investigation rules that there is reasonable grounds to suspect the teacher of drinking on the job.
   c. The accusers' names will be provided to the teacher's attorney only after he has filed for them.
   d. The accusers' names will be provided to him.

a _____ 13. In June, a nontenured teacher has not been informed of her employment status for the following year. On August 16, she is informed that she will not be rehired by the school district because of her "ineffective classroom management." How has this situation violated the Supreme Court decision of *Goldberg* v. *Kelly*?

a. The teacher was not given timely notice of her dismissal.
b. The teacher was not given a clear reason for her dismissal.
c. The teacher was not given a chance to improve her deficiencies in teaching.
d. The teacher was not given the chance to demonstrate her teaching abilities to the school board.

c _____ 14. Which of the following would probably render a teaching contract void?

a. The contract specifies a salary well below the average and fewer benefits than are customarily offered.
b. The contract lists responsibility for several different curricular and extracurricular areas.
c. The contract uses clear but unspecific language.
d. The contract states a beginning date for the commencement of the contract but does not specify an ending date.

d _____ 15. Megan has been offered a continuing contract whereas Josie has been given a tenure contract. What is the distinction between the two teachers' contracts?

a. Megan's contract stipulates what she must do to continue teaching at the school, whereas Josie's indicates that she has seniority in her teaching job.
b. Megan's contract indicates that her teaching position is probationary, whereas Josie's indicates that she will always have her teaching job as long as she chooses to teach.
c. Megan's contract specifies her rights and responsibilities as a teacher in that school district, whereas Josie's contract does not detail her rights and responsibilities.
d. Megan's contract states that she will teach for a specific, limited time period, whereas Josie's indicates that she has a long-term right to teach within that school district.

b _____ 16. Having tenure means that

a. the teacher can never be relieved of his or her teaching position until the teacher decides to quit or retire.
b. the teacher's permanent holding of a teaching position is considered part of his or her property.
c. the teacher can be dismissed only if there is a reduction in force.
d. the teacher can be dismissed only if he or she is grossly incompetent.

d _____ 17. Shoshona and Patti are both tenured foreign language teachers. In the Latin courses, which Shoshona teaches, there has been a 30 percent decrease in student enrollment. Patti has assigned numerous papers to students without ever grading them, has shown films in class week after week, or many times has given the students a study hall. According to tenure law, what can their administrators do regarding both teachers' future teaching assignments?

a. Because of tenure, Shoshona can*not* be laid off even if there is a reduction in force. However, despite tenure, Patti may lose her job if the administrators demonstrate that she is incompetent.
b. Shoshona can be laid off; however, Patti has a contractual right to teach and cannot be fired because of classroom performance.
c. Tenure protects and ensures the teaching jobs of both Shoshona and Patti.
d. Tenure does not protect the jobs of teachers who are proven to be incompetent or when schools have a reduction in force.

c _____ 18. In which of the following instances is the teacher most likely to be held liable?

a. Two students begin to speak to each other hostilely. The teacher tells them to stay away from each other. Even though they appear to have calmed down during the class, they begin fighting as soon as they leave class.
b. While a teacher is circulating through the classroom assisting students with their work, a student unexpectedly jumps out of her seat to show a friend a dance move. In doing the move, she dislocates her shoulder.
c. A teacher ignores two students who begin to wrestle playfully, and one of them breaks a wrist.
d. A student enters the teacher's class very angry about a fight he has just had with his father. In his emotional state, he puts his fist through a window, cutting his hand.

b _____ 19. In considering whether a teacher should be held liable for a student injury, which of the following facts will a judge consider most important?

a. the pupil-to-teacher ratio in the classroom
b. whether the teacher had established rules for the students
c. the age of the students in the teacher's classroom
d. whether the teacher had determined the extent and severity of the student injury

d _____ 20. As a social studies teacher strolls through the halls during lunch, he finds a group of students clustered around two boys who are fighting. When he intervenes to stop the fighting, the teacher must also be aware of

a. the right to due process.
b. the *in loco parentis* position.
c. his liability insurance.
d. the use of reasonable force.

a _____ 21. When a teacher thinks about her actions, considering the physical size and strength of both the student and herself, *before* she gets involved in stopping a student's physical aggression, she is demonstrating
a. a consideration of reasonable force.
b. procedural due process.
c. a concern for moral empathy.
d. an awareness of her contractual agreement with the school board.

c _____ 22. A teacher reports to the principal an incident of personal assault by a student. The notation made by the principal about this event may say something like this:
a. "Student strikes teacher."
b. "Student calls teacher an obscene name."
c. "Student threatens teacher."
d. "Student is injured by teacher."

a _____ 23. Willful attack resulting in harm to a person is called
a. battery.
b. liability.
c. injury.
d. assault.

c _____ 24. As a result of the *Pickering* decision, teachers were reassured of their right to
a. promote their personal beliefs in class.
b. wear long hair or unusual apparel in class.
c. express their opinions on civic matters freely outside the classroom.
d. choose teaching materials freely.

d _____ 25. Which of the following instances would be protected by the *Pickering* decision?
a. A teacher would be able to select the movie *The Crucible* for a history unit on the Salem witchcraft trials.
b. A teacher would be able to report suspected child abuse without fear of recrimination by the parents.
c. A teacher would be assured that she would have a chance to defend herself before being dismissed from a teaching position.
d. A teacher would know that she could march in a parade calling for increased federal spending on AIDS research without recrimination from the school administration.

b _____ 26. A small group of angry parents threatens to sue a school board for their support of an English teacher and her choice of texts for her class, including the work of J. D. Salinger and Judy Blume. The parents claim that Salinger's *Catcher in the Rye* and Blume's *Forever* are inappropriate to teach in school because of their subject matter. If this case reached the courts, what would a judge consider in deciding the case?

a. a review of the personal lives of both Salinger and Blume
b. the relevance of the two books to the formal course objectives
c. the literature selections of other teachers in the department
d. the merit and quality of each literature selection, as viewed by literary critics and scholars

b _____ 27. A group of angry parents comes to a school board meeting, demanding that Ms. Montero never teach *Romeo and Juliet* in school again, for it glorifies teen suicide. This demand of the parents demonstrates

a. the *in loco parentis* position.
b. an infringement of the teacher's academic freedom.
c. an infringement of procedural due process.
d. a violation of Ms. Montero's teaching contract.

a _____ 28. Although challenges to censorship have appeared to be on the upswing in recent history, members of particular educational organizations are staunchly opposed to removing a book from a school or library because

a. it implies that suppressing an idea is an acceptable way of dealing with controversy.
b. they believe that teachers and school librarians should have complete academic freedom from any parental or community input.
c. many of the books that come under censorship challenges are the very books that are of high interest to students, prompting them to read.
d. they do not want to include parents in education or curricular discussions.

c _____ 29. A school librarian is completing his book order for the next academic year. According to recent trends concerning censorship challenges, which of the following would most likely meet with community opposition?

a. *The Beginning of the World,* a science book including an explanation of evolution
b. *Killing Streets,* a graphic young-adult novel about teens growing up amidst gang warfare, drive-by shootings, and random acts of violence
c. *Join Us,* a nonfiction book about various religious sects and cults, including satanic groups
d. *The First Nine Months,* a text on the development of humans from conception to birth

a _____ 30. A group of irate citizens comes to a school board meeting with complaints about faculty. On which of the following complaints might current court decisions permit the board to act?
a. Marcus Eiflander has extremely long hair and fingernails, and he wears soiled and torn jeans to school.
b. Serge Moses lives outside of town in a group home "that is part of a religious cult."
c. Sue Johnson, who is gay, lives with her female partner in a nearby town.
d. Bernice Franklin, a union representative, has appeared on local morning talk shows severely criticizing both the faculty and the administration for their "inertia."

c _____ 31. According to recent court rulings, which of the following situations is *not* protected as a teacher's right?
a. to choose any lifestyle, as long as it is not advocated for students
b. to express any sexual orientation, as long as it is not advocated for students
c. to wear any hairstyle or dress in any fashion, as long as it is not advocated for students
d. to belong to any political party, as long as the party is not advocated for students

d _____ 32. Which of the following teachers has the greatest likelihood of being dismissed from his or her teaching position?
a. Rosa has been out sick several times but neglected to call in for a substitute teacher.
b. Jerry often drinks alcohol from Friday night through Saturday and is drunk most weekends.
c. Mike occasionally loses his temper with his students and yells at his class.
d. A year ago, Shelly had a one-night sexual affair with one of her students, but it never happened again.

c _____ 33. A teacher is arrested in the teachers' restroom for possession and use of cocaine. It is the first offense for the teacher. According to the text, which response would be the most typical from the school board and school administration?
a. a leave of absence without pay offered to the teacher until the legal matters are resolved
b. the requirement that, in addition to any other consequences of the teacher's arrest, she enroll in a drug rehabilitation program for at least six weeks
c. dismissal from her teaching position
d. a leave of absence with pay for three months or until she appears in court, whichever comes first

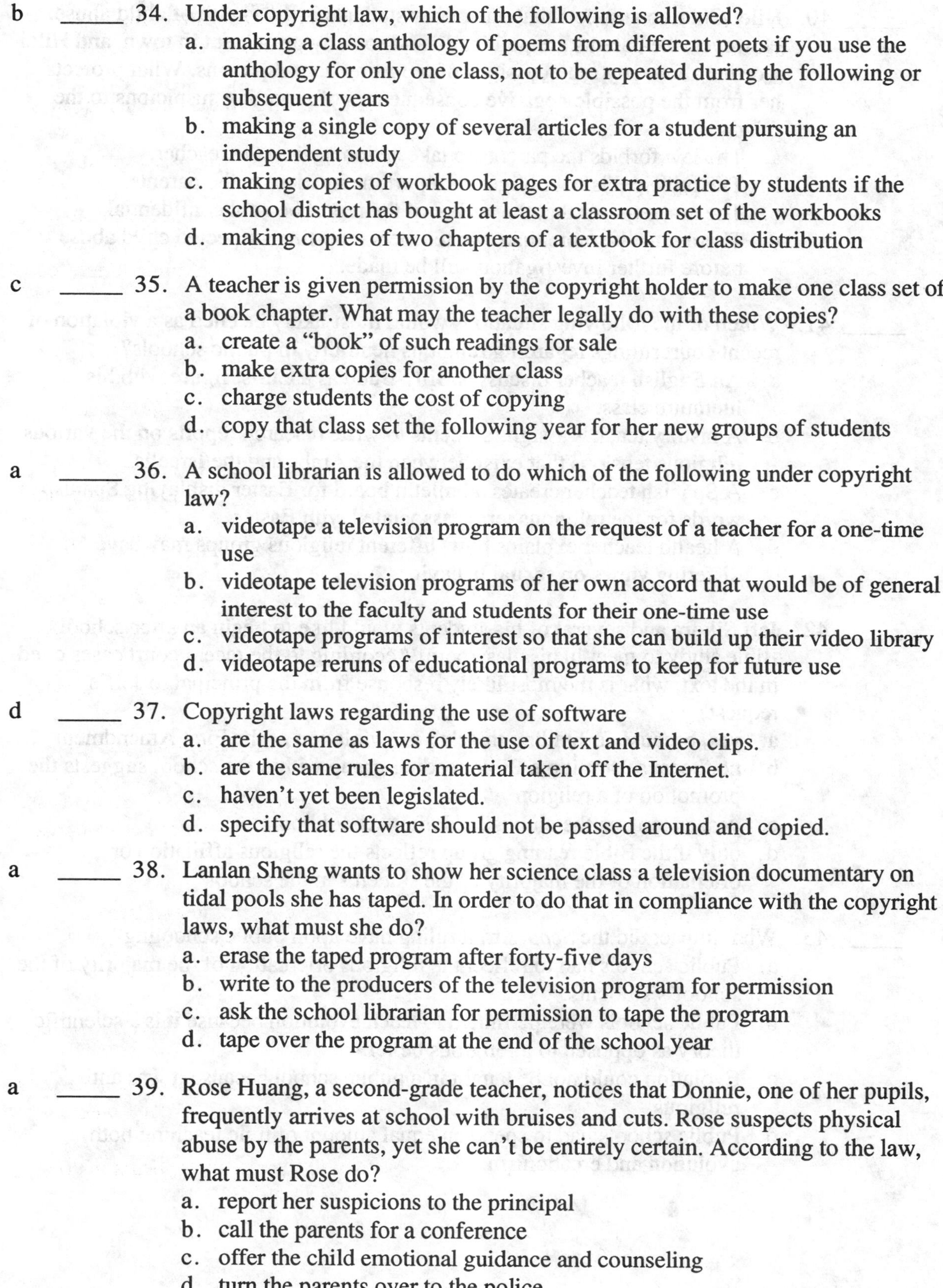

b _____ 34. Under copyright law, which of the following is allowed?
- a. making a class anthology of poems from different poets if you use the anthology for only one class, not to be repeated during the following or subsequent years
- b. making a single copy of several articles for a student pursuing an independent study
- c. making copies of workbook pages for extra practice by students if the school district has bought at least a classroom set of the workbooks
- d. making copies of two chapters of a textbook for class distribution

c _____ 35. A teacher is given permission by the copyright holder to make one class set of a book chapter. What may the teacher legally do with these copies?
- a. create a "book" of such readings for sale
- b. make extra copies for another class
- c. charge students the cost of copying
- d. copy that class set the following year for her new groups of students

a _____ 36. A school librarian is allowed to do which of the following under copyright law?
- a. videotape a television program on the request of a teacher for a one-time use
- b. videotape television programs of her own accord that would be of general interest to the faculty and students for their one-time use
- c. videotape programs of interest so that she can build up their video library
- d. videotape reruns of educational programs to keep for future use

d _____ 37. Copyright laws regarding the use of software
- a. are the same as laws for the use of text and video clips.
- b. are the same rules for material taken off the Internet.
- c. haven't yet been legislated.
- d. specify that software should not be passed around and copied.

a _____ 38. Lanlan Sheng wants to show her science class a television documentary on tidal pools she has taped. In order to do that in compliance with the copyright laws, what must she do?
- a. erase the taped program after forty-five days
- b. write to the producers of the television program for permission
- c. ask the school librarian for permission to tape the program
- d. tape over the program at the end of the school year

a _____ 39. Rose Huang, a second-grade teacher, notices that Donnie, one of her pupils, frequently arrives at school with bruises and cuts. Rose suspects physical abuse by the parents, yet she can't be entirely certain. According to the law, what must Rose do?
- a. report her suspicions to the principal
- b. call the parents for a conference
- c. offer the child emotional guidance and counseling
- d. turn the parents over to the police

c _____ 40. Hildi Chinigo suspects that one of her students is the victim of child abuse. However, the parents are politically and socially prominent in town, and Hildi worries about any repercussions of reporting her suspicions. What protects her from the possible negative consequences of reporting suspicions to the principal?
a. The law forbids the parents to take action against the teacher.
b. The principal is not obliged to report the incident to the parents.
c. The law requires that the source of the report be kept confidential.
d. There must be more than two teachers reporting suspected child abuse before further investigation will be made.

c _____ 41. Which of the following situations would most likely be cited as a violation of recent court rulings regarding religious neutrality in public schools?
a. An English teacher discusses Billy Budd as a Christ figure with his literature class.
b. A history teacher assigns students to write research reports on the various religious tensions that exist between the Arabs and the Israelis.
c. A Spanish teacher creates a bulletin board for Easter displaying Spanish words for the religious terms associated with Easter.
d. A health teacher explains how different religious groups may have differing views on sexual behavior.

b _____ 42. Jeff Sikora and several of his students would like to begin an after-school Bible study to meet in his classroom. According to the recent court cases cited in the text, what is the most likely response from the principal to Jeff's request?
a. yes, because forbidding the club is a violation of the First Amendment
b. no, because starting a Bible reading group within the school suggests the promotion of a religion
c. yes, as long as the club is held after school hours
d. only if the Bible reading group reflects the religious affiliation or orientation of the majority of the students in the school

b _____ 43. What impact did the *Scopes* trial ruling have upon public schooling?
a. Public schools had to reflect the religious orientation of the majority of the school's students.
b. Public schools were permitted to teach evolution because it is a scientific theory as opposed to a religious belief.
c. Evolution could not be taught in a public school because it was anti-religious.
d. Public schools had to spend an equal amount of time teaching both evolution and creationism.

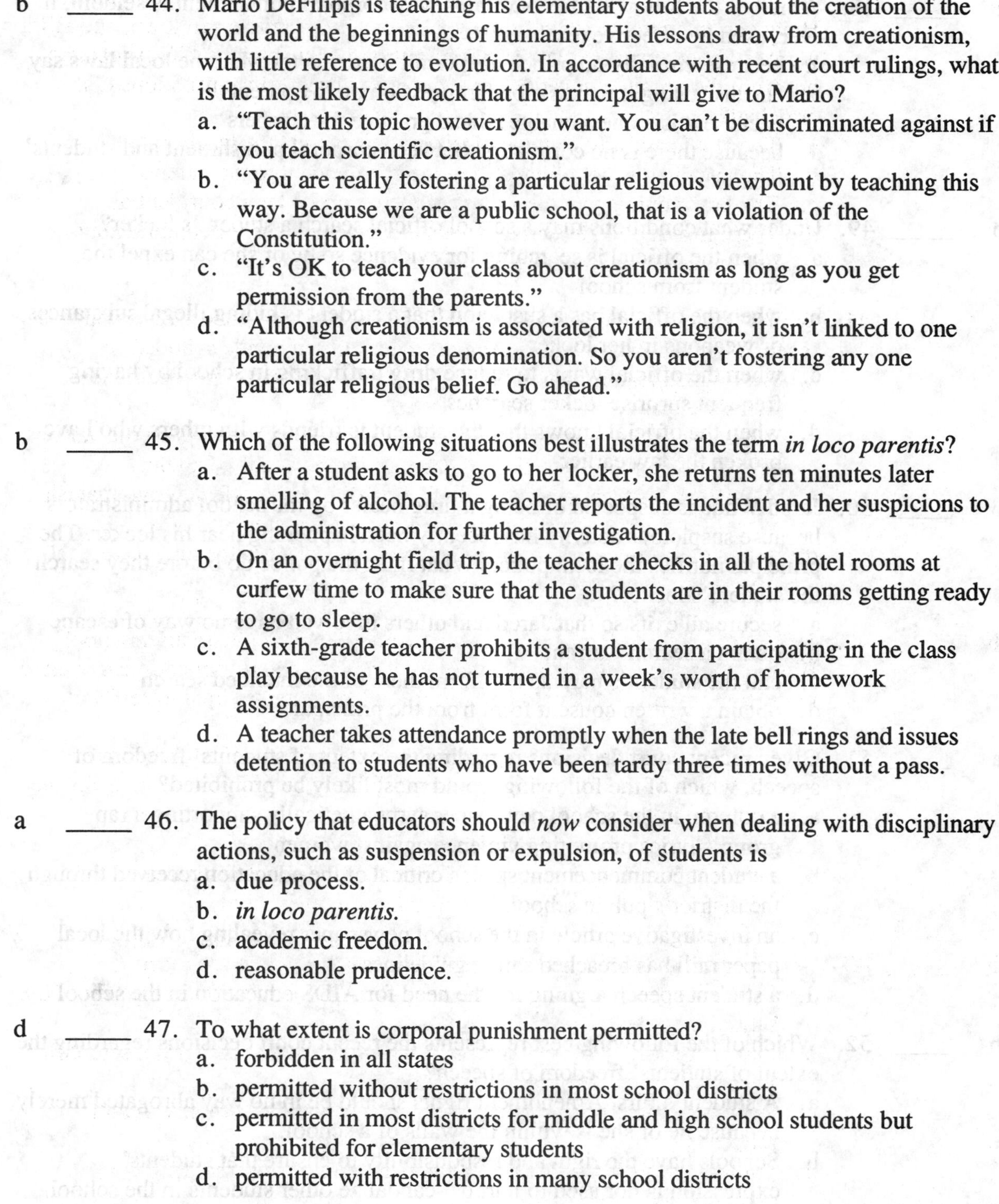

b _____ 44. Mario DeFilipis is teaching his elementary students about the creation of the world and the beginnings of humanity. His lessons draw from creationism, with little reference to evolution. In accordance with recent court rulings, what is the most likely feedback that the principal will give to Mario?

a. "Teach this topic however you want. You can't be discriminated against if you teach scientific creationism."

b. "You are really fostering a particular religious viewpoint by teaching this way. Because we are a public school, that is a violation of the Constitution."

c. "It's OK to teach your class about creationism as long as you get permission from the parents."

d. "Although creationism is associated with religion, it isn't linked to one particular religious denomination. So you aren't fostering any one particular religious belief. Go ahead."

b _____ 45. Which of the following situations best illustrates the term *in loco parentis*?

a. After a student asks to go to her locker, she returns ten minutes later smelling of alcohol. The teacher reports the incident and her suspicions to the administration for further investigation.

b. On an overnight field trip, the teacher checks in all the hotel rooms at curfew time to make sure that the students are in their rooms getting ready to go to sleep.

c. A sixth-grade teacher prohibits a student from participating in the class play because he has not turned in a week's worth of homework assignments.

d. A teacher takes attendance promptly when the late bell rings and issues detention to students who have been tardy three times without a pass.

a _____ 46. The policy that educators should *now* consider when dealing with disciplinary actions, such as suspension or expulsion, of students is

a. due process.

b. *in loco parentis.*

c. academic freedom.

d. reasonable prudence.

d _____ 47. To what extent is corporal punishment permitted?

a. forbidden in all states

b. permitted without restrictions in most school districts

c. permitted in most districts for middle and high school students but prohibited for elementary students

d. permitted with restrictions in many school districts

c _____ 48. Which of the following best explains why corporal punishment is seldom, if ever, used by effective teachers?
a. because virtually no principals permit it, no matter what the local laws say
b. because using it makes a bad impression on the parents
c. because it is a questionable ethical practice for teachers
d. because there is no correlation between corporal punishment and students' behavior

b _____ 49. Under what conditions may a school official search a student's locker?
a. when the official is searching for evidence so he or she can expel the student from school
b. when the official has a suspicion that a student is hiding illegal substances or weapons in her locker
c. when the official wants to reduce drug trafficking in school by having frequent surprise locker searches
d. when the official knows that the student is friends with others who have broken the law earlier

b _____ 50. Jared Wade is suspected of being a drug dealer by the school administrators because suspicious activity has recently been happening near his locker. The principal notifies the local police. What must the police do before they search the student's locker?
a. secure all exits so that Jared and others involved have no way of escape
b. obtain a search warrant
c. call the student's parents to inform them of the intended search
d. obtain a written consent form from the principal

a _____ 51. Given recent court decisions regarding the extent of students' freedom of speech, which of the following would most likely be prohibited?
a. a column in the school newspaper sympathetically supporting a rap group's lyrics promoting violence against women
b. a student commencement speech critical of the education received through the district's public schools
c. an investigative article in the school newspaper revealing how the local paper mill has breached safety guidelines
d. a student speech arguing for the need for AIDS education in the school

b _____ 52. Which of the following best represents the recent court decisions regarding the extent of students' freedom of speech?
a. A student's First Amendment rights should be in no way abrogated merely because he or she is within the walls of a school.
b. Schools have the right and responsibility to ensure that students' expression is not used to hurt or scandalize other students in the school.
c. An individual student's writing or speech is covered by the First Amendment, but symbolic speech is not.
d. A minor's right to free speech is not as extensive and far-reaching as an adult's; therefore, public schools have the right to restrict students' free speech so that it is consistent with the goals of the school.

c _____ 53. Natalie Leach is a second-grader who is infected with the AIDS virus. According to recent court rulings, what is the most likely event to occur?
- a. She will receive home tutoring to prevent her from coming in contact with other schoolchildren.
- b. She may attend public school, but she will be placed in a special classroom, separated from the rest of the students.
- c. She will attend public school like any other child.
- d. She will attend a special public school exclusively for children with AIDS and other communicable diseases.

a _____ 54. Which of the following most specifically pertains to protecting the rights of children with AIDS?
- a. The Individuals with Disabilities Education Act (IDEA)
- b. The Elementary and Secondary Education Act
- c. Title IX
- d. The Tinker case

a _____ 55. Under the terms of the Buckley amendment, what might happen to a school that refused parents access to the school files on their own children?
- a. The school is denied federal funds.
- b. The school is closed.
- c. The school loses accreditation.
- d. The school officials are arrested.

d _____ 56. Kristi Mandelbaum keeps extensive personal notes on the progress of her students. A parent of one student finds out about her notes and demands to see the notes Kristi has kept on her son. Which of the following responses of Kristi is most reflective of the Family Educational Rights and Privacy Act?
- a. "Certainly, here are all my notebooks."
- b. "I will let you see what I have written about your son, but I cannot show you what I have written about the other students."
- c. "Your request must be approved by the school board before I can share any of my notes with you."
- d. "I'm sorry, but these are my personal notes, so I am not required to share them with you."

Short-Answer Questions

Respond to each of the following questions briefly, but specifically, in complete sentences.

57. According to Kenneth Howe, a teacher who strives to be ethical must have "an appreciation for moral deliberation." What does that phrase mean? Give an example to illustrate.

(suggested answer) The text states that "appreciation for moral deliberation" means that the teacher must be able to see a situation as containing conflicting and competing moral

interests. The teacher must be able to see the complexities of moral problems and take care that the rights of all parties are protected. Examples to demonstrate that definition will vary, but all examples should illustrate the teacher's ability to see moral problems as containing competing moral claims.

58. To what extent is academic freedom available to public school teachers?

(suggested answer) Academic freedom is available to some degree to public school teachers, although they certainly have less freedom in their choice of teaching materials than teachers in private schools, colleges, or universities. Academic freedom in a public school is moderated by particular questions regarding the relevance of the material to the stated course goals, the appropriateness of the material for the students involved, the quality of the material, and the purpose of the teacher in using the material.

59. How has the Buckley amendment proved somewhat problematic for teachers?

(suggested answer) Because students now have the right to see everything in their student files, teachers are more careful about what they write there. In many cases, that is a positive change. However, teachers are also cautious about what they write for fear of potential lawsuits. As a result, to protect themselves teachers may concentrate on writing vague or extremely general comments about students. The Buckley amendment may have inhibited many teachers from writing fully and honestly about students for fear that something in their descriptions would in some way offend a student or parent.

60. How do copyright laws pertain to information a teacher may get from computer on-line services?

(suggested answer) The same fair use guidelines that govern written text apply to the information obtained from information retrieval systems. It is the teacher's responsibility to ensure that she or he is properly adhering to those copyright laws.

Essay Questions

Read each of the following questions, and respond by composing an organized essay that includes an introduction, fully developed paragraph(s), and a conclusion.

61. In practicing their profession, teachers frequently face issues that have ethical or legal dimensions. Listed here are five situations that require ethical or legal decisions. For each, tell whether the decision involves professional ethics or law and explain what the ethical or legal consideration is. For each, describe one solution that represents sound legal or ethical thinking.

    a. One of your students appears to be abused at home.

    (answer) Law. Teachers are required to report suspected abuse. Tell the principal.

b. You think you see a student cheating on a test. The evidence is fairly convincing, but there is room for doubt.

(answer) Ethics. Teachers are supposed to help students achieve their best and also to behave honestly. Several different responses might be ethical.

c. You write a letter to the editor of the local paper expressing your view that sexual preference is a private matter and should not be used as a basis for employment. Your letter elicits a response, and you would like to continue the dialogue in another letter. Your principal reports this civic activity to the superintendent.

(answer) Law. Teachers are permitted public expression of conviction, just as are all citizens. You may write your second letter and may decide to remind the principal that you never use the classroom as an arena to advocate your beliefs.

d. You have used only one or two of your sick leave days this year, and today is the first warm, lovely day of spring. You would like to take what you privately call a "mental health day."

(answer) Ethics. You have agreed to serve in good faith, and only you can judge when you are capable of working and when you are not. However, you are clearly bound to teach when you can. In real life, people decide differently on this common problem. Any answer supported by an ethical interpretation is correct.

e. After months of good-faith negotiation, your professional association has determined that only a strike can persuade the school board of the teachers' seriousness about getting improved working conditions. The board continues to put off making any decisions and has said that working conditions are good as they are. You agree that the current board offers are not fair. The strike is supported by a clear majority of members. You feel very uneasy about joining it because you are by nature very reserved and quiet in public.

(answer) Ethics. By becoming a member, you have agreed to work collectively. The call for a strike is warranted by the board's inaction. As this case is described, joining the strike is probably the ethical response.

62. Explain current court interpretations of issues involving religion in schools. Mention specifically teaching creationism, praying in school, Bible reading, and discussion of religious practices.

(suggested answer) Current interpretations require teachers to steer away from any behavior that advocates a particular set of beliefs or practices. Creationism is defined as a religious belief and evolution as a scientific theory. Creationism thus must *not* be taught; evolution may be taught. No form of prayer or silent prayer is permitted at a formal event because it puts social pressure on all students to participate. Bible reading as a form of prayer is forbidden. The Bible may be studied as literature. Religious practices may be discussed as features of a pluralistic society but not conducted as forms of observance.

63. How does the right to due process affect a school administrator's dismissal of a teacher? What is the difference between substantive and procedural due process?

    (suggested answer) The right to due process means that an individual's rights should not be violated and that the individual should be treated fairly. Due process affects the way in which a school board may dismiss a teacher, because the teacher must know why he or she is being fired, must have timely and adequate notice of his or her dismissal, must have the opportunity to defend himself or herself and to cross-examine witnesses, must also be allowed the counsel of an attorney, and must have an impartial decision maker. Substantive due process concerns the fairness of the issue itself. For example, it would violate substantive due process for the school board to dismiss a teacher because she became a Muslim. Procedural due process has to do with the fairness of the procedure followed. A school board can inform a teacher that it wants to dismiss her. But it would violate procedural due process for the school board to inform the teacher that her hearing at which she could defend herself was scheduled for the next day, because that would not give her adequate time to prepare her own defense.

Alternative Assessment Ideas

The following activities are suggestions for student portfolio activities. They are a means of providing alternative assessment of the students' capabilities.

Independent Reading

Read and respond to any of the following selections from Ryan/Cooper, *Kaleidoscope: Readings in Education* (Houghton Mifflin, 1998). You may want to use the Article Review Form on page 269.

Cates, Markell, and Bettenhausen—"At Risk for Abuse"

Strike—"The Ethics of Teaching"

Reflective Papers

Choose one of the following topics to write a reflective paper (2–5 pages). The purpose of the paper is to help you assimilate new knowledge by blending it with your previous knowledge and experiences.

1. Consider the information that has been presented in Chapter 12 concerning the ethics of teaching. What are some of the ethical imperatives that you see as vital in teaching and in being a teacher?

2. What experiences have you had—either as a student or as an observer in schools—that especially underscored the ethical dimensions of teaching?

3. Select several of the legal rulings presented in the chapter. Explain how they would apply in your work as a teacher. You may wish, instead, to discuss how they apply to the field-site school in which you are observing.

Journal Writing

Suggestions for journal topics for students' selection:

1. What do you think will be one of the toughest ethical challenges for you as a professional and why?

2. Do you think recent interpretation of the law has infringed on the teacher's civil rights? Why? or why not?

3. Do you think the laws regarding discipline in schools have made classroom management easier or harder? Why?

Chapter 13 How Should Education Be Reformed?

Multiple-Choice Items

Read each item carefully. On the appropriate line, write the letter of the choice that represents the best answer.

b _____ 1. School reform is a complex task to undertake because
- a. key administrators do not see a need for reform.
- b. it is difficult to have consensus on what constitutes a "good" education.
- c. measuring student achievement in discrete skills is nearly impossible.
- d. there is no agreement on how many years students should attend school.

a _____ 2. The complexity and difficulty of school reform can be evidenced by
- a. the philosophical debate over what constitutes a "good" education or a "good" school.
- b. the lack of communication between faculty and administration.
- c. lack of leadership in the Department of Education.
- d. the number of unlicensed teachers teaching in private schools.

d _____ 3. The long-term goals that undergird school reform are threefold:
- a. develop academic excellence, world dominance, and social graces.
- b. nurture self-esteem, confidence, and a positive outlook on life.
- c. develop the good worker, educate the people, and increase productivity.
- d. develop the democratic citizen, the good worker, and the private person.

d _____ 4. Which of the following is *not* a key element of true school reform as defined by Ryan and Cooper?
- a. active learning
- b. learning to learn
- c. community building
- d. accounting

b _____ 5. The "call to excellence" movement places high expectations on both students and teachers. Students are expected to perform at higher levels, and teachers are expected to
a. live in the community in which they teach.
b. engage and challenge students.
c. help students succeed on standardized tests.
d. weed out less competent students.

c _____ 6. The "call to excellence" movement sees the role of self-esteem in learning as
a. a necessary prerequisite. Students must feel good about themselves in order to learn.
b. insignificant. Learning is an intellectual process, and self-esteem is affective.
c. a by-product of excellence. When students achieve excellence, they gain greater self-esteem.
d. a deterrent. Focusing on self-esteem detracts students from learning.

a _____ 7. In a constructivist approach to learning, learners
a. take responsibility for their learning and make their own meaning from new knowledge.
b. learn new facts and knowledge without questioning them.
c. question all new information.
d. believe that there are no universal truths; all truths are relative.

d _____ 8. Mildred teaches a fifth-grade class in which she applies a constructivist approach to learning. What would Mildred's classroom probably look like?
a. Students sit quietly in their seats and work independently on worksheets.
b. Mildred does a lot of whole-class instruction, presenting lecture-type lessons.
c. Students make frequent use of library resources to prepare written reports on various topics in social studies and science.
d. Students work on projects in small groups or independently. There are a lot of "hands-on" activities.

b _____ 9. Authentic assessment grew out of a concern that
a. student performance was declining on standardized tests.
b. teachers were teaching to the tests and emphasizing lower-order thinking skills to the detriment of higher-order thinking and problem-solving skills.
c. multiple-choice tests were too difficult for the majority of students.
d. students were focusing on critical-thinking skills and not performing well on competency tests.

b ______ 10. Portfolio assessment allows the teacher to determine a student's progress toward certain learning goals or standards. Still, concerns about authentic assessment remain, in particular

a. the feasibility of quantifying scores from authentic assessments.
b. the reliability and validity of the assessments from site to site and evaluator to evaluator.
c. the ability of the students to complete the portfolio on time.
d. the interest of teachers in authentic assessment.

c ______ 11. Smaller schools are a recommended component of school reform because they

a. are less expensive to operate.
b. require a smaller administrative staff and less cost.
c. allow for a greater sense of community within the school.
d. make it easier to keep track of books and supplies.

d ______ 12. Reformers criticize large schools and fault them with being partly responsible for the decline in academic achievement because they

a. foster poor discipline and classroom management problems for new teachers.
b. are so costly to run that money cannot be spent on updating books and school supplies.
c. cause students to be constantly late for class because of the distance between classrooms.
d. create an aura of impersonality in which students feel lost, disengaged, and unmotivated.

d ______ 13. The Kennedys live in an upper-middle-class suburb of a large metropolitan area. They bought a house in that community because the school system has an excellent reputation and they felt that their two children, ages seven and nine, would receive a quality education. Their older child is very bright and should be in a gifted program, but the community no longer has one. The Kennedys are investigating a private school for this child. The Morgans live in an urban area not far from the Kennedys. Their oldest child will begin school in September, and the Morgans are worried about sending her to the local public school, a K–8 school with close to 1,000 students and a reputation for violence. However, they cannot afford to move out of the city. Which of the two families would benefit more from a school choice plan?

a. the Morgans, because they could send their older child to a smaller, safer school
b. the Kennedys, because they could send their older child to a school with a gifted program
c. Neither would get any more benefits from a school choice plan.
d. Both would benefit from a school choice plan for the reasons stated above.

c _____ 14. Proponents of school choice argue that if parents can choose their children's school, then
a. some teachers will have to work sixteen hours a day.
b. parents will be able to move from one community to another more easily.
c. free-market principles of competition will help to improve the quality of education.
d. some schools will be able to make a lot of money.

a _____ 15. Charter schools, one option of school choice, have certain advantages over public schools because they
a. have considerable autonomy to operate as they wish.
b. have more money to operate than the other public schools.
c. are usually larger and more economical than other public schools.
d. have a clearly delineated hierarchical structure.

c _____ 16. A second school choice option is the voucher plan, in which parents would
a. vouch for their children when they enroll them in the school of their choice.
b. receive a voucher for their children's books and school materials.
c. receive a voucher worth a specified amount and use it to enroll their children in whatever school they choose.
d. vouch for the quality of the instruction the children would be receiving.

c _____ 17. Computer-assisted education follows in the same vein as the constructivist approach to learning, since
a. both focus on enhancing students' memorization skills, which are particularly weak.
b. neither requires a group learning environment.
c. both require that the students take responsibility for their own learning.
d. both require that the teacher possess extensive knowledge about his or her subject matter.

b _____ 18. Ryan and Cooper contend that the New Basics, a set of academic learning skills, ought to be a major component of school reform because these skills
a. provide job training to make high school students more marketable.
b. can train students' thinking to make them more efficient learners.
c. keep students from mixing up facts.
d. help students do better on standardized tests.

b _____ 19. Character educators would like to redefine a "good" student as being one who
a. excels in a particular sport.
b. has a good sense of right and wrong.
c. gets good grades in school.
d. is considered a "good kid" by his or her teachers.

d _____ 20. Joshua is a high school history teacher who believes that his role as teacher extends to teaching his ninth-grade students certain core values, such as honesty, justice, kindness, and respect. Which of the following would most likely be found in Joshua's classroom?
a. a multiple-choice test on important events in World War II
b. a geography unit identifying all the major battles of World War II
c. a fine arts unit in which students become familiar with the music and dance of the United States in the 1940s
d. a discussion of the responsibilities of the United States toward Europe in the early 1940s

b _____ 21. Although much debate revolves around whether schools should teach values, and if so which values, character educators maintain that students
a. have a moral "Teflon coating" and absorb little teaching of values.
b. are constantly and unavoidably learning values from their teachers, so it would be beneficial to formalize this instruction in the curriculum.
c. practice good moral behavior already and have little need for character education.
d. have such a narrow focus on academics that they block out any other instruction.

c _____ 22. A second approach to character education is service learning, in which students participate in a service activity. The goal of service learning is
a. to teach students the core values of honesty, respect, and kindness.
b. to instill in students a work ethic.
c. to give students the opportunity to practice the core values that they have been taught.
d. to provide students with work experience in an ethically good environment.

c _____ 23. *A Nation at Risk* was published in 1983 and declared that the United States was
a. in peril of being attacked by hostile nations in the near future.
b. in serious peril of losing the state of California.
c. losing its economic and military competitiveness in the world market.
d. facing serious and significant problems in the major urban areas.

a _____ 24. The Education Summit of 1989 marked the most visible efforts to bring about education reform at a national level. The summit ended with
a. a commitment by the governors present to work toward meeting the six established goals by the year 2000.
b. a commitment by the governors present to remain in office until the year 2000 in order to bring about change in the educational system of their respective states.
c. an ambiguous statement from the governors present indicating an absence of consensus on educational reform.
d. disagreement over what needs to be done to reform the educational system of the United States.

c _____ 25. A number of national curriculum reform efforts have come from
a. the federal government.
b. elementary school teachers.
c. national groups of associations representing academic areas such as science, math, and social studies.
d. national curriculums in other countries around the world.

b _____ 26. The participation of the National Board for Professional Teaching Standards in the reform movement represents the recognition that
a. teachers need a longer preparation period.
b. substantive reform in education requires the participation of teachers.
c. teachers need to get paid more for their work.
d. educational reform is in conflict with the interests of teachers.

c _____ 27. State reform efforts, focusing on the call to excellence, share a number of common elements, which include
a. more students to graduate, more time in school, and higher salaries for teachers.
b. better test results for students and teachers, and more graduates.
c. more time in school, more courses to graduate, and competency testing for teachers.
d. more homework, career ladders for teachers, and higher standards.

d _____ 28. Many state reform efforts have tried to improve the quality of instruction in the schools. A frequently heard proposal calls for a career ladder in teaching that would
a. allow the more experienced teachers to teach in the better classrooms.
b. extend the salary schedule for teachers to an unlimited number of steps.
c. make it easier for teachers to assume administrative positions in the same schools.
d. allow expert teachers to be recognized for their experience and knowledge by giving them new roles, responsibilities, and rewards while remaining in the classroom.

a _____ 29. One residual of the state reform efforts has been
a. a loss of local authority and autonomy as more and more funding for reform comes from the state.
b. an increase in the number of teachers teaching at the elementary level.
c. more teachers leaving the teaching profession.
d. greater recognition of the strengths and weaknesses of teacher education programs.

c _____ 30. The limited involvement of teachers in state reform efforts would indicate that most of the reforms have been
a. unsupported by the rank and file.
b. ineffective.
c. top-down.
d. bottom-up.

b _____ 31. The Kentucky Education Reform Act is notable because it
- a. has state-mandated testing in grades 4, 8, and 12.
- b. consists of both top-down and bottom-up strategies to bring about reform.
- c. was declared unconstitutional in Kentucky.
- d. was initiated by the state legislature.

a _____ 32. Local reform efforts have not been very well supported because of
- a. weak fiscal environments.
- b. frequent criticism of private education.
- c. regular teacher strikes.
- d. a lack of interest on the part of parents.

d _____ 33. The teachers at Nine Acres school district are very concerned about the quality of education that the students are receiving. The outdated books and inadequate technology in the schools put the students at a disadvantage. The teachers have formed a committee and have worked many hours to produce a thorough proposal to bring the Nine Acres school system into the 21st century. They have presented the proposal to the school committee, who read it and responded, "We can't do it." According to Ryan and Cooper, what is most likely the reason that the school committee turned down the teachers' proposal?
- a. The school committee does not see any need to reform the system.
- b. The school committee prefers to hire a consulting firm to do a needs assessment of the system and work from the consultant's proposal.
- c. The school committee dislikes the teachers and would never agree to any teacher's suggestions or recommendations.
- d. The school system lacks the funds to finance the proposal.

c _____ 34. Any successful reform of education will require
- a. the approval of Congress.
- b. funding from the federal government.
- c. the active participation of the teachers involved.
- d. the creation of a new body to oversee the changes.

Short-Answer Questions

Respond to each of the following questions briefly, but specifically, in complete sentences.

35. Explain why the New Basics are seen as a way of improving the schools.

(suggested answer) The New Basics are a variety of skills that can make the brain a more efficient tool by improving memory strategies. These skills include note taking, study reading, test preparation, researching, systematic problem solving, creating thinking, and goal setting. Proponents of the New Basics believe that these skills can help learners access more knowledge more easily, an essential ability in most, if not all, work situations.

36. Describe the three major strands of national reform efforts.

    (suggested answer) The first is that of the nation's governors, recommendations that have since been reformulated into a federal act. America 2000 was a commitment by the nation's governors to strive to attain common goals set at the economic summit in 1989. It is important to note that the nation's governors formulated America 2000, since states have sole authority over education. A second strand of national reform comes from research and discipline associations, groups of scholars who are proposing curriculum frameworks, guidelines, or standards that are based on essential or appropriate knowledge in that discipline. The third strand is the National Council on Educational Standards and Testing, which was established by Congress to develop specific standards to achieve the national goals in education and assessment tools to measure progress toward meeting the standards. Both the standards and the assessment of these standards remain voluntary.

37. Explain what is meant by a constructivist approach to learning.

    (suggested answer) A constructivist approach to learning recognizes that humans are meaning makers. Constructivists maintain that learners do not simply take in new knowledge and information, but that they actively construct it, using their prior knowledge and experiences to make sense of the new knowledge. In this way, learners take responsibility for their own learning since they are making meaning for themselves. A constructivist classroom encourages experiential learning and Socratic questioning.

Essay Questions

Read each of the following questions, and respond by composing an organized essay that includes an introduction, fully developed paragraph(s), and a conclusion.

38. School choice is a very controversial and complex topic of debate. Not only is the theory of greater competition bringing about better schools untested, but the multitude of options for choice tends to make the discussion very murky. Take one aspect of the debate (for example, intradistrict school choice,[1] vouchers in public schools, or charter schools) and present the two sides of the debate. Which position do you find to be the more convincing? Why?

    (suggested answer) Answers will vary significantly, but students must first present the two sides of the debate and then choose one side and explain the reasons for their choice.

39. One of the most frequently debated components of educational reform is character education. The debate revolves around two important questions. Identify these two questions and present the opposing positions on each question.

---

[1]Intradistrict plans allow parents to choose any school within a district. Some large urban areas, such as Boston and Cambridge, have instituted intradistrict school choice plans with some success.

(suggested answer) The first question deals with whether or not the school as an institution is an appropriate venue for character education. Opponents argue that character education is primarily the responsibility of the family and of religious institutions, not the school. Supporters insist that, historically, the schools always had a moral component that was lost sometime in the 1960s. They agree that the family should be the primary moral educator but too frequently is abandoning that role, leaving many children in a moral and ethical vacuum. Therefore, the schools must reclaim their moral responsibility to educate the whole child.

The second question revolves around what values to teach if values are indeed taught in school. Opponents maintain that values are culturally and religiously based, and teaching values in school would necessarily mean teaching values particular to a certain religion to the detriment of others. Supporters argue that there is a core of civic values, such as honesty, respect, tolerance, kindness, and justice, that are common to all cultures and religions.

Alternative Assessment Ideas

The following activities are suggestions for student portfolio activities. They are a means of providing alternative assessment of the students' capabilities.

Independent Reading

Read and respond to any of the following selections from Ryan/Cooper, *Kaleidoscope: Readings in Education* (Houghton Mifflin, 1998). You may want to use the Article Review Form on page 269.

Berliner—"Mythology and the American System of Education"

Eisner—"Standards for American Schools"

Hill—"The Educational Consequences of Choice"

Lickona—"The Return of Character Education"

Mehlinger—"School Reform in the Information Age"

Molnar—"Charter Schools"

Nathan—"Early Lessons of the Charter School Movement"

Noddings—"Teaching Themes of Care"

Ryan—"Mining the Values in the Curriculum"

Sizer—"New Hope for High Schools"

Smith and Meier—"School Choice"

Reflective Papers

Choose one of the following topics to write a reflective paper (2–5 pages). The purpose of the paper is to help you assimilate new knowledge by blending it with your previous knowledge and experiences.

1. Think about your own education and what values and morals you were taught in school either explicitly or implicitly through the teachers' behaviors, the school climate, or district funding of educational activities. What behaviors were encouraged and consequently valued among the students? Between the students and teachers? Between teachers and administrators? How would you describe the moral environment of your high school?

2. You have no doubt had the experience of hearing someone recount an event that you were present at or participated in, yet that person's retelling of the event diverges significantly from your recollection of the event. Taking a constructivist's approach to learning, how can we explain these differences? Is it that one person is telling the truth and the other isn't?

3. Have you ever been evaluated through portfolio assessment? What was the experience like? How did you react to the portfolio process? Did you feel that the portfolio accurately conveyed your ability in that subject area? Was that approach to assessment more or less stressful than a final exam? Why?

Journal Writing

Suggestions for journal topics for students' selection:

1. Into which of the seven elements of educational reform would you put the most effort to achieve the greatest improvement? Why?

2. Do you feel the initiatives to improve the quality of education will be successful? Why?

3. How will you go about teaching character education in your own classroom?

Chapter 14 What Are Your Job Options in Education?

Multiple-Choice Items

Read each item carefully. On the appropriate line, write the letter of the choice that represents the best answer.

d _____ 1. A recent college graduate targets a particular district for his job search because he knows a number of teachers are retiring and the student enrollment is increasing. What other information should he look at that could impact on his being hired?
   a. the number of alternative-route certificate teaching candidates in the area
   b. the pupil-teacher ratio in the schools
   c. the educational level attained by most teachers in the district
   d. the strength of the local school budget and the local economy

c _____ 2. Why hasn't the anticipated teacher shortage of the 1990s materialized?
   a. Public school teachers are not retiring.
   b. The school-age population is not growing.
   c. The weak economy has restricted school budgets, leading to cutbacks.
   d. Smaller student-teacher ratios have become the norm.

c _____ 3. The increase in teaching positions expected over the next ten years is due to
   a. declining student enrollments.
   b. declining teacher retirements.
   c. increasing student enrollments.
   d. declining standardized test results.

c _____ 4. Jezebel has just started college and is interested in pursuing a career in teaching. Her advisor tells her that she shouldn't have any trouble getting a job when she graduates. Why does her advisor think that?
- a. Municipal funding for education is expected to increase 15 percent in the next ten years.
- b. Teachers' salaries are expected to rise 20 percent in the next ten years.
- c. Teaching positions are expected to increase by 13 percent by 2004.
- d. The student-teacher ratio will decrease to 15 to 1.

a _____ 5. Minority teachers serve as positive role models for both minority and white students because
- a. minority students develop self-esteem and white students break stereotyping and racism.
- b. white students develop self-confidence and minority students achieve better results.
- c. both minority and white students perform better academically.
- d. minority students break stereotyping and teach white students minority culture.

b _____ 6. The shortage of minority teachers is problematic because
- a. there are many minorities in urban areas.
- b. many minority students have no positive minority role models.
- c. too many white students do not have positive white role models.
- d. minority teachers represent a disproportionately large percentage of the teaching population.

a _____ 7. Which of the following has contributed to the decline in the number of minority teachers?
- a. wider recruitment of minorities in other professions and the increased use of competency testing for teachers
- b. the decline of minority students enrolled in education because of the anticipated teaching surplus in the 1990s
- c. the lack of respect and worth given to teachers and the increased use of alternative licensure in hiring teachers
- d. the refusal of many school systems to recognize alternative licenses of teachers

a _____ 8. Abraham Lincoln Junior High School is located in a large, racially mixed city. During the late 1960s, Lincoln's faculty was almost entirely African American. Now, twenty years later, the faculty is almost entirely white. What is the most probable cause for this shift in the faculty population?

a. During the merging of Lincoln Junior High, an all-black school, with City Junior High, an all-white school, during the integration efforts of the 1960s, many of the black faculty members were dismissed.
b. Many of the African-American teachers advanced into administrative positions, and the others chose to leave teaching.
c. The African-American teachers were heavily recruited by representatives of other fields who wanted to diversify the staffs of their agencies or businesses.
d. The community shifted its racial composition, and white teachers were hired to reflect the racial balance of the community.

c _____ 9. LaMar, an African American, is majoring in English at a state college. He took an education course and really enjoyed the experience and so is thinking about a teaching career after college. What are LaMar's chances of getting a teaching job when he graduates?

a. Good. The call for excellence recommends smaller class sizes, so more teachers will probably be hired.
b. Mediocre. The teaching job market does not look very promising over the next ten years.
c. Excellent. Minority teachers are always needed in urban or suburban school systems.
d. Weak. There is a surplus of English teachers in most parts of the country.

c _____ 10. After ten years of working in journalism, Ellen decided to pursue a teaching career. She received her teaching license through the alternative licensing program and is currently seeking a teaching position. She has a degree in English and would like to teach middle school English in a rural school district. Which of the following will work most in her favor as she searches for a job?

a. her experience working in journalism
b. her status as an alternative-route teaching candidate
c. her willingness to teach in a rural community
d. her interest in teaching in a middle school

d _____ 11. The school board and superintendent of Basking Ridge are planning for next year's personnel hiring. Before determining how many new teachers they are in the position to hire, they need to know

a. current student-enrollment figures.
b. the amount of tax revenue from the community allocated to the schools.
c. the anticipated number of teaching candidates available in the area.
d. current student-enrollment figures and the amount of tax revenue from the community allocated to the schools.

a _____ 12. It is helpful to verify published reports on teacher supply and demand with your own research on local conditions because
- a. projections are based on information that changes unpredictably.
- b. published reports are inherently unreliable.
- c. local communities sometimes exaggerate the facts in publications to make their community appear more desirable.
- d. many communities are ignored in the broadly based statistical surveys.

d _____ 13. Published reports on teacher supply and demand may be soon outdated because
- a. teachers' retirement rates are unpredictable.
- b. economic problems in a community may reduce demand for new teachers.
- c. of the increasing birth rate.
- d. teachers' retirement rates are unpredictable, and economic problems in a community may reduce demand for new teachers.

c _____ 14. Sally White and David Tepper both were hired as recent college graduates by the same school district in 1982. After ten years of teaching, Sally earns considerably more than David. Which of the following could explain this salary difference?
- a. Sally has advised the AFS club and debate team over the course of her tenure.
- b. Sally has been awarded merit pay increases for her outstanding teaching.
- c. Sally has earned a master's degree in her field.
- d. Sally teaches high school whereas David teaches elementary.

d _____ 15. Most public school teachers' salaries are based on level of education and
- a. grade level or academic subject taught.
- b. additional coaching or advising activities.
- c. recommendations and evaluations of administrators.
- d. years of teaching experience.

b _____ 16. Vicky is graduating in June and is looking for a teaching position for September. She has made several copies of her one-page résumé, written a standard cover letter, acquired letters of reference from a professor and her cooperating teacher, and sent out this packet to school systems in the area. Vicky has not gotten any response from any school district while many of her friends have. Vicky probably should have
- a. expanded her résumé so that it was two pages long and described her accomplishments in more detail.
- b. written only one cover letter at a time, tailoring each one specifically to the school district to which it would be sent.
- c. substituted the letter of recommendation from her professor with one from a previous employer illustrating her work history.
- d. called the school district to try to set up an appointment with the superintendent.

c _____ 17. Among the features of an effective job search are
- a. a detailed résumé that includes complete information about you.
- b. generic form-letter-type cover letters.
- c. cover letters typed individually for each potential employer and a placement file that includes all of your credentials.
- d. a list of all the positions you are applying for.

d _____ 18. Randy has a job interview for a teaching position in a school system he knows very little about. Before the interview, what should Randy do?
- a. talk to his professors about contemporary education issues
- b. talk to his teacher friends in another state to find out about work conditions there
- c. investigate graduate programs nearby
- d. find out as much as he can about the town and its population

b _____ 19. Ryan and Cooper suggest that an effective way of preparing for a job interview is to
- a. do stress-relieving exercises for a week before.
- b. role-play the interview with a friend to practice your skill in answering questions.
- c. buy a new pair of shoes.
- d. talk to your college professor about job openings.

c _____ 20. Licensure requirements exist for teachers because
- a. the requirements help screen out people who would make poor teachers.
- b. people must demonstrate the ability to follow complex procedures before they teach.
- c. the requirements ensure that prospective teachers meet certain minimum competencies.
- d. licensure fees are an important source of income for state education agencies.

b _____ 21. License requirements are designed to ensure that all teachers
- a. are skilled in their work.
- b. receive training that should lead to competence.
- c. have substantial knowledge of important subjects such as history and math.
- d. are concerned about the welfare of their students.

b _____ 22. According to the text, alternative licensure programs vary widely from state to state and are designed to meet the various conditions under which traditional teacher education will not or cannot suffice. Which of the following is the *least* likely to be a rationale for a state's alternative teaching route?
- a. the provision of licensed teachers when the state suffers a teacher shortage
- b. the need for teaching licenses by adults making a career change
- c. the design of an alternative license program for secondary school teachers
- d. the enhancement of a college-approved teacher education program

d ______ 23. Alternate teaching licensure programs indicate a belief by some legislators that
a. adults with training in other fields are better qualified to teach than teachers.
b. teacher preparation is too long and arduous for most people.
c. traditional teacher education courses are ineffective in preparing people to teach.
d. subject-matter knowledge is sufficient to teach.

a ______ 24. Julio is a sophomore in college and has decided to become a biology teacher. What could he do now to enhance his marketability for a teaching position in two years?
a. take additional chemistry courses so that he can become licensed in both biology and chemistry
b. research the anticipated teaching shortages in various states
c. prepare a credential file including a résumé and letters of recommendation from current professors
d. transfer to a school in a state that is expecting a teacher shortage

c ______ 25. It is near the end of the school year, and the principal of a K–8 school has just been told that because of budgetary constraints she will have to lay off several nontenured teachers. Which of the following teachers would be most likely to keep her job?
a. a health teacher who also coaches after-school sports
b. a kindergarten teacher
c. a language arts or English teacher who is also licensed to teach science
d. an art teacher who directed the school pageant

d ______ 26. The education one receives to become a teacher can also contribute to effectiveness as
a. a curriculum specialist.
b. a corporate trainer.
c. a researcher.
d. a curriculum specialist, a corporate trainer, or a researcher.

d ______ 27. Experienced teachers will find that their skills transfer well into such settings as
a. federal agencies.
b. philanthropic organizations.
c. businesses.
d. all of the above.

c _____ 28. Cinnamon is a senior in college and is interested in a career in school administration. What must she do in order to achieve her goal?
a. send out résumés and actively seek an administrative position
b. work in the private sector for a few years, then apply for administrative positions
c. pursue a teaching career for a couple of years and then move into administration
d. apply to a master's program to earn an advanced degree in school administration

b _____ 29. Other nonteaching jobs in education, such as staff developer, curriculum coordinator, or guidance counselor, usually require
a. a cut in salary.
b. teaching experience and an advanced degree.
c. a terminal degree in the field of practice.
d. key contacts in the right places.

a _____ 30. Which of the following is *not* a suggested strategy for bringing more minorities into teaching?
a. creating segregated schools
b. higher teaching salaries
c. more valued status for teachers
d. assistance programs for competency tests

Short-Answer Questions

Respond to each of the following questions briefly, but specifically, in complete sentences.

31. Imagine that an education professor at a state college has just received a statistical report projecting demand for teachers for the next ten years. In the report, the professor sees that there is expected to be a considerable surplus of elementary teachers in the college's geographical region. The next day, a student comes to the professor, wishing to declare her major in elementary education. Other than self-serving interest (the professor's need to keep the teaching position), what would be a justifiable reason for the professor to admit the student into the elementary education program?

(suggested answer) Although statistical reports can be helpful in determining trends, at times, statistical data change rapidly. Therefore, it is unwise to base a career decision solely on a review of *projected* teacher supply and demand. The professor could inform the student of the projections without discouraging her from becoming a teacher. Also, the professor does not know if the student would be willing to relocate, which could aid her chances of finding a teaching position. Finally, as the text mentions, there is never a surplus of good teachers. Society will always need talented teachers, and this prospective elementary school teacher could become a gifted one.

32. Briefly describe the role of alternative teaching licensure. What is its purpose? How effective has it been to date in preparing teachers?

    (suggested answer) One of the major purposes of alternative teaching licensure is supplying teachers when states experience shortages. Because of many of the commission reports during the early to mid-1980s, which sharply criticized the quality of education majors and the quality of teaching in public schools, alternative licensure received attention as a way of luring liberal arts graduates and people with extensive backgrounds in math and science into teaching. The alternative license programs vary widely from state to state, and at this point there are few data demonstrating their effectiveness in preparing teachers.

33. Let's say that although you have performed well as a teacher, at the end of your second year of teaching, you decide to pursue another career. Given the training you have had as a teacher, identify another field or occupation in which you could be successfully employed and explain why.

    Answers will vary, but students should mention the skills they have learned in teacher training, including managing people, planning, organizing and implementing those plans, researching, speaking in public, and communicating in general.

Essay Questions

Read each of the following questions, and respond by composing an organized essay that includes an introduction, fully developed paragraph(s), and a conclusion.

34. The text includes sobering data on the number of minority teachers in America. According to the text, 87 percent of all teachers are white, and the percentage of minority teachers continues to shrink. How do minority teachers fulfill a vital role in education, and what would be your suggestions for recruiting more minority teachers into the field?

    (suggested answer) Students should discuss the function minority teachers serve as role models for both minority and white children. The need for positive role models is particularly strong in troubled school districts where children sometimes have few positive influences in their lives. In addition, minority teachers also reflect the diversity of the U.S. population.

    Answers will vary on recruiting more minority teachers into the field.

35. Ryan and Cooper speak of the unpredictability of employment trends in teaching in the United States. What are the factors that affect the supply and demand of teachers, and why is the field dominated by unpredictability?

    (suggested answer) Answers will vary, but students should speak about the social and economic factors that influence supply and demand. Students should recognize the dependence of public school funding on the economic well-being of the community and country. Therefore, when there is an economic downturn, public school budgets suffer and teaching positions are lost. Students should also mention the current demographics of the

teaching population, which will potentially lead to a large number of retirements in the near future. However, the economy will continue to play a dominant role in the availability of teaching positions.

Alternative Assessment Ideas

The following activities are suggestions for student portfolio activities. They are a means of providing alternative assessment of the students' capabilities.

Independent Reading

Read and respond to any of the following selections from Ryan/Cooper, *Kaleidoscope: Readings in Education* (Houghton Mifflin, 1998). You may want to use the Article Review Form on page 269.

Darling-Hammond—"What Matters Most"

Ducharme—"The Great Teacher Question"

Haberman—"Selecting Star Teachers"

Wise—"Six Steps to Teacher Professionalism"

Reflective Papers

Choose one of the following topics to write a reflective paper (2–5 pages). The purpose of the paper is to help you assimilate new knowledge by blending it with your previous knowledge and experiences.

1. What are your views on alternative-route licensure? Should it exist? For whom? Under what conditions? Keeping in mind that you are following the traditional route to licensure, learning a great deal about education, do you think that a person who has not had a similar educational experience can be as effective a teacher as someone who has studied education at college?

2. What strengths (and weaknesses) do you bring into teaching? Think about your own personality and describe the qualities that can help you be an effective teacher.

Journal Writing

Suggestions for journal topics for students' selection:

1. What are the factors that favor you to get a job in the district of your choice?

2. How do you feel about substitute teaching?

3. Answer at least three of the sample interview questions from the chapter.

Chapter 15 What Can the New Teacher Expect?

Multiple-Choice Items

Read each item carefully. On the appropriate line, write the letter of the choice that represents the best answer.

c _____ 1. Why is the "shock of the familiar" that new teachers usually experience similar to culture shock?

a. New teachers usually realize and then are shocked that they know little about their own culture, although it seemed so familiar.
b. New teachers are usually shocked by how similar their lives as teachers are to their lives as students, similar to the shock one experiences at finding similarities in a new community.
c. New teachers usually feel disoriented by their role as teacher, similar to the disorientation newcomers to a country experience.
d. New teachers usually expect schools to be familiar, yet they are shocked to find that dramatic, foreign changes have occurred in schools since they were students.

c _____ 2. During Patty Miller's first week of teaching, she finds it odd to walk past the cafeteria and into the faculty lunchroom. Even more peculiar is having students call her "Ms. Miller." What is Patty likely experiencing?

a. extreme insecurity about her ability as a teacher
b. delayed stress syndrome
c. culture shock
d. overexcitement from her first week of teaching
e. feelings of regret that she entered teaching

a ______ 3. In one day, principal Toni Radano explained the statewide curricular changes to a group of teachers, fielded an angry phone call from a parent about a teacher, and publicly recognized two teachers for their outstanding work directing the school play. Which of the following best describes her roles on this particular day?
a. coach, crisis manager, evaluator
b. educator, facilitator, judge
c. initiator, buffer, reward dispenser
d. helper, sacrificial lamb, evaluator

c ______ 4. Mr. Gulick usually represents the school to the local press. He also orders instructional supplies for the school, facilitates student-teacher disagreements, observes and evaluates teachers, and meets directly with parents at times. Based upon that description, what is Mr. Gulick?
a. a master teacher
b. a curriculum coordinator
c. a principal
d. a superintendent

a ______ 5. In what way does the principal act as a liaison between the larger school organization and the faculty? He or she
a. guides teachers toward achieving districtwide goals.
b. is chosen to be the "sacrificial lamb" if the public isn't satisfied with the school.
c. frequently visits teachers to make classroom observations.
d. keeps up-to-date on current research and reform initiatives.

b ______ 6. Because of the complexity of the principal's role, a teacher may lack the principal's support in certain instances. Which of the following describes the most likely instance in which a teacher would lack administrative support?
a. A student with a serious behavior problem fails to live up to the terms of a learning contract.
b. The teacher does not want to complete the routine paperwork demanded by the office because it interferes with planning.
c. A custodian regularly fails to perform routine tasks clearly defined in the posted description.
d. An irate parent charges into the teacher's classroom, disrupting the class.

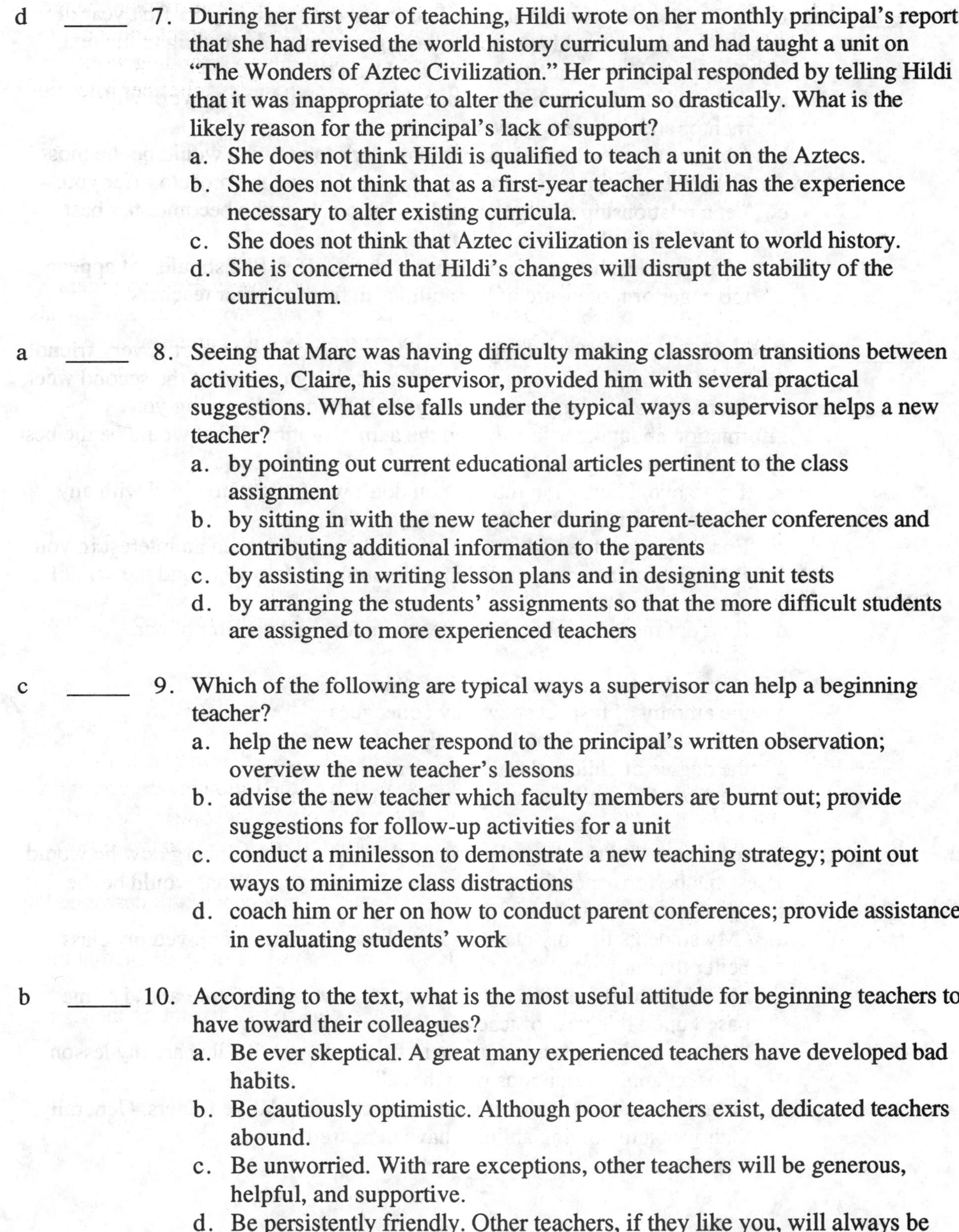

d _____ 7. During her first year of teaching, Hildi wrote on her monthly principal's report that she had revised the world history curriculum and had taught a unit on "The Wonders of Aztec Civilization." Her principal responded by telling Hildi that it was inappropriate to alter the curriculum so drastically. What is the likely reason for the principal's lack of support?

a. She does not think Hildi is qualified to teach a unit on the Aztecs.
b. She does not think that as a first-year teacher Hildi has the experience necessary to alter existing curricula.
c. She does not think that Aztec civilization is relevant to world history.
d. She is concerned that Hildi's changes will disrupt the stability of the curriculum.

a _____ 8. Seeing that Marc was having difficulty making classroom transitions between activities, Claire, his supervisor, provided him with several practical suggestions. What else falls under the typical ways a supervisor helps a new teacher?

a. by pointing out current educational articles pertinent to the class assignment
b. by sitting in with the new teacher during parent-teacher conferences and contributing additional information to the parents
c. by assisting in writing lesson plans and in designing unit tests
d. by arranging the students' assignments so that the more difficult students are assigned to more experienced teachers

c _____ 9. Which of the following are typical ways a supervisor can help a beginning teacher?

a. help the new teacher respond to the principal's written observation; overview the new teacher's lessons
b. advise the new teacher which faculty members are burnt out; provide suggestions for follow-up activities for a unit
c. conduct a minilesson to demonstrate a new teaching strategy; point out ways to minimize class distractions
d. coach him or her on how to conduct parent conferences; provide assistance in evaluating students' work

b _____ 10. According to the text, what is the most useful attitude for beginning teachers to have toward their colleagues?

a. Be ever skeptical. A great many experienced teachers have developed bad habits.
b. Be cautiously optimistic. Although poor teachers exist, dedicated teachers abound.
c. Be unworried. With rare exceptions, other teachers will be generous, helpful, and supportive.
d. Be persistently friendly. Other teachers, if they like you, will always be able to help lighten your workload by giving you materials.

b _____ 11. Darla Desiderio is somewhat apprehensive about surviving her first year of teaching, and she would appreciate having a mentor. According to the text, which approach would be the wisest for Darla?

a. Announce in the teacher's lounge that you would like to work with a mentor and choose whoever volunteers.
b. Observe teachers in their day-to-day work to see who would be the most receptive to being a mentor and who would have the most to offer you.
c. Let a relationship emerge naturally. The teacher who becomes her best friend will be the best mentor for Darla.
d. Wait for a teacher to approach her with the offer. She should not appear too eager or too unsure of her abilities in front of other teachers.

c _____ 12. It is your first year of teaching. A few days before classes start, a very friendly teacher stops by to welcome you to the school. By the end of the second week of school, she stops by your room regularly, frequently giving you information about other faculty and the administration. What would be the best approach for dealing with this teacher?

a. Try to avoid her in the future. You don't want to get involved with any teacher who is too friendly this early in the year.
b. Encourage her friendship. She's friendly and has taken an interest in you.
c. Be polite but reserve your friendship until you know her and the school system better.
d. Find out more by asking other teachers for their opinion of her.

c _____ 13. What is the best measure of a teacher's success?

a. the amount of respect shown by colleagues
b. ratings earned on formal evaluations
c. the degree of children's advancement as learners
d. the size of the raise in salary for the second year

d _____ 14. During a year-end meeting, the principal asked Mark Steinberg how he would assess his performance as a teacher over the past year. What would be the strongest answer from Mark?

a. "My students like my class. In fact, they tell me they enjoyed my class better than any other."
b. "My department chairman told me that I have a fine future ahead of me based upon this year of teaching."
c. "Other members of the department frequently ask if I'll share my lesson plans and unit evaluations with them."
d. "I've just finished reviewing my students' cumulative folders. Generally, their problem-solving abilities have increased."

c _____ 15. Many beginning teachers are concerned that they will lack subject-matter knowledge. In reality, though, most beginning teachers have the most difficulty with which of the following?
a. learning how to work in a bureaucracy
b. designing adequate lesson plans
c. maintaining classroom discipline
d. evaluating student work

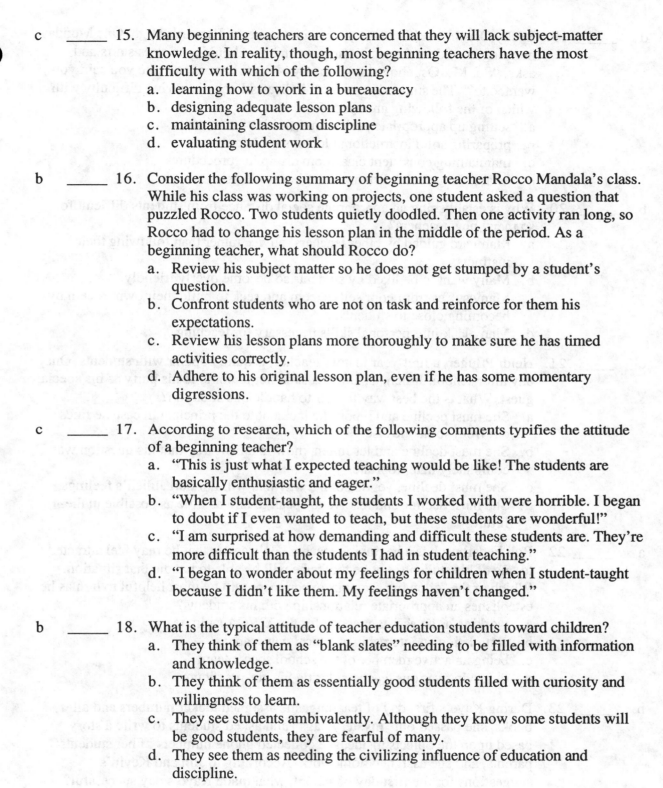

b _____ 16. Consider the following summary of beginning teacher Rocco Mandala's class. While his class was working on projects, one student asked a question that puzzled Rocco. Two students quietly doodled. Then one activity ran long, so Rocco had to change his lesson plan in the middle of the period. As a beginning teacher, what should Rocco do?
a. Review his subject matter so he does not get stumped by a student's question.
b. Confront students who are not on task and reinforce for them his expectations.
c. Review his lesson plans more thoroughly to make sure he has timed activities correctly.
d. Adhere to his original lesson plan, even if he has some momentary digressions.

c _____ 17. According to research, which of the following comments typifies the attitude of a beginning teacher?
a. "This is just what I expected teaching would be like! The students are basically enthusiastic and eager."
b. "When I student-taught, the students I worked with were horrible. I began to doubt if I even wanted to teach, but these students are wonderful!"
c. "I am surprised at how demanding and difficult these students are. They're more difficult than the students I had in student teaching."
d. "I began to wonder about my feelings for children when I student-taught because I didn't like them. My feelings haven't changed."

b _____ 18. What is the typical attitude of teacher education students toward children?
a. They think of them as "blank slates" needing to be filled with information and knowledge.
b. They think of them as essentially good students filled with curiosity and willingness to learn.
c. They see students ambivalently. Although they know some students will be good students, they are fearful of many.
d. They see them as needing the civilizing influence of education and discipline.

d _____ 19. Becky Osuchowski is a first-year math teacher at Bernards High. One Monday morning, a student drapes his arm around her shoulder as class starts and asks, "So, Ms. Osuchowski, go to any clubs this weekend like you said you wanted to?" The student's comment indicates Becky is having difficulty with which of the following areas?

a. setting up appropriate prelesson activities for students
b. preparing solid instructional lessons for her classes
c. maintaining consistent classroom discipline procedures
d. establishing social distance from her students

b _____ 20. Why is establishing an appropriate social distance from students difficult for so many new teachers?

a. Many are guided by other teachers' advice rather than following their instincts.
b. Many want to be liked by students so become overly friendly.
c. Many suffer from poor self-esteem and seek to build their own esteem by becoming close to students.
d. Many lack interpersonal skills necessary for teaching.

c _____ 21. Heidi Pfluger, a first-year history teacher, is quite popular with students. One day after school, Julien, a student, asked her to come to his party as his special guest. What is the best way for her to handle this situation?

a. She must decline and report the incident to the principal in case he finds out from someone else.
b. She must decline and let Julien know in a firm way that his question was completely inappropriate.
c. She must decline, yet do so in a way that will not hurt Julien's feelings.
d. She must decline and resolve to speak to him as little as possible in the future.

a _____ 22. Bob Federbusch is a beginning teacher. He's aware that he may feel attracted to one of his students, yet he thinks he will be able to handle that situation. Which of the following previous experiences will be most helpful to him as he establishes an appropriate relationship with his students?

a. working as an assistant coach for the YWCA swim team
b. completing an internship at a local newspaper
c. being an active member of the school soccer team
d. observing various teachers during his pre-practicum

b _____ 23. During Kaye's first day of teaching, she assigned locker numbers and all books, she passed out "mystery bags" and asked students to write a story based upon the objects inside, she collected phone numbers of her students' parents, and she assigned homework. According to Jim and Kevin's suggestions for the first day of school, what made Kaye's day successful?

a. She dealt with administrative details and taught an interesting lesson.
b. She taught an interesting lesson and collected parents' phone numbers.
c. She collected parents' phone numbers and assigned homework.
d. She taught an interesting lesson and assigned homework.

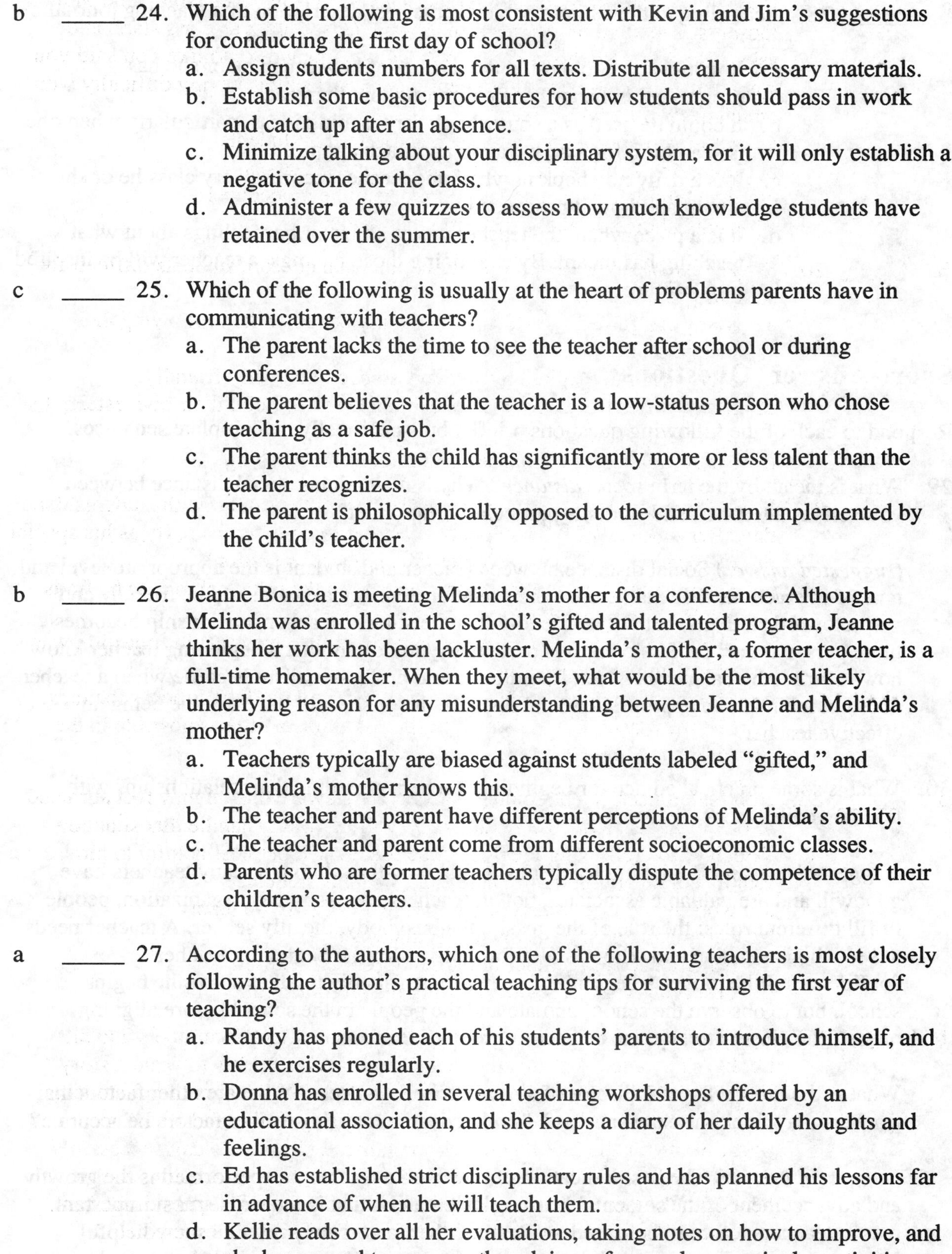

b _____ 24. Which of the following is most consistent with Kevin and Jim's suggestions for conducting the first day of school?

a. Assign students numbers for all texts. Distribute all necessary materials.

b. Establish some basic procedures for how students should pass in work and catch up after an absence.

c. Minimize talking about your disciplinary system, for it will only establish a negative tone for the class.

d. Administer a few quizzes to assess how much knowledge students have retained over the summer.

c _____ 25. Which of the following is usually at the heart of problems parents have in communicating with teachers?

a. The parent lacks the time to see the teacher after school or during conferences.

b. The parent believes that the teacher is a low-status person who chose teaching as a safe job.

c. The parent thinks the child has significantly more or less talent than the teacher recognizes.

d. The parent is philosophically opposed to the curriculum implemented by the child's teacher.

b _____ 26. Jeanne Bonica is meeting Melinda's mother for a conference. Although Melinda was enrolled in the school's gifted and talented program, Jeanne thinks her work has been lackluster. Melinda's mother, a former teacher, is a full-time homemaker. When they meet, what would be the most likely underlying reason for any misunderstanding between Jeanne and Melinda's mother?

a. Teachers typically are biased against students labeled "gifted," and Melinda's mother knows this.

b. The teacher and parent have different perceptions of Melinda's ability.

c. The teacher and parent come from different socioeconomic classes.

d. Parents who are former teachers typically dispute the competence of their children's teachers.

a _____ 27. According to the authors, which one of the following teachers is most closely following the author's practical teaching tips for surviving the first year of teaching?

a. Randy has phoned each of his students' parents to introduce himself, and he exercises regularly.

b. Donna has enrolled in several teaching workshops offered by an educational association, and she keeps a diary of her daily thoughts and feelings.

c. Ed has established strict disciplinary rules and has planned his lessons far in advance of when he will teach them.

d. Kellie reads over all her evaluations, taking notes on how to improve, and she has agreed to serve as the advisor of several co-curricular activities.

a ______ 28. According to the authors, which is the best description of a teaching journal's use?
a. It would serve to remind the teacher of how much he or she has progressed in his or her field throughout the year.
b. It could be used as a sourcebook for teaching ideas, particularly when one is searching for a new way to approach a topic.
c. It is a daily notebook in which the teacher records every class he or she taught and how it proceeded.
d. It is a place where the teacher writes all his or her feelings about what teaching has meant. By examining those feelings, a teacher will be inspired in the future.

Short-Answer Questions

Respond to each of the following questions briefly, but specifically, in complete sentences.

29. What is meant by the term *social distance*? Why is maintaining social distance between yourself, as a teacher, and students particularly important?

(suggested answer) Social distance between teacher and student is the appropriate level and tone of interactions that characterize their relationship. A teacher should be friendly and warm toward students, but not so friendly that the student-teacher relationship becomes more personal than professional. It is particularly important that a beginning teacher know how to strike the balance between friendliness and professionalism because when a teacher does not maintain an appropriate social distance, he or she will have trouble being an effective teacher.

30. What is some practical advice for beginning teachers regarding their relationships with teaching colleagues?

(suggested answer) Beginning teachers should know that although many teachers have goodwill and are valuable associates, not all teachers are. As in any organization, people fulfill different roles: the role of the gossip, the busybody, the ally seeker. A teacher needs to see who is genuine and who has ulterior motives for the beginning teacher's confidences. It behooves a beginning teacher to be friendly to all as she or he begins school, but to observe the school climate and the people in the school before aligning oneself too closely to any one teacher or group of teachers.

31. What is the most reliable indicator of a new teacher's success? What are other factors that teachers may think measure success? To what degree may those other factors be accurate?

(suggested answer) The best indication of how well a teacher has performed is the growth and advancement of the students' learning. Ultimately, that is the single most important reason teachers teach: to help students learn. Other factors may provide some helpful information, but they are not always accurate measures of how much the students have

learned. Such other factors include the teacher's reputation among colleagues, the teacher's written evaluations, the popularity of the teacher with students, and the relationship of the teacher with students' parents.

32. Why are teacher education students' attitudes toward children typically much more positive than those of first-year teachers?

    (suggested answer) The answer lies in two potential areas: philosophy and experience. Many times prospective teachers' underlying philosophy emanates from Romanticism. They conceive of children as essentially good, thwarted by the stifling influence of education, curious and willing to learn if supported and nurtured in the proper environment. Although that is a tenable philosophy for many and has had a long history in education, most prospective teachers have not had the opportunity to test out their philosophy, to match it against real situations. For that reason, they may feel shocked when their best attempts to nurture students are rebuffed.

    Furthermore, most prospective teachers have not had extended experience as authority figures with children and adolescents. They may experience some awkwardness moving from student to teacher and the change in authority that requires. For that reason, the authors suggest any experience, such as coaching, tutoring, and camp counseling, can help prospective teachers make that transition.

Essay Questions

Read each of the following questions, and respond by composing an organized essay that includes an introduction, fully developed paragraph(s), and a conclusion.

33. Explain the kinds of problems that a first-year teacher might face in three of the following six areas: shock of the familiar, instruction, and dealing with students, administrators, teaching peers, and parents. Include a definition of culture shock.

    (Answers will vary.)

34. Parents and teachers often have communication problems that stem from one of three areas. Tell what the areas are, and give an example of a problem in each area.

    (suggested answer) Different perspectives, differing evaluations of the student's work, different socioeconomic status. Examples will vary.

35. To what degree are the principal's and teacher's roles in a school system complementary? To what degree can each help the other do the best possible job?

    (suggested answer) Whereas both principals and teachers are educators, their function in the school organization is different. Teachers work individually with particular students, instructing them and designing activities to help their individual class or classes advance.

They are the primary instructor in a school organization, and, as a result, they will know details about their students' learning that others will not know. They are typically most concerned with how the curriculum impacts their classroom or their department.

Principals are, in large degree, the managers of the school building. They oversee the general processes of education, trying to keep the entire school heading toward district and state curricular goals. They are responsible for evaluating the teachers' performance as well as being the official spokesperson to the community of that school. Teachers and principals are most helpful to each other when they recognize what the other one brings to education. Principals can look to teachers to provide feedback and input on the implementation of the curriculum. Teachers can discuss, with more authority than other school personnel, how students are learning under particular conditions and what students are undergoing at any particular time. Principals can provide the general leadership a school needs by articulating general goals, fostering a sense of purpose, making connections between individual teachers and departments, and otherwise working to create a unified school.

Alternative Assessment Ideas

The following activities are suggestions for student portfolio activities. They are a means of providing alternative assessment of the students' capabilities.

Independent Reading

Read and respond to any of the following selections from Ryan/Cooper, *Kaleidoscope: Readings in Education* (Houghton Mifflin, 1998). You may want to use the Article Review Form on page 269.

Crowley—"Letter from a Teacher"

Shively—"Why I Entered Teaching, Why I Stay"

Reflective Papers

Choose one of the following topics to write a reflective paper (2–5 pages). The purpose of the paper is to help you assimilate new knowledge by blending it with your previous knowledge and experiences.

1. This is based upon the role play described in the Instructional Resources section. After your class has debriefed the role play, think about your reactions or responses to this role play more thoroughly. If you were an observer, how, given your personality, would you have dealt with the situation presented? Do you think it would have been an effective way of dealing with the situation? To what extent would your behavior match the "ideal" way of handling the events, however you define that? If you participated in the role play, consider the events as they occurred. How did they reveal outcomes that you may not have anticipated or expected? If this had been an actual situation, what would you have found

most challenging? How do you think you would have behaved? For all, to what degree did the events in the role play match your conception of how a teacher should work with students? What can you take away from this experience?

2. In the chapter, the authors suggest that prospective teachers "begin now" to analyze their own personality and its match with teaching. Specifically, they encourage you to make a systematic study of your strengths and weaknesses that you can articulate. Think about your personality and write a reflective paper describing what you identify as your biggest strength and your biggest weakness. To what degree do you see your personality characteristics advancing or possibly impeding your teaching? After you've written your paper, share it with your cooperative learning group. Are there any suggestions the group can provide? To what extent do you share similar traits?

3. After observing in your field-site school, see if you can identify a situation where the teacher's perception of a child and a parent's perception may differ. Observe the child and his or her interaction with the teacher over several visits. Then write two "letters," one from the perspective of the teacher about the child and one from the perspective of the parent, describing the child. Share your "letters" with your cooperative learning group. What are the possible implications of regarding a child's behavior through the lens of a teacher or of a parent?

Journal Writing

Suggestions for journal topics for students' selection:

1. Of the challenges for new teachers reviewed in the chapter, which do you think will be the most difficult for you? Why?

2. What is your greatest "fear" in becoming a teacher? What can you do about this?

3. What part of a teacher's job or tasks do you most look forward to doing?

Chapter 16 What Does It Mean to Be a Professional?

Multiple-Choice Items

Read each item carefully. On the appropriate line, write the letter of the choice that represents the best answer.

d _____ 1. Changes in teacher education from colonial times to the present might be summed up by this statement:

a. Then, as now, a considerable amount of formal education was required.
b. Then, teachers were well paid and highly regarded; this is not as true, in a relative sense, now.
c. Then, teachers were poorly paid, poorly educated, and expected to act as models of decorum; now, they are better paid and better educated, though expectations are declining.
d. Then, teachers were not very well educated but had to be models of moral fortitude; now, teachers are more highly paid and regarded, as requirements for certification/licensure become more demanding.

b _____ 2. A teacher during the colonial time period most likely

a. was well educated and well behaved by community standards.
b. had little education beyond the older students and was expected to act conservatively.
c. was well respected for his or her scholarship and virtue.
d. was poorly educated and had questionable moral practices according to the community.

c _____ 3. In the early nineteenth century, an educated citizenry was considered essential to maintaining a democracy. The heightened attention to schooling led to calls for
a. smaller classrooms so that students could learn better.
b. better-paid teachers who would remain in the classroom longer.
c. better-trained teachers who could teach students more.
d. greater parental participation in the schooling of their children.

a _____ 4. As the common school movement grew in the nineteenth century, how did it affect teaching?
a. Education was seen as essential to the maintenance of democracy, so more schools were created.
b. Teachers were expected to teach students to become more efficient farmers and laborers.
c. Teachers were expected to teach students to read the Bible and to instill in them moral virtue.
d. Education was considered the cause of the social difficulties and was to be provided only to wealthy children.

c _____ 5. Which was *not* a factor to explain the influx of women into teaching?
a. More schools were being created, and many more teachers were needed.
b. Women could be paid less than men.
c. Teacher salaries were quite high.
d. Men were being called into the army.

a _____ 6. The nineteenth century witnessed an influx of women into teaching. What was one of the probable reasons for this influx?
a. Men were demanding too much money.
b. Women were seen as better teachers.
c. Growing numbers of schools needed teachers, and there were not enough male teachers.
d. Men were being called into military service.

c _____ 7. Normal schools originated in Europe and were so named because they
a. trained teachers to work with only "normal" children.
b. were not unusual—for example, not offering very specialized courses—but were "normal" in their curriculum.
c. taught students the "norms," or rules, of teaching.
d. were the usual or ordinary training programs for teachers.

b _____ 8. During the late 1800s, most female teachers received their teacher training in
a. high school.
b. normal schools.
c. English academies.
d. two-year colleges.

c ______ 9. The most important change in teacher training in the twentieth century was
a. the inclusion of longer periods of practice teaching.
b. the strengthening of the normal schools for teacher training.
c. the shift from teacher *training* to teacher *education*.
d. the establishment of teacher certification for prospective teachers wanting to find employment.

a ______ 10. The shift from teacher training to teacher education is significant because it
a. signaled a change in substance of what teachers were expected to know.
b. led to more men becoming teachers.
c. increased enrollment in universities since teachers needed a four-year degree.
d. raised the standard of intellectual level in the schools.

b ______ 11. An indication of teachers' power in the classroom is
a. a steady and reliable influence on national and state elections.
b. the selection of lessons to emphasize.
c. the hiring of principals.
d. the selection of school board members.

c ______ 12. Negotiations between the Hillsborough Teachers Association and the Hillsborough school board have reached an impasse. Neither side feels as though any progress has been made in the past six weeks. As a result, the teachers association is calling for a work-to-rule. What kind of power is demonstrated by this action?
a. economic
b. community
c. political
d. academic

d ______ 13. According to the text, which is *not* a defining characteristic of a profession?
a. the ability to provide a unique, essential service
b. a long period of training
c. professional organizations
d. high salaries

d ______ 14. Which of the following must be included for an occupation to be a profession?
a. high status of those in the field
b. the potential for great financial reward
c. strict control of the numbers of people allowed into the field
d. extensive special training required, using one's intellectual ability

a _____ 15. A teacher and her sister are debating whether teaching is a profession. Which of the following reasons will the teacher most likely use to build her argument that teaching is a profession?
- a. Teachers perform an essential service for society: that of educating the youth.
- b. Teachers are paid well for their services.
- c. Teachers enjoy high status for the valuable work they do.
- d. Teachers are self-governing; they have significant power over their own careers and those of their colleagues.

d _____ 16. Teaching may be called a profession because teachers
- a. receive specialized training in a relatively short period of time.
- b. exercise minimal autonomy in their classrooms.
- c. govern themselves through evaluations and peer reviews.
- d. are specialists who pass on key intellectual skills.

b _____ 17. If someone wanted to *discount* the claim that teaching is a profession, which of the following statements could he or she use?
- a. The teacher's work emphasizes service, not rewards.
- b. The teacher's power is limited.
- c. The teacher earns an impressive salary.
- d. The teacher's job is not essential to the community.

d _____ 18. Some of public teachers' harshest critics state that teachers do not fool the public even if they fool themselves; teaching is not a profession, and it will not be until teachers
- a. recognize the fallibility of man.
- b. build better relations with the parent community.
- c. develop more compassion for the students with whom they work.
- d. can govern their own, including weeding out incompetent teachers.

c _____ 19. The recommendations made in the text for ensuring the place of teaching among the professions are
- a. higher pay, more strikes, and better negotiations.
- b. fewer workdays, higher pay, and better training.
- c. more self-governance, better training, and better policing of teachers.
- d. higher pay, fewer workdays, and better negotiations.

d _____ 20. The new Teachers Association president is greatly concerned with helping teaching become a profession. What would be the best area that she could work on to help achieve that goal?
- a. working for greater retirement benefits for twenty-five-year veteran teachers
- b. developing a pay scale that pleases teachers and school board members
- c. developing a program by which teachers could work with parents for their child's academic and social adjustment
- d. creating a better system for weeding out incompetent teachers in the district

c _____ 21. Ryan and Cooper suggest that teaching be considered a *semiprofession* because
a. teachers work only part-time.
b. many teachers have another job besides teaching.
c. in some ways it fits the criteria and in other ways it does not.
d. some teachers are professionals and others are not.

d _____ 22. By saying that teaching is *in the process of becoming a profession*, Ryan and Cooper want to highlight
a. the legislation that Congress is working on to make teaching a profession.
b. the continuous education of teachers, which makes them more and more effective.
c. a case before the Supreme Court that will soon decide if teaching is a profession.
d. the significant changes that teaching has experienced over the years.

d _____ 23. The National Board for Professional Teaching Standards is developing board certification assessments for teachers in order to
a. relieve the states of the responsibility of certifying teachers.
b. create a career ladder for more qualified and talented teachers.
c. identify the knowledge base of teaching.
d. help teachers gain professional credentials.

b _____ 24. The National Board for Professional Teaching Standards designation will be earned by a teacher after
a. earning the recommendation of his or her building principal.
b. undergoing an extensive assessment procedure, including observations, interviews, and submitting a portfolio.
c. earning a master's degree and undergoing a rigorous examination of his or her teaching abilities.
d. undergoing an extensive assessment and being nominated by fellow teachers.

b _____ 25. One potential benefit of the National Board for Professional Teaching Standards is
a. more people choosing teaching as a career.
b. a highly regarded, nationally recognized measure of a teacher's competency.
c. fewer strikes in schools.
d. the board of examiners being made up of practicing teachers.

d _____ 26. Melanie is applying for board certification from the NBPTS. What will she probably have to do?
a. She will have to take a written exam to evaluate her knowledge of her subject area.
b. She will have to have an oral interview with a group of school board members from her town.
c. She will have to send in videotapes of her teaching in her classroom.
d. She will probably have to do all of the above.

a _____ 27. Critics of the National Board for Professional Teaching Standards argue that
a. teaching has no recognized common knowledge base on which to ground assessments.
b. teaching has no need for any kind of standards.
c. historically, teaching has been dominated by women.
d. these standards seek to make teaching even more elitist than it already is.

b _____ 28. The two major organizations representing teachers are
a. the AFT and the ASCD.
b. the NEA and the AFT.
c. the AERA and the ASCD.
d. the ASCD and the NEA.

a _____ 29. The NEA is well known for its initial resistance to
a. collective bargaining for teachers' salary negotiations.
b. efforts to improve preservice teacher education.
c. the establishment of the National Board for Professional Teaching Standards.
d. multicultural education.

c _____ 30. As an indication of its focus on service to its members, the NEA has recently created the National Center for Innovation. This center is concerned with
a. instituting voucher programs.
b. bringing innovation into preservice teacher education programs.
c. restructuring and renewing public education.
d. evaluating innovative instructional strategies.

a _____ 31. The AFT is best known for its
a. active support for bread-and-butter issues for teachers.
b. strong support of teacher competency exams.
c. support for greater control of schools by neighborhood groups.
d. representation of a broad group of people associated with education: teachers, aides, administrators, clerical staff.

b _____ 32. The AFT is known as more aggressive than the NEA because it
a. instituted QUEST (Quality Education Standards in Teaching).
b. instituted collective bargaining for teachers' salaries.
c. has supported greater decision making by teachers.
d. works against parents having choices in public schools.

d _____ 33. Ryan and Cooper contend that the issue of teacher professionalism may be affected by
a. the growing immigrant population.
b. the anticipated retirement of a large percentage of teachers.
c. salary negotiations in large urban areas.
d. the new teacher empowerment movement.

c _____ 34. The need for continuous education for teachers seems to be even greater in the 1990s because of
a. the number of poorly trained people being hired to teach.
b. the high cost of a college education.
c. the social problems that dominate and affect the learning of many students.
d. the growing class size, especially in rural areas.

b _____ 35. Which of the following would *not* be considered a way for an elementary school teacher to continue to grow professionally?
a. attend a summer workshop in cooperative learning
b. become a licensed real estate agent
c. serve as a cooperating teacher for a student teacher
d. enroll in a master's program at a local college

Short-Answer Questions

Respond to each of the following questions briefly, but specifically, in complete sentences.

36. How did Catharine Beecher contribute to teacher education?

(suggested answer) Catharine Beecher lived during the 1800s and devoted her life to the advancement and improvement of women's education and educational reform. She founded the Hartford Female Seminary. It provided for the education of women. Beecher emphasized that if women were to be teachers, their education needed to be stronger and modeled more on the college education of men. She established female seminaries in New England and the Midwest that were attached to a model school, supported by the families of the children who attended. Beecher developed a course of teacher education at these seminaries that could be replicated throughout the country. She promoted the idea of a teacher as a specialist in an academic discipline. Beecher made a deep impact on both teacher training and the education of women.

37. According to Bob Chase, why should a new teacher join the NEA?

(suggested answer) Teachers should join the NEA because they want to be part of making the changes that are coming in education. Teachers join because they want to make a difference.

38. Why is teaching a profession dominated by women? Relate the historical events that led to teaching being a "feminine" profession.

    (*suggested answer*) Answers may vary, but should contain a discussion of the common school movement, when many schools were created and the need for teachers was great. Because women could be employed at less cost and were willing to work for that salary, many of them were recruited. Because teaching was seen as a transient occupation, it was well suited to young women who would teach for a few years before getting married. Likewise, women were seen as being more nurturing and better suited to teaching younger children.

Essay Questions

Read each of the following questions, and respond by composing an organized essay that includes an introduction, fully developed paragraph(s), and a conclusion.

39. List four of the elements that characterize a profession. For each one, summarize the arguments both for and against calling teaching a profession.

    (suggested answer) A profession provides a definite, unique, essential service; relies on intellectual skills; requires special training; permits autonomy for members; assumes personal responsibility for consequences; emphasizes services rather than rewards; is self-governing; and has a code of ethics. Evidence in support of calling teaching a profession includes the fact that teachers are specialists who pass on key skills, they teach thinking skills, they train continuously, they exercise a great deal of personal control, they are accountable for effectiveness, and they attempt to influence law and licensure and to maintain standards. Evidence arguing against calling teaching a profession includes that everyone and everything is a teacher, many people have education equal to that of teachers, little training is required, teachers' power is greater only than that of students, teachers' influence on professional governance is limited, there are no repercussions for ineptitude, there is limited interest in excellence, and teachers have low status and low pay.

40. The NEA and the AFT both represent large numbers of teachers. Each ranks its priorities in slightly different ways, emphasizing slightly different factors. Describe the similarities and differences between the organizations with respect to size, age, representation, history of issues, positions on educational reform, and collective bargaining.

    (suggested answer) The NEA represents nearly two-thirds of elementary and secondary teachers in the United States. It seems more conservative about educational reform than the AFT. The NEA was founded in the mid-1800s. It resisted collective bargaining at first. The AFT, representing about 12 percent of all teachers, is a strong advocate of educational reform. It was begun in the mid-1900s. The AFT is a member of the AFL-CIO and brought collective bargaining into teachers' salary negotiations. The AFT is noted for hard bargaining over bread-and-butter issues and is a defender of academic freedom and of greater participation by teachers in decision making.

Alternative Assessment Ideas

The following activities are suggestions for student portfolio activities. They are a means of providing alternative assessment of the students' capabilities.

Independent Reading

Read and respond to any of the following selections from Ryan/Cooper, *Kaleidoscope: Readings in Education* (Houghton Mifflin, 1998). You may want to use the Article Review Form on page 269.

Wise—"Six Steps to Teacher Professionalism"

Buday and Kelly—"National Board Certification"

Reflective Papers

Choose one of the following topics to write a reflective paper (2–5 pages). The purpose of the paper is to help you assimilate new knowledge by blending it with your previous knowledge and experiences.

1. Think about your position on teaching as a profession. Do you maintain that teaching is a "profession"? Why do you think so? Why could the argument be made that it is not a profession? What do you think needs to be done so that the debate could be put to rest?

2. Do you see yourself joining one of the professional associations when you become a teacher? Why would you join one? Discuss your perceptions of these associations and what you feel they contribute to teaching.

3. Ryan and Cooper have traced the history of teaching and teacher education in the United States up to the present. How do you see the future of teaching and teacher education? Keeping in mind that many of the changes made in schools were *in response* to societal changes, what do you anticipate will be the most influential elements affecting education in the next century, and how will teaching and teacher education be affected?

Journal Writing

Suggestions for journal topics for students' selection:

1. Do you think you will join the NEA or AFT (whichever one is the collective bargaining agent in your district)? Why or why not?

2. Will it make a difference in how you do your job if teaching is perceived as a profession?

3. Describe how you think teacher education programs will change over the next twenty years.

Appendix *Teaching with Case Studies*

The case study approach has been gaining popularity in teacher education programs. Long a common approach in law, medicine, counseling, and psychology, it is now being used more frequently in teacher preparation and even in teacher in-service programs. By reading a case study, prospective teachers can appreciate the complexities of teaching and can learn more about the contingencies involved in teaching. As they discuss the issues and propose viable solutions, prospective teachers can apply their theoretical knowledge of teaching in realistic contexts and can explore alternate courses of action, thereby expanding their thinking about teaching.

The case studies we have included deal with topical themes that confront teachers: pedagogical issues such as educational philosophy, teaching styles, grading practices, classroom management, and ability grouping, and practical or professional issues such as disagreements with the principal and decisions to strike.

When using a case study with your students, we suggest that the first part of the discussion focus on identifying the issues at hand and the key players involved as well as other factors that affect the issues. The second part can explore the issues themselves, discussing the different positions on the issues and the rationale (if there is one) for these positions. Finally, possible solutions can be evoked with the subsequent consequences of these solutions.

For use with Chapters 4, 5, or 12

Leigh Scott

A high school social studies teacher gives a higher-than-earned report card grade to a mainstreamed student on the basis of the boy's effort, and is confronted by another student with identical test grades who received a lower report card grade.

Leigh Scott felt the flush slowly leave her face as she watched Aaron Washington leave the classroom, slamming the door behind him. It was the end of the second grading cycle; students had received their report cards the day before. Leigh had just taken off her coat and was on her way to the teachers' room to get a cup of coffee before the bell rang when Aaron came into the room.

He began, "We got to talk about my American government grade." It was clear that he was angry.

Leigh moved to her desk and responded, "Hi, Aaron, What's up? You're upset about your grade?"

"You gave me a D."

"You did D work."

"So did Dale, and he got a C." Aaron was leaning over the desk toward Leigh.

"Aaron, this is not a good time to talk about this. The bell is going to ring in a few minutes. Why don't you see me after school this afternoon."

Aaron shook his head at her suggestion. "I have practice after school. We have to talk now."

Now it was Leigh's turn to shake her head. "This is not a good time; I have to get ready for homeroom. Besides, there's not really anything to talk about."

Aaron straightened up, took a couple of steps back from the desk, and said, "You gave a white kid who got the same grades I did a C, and you gave me a D. I even did more homework than Dale. I say we *do* have something to talk about."

Leigh capitulated. "Come in tomorrow morning at 7:30, and we'll talk before homeroom period."

Aaron nodded, strode out of the room without another word, and let the door slam as he left.

Leigh had been teaching social studies at Littleton High School for eleven years, and this was the first time a student accused her of racial bias. Students sometimes complained about their grades, and Leigh was always willing to reconsider a grade. But she never had a student suggest she was biased. Leigh had spent her entire teaching career at Littleton, so she had been teaching classes that were mixed racially and ethnically for a long time. She considered herself color blind when it came to assigning grades.

At Littleton High School, students were placed into one of four academic tracks: honors, above average, average, and remedial. Teachers were responsible for five classes a day, with the honors classes typically assigned to senior faculty. Newer faculty taught mostly average and remedial sections. Leigh taught a senior-level honors American history course, two freshman above-average sections of world history, and two sophomore average-level sections of American government.

Leigh graded her two sophomore American government sections on the following requirements each cycle:

- Tests (usually three or four, depending on the material)
- Homework (collected three times a week)
- A project
- Participation in class discussions based on the textbook readings

The textbook was written on an eighth-grade reading level. Leigh's tests were a combination of vocabulary, multiple-choice, and short-answer items. Leigh didn't require that students in the average sections answer essay questions. Students selected projects from among several choices: writing papers, constructing something appropriate to the topic, making a presentation to the class, or writing book reports on pertinent readings.

During homeroom period, Leigh consulted her grade book and confirmed that Aaron's information was accurate. Neither he nor Dale had done particularly well this grading cycle. Both had received mostly D grades with an occasional C. Neither participated in class discussions unless called on. However, she knew that she had given Dale the higher grade because of his effort, not because of his color. Dale was a learning disabled student mainstreamed into Leigh's class.

Typically a mainstreamed student would be placed in a remedial section, but Dale's case was an exception. He was in an average-level class because his resource room teacher, Meg Dament, requested the placement, feeling that Dale needed a more academic environment and a higher-achieving peer group than he would have had in a remedial section. Meg and Leigh had known each other since Leigh came to Littleton. Leigh admired Meg's dedication and her tenacity on behalf of her students. It was clear that Meg cared deeply about the students she served and wanted them to have whatever educational normality she could engineer for them. Meg was able to mainstream her "best" students into average-level, not remedial, classes. She actively sought teachers who would be responsive to her students' needs and to their efforts. It was not easy to convince high school teachers to work with classified students, but of the four resource room teachers in the high school, it was Meg who made the most regular class placements.

When Meg requested Leigh as Dale's teacher, Leigh understood that Dale was not a very good reader and that he would not volunteer in class. Leigh and Meg spoke regularly about Dale's progress, as well as the classroom requirements. Meg helped Dale prepare for Leigh's class, and he was showing real improvement since the first cycle, when his grade had been a low D.

Additionally, Dale's attitude in class was positive. He had learned to exhibit "teacher-pleasing behaviors": He looked attentive, he tried to take notes, he almost always carried his textbook and notebook and a pencil, and he never disrupted the class. Aaron had a different style: He would put his head on his desk during class discussions, he seldom brought materials to class, and he often talked to friends while Leigh was lecturing.

Nevertheless, their grades during the cycle were nearly identical, and Aaron was demanding an explanation. Leigh drove home that day wondering what she would tell Aaron during their appointment the following morning. Aaron's anger, coupled with his charge of racism, exacerbated her anxiety about their meeting. She also knew that she would have to figure out what she might do to prevent this from happening in the future, since she anticipated that she would continue to have mainstreamed students in her classes and she believed they should be rewarded for effort and improvement.

Discussion Questions

Two issues dominate this case: grading practices and mainstreaming, both of which are complicated by the charge of racism that Aaron has leveled at Leigh.

Grading

What is Aaron's complaint with his grade? Does he have a legitimate complaint? Is Leigh Scott's grading system fair? What is her grading system? Is it clearly articulated to the students? On what does Leigh base her grades? What is she rewarding in students, outcomes only or progress toward a specified outcome? Is she consistent in her grading practices? What are the strengths and weaknesses of her system?

Mainstreaming

Should mainstreamed students be evaluated on different criteria or the same ones as the regular education students? Who should decide the criteria? How should they be decided? What role does the mainstreamed student's individualized education plan (IEP) play in grading? What is more important for mainstreamed students: feelings of social well-being or academic achievement?

Teacher-Student Interactions

How should Leigh respond to Aaron? Should she respond to his demands for an explanation of her grading? Should Aaron be encouraged (allowed) to challenge Leigh's grading? How should Leigh respond to Aaron's charges of racism?

How should Leigh prepare for the meeting with Aaron? Where should it be? Who should be present? Should she be willing to change Aaron's grade?

For use with Chapter 4

Marsha Warren

An experienced third-grade teacher is overwhelmed by the problems created by her heterogeneous class, which includes seven students who have unique home and personal situations that are affecting their schooling.

José glared at Tyrone. "Quit looking at me, you jerk!"

"I wasn't lookin' at nothin', creepy," replied Tyrone vehemently.

Marsha Warren looked up sharply at the two boys and made a cutting gesture through the air. "That's enough from both of you. You should both be looking at your books, not each other."

"I was lookin' at my book!" protested Tyrone.

"Just stop!" repeated Marsha. "Please continue reading, Angela."

Angela rolled her eyes at no one in particular and resumed reading aloud in a bored, expressionless tone. Her progress was slow and halting.

Marsha Warren was a third-grade teacher at the Roosevelt Elementary School in Littleton. She was trying to conduct a reading group with the eight slowest readers in her class of twenty-two while the other children worked in workbooks at their seats. But each time an argument erupted among the children in the reading group, most of the children at their desks snapped to attention to watch the sparks fly.

"You can stop there, Angela," interrupted Marsha as Angela came to the end of a paragraph. "Bettie Ann, will you read next?" As she spoke, Marsha also put a hand out to touch another child, Katie, on the shoulder in an attempt to stop her from bouncing in her chair.

Bettie Ann didn't respond. She was gazing out the window at the leafless November landscape, sucking her thumb and twirling her hair with her other hand. "Bettie Ann, I'm talking to you," repeated Marsha.

"Your turn," yelled José, as he poked Bettie Ann's shoulder.

"Shut up, José," interjected Sarah. Sarah often tried to mediate between the members of the group, but her argumentative streak pulled her into the fray as often as not.

"Quiet!" insisted Marsha in a hushed, but emphatic tone. As she spoke, she turned her head to glance over her shoulder at the rest of the class. The hum of conversation was growing in the room. Tension crept into her voice as she addressed the reading group. "We're distracting the other children. Do we need to discuss rule 3 again? Everyone pull out the class rules from your notebook, now."

The chemistry in the reading group—and in the class in general—had been so explosive since September that Marsha had gone beyond her normal first-of-the-year review of rules and procedures. All the children in the class had copied four class rules into their notebooks, and she had led long discussions of what they meant. Rule 3 was "Be considerate of other people."

Loud groans from the reading group greeted Marsha's mention of rules. Simultaneously, a long BANG sounded in the back of the room. Marsha turned and saw a student reaching to the floor for a book as his neighbor snickered. She also noticed three girls in the far-left row leaning into a conversation over a drawing, and she saw most of the students quickly turn back to their work, as if they were not enjoying the entertainment of the reading group once again.

"That's it!" Marsha exclaimed. She slammed her hand down on the reading-circle table and stood to face the entire class. "Put your head on your desks and don't say another word—everyone!" By the time she finished her sentence, Marsha realized she had been shouting, but she didn't care. Her class glazed at her in stunned disbelief. Mrs. Warren had always been so gentle! "Now!"

Marsha quickly turned and walked from the room, not bothering to look back to see if her command had been obeyed. She closed the door to her classroom, managing not to slam it, and tried to control her temper and collect her thoughts. "What in God's name am I going to do with this class?" she asked herself. "I've got to calm down. Here I am in the hallway with twenty-two kids inside who have driven me out—they've absolutely won." Marsha suddenly felt paralyzed.

Marsha tried to remember if there was ever a time in her eleven years of teaching when discipline and control were such a challenge. "It's not as though I were a rookie. I ought to know what to do!" she agonized. But Marsha had tried everything she had ever learned or done before to interest and control this group, and the class as a whole, yet there she was, standing in the hall.

Marsha's third-grade class was indeed a difficult group of children. There were a few students who liked school and really tried to learn, but overall it was a class full of children who were just not focused on learning. It was impossible to relax with them. If Marsha let down her guard and tried to engage them on a more friendly or casual level, the class would disintegrate. Marsha's natural inclination in teaching was to maintain a friendly, relaxed manner; she usually enjoyed her students and her enjoyment showed. But with this class she constantly had to be firm and vigilant ("witchlike," she thought) in order to keep the students under control.

Academically the class was fairly average, but Marsha did have two instructional challenges: There were three really bright students, whom Marsha tried to encourage with extra instruction and higher expectations, and there were three students (besides the Hispanic children in her slow-reading group) who spoke little or no English. The most remarkable characteristic of the students, though, was their overall immaturity. Each child seemed to feed off the antics of the others, and every issue was taken to its extreme. For example, whenever one child laughed, the entire class would begin to giggle uncontrollably. The students' behavior was simply inappropriate for their age and grade.

The core of Marsha's problem was the lowest-level reading group. This group provided the spark that set off fireworks in the entire class, day after day. The slow readers were rude and disruptive as a group, and they were instigators on their own.

When Marsha thought of each child in the lowest reading group individually, she was usually able to summon some sympathy and understanding. Each of the eight had an emotional or academic problem that probably accounted, at least in part, for his or her behavior.

José, for instance, topped her list of troublemakers. He was a loud, egocentric child. His mother, Marsha thought, probably had surrendered long ago, and his father did not live with them. José had little respect for or recognition of authority; he was boisterous and argumentative; and he was unable to take turns under any condition. When something didn't go his way, he would explode. This low flash point, Marsha felt, was just one of many signs of his immaturity, even though José was repeating the third grade and was actually older than his classmates.

José had a slight learning disability in the areas of organizational skills, but Marsha didn't think this justified his behavior. His mother spoke only Spanish, and—although José was fluent in both Spanish and English—when Marsha sent notes home, she would first have to find someone to translate for her. Conferring with José's mother on the telephone was out of the question.

Angela was also repeating the third grade, and Marsha thought the child's anger over this contributed to her terrible attitude in class. The child just refused to learn. She could be a low-average achiever if she would apply herself, but it was clear that Angela's agenda was not school. She was concerned with her hair, her looks, her clothes—preoccupations that Marsha found inappropriate for a third-grader. Angela came from a middle-class black family, and her parents were also angry that she had been held back; consultations with them were not usually fruitful. Angela seemed truly upset if Marsha asked her to do any work, and Marsha was sure her frustration with the child was occasionally apparent.

Tyrone, on the other hand, was a very low average learner, but he, at least, worked to his capabilities. He even tried to mediate arguments among the members of the group. But Tyrone had a very stubborn streak, which was typical, Marsha thought, of slow learners. If he was on the wrong track, he just would not get off of it. She frequently asked him to redo work and helped him with his errors, but when he presented it to her the next day as though it were different, it would contain the same mistakes.

Sarah, too, knew right from wrong and generally wanted to do her work, but she was easily pulled into the fray. Sarah had appointed herself protector of Bettie Ann, an overweight, emotionally insecure child who had difficulty focusing on the topic at hand. Bettie Ann was the baby of her family, with several near-adult siblings at home. Marsha wondered if Bettie Ann's position in the family was the reason she assumed no responsibility for her own actions and no control over her own fate. Bettie Ann seemed hungry for Marsha's attention, but she exhibited no independence or initiative at all.

Katie was one of the brighter students in the reading group, but her hyperactivity caused her to be easily distracted and argumentative. She could neither sit still physically nor pay attention mentally. Katie had a rich home background, full of books and middle-class aspirations, but Marsha thought she also encountered pressure at home to perform, perhaps to levels beyond her capability.

Rhea, another child with at least average intelligence, was one of the more heart-rending cases. Her mother was an alcoholic who neglected her, and Rhea had to do the housework and care for her older brother, who was in a special education class. She had no time for homework, and there were no books or even conversation at home. Rhea had been held back in the second grade, and while she tried to do her work, the language deficit at home was so severe that she kept falling further behind.

Finally, there was Maria, a petite immature native of El Salvador. She had average intelligence and a cooperative spirit, but Spanish was spoken in her home and her limited English vocabulary severely limited her progress.

Marsha tried to analyze what it was among these children that fostered such animosity. Not a day passed that they didn't argue, fight, or insult one another. The reading group was not the only arena for these combatants; they fought in the playground, in line, on the bus, and in the cafeteria. They were troublemakers in previous grades, and some of the teachers at Roosevelt called them "Infidels."

They tended to be at their worst as a group, and so Marsha had tried separating them, but with little improvement. Three weeks before, in early October, she rearranged and reorganized all three reading groups, distributing the students in the lowest section among three new groups. But she found that the inappropriate behavior did not stop; it only spread. Now all three of her reading groups, rather than one, were disrupted, and mixing her slow and average readers dramatically reduced the pace of both groups. Finding this arrangement unfair to her other students, she reorganized back to her original group assignments last week.

Marsha also tried other remedies. She introduced popular reading material for the reading groups and tried innovations such as having the children act out the stories they read. She wrote a contingency contract with the groups when she reconstituted them last week, promising that they could use the school's audiovisual equipment to make filmstrips illustrating their current book if they behaved, but so far that wasn't working either.

Marsha did not think she was generally too lax. She had procedures for incomplete work (the students had to come to her room during lunch hour or after school to finish); she had rules for appropriate behavior in school; and she never hesitated to involve parents. She praised the children for completing work, and she sent positive notes home when they did so. She also sent home disciplinary cards (much more frequently, unfortunately), which parents were supposed to sign, and she telephoned parents when she thought it would help.

Marsha also tried punishment. She sent individual troublemakers to the office, and she held detention during lunch. She isolated children for misbehavior by separating their desks from the rest of the class, and she used denial of privileges (the children really liked using the class computer, so she withdrew that privilege frequently). Marsha even tried talking honestly with the children, giving them pep talks about the value of education and their need to read and write and think in order to participate in life. But nothing was fundamentally altering the course of the class's behavior.

Besides having the desire to teach the "Infidels," Marsha knew that the progress of the rest of the class was being slowed because of the time she was forced to spend on policing. Her patience, her ideas, and her fortitude were fast evaporating, and she knew she had to solve the problem even though she felt like giving up.

Marsha stood on tiptoe to look through the window of the classroom door. The children were sitting in their places looking at each other uneasily and at the door, clearly wondering what would happen next. With a sigh, Marsha turned the knob.

Discussion Questions

The first task with this case is to decide what is happening in Marsha's classroom—that is, what are the different problems that Marsha has to manage? Once the problems have been identified, the discussion can turn to possible solutions. A suggested outline for discussion contains the following:

Problem Identification

What are the problems in the class, from Marsha's perspective? What is known about the students in the class? How can the behavior of the "Infidels" be explained?

How has Marsha contributed to these problems? What has she already tried to solve the problems? Why weren't her efforts successful? How does Marsha explain her lack of progress?

Solutions

Short-term: Marsha has to return to the classroom. What should she do when she walks back into the room?

Long-term: What can Marsha do to improve the environment of her classroom? What areas should she focus on first? Classroom management? Ability grouping? Motivation? What specific plans could she try?

For use with Chapters 4 or 12

From *Case Studies for Teacher Problem Solving* by Rita Silverman, William M. Welty, and Sally Lyon. Copyright © 1992. Reproduced with permission of The McGraw-Hill Companies.

Erica Kaiser

Erica Kaiser was busy teaching her fifth-period Spanish class at Centerville Middle School. It was a seventh-grade class and the students were engrossed in some language puzzles that Erica had made up for them. She was pleased to see them working so hard at the puzzles because she had spent a lot of time developing them. As Erica wandered around the classroom, checking on the groups' progress, she thought about her work. She was in her second year of teaching and had already received notes from parents praising her work, and very positive feedback from her department coordinator. She enjoyed teaching at the middle school level and working with her colleagues, many of whom had become Erica's good friends. She was delighted with the professional development opportunities which the Centerville school district offered and regularly took part in these activities. Erica thought she had found her niche.

As she was circulating around the class, Dr. Fraelich, the principal, came in. Erica started toward the door, but he waved her away. She knew what that meant: he was just on one of his spot visits. He didn't stay long, but then he rarely did. He circled around the class, chatted with a few students, checked their work, and then he was off to another class. As he strolled out the door, he stopped near Erica and murmured, "Well, Miss Kaiser, looks like you've got the troops under control today. But then again, they're not doing much, are they? I'll come back another day when you're doing some real teaching! After all, it's Friday, and I'm sure you have other things on your mind besides verb conjugations!" He winked playfully at her and left the room.

Erica gaped at the open door. She had worked on these vocabulary puzzles for two weeks; they were hardly spur-of-the moment "busy work" for the students. Besides, her social life after school hours was none of his business. The bell rang and brought Erica back to the classroom as the students filed out. Erica tried to forget Dr. Fraelich's remark, yet, as the afternoon wore on, Erica found her irritation growing as she thought about the incident and other similar comments Dr. Fraelich had made in the past. She tried to excuse him to herself, since he was an older man and basically nice. Maybe he just didn't realize that he sounded patronizing.

As the weeks went by, Dr. Fraelich's comments seemed to become more frequent and more irritating. Erica tried to remain pleasant, but she found herself cutting her conversations with him short out of fear of saying something that she might regret. The situation came to a head in May when Erica received her yearly evaluation from Dr. Fraelich. Because she was an untenured teacher, Erica received a "full" evaluation every year which consisted of a checklist and a narrative evaluation. She scanned down the checklist and was pleased to note that she had received "outstanding" for every item there. She turned to the next page to read Dr. Fraelich's written comments about her teaching. She read:

> Miss Kaiser is a fine, courteous young woman. She comes to school promptly every day, and she hands in her plan book on the date assigned. She has eagerly volunteered for after-school events and has the knack of adding a special touch to every activity, whether it's bringing in some homemade baked goods or staying behind to help with the clean-up crew. Finally, Miss Kaiser's professional appearance is to be commended. Her dress is neat, modest, and attractive. I recommend her without hesitation for a contract for the 1994–95 school year.

Erica's stomach churned. She stared at her evaluation in disbelief. She knew that Dr. Fraelich could be patronizing at times, but she couldn't believe what he had written. This report was part of her permanent record and he was talking about her culinary talents! He made no reference at all to her teaching, her professional development activities, or her participation on the school committees. She shoved the report in her briefcase and headed out the door.

On her way home, Erica tried to remember what he had written in her evaluation last year, but she couldn't. She could only remember being so nervous about the two classroom observations he did that when she saw that he had recommended her to be rehired, she only gave a cursory glance at the rest of the report. She was overjoyed to have survived her first year and to be coming back for a second year.

That evening, she showed her evaluation to Mike and Laurie, two close college friends.

"I don't believe he wrote this!" exclaimed Laurie. "I thought it was bad in med. school, but this is ridiculous! Where has this guy been? Doesn't he know about sexual harassment? Can't you file some sort of complaint? What's he going to write next year? A recommendation that you make coffee and sew curtains?"

Mike stared at Erica and shook his head. "Yeah, that's really too bad because except for him, you're happy at Centerville, aren't you? And your position seems secure, unlike mine. I'm pretty sure I'm getting pink-slipped next week. I have the least seniority in the science department and every department has to cut one teacher. Modern languages has to cut two."

Laurie interrupted Mike. "So, what are you saying, Mike? That she should just ignore this? This is part of her permanent record. What happens when she applies for another job and they call here for a reference and find out she bakes good cookies and dresses nicely? I certainly wouldn't be impressed by that!"

"No, no, no. The guy's definitely chauvinistic and patronizing and everything else. I'm just saying that before Erica does anything, she should find out more about what's going on. I mean, the bottom line is that he did recommend that her contract be renewed, so would it hold up as sexual discrimination or harassment? I'm not sure. Besides," he added as he picked up the report to look at it more carefully, "don't you have to sign the report and give it back to him? Why don't you write on the report that you're not happy with it because it doesn't evaluate your teaching? Or maybe you could just talk to the principal about it and ask him to redo it or something. That's what we do at my school if we have a problem with our annual reports."

"Mike is right," Erica sighed. "First I need to find out what procedures are in place to deal with this. I can check with Bill, who's our teachers' association rep. But I really wonder what other teachers' evaluation reports are like. Is he this way just with me or with everyone?"

Over the next few days, Erica learned a lot. She found out from Bill the district policy regarding teacher evaluations (which was in her teacher handbook, but she had never paid much attention to it). He told her that teachers had to sign and return their reports within ten working days. If a teacher was unhappy with the report, he or she could draft a rebuttal, sign that, and not the evaluation report, and submit the two of them. The next step, he explained, was up to the principal, who could rewrite the report and, assuming the teacher was satisfied with the revised report, submit that one to the superintendent. However, if the principal felt that the evaluation was an accurate representation of the teacher's performance, then the two reports, the principal's original and the teacher's rebuttal, would be submitted. At that point, it was up to the superintendent to resolve the issue by either meeting with the two people concerned or having a third party observe the teacher in question and write up an evaluation.

"But, just a friendly reminder before you do anything, Erica. Dr. Marston, our superintendent, and Dr. Fraelich came to Centerville at the same time and have both been here for a long time. They are frequent golf partners, if that makes any difference to you. But, whatever you decide, keep me informed in case you need the support of the teachers' association."

"I will, Bill, and thanks for the information—and the advice."

At lunch, she asked some of her closer friends about their evaluation reports and found that hers was not unique, nor was her reaction.

"Yeah, that fries me, too," remarked Tracy. "He always says that I 'dress sensibly.' That's so demeaning. But, you know, Erica, other than those stupid remarks, he doesn't bother me. I can teach and be left to do what I like just about all of the time. Besides, he would always recommend that my contract be renewed. Of course now that I'm tenured, that is less of a concern for me."

"But what about those of us who aren't tenured?" asked Maggie. "Why should we have to put up with those kinds of comments when we all know that they're inappropriate? It's not fair that someone like that is the one deciding whether or not we will have jobs in the fall."

Erica looked over to Drew. "Well, what do you think, Drew? Are you comfortable with what he says?"

Drew looked at her sheepishly. "I don't know what to say. My evaluation reports have been fine. He always gives a full evaluation of my teaching and lists all the extracurricular and professional activities I participate in. I hate to say it, but I have no complaints about my evaluations. I really don't."

"Boy, that makes it sound even worse, doesn't it?" Erica commented. "Now what do we do? What do *I* do?"

"I don't know, but I do know that you should really think this through before you do anything," Drew advised, "and I don't say that to sound patronizing. You know about Dr. Fraelich and Dr. Marston, don't you?"

"Yeah, more or less," Erica responded.

"But do you know about Lucy? She got fed up with Bob, too, and called him a chauvinist. Actually, she did more than that. She filed a grievance against him. Not much really came of it, though, except that Lucy got transferred to the high school the following year when she hadn't even requested it."

"And then there was Charlotte," Tracy added. "Remember her?"

Mary Jane continued, "First, she also complained about her evaluations and about Dr. Fraelich's comments. Then she was assigned to all the lousy duties and Bob started being very subtly vigilant about making sure she was at the bus stop, at detention, you know, the whole deal. Then, the next year, we had a classroom shortage, and Bob reassigned Charlotte to this closet space instead of a classroom, saying that she had the smallest number of students, so she didn't need her own classroom. Ever since, her 'space' has been down in the corner of the book closet.

"And Charlotte applied to be language arts coordinator four years ago. Even though she was the most qualified, they hired someone else, saying they wanted someone from the outside."

Drew added, "We're not exactly sure that Bob had anything to do with that, but it does seem awfully coincidental."

Erica looked at them squarely. "So you're telling me he's not a man to make enemies with, that he has friends in high places, is that right? So what do I do?"

"Well, if you'll forgive my sports analogy," Drew said, "the ball is in your court. What do you want to do? You have been recommended to be rehired."

Discussion Questions

Problem Identification

What is Erica's problem? Why is it a problem? Is this really a case of gender bias or sexual harassment? What are important factors that Erica needs to keep in mind?

Problem Solution

What should Erica do? Her options are clear: either let it go or write a rebuttal. Or is there another option? What are some potential consequences if she does nothing? If she writes a rebuttal? If she talks to Dr. Fraelich?

For use with Chapter 12

Kowalski, Theodore J., Roy A. Weaver, and Kenneth T. Henson, *Case Studies on Teaching*. Copyright © 1992 by Longman, a division of Addison-Wesley Publishing Co., Inc. Used by permission of the author.

Karen Washington

Karen's first year of teaching starts off very well, but the threat of a strike forces Karen to examine her priorities and to make some hard decisions fast.

Karen Washington faces what she believes is the greatest decision of her life. She must decide if she will participate in a teachers' strike. The predicament angers Karen. She sits alone in her newly acquired apartment mulling over her options and trying to determine how she got herself into this situation.

Just four months ago, Karen graduated from North State College after completing her student teaching. Everything seemed magnificent. She had received an outstanding evaluation for student teaching; she was going to graduate summa cum laude; she had four solid job opportunities; and most important, she was convinced that she had made an excellent career choice. Karen was in love with teaching!

The youngest of four children, Karen had been reared in the industrial area of Pittsburgh. Her father was an ardent union loyalist who, after thirty-one years of employment in the steel mills, was forced to take an early retirement. Her mother, who managed to complete her high school education after she got married, works as a clerk in a meat packing company—a job she has held for twenty-two years. In the Washington household, education is a high priority. Karen's siblings all attended college. One of her brothers left after his freshman year to join the army, and after twelve years, has decided to make the military his career. Karen's sister is a nursing supervisor in a suburban hospital and her other brother is finishing his Ph.D. in sociology at the University of Texas.

Karen has a very close relationship with her mother. She would preach to Karen, "Getting your degree is your ticket to job security. Look at what happened to your father. Thirty-one years and they just tell him he has to retire."

As Karen sits in her room pondering the issue before her, memories of home and college are comforting. But she also thinks about the major decision she made just two months ago—accepting a teaching position in the Glennville schools. Karen had applied for four positions. Each school district had pursued her vigorously. In a way, she had been surprised because the districts were located in quite different environments. One of the school systems was large and urban; one was an affluent suburban district; one was a "blue collar" suburb; and Glennville was a quiet, sleepy little community of 5,000 nestled in the mountains of central Pennsylvania. Perhaps it had been her mother's urgings to seek job security that had prompted Karen to select Glennville. After all, it offered the lowest salary of the four.

The first month of teaching had been superb. Karen had a second-grade class with nineteen healthy and happy students. She had become very good friends with the other second-grade teacher, Martha McKewan, a veteran of twenty-seven years in the classroom. To the unending pleasure of her mother, Karen had also become a member of the choir at the local church in Glennville and had begun dating the assistant pastor, David Simms.

As a matter of routine, Karen had joined the Glennville Teachers' Association (GTA) the first day she reported to work. She hadn't asked any questions—it seemed like the thing to do. About the second week of school, Karen began receiving an association newsletter entitled, "Negotiations Update." The publication had made it clear that the GTA was most unhappy with the progress of its salary negotiations with the school board. Discussions in the lunchroom and teachers' lounge centered almost entirely around the contents of the newsletter. It was obvious that tensions were mounting.

During a routine visit with the principal, Mrs. Armand, Karen had raised the issue of negotiations. "I just don't understand it," Mrs. Armand said. "I've been in this community longer than I care to admit and nothing like this has ever happened before. I really think we're headed for a showdown. The school board has decided to get tough."

Karen asked, "What do you mean by getting tough?"

Mrs. Armand thought a moment and responded. "We never had negotiations here until five years ago. The board reluctantly participates in the process. Each year they get a little more bitter. This is not a union town. Even though our salaries are not very high, and even though the board knows that, they find if difficult to accept collective bargaining. Maybe they feel they have to teach the GTA a lesson."

Karen was surprised that the situation was so severe. She asked further, "If there is a strike, Mrs. Armand, what do you recommend that I do?"

"Karen, you know, I have to be on the board's side in this matter," she responded. "I don't believe in strikes. You have to decide what is best for you. As a first-year teacher, you'd better be careful."

Two days after her conference with the principal, the officers of the GTA held a strike vote. Karen did not vote because she was torn by mixed emotions. The teachers voted overwhelmingly to strike. A majority of the teachers believed that the board would not make salary concessions without a strike. The strike would begin in the morning.

Sitting in her room alone now, Karen also recalls other pleas she had made for advice.

Mrs. McKewan, a professional role model for Karen, had told her, "I'm going out on strike. I never thought I would. But this has become a matter of honor and professional integrity." Karen's recently acquired friend, Reverend Simms, had responded by saying that a strike would not go over very well in the community. "As a first-year teacher, Karen, you could be very vulnerable," he advised.

Karen had reluctantly called home and discussed the matter with her parents. Even they disagreed on what she should do. Her father told her to honor the strike; her mother told her to protect her job.

Ralph Hopson, president of the GTA, had said, "Karen, your best friends are in the GTA. Stand with us and we'll stand behind you. Don't make the mistake of turning your back on your professional colleagues."

All of this would not be so bad if Karen didn't really like her job, the community, and most important, the children in her classroom. Karen had received two letters from parents urging her not to go on strike. One father had pleaded, "Only the children suffer in a strike. Why should they be made the innocent victims of a political fight?"

Just two weeks ago, everything was so perfect, so rosy. Karen wanted her experiences in Glennville to continue to be positive. Yet she knew she had to make a decision that could change her future in this community.

Discussion Questions

The major issue here has to do with where Karen's professional loyalties should lie. Should she honor the strike and support her colleagues, thereby signaling her adherence to her professional community, or should she honor her professional obligations to teach the students?

Problem Identification

What are the arguments in favor of Karen supporting the strike? Consider professional as well as personal arguments. What are the arguments against Karen supporting the strike? Once again, consider both personal and professional arguments. Who else could Karen consult to help her make her decision?

Solution

What advice would you give Karen? Should she support the strike or not? What do you imagine to be the consequence of her supporting the strike? Of her not supporting the strike?

Instructor Evaluation of Those Who Can, Teach, *Eighth Edition*

Please complete the questionnaire and mail it to: Marketing Services, College Division, Houghton Mifflin Company, 222 Berkeley Street, Boston, MA 02116-3764.

1. Indicate how often you use each of these features in this instructor's manual.

	Frequently	*Occasionally*	*Never*
Chapter Outline	______	______	______
Supplementary Lecture and Discussion Topics	______	______	______
Student Activities	______	______	______
Ready-to-Copy Assignment Sheets	______	______	______
Additional Resources for Instructors	______	______	______
Media Resources	______	______	______

2. Do you provide or require your students to use the following student resources in this manual?

Study Guides	______	______	______
Sample Chapter Quizzes	______	______	______

3. Which of the following assessment resources do you use?

Test Bank Questions on Disk	______	______	______
Test Bank Questions in Print	______	______	______
Multiple-Choice Items	______	______	______
Short-Answer Questions	______	______	______
Essay Questions	______	______	______
Alternative Assessment Ideas:			
Independent Reading	______	______	______
Reflective Papers	______	______	______
Journal Writing	______	______	______

4. Do you use the case studies in the Appendix?	______	______	______
5. Do you use *Kaleidoscope* in conjunction with this course?	______	______	______

6. Please indicate the following information about yourself to help us better understand who uses our manual and how we can support you.

Rank:			
	Graduate Assistant	____	
	Lecturer	____	
	Assistant	____	
	Associate	____	
	Professor	____	
	Full Time	____	
	Part Time	____	
	Tenured	Yes ____	No ____

7. How many years have you taught this course? ____

8. How many sections of this course do you teach in one year? ____

9. Do you consider the foundations of education to be your major area of expertise?
Yes ____ No ____

10. What else would you like to suggest we add to the *Instructor's Resource Manual* to assist you?

11. Is there anything we should delete?

12. We would like to know how you rate our textbook in each of the following areas:

	Excellent	*Good*	*Adequate*	*Poor*
a. Selection of topics	____	____	____	____
b. Detail of coverage	____	____	____	____
c. Order of topics	____	____	____	____
d. Writing style/readability	____	____	____	____
e. Accuracy of information	____	____	____	____
f. Study aids and test questions	____	____	____	____
g. Illustrations and cartoons	____	____	____	____
h. Student reaction to book	____	____	____	____
i. Examples/applications	____	____	____	____
j. Explanations of concepts	____	____	____	____

13. We invite you to cite specific examples that illustrate any of the above ratings.

14. Describe the strongest feature(s) of the book.

15. Describe the weakest feature(s) of the book.

16. What other topics should be included in this text?

17. What recommendations can you make for improving this book?